Bronze Age Rural Ecology and Village Life at Tell el-Hayyat, Jordan

Steven E. Falconer
Patricia L. Fall

with contributions by
Ilya Berelov and Mary C. Metzger

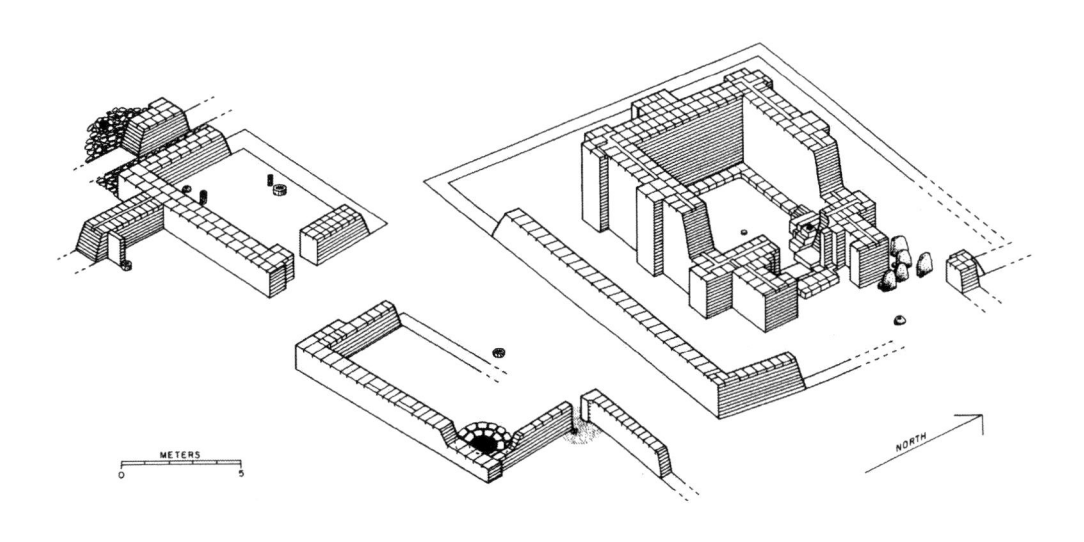

BAR International Series 1586
2006

This title published by

Archaeopress
Publishers of British Archaeological Reports
Gordon House
276 Banbury Road
Oxford OX2 7ED
England
bar@archaeopress.com
www.archaeopress.com

BAR S1586

Bronze Age Rural Ecology and Village Life at Tell el-Hayyat, Jordan

© S E Falconer P L Fall 2006

ISBN 1 84171 799 1

Printed in England by Chalvington Digital

All BAR titles are available from:

Hadrian Books Ltd
122 Banbury Road
Oxford
OX2 7BP
England
bar@hadrianbooks.co.uk

The current BAR catalogue with details of all titles in print, prices and means of payment is available free from Hadrian Books or may be downloaded from www.archaeopress.com

Tell el-Hayyat during excavation in 1983, amid the productive agricultural fields of the broad alluvial plain of the Jordan Valley, facing southwest (photo by Jon Kline).

DEDICATED

To our parents

Bob and Judy Falconer

Sam and Barbara Fall

TABLE OF CONTENTS

List of Figures viii

List of Tables xvi

List of Appendices xviii

Preface and Acknowledgements xix

CHAPTER I: Village Communities in the Bronze Age Levant: Ecology and History 1

    Introduction 1
    Physical Geography 1
        Local Environmental Conditions at Tell el-Hayyat. 4
    Agrarian Society in the Southern Levant 5
    Past Environment of the Jordan Rift 6
        Palynological Records for the Late Pleistocene and Early Holocene 6
        Palynological Records for the Bronze Age and Subsequent Periods 7
            Pollen Spectra from the Dead Sea Area 7
            Pollen Spectra from the Sea of Galilee 9
        Temporal and Spatial Vegetation Dynamics along the Levantine Rift 10
        Evidence for Climatic Change during the Bronze Age 10
    The Levantine Bronze Age 11
    Middle Bronze Age Urbanism and Ruralism 13
    Late Third and Early Second Millennium Settlement in the Jordan Valley 15
        Early Bronze IV Settlements 15
        Middle Bronze II Settlements 15

CHAPTER 2: Interpretative Framework for Exploring Bronze Age Ruralism 18

    Introduction 18
    Tell el-Hayyat: Discovery and Previous Research 18
    Excavations at Tell el-Hayyat 18
    Excavation Methods, Concepts and Terminology 24
    Units of Spatial Analysis 26
    Classification and Analysis of Material Remains 29
        Pottery 29
        Animal Bones 30
        Floral Remains 30
        Stone Tool Industries and Other Remains 31
        Multiple Lines of Evidence and Analysis 32

CHAPTER 3: Domestic and Public Architecture at Tell el-Hayyat 33

    Temples and Households: The Architectural Sequence 33
        Phase 6 (late Early Bronze IV) 33
        Phase 5 (early Middle Bronze IIA) 33
        Phase 4 (Middle Bronze IIA) 38
        Phase 3 (Middle Bronze IIA/B) 42
        Phase 2 (Middle Bronze IIB/C) 42
        Phase 1 (Middle Bronze IIC) 42
        Phase 0 (Post-Bronze Age) 43
    Tell el-Hayyat Village Architecture Overview 43

CHAPTER 4: Ceramic and Radiocarbon Chronology for Tell el-Hayyat 44

    Steven E. Falconer and Ilya Berelov

Introduction 44
Ceramic History at Tell el-Hayyat 44
    Phase 6 Pottery 44
    Phase 5 Pottery 46
    Phase 4 Pottery 49
    Phase 3 Pottery 52
    Phase 2 Pottery 57
    Phase 1 Pottery 59
    Decorative Techniques at Tell el-Hayyat (Phases 6-1) 60
Chronological Implications 61
Radiocarbon Chronology from Tell el-Hayyat 62
Tell el-Hayyat Phases and Chronology 63

CHAPTER 5: Economy and Subsistence at Tell el-Hayyat 65

    Patricia L. Fall and Mary C. Metzger

Agricultural Crops and the Expansion of Orchards 65
    The Domestication of Fruit Trees in the Levant 65
    Orchard Development and the Rise of Cities 66
        Levantine Arboriculture 67
    Crop Management at Tell el-Hayyat 69
Faunal Remains from Tell el-Hayyat 72
    Domestic Animals 73
    Wild Fauna 80
        Insectivores 80
        Rodents 80
        Ungulates 80
        Carnivores 80
        Birds 81
Conclusions 81

CHAPTER 6: Temple Economy and Ritual at Tell el-Hayyat 83

Introduction… 83
The Organization of Ritual 83
Temples and Ritual Behavior 84
The Bronze Age Temples at Tell el-Hayyat 86
    Phase 5 (early Middle Bronze IIA: ca. 2000-1900 B.C.) 87
    Phase 4 (Middle Bronze IIA: ca. 1900-1800 B.C.) 88
    Phase 3 (Middle Bronze IIA/B: ca. 1800-1700 B.C.) 96
    Phase 2 (Middle Bronze IIB/C: ca. 1700-1600 B.C.) 99
The Temples in Overview 101
Temples and Community 102
Patterns of Ritual Behavior and the Roles of Temples 103
    Animal Deposition and Temple Ritual 104
    Plant Deposition and Temple Ritual 105
    Pottery Deposition and Temple Ritual 106
        Cooking Vessels 107
        Storage Vessels 108
        Objects of Symbolic and Intrinsic Value 109
Ritual and Community at Tell el-Hayyat 109

CHAPTER 7: Household Economy at Tell el-Hayyat 111

    Introduction 111
    Historical and Ethnographic Insights on Ruralism 111
    Bronze Age Ruralism at Tell el-Hayyat 113
        Animal Management and Consumption 114
        Consumption and Exchange of Cultivated Plants 117
    Pottery Manufacture and Function 118
        Cooking Vessels 119
        Storage Vessels 119
    Household Material Culture 119
    Conclusions 123

CHAPTER 8: Bronze Age Agrarian Ecology along the Jordan Rift 124

    Introduction 124
    Bronze Age Agriculture 124
    Conclusions 128

REFERENCES CITED 130

APPENDICES A-G 143

APPENDICES A-S ON CD

LIST OF FIGURES

FRONTISPIECE Tell el-Hayyat during excavation in 1983, amid the productive agricultural fields of the broad alluvial plain of the Jordan Valley, facing southwest (photo by Jon Kline).

FIGURE A.1 Tell el-Hayyat Project Co-Director Bonnie Magness-Gardiner and William Dever, professor at the University of Arizona, at the Deir Alla dighouse, 1983 (photo by Jon Kline)..................xxi

FIGURE A.2 Khamis Fahid, Fuad Awadd, "Sheikh" Sadek Abdullah, Mohammed Jumrah, Ali Abdul Rusool (Abu Said) and Mohammed Darwish at the Meshara "dighouse," 1982 (l-r; photo by Bob Erskine). xxi

FIGURE A.3 Field staff for Tell el-Hayyat excavations, 1982. Land Rover roof (l-r): Ghazi Meisin, Steve Falconer, Pat Fall, Fuad Awadd, workman from Meshara. Standing (l-r) John Whittaker, Khamis Fahid, Tom Davis, Abu Jamal, Ron Gardiner, "Sheikh" Sadek Abdullah, Bonnie Magness-Gardiner, workman from Meshara, Mohammed Darwish, Mary Metzger, Mohammed Jumrah, Bob Erskine; Front Row: workman from Meshara, Kathy Kamp, two boys from Meshara, Ali Abdul Rusool (Abu Said), workmen from Meshara (photo by Bob Erskine)..xxii

FIGURE A.4 Field staff for Tell el-Hayyat excavations, 1983. Standing (l-r) "Sheikh" Sadek Abdullah, Bonnie Wistoff, Tom Davis, Ron Gardiner, Bob Erskine, Risa Carlson, Chuck Mobley, Fuad Awadd, Ali Abdul Rusool (Abu Said); Seated (l-r) Glen Peterman, Jenny Davis, Bonnie Magness-Gardiner, Steve Falconer, Pat Fall, Mary Metzger, Mohammed Darwish (photo by Jon Kline). xxii

FIGURE A.5 Full field crew for Tell el-Hayyat excavations, 1985; photo taken at Tell Abu en-Ni'aj (photo by Karen Scholz). xxiii

FIGURE A.6 Meshara "dighouse" at the end of the 1982 season at Tell el-Hayyat; Mary Metzger (l) and Bonnie Magness-Gardiner (r) (photo by Bob Erskine). xxiii

FIGURE A.7. Tell Deir 'Alla at sunset, as seen from the roof of the Deir 'Alla dighouse, 1983 (photo by Karen Scholz). xxiii

FIGURE A.8 Tell el-Hayyat field and house staff, 1985; photo taken at Deir 'Alla dighouse. Back row (l-r) Karen Scholz, Mohammed Jumrah, Mary Metzger, Steve Falconer, Pat Fall, Glen Peterman, John Meloy, Ron Gardiner, Gaetano Palumbo. Front row (l-r) Saad Hadidi, Haj Faris Joudeh, Jalal Jumrah, Rima Jumrah, Susan Morton, Lynn Grant, Paula Marcoux, Jonathan Mabry, Bonnie Magness-Gardiner, Umm Salem (photo by Karen Scholz). xxiv

FIGURE A.9 Mary Metzger excavating at Tell el-Hayyat, 1983 (photo by Jon Kline). xxiv

FIGURE 1.1 Physical geography of the southern Levant showing the Coastal Plain, the Rift Valley and the Jordan Plateau (map produced by Mariela Soto)..2

FIGURE 1.2 Archaeological sites and coring localities along the Jordan Rift. Inset shows location of Tell el-Hayyat on the *ghor*, the fertile alluvial terrace of the Jordan River (drafting by Barbara Trapido-Lurie). 3

FIGURE 1.3 View of the *zor* from the edge of the *ghor* at Tell Abu en-Ni'aj, facing west (photo by Karen Scholz). The edge of the riparian trees indicates the position of the Jordan River as it flows through the middle of the *zor*. 4

FIGURE 1.4 Tell el-Hayyat in the Jordan Valley during excavation in 1985; village of Mashara in background. Photo taken from Tell Abu en-Ni'aj looking northeast to the eastern escarpment of the Jordan Rift (photo by Karen Scholz). 5

FIGURE 1.5 Pollen diagram from Ein Gedi, Dead Sea (data from Baruch 1990; drafting by Barbara Trapido-Lurie)..8

FIGURE 1.6 Pollen diagram from Dead Sea (after Heim et al. 1997: fig. 3; drafting by Barbara Trapido-Lurie). 8

FIGURE 1.7 Pollen diagram from borehole U.P. 15 in the Huleh Basin (data from Horowitz 1971; 1979: fig. 6.20; drafting by Barbara Trapido-Lurie). 9

FIGURE 1.8 Pollen diagram from the Sea of Galilee (Lake Kinneret) (data from Baruch 1990; drafting by Barbara Trapido-Lurie)..9

FIGURE 1.9 Physiographic regions within the southern Levant from the Mediterranean Sea east to the Jordan Rift Valley (map created by Steve Savage)...11

FIGURE 1.10 Digital image 10m resolution (CNES/SPOT Image 1992-1994) showing locations of Early Bronze IV sites in the southern Levant, with sites mentioned in the text highlighted (data from Steve Savage; map created by Mariela Soto)..12

FIGURE 1.11 Digital image 10m resolution (CNES/SPOT Image 1992-1994) showing locations of Middle Bronze Age sites in the southern Levant, with sites mentioned in the text highlighted (data from Steve Savage; map created by Mariela Soto). 13

FIGURE 1.12 Rank-size curves for Early Bronze III and Middle Bronze IIB-C settlements in the southern Levant (see discussion in Falconer and Savage 1995; drafting by Barbara Trapido-Lurie). 14

FIGURE 1.13 Rank-size curves for Early Bronze II, Middle Bronze IIA and Middle Bronze IIB-C settlements in the Jordan Valley (see discussion in Falconer and Savage 1995; drafting by Barbara Trapido-Lurie). 14

FIGURE 2.1 The first day of excavation in Area A at Tell el-Hayyat, January 1982, facing north; Ron Gardiner (l) and Pat Fall (r) (photo by Bob Erskine). 19

FIGURE 2.2 Excavation of Areas C and D early in the 1982 season at Tell el-Hayyat, facing southwest (photo by Bob Erskine). 19

FIGURE 2.3 Topographic map of Tell-el-Hayyat showing the *tell*'s setting among agricultural fields. Excavation areas shown: Areas A and B (domestic trash and Phase 4 pottery kiln); Areas C, D, E, F, G, H, I, J, K, S and T (domestic architecture); Areas L, M, N, P, Q and R (temples); Area U (Phase 2 temple enclosure wall) (drafting by Barbara Trapido-Lurie). 19

FIGURE 2.4 Excavation of Areas B (foreground; supervisor Kathy Kamp) and A (background; supervisor Ron Gardiner) at Tell el-Hayyat, 1982, facing east (photo by Bob Erskine)................................ 19

FIGURE 2.5 Sheikh Sadek, Bonnie Magness-Gardiner and Abu Said (l to r) excavating Areas C and D after removal of intervening balk at Tell el-Hayyat, 1982, facing east (photo by Bob Erskine). . 20

FIGURE 2.6 Excavation of Areas D (foreground; supervisor Bonnie Magness-Gardiner with notebook) and C at Tell el-Hayyat, showing domestic household features, 1982, facing east (photo by Bob Erskine). 20

FIGURE 2.7 Teatime on the southern slope of Tell el-Hayyat, 1982, facing west; (photo by Bob Erskine). ... 21

FIGURE 2.8 Mansaf lunch outside Meshara "dighouse" during visit by Bill Dever, 1982; Khamis Fahid, Ali Abdul Rusool (behind Khamis), Fuad Awadd, "Sheikh" Sadek Abdullah, Bill Dever, Mohammed Jumrah, Bonnie Magness-Gardiner (l-r) (photo by Bob Erskine). 21

FIGURE 2.9 Excavation of Areas C-E and G-K at Tell el-Hayyat, 1983, with Areas H-K shown to the right, facing north (photo by Jon Kline). 21

FIGURE 2.10 Egyptian workmen during breakfast on the western slope of Tell el-Hayyat, 1983; facing north (photo by Jon Kline). 22

FIGURE 2.11 Tom Davis (on balk) and Ron Gardiner (below) excavating the Phase 4 pottery kiln in Area A at Tell el-Hayyat, 1983, facing southeast (photo by Jon Kline). 22

FIGURE 2.12 Excavation showing the discovery of the Phase 2 south temple wall in Areas L and M at Tell el-Hayyat, 1983; Steve Falconer cleaning pit dug into temple wall; facing east (photo by Jon Kline). 22

FIGURE 2.13 Bonnie Magness-Gardiner and Paula Marcoux shop for vegetables in Deir 'Alla, 1985 (photo by Karen Scholz). 23

FIGURE 2.14 John Meloy and Glen Peterman tend to yet another flat tire and other mechanical challenges of our trusty pickup truck at the Deir 'Alla dighouse, 1985; Haj Faris (dighouse caretaker) and Gaetano Palumbo supervise (photo by Karen Scholz). 23

FIGURE 2.15 Early in the 1985 excavations at Tell el-Hayyat; (l-r) Jake Jacobson (visitor), David McCreery (visitor), Steve Falconer, Bonnie Magness-Gardiner, Don Whitcomb (visitor), Linda McCreery (visitor) and John Meloy (in excavation unit) (l to r) (photo by Karen Scholz). 23

FIGURE 2.16 Excavations at Tell el-Hayyat in 1985 after removal of balks. Domestic architecture in foreground; temple enclosure wall running across the middle of the excavated area; beginning of exposure of Phase 4 temple in background, facing northwest (photo by Karen Scholz).......... 24

FIGURE 2.17 Large-scale balk removal to expose Phase 2 temple architecture at Tell el-Hayyat, 1985 (photo by Karen Scholz). 24

FIGURE 2.18 Example of locus sheet used during the excavation of Tell el-Hayyat. 25

FIGURE 2.19 Jenny Davis sieving sediment at Tell el-Hayyat, 1983 (photo by Jon Kline). 26

FIGURE 2.20 Lynn Grant, Bonnie Magness-Gardiner, Steve Falconer and Gaetano Palumbo (l to r) analyzing pottery from Tell el-Hayyat on the roof of the Deir 'Alla dighouse, 1985 (photo by Karen Scholz). 26

FIGURE 2.21 Architectural plans for phases 5-2 at Tell el-Hayyat showing sectors used in spatial analyses (drafting by Barbara Trapido-Lurie). 27

FIGURE 2.22 Architectural plans for phases 5-2 at Tell el-Hayyat showing temple and domestic architecture, including temple interiors and courtyards and domestic interiors and exteriors (drafting by Barbara Trapido-Lurie). 28

FIGURE 2.23 Pottery reading with Steve Falconer, Pat Fall, Bill Dever (visitor) and Bonnie Magness-Gardiner (l to r) at the Deir 'Alla dighouse, 1983 (photo by Jon Kline). 30
FIGURE 2.24 Glen Peterman and Lynn Grant (l to r) processing flotation samples at the Deir 'Alla dighouse, 1985 (photo by Karen Scholz). 31

FIGURE 3.1 Plan views of phases 5-2 at Tell el-Hayyat detailing architectural features in households and temples. Excavated foundations are stone (dark), mudbrick (stippled) and reconstructed (lined). Note depressions for potstands in Phase 5 temple, pedestal bases in center of Phase 4 and 3 temples, and in forecourt of Phase 2 temple. In temple forecourts standing stones are shown as dark; flat-lying stones shown in outline. Domestic features include small postholes, circular tabuns; in Phase 4 a rectangular basin drains west into a deep circular pit (drafting by B. Trapido-Lurie). 34
FIGURE 3.2 View across the Phase 5 temple at Tell el-Hayyat showing the stratification of all four temples in the north balk face of Areas N, P and Q. Conclusion of excavations, 1985, facing north, Glen Peterman (l), Steve Falconer (r). Note stratified remains of Phase 4, 3 and 2 temples in north and west balks. Phase 4 standing stone in north balk; Phase 5 structure in northeast corner (photo by Karen Scholz). 35
FIGURE 3.3 Stratigraphic cross-section across the north balk face of Areas N, P and Q, Tell el-Hayyat; drawn at the conclusion of the 1985 excavation season. 35
FIGURE 3.4 Drawing stratigraphic cross-sections at Tell el-Hayyat, 1985, facing southeast. Left to right: Pat Fall drawing south balk face of Area R; Bonnie Magness-Gardiner drawing north balk face of Area S; Ron Gardiner taking notes in Area T (photo by Karen Scholz). 36
FIGURE 3.5 Stratigraphic cross-section across the south balk face of Areas K and I at Tell el-Hayyat; drawn at the conclusion of the 1983 excavation season. 36
FIGURE 3.6 Stratigraphic cross-section across the north balk face of Area F at Tell el-Hayyat; drawn at the conclusion of the 1982 excavation season. 37
FIGURE 3.7 Stratigraphic cross-section across the south balk face of Area A at Tell el-Hayyat; drawn at the conclusion of the 1982 excavation season. The northern half of Area A was excavated in 1982, exposing the northern half of the Phase 4 kiln. Excavation of the southern half of Area A in 1983 revealed the remaining portion of Tell el-Hayyat's kiln. 37
FIGURE 3.8 Excavation of the Phase 4 temple at Tell el-Hayyat, 1985, facing northwest. Note clear Phase 4 mudbricks and standing stones in temple forecourt to the right. Single course stone foundation for Phase 3 temple shown directly on top of remains of Phase 4 temple north wall. Stone foundations and foundation trench for Phase 2 temple revealed in north and west balk faces. Two stratified Phase 2 temple plaster floors shown in north balk face (photo by Karen Scholz). 38
FIGURE 3.9 Shallow mudbrick basin with channel draining into a deep trash pit in the East Building, Phase 4 at Tell el-Hayyat, 1985, facing east (photo by Karen Scholz). 38
FIGURE 3.10 Deep trash pit excavated by Ron Gardiner (l) and Tom Davis (r) in the East Building, Phase 4 (Locus K064) at Tell el-Hayyat, 1983, facing southeast (photo by Jon Kline). 39
FIGURE 3.11 Mudbrick-encircled trash pit in the West Room, Phase 4 at Tell el-Hayyat, 1982, facing west. Note Phase 4 exterior paved alleyway in the foreground. Small square sounding reveals Phase 5 deposition (photo by Jon Kline). 39
FIGURE 3.12 Phase 4 pottery kiln interior at Tell el-Hayyat, 1982, showing brick walls and mud plastered interior wall of firing chamber, plus trash fill post-dating the kiln's use, facing south (photo by Bob Erskine). 39
FIGURE 3.13 Phase 4 pottery kiln at Tell el-Hayyat following excavation in 1983, facing southeast (photo by Jon Kline). Note brick work for firing chamber that was built back against tell sediments to the left. 39
FIGURE 3.14 Phase 4 pottery kiln at Tell el-Hayyat cut in cross-section following excavation in 1983, facing northwest (photo by Karen Scholz). Note plastered interior wall of firing chamber, access for stoking fuel from the left, three flues along edge of firing chamber in foreground. ... 40
FIGURE 3.15 Examples of ceramic wasters from Area A kiln debris, Tell el-Hayyat. Storejar handle on left displays the effects of bloating due to trapped gases or liquids; storejar body sherd on right exemplifies slumping due to excessive firing. 40
FIGURE 3.16 Human skeletal remains uncovered amid trash in Phase 4 pottery kiln at Tell el-Hayyat, 1982 (photo by Bob Erskine). 40
FIGURE 3.17 Skull, hand and wrist bones of a young adult male found buried in the Phase 4 pottery kiln at Tell el-Hayyat, 1982 (photo by Bob Erskine). 40
FIGURE 3.18 Remains of burned, chaff-plastered Phase 3 house (Sector EB) at Tell el-Hayyat, 1983, facing south (photo by Jon Kline). 41

FIGURE 3.19 Remains of two tabuns excavated in Phase 3 alley (Sector CA) at Tell el-Hayyat, 1983, facing north (photo by Jon Kline)..41

FIGURE 3.20 Stone foundations and mudbrick walls for Phase 2 domestic architecture at Tell el-Hayyat, 1983, facing west. Bonnie Wistoff in Phase 2 East Building (foreground left), Bonnie Magness-Gardiner at western end of temple enclosure wall (middle right), and Bob Erskine, Mary Metzger and workers excavating West Building 1 and West Building 2 (background) (photo by Jon Kline)..43

FIGURE 4.1 Early Bronze IV trickle painted cups (a, b), storejars (c-h, l-r), holemouth jars (i-k), small jar (s) and ledge handles (t-w) from Phase 6 at Tell el-Hayyat. Scale 1:5......................................45

FIGURE 4.2 Phase 5 pottery from Tell el-Hayyat, including transitional Early Bronze IV/Middle Bronze II forms and early Middle Bronze IIA vessels: bowls (a-d, h-j), closed globular vessels (e-g), cooking pots (k-m), storejars (n-y) and holemouth jar (z). Scale 1:5..47

FIGURE 4.3 Early Middle Bronze IIA hand-built carinated bowls found in conjunction with the Phase 5 temple at Tell el-Hayyat. Note the associated fragmentary incense burner found on a surface in the Phase 5 temple interior...48

FIGURE 4.4 Middle Bronze IIA bowls (a-h, k-p), kraters (i-j) and flat-bottomed cooking pot (q) from Phase 4 at Tell el-Hayyat. Scale 1:5...50

FIGURE 4.5 Middle Bronze IIA juglets (a, b), storejars (c-s) and widemouth jars (t-y) from Phase 4 at Tell el-Hayyat. Scale 1:5, except as noted (s)..51

FIGURE 4.6 Middle Bronze IIA-B bowls (a-f), deep bowls/kraters (g-l), carinated and globular bowls (m-q) and bowls bases (r-v) from Phase 3 at Tell el-Hayyat. Scale 1:5...53

FIGURE 4.7 Middle Bronze IIA-B flat-bottomed cooking pots (a-l) and globular cooking pots (m-p) from Phase 3 at Tell el-Hayyat. Scale 1:5...54

FIGURE 4.8 Middle Bronze IIA-B jugs (a-c), storejars (d-q), widemouth jars (r-t) and jug/jar base (u) from Phase 3 at Tell el-Hayyat. Scale 1:5..55

FIGURE 4.9 Middle Bronze IIB-C votive bowls (a-g), carinated and globular bowls (h-l), votive lamps (m, n), bowl bases (o, r-u), Chocolate on White ware (p, q), juglets (v-x) and pot stand (y) from Phase 2 at Tell el-Hayyat. Scale 1:5..56

FIGURE 4.10 Cache of votive vessels (five shallow bowls, three carinated bowls and two lamps) from Tell el-Hayyat found buried in the Phase 2 temple forecourt, at the foot of the front temple wall......57

FIGURE 4.11 Miniature hand-built, high-necked carinated bowl from Phase 2 at Tell el-Hayyat....................58

FIGURE 4.12 Examples of Carinated Bowls from Phase 2 at Tell el-Hayyat; note three holes drilled through the base of the bowl on the right..58

FIGURE 4.13 Three button-based juglets from Phases 3 and 2 at Tell el-Hayyat...59

FIGURE 4.14 Juglet and pot stand from Phase 2 at Tell el-Hayyat...59

FIGURE 4.15 Middle Bronze IIC platter bowls (c-e), large carinated bowl (b), globular vessel (f), ring and concave bowl bases (g, h), juglet button base (i) and flat-bottomed cooking pot (j) from Phase 1 at Tell el-Hayyat. A single example of a mortarium (a) belongs to the Persian Period. Scale 1:5...60

FIGURE 4.16 Examples of painted and applied decorative techniques commonly utilized on the pottery from Tell el-Hayyat..61

FIGURE 5.1 View of Tell el-Hayyat looking across the fields of the *ghor* in the foreground to the hills of Israel and Palestine in the background, facing west. Note the backdirt piles framing Tell el-Hayyat during the 1985 excavations. The Jordan River flows at the foot of the trees in the middle distance at the right (photo by Karen Scholz)..65

FIGURE 5.2 Patchwork of remnant Mediterranean forests, olive groves, and agricultural fields near Ajlun, Jordan about 1000 masl on the Jordan Plateau overlooking the northern Jordan Valley (photo by Pat Fall)..67

FIGURE 5.3 Domestic olive (*Olea europea*) trees near Umm Qeis, Jordan, like those planted in Classical period orchards (photo by Pat Fall)..68

FIGURE 5.4 Domestic grape (*Vitis vinifera*) vine (photo by Pat Fall)..68

FIGURE 5.5 Domestic fig (*Ficus carica*) tree (photo by Pat Fall)..69

FIGURE 5.6 Local farmer plowing the fields west of Tell el-Hayyat, 1982, facing west (photo by Bob Erskine)..69

FIGURE 5.7 The Zarqa River near its confluence with the Jordan River in the Jordan Valley, facing northeast (photo by Pat Fall)..70

FIGURE 5.8 Pat Fall recovering seeds from Tell el-Hayyat by water flotation (photo by Steve Falconer).......70

FIGURE 5.9 Density ratios of wheat and barley by phase at Tell el-Hayyat (drafting by Barbara Trapido-Lurie)..72

FIGURE 5.10 Density ratios of olive and grape seeds by phase at Tell el-Hayyat (drafting by Barbara Trapido-Lurie). 72

FIGURE 5.11 Mary Metzger at the Deir 'Alla dighouse with pots from Deir 'Alla on the top three shelves and bones from Tell el-Hayyat on the bottom two shelves, 1985 (photo by Jon Kline). 73

FIGURE 5.12 Relative frequencies of domestic animal bones by phase at Tell el-Hayyat (data based on NISP; drafting by Barbara Trapido-Lurie). 74

FIGURE 5.13 The goat (*Capra hircus*) was a major source of meat and dairy products at Tell el-Hayyat, and became favored for ritual consumption associated with Hayyat's temples (photo by Mary Metzger). 75

FIGURE 5.14 Sheep (*Ovis aries*) management became accentuated at Tell el-Hayyat, reflecting increased production of wool, one of the major trade commodities of the secondary products revolution. View from the top of Tell Abu en-Ni'aj[N], 1985, facing southeast (photo by Karen Scholz). 75

FIGURE 5.15 Evidence for consumption of pig (*Sus scrofa*) illustrates a trend of increased household economic autonomy at Tell el-Hayyat (photo by Will Falconer). 79

FIGURE 5.16 The remains of cattle (*Bos taurus*) at Tell el-Hayyat indicate their use as traction animals and their declining importance as sources of beef often associated with urban elites. Cattle in the modern village of Mashara, facing north (photo by Jon Kline). 79

FIGURE 6.1 Regional map of Syria and the southern Levant showing locations of archaeological sites with temples mentioned in text (drafting by Barbara Trapido-Lurie). 84

FIGURE 6.2 Plan view of Middle Bronze Age temple and domestic architecture at Tell el-Hayyat, Phases 5-2 (drafting by Barbara Trapido-Lurie). 85

FIGURE 6.3 Isometric reconstruction of Phase 5 (early Middle Bronze IIA) temple at Tell el-Hayyat (drafting by Chuck Sternberg). 86

FIGURE 6.4 Tell el-Hayyat Phase 5 temple, facing west. Note temple interior with platform in northeast corner and low curb along south and west walls; Steve Falconer in foreground, Glen Peterman at back of temple (photo by Karen Scholz). 86

FIGURE 6.5 Standing stone and adjacent flat-lying stones in northeast portion of Phase 5 temple forecourt at Tell el-Hayyat, facing east (photo by Karen Scholz). 87

FIGURE 6.6 Ceramic incense burner from surface in Phase 5 temple interior at Tell el-Hayyat (photo by Karen Scholz). 87

FIGURE 6.7 Copper alloy plates resembling miniature "oxhide" ingots from Phase 5 temple interior surface (l) and jar in Phase 4 temple altar (r) at Tell el-Hayyat (photo by Karen Scholz). 87

FIGURE 6.8 Copper alloy anthropomorphic figurine, possibly depicting the Canaanite goddess Astarte, found embedded in the mudbrick curb inside the Phase 5 temple at Tell el-Hayyat (photo by Karen Scholz). 88

FIGURE 6.9 Front and back views of copper alloy anthropomorphic figurine found embedded in the mudbrick curb inside the Phase 5 temple at Tell el-Hayyat. Front and end views of carved limestone mold for casting anthropomorphic figurines; mold found in forecourt of the Phase 3 temple (drawings by Jonathan Mabry). 88

FIGURE 6.10 Tell el-Hayyat Phase 4 temple, facing west. Note temple interior with central depression for pedestal, low mudbrick curb, mudbrick altar in northeast corner; Paula Marcoux in foreground, Steve Falconer behind back temple wall (photo by Karen Scholz). 89

FIGURE 6.11 Isometric reconstruction of Phase 4 (Middle Bronze IIA) temple and domestic structures at Tell el-Hayyat (drafting by Chuck Sternberg). 89

FIGURE 6.12 Inset-offset niching of southern temple *anta* framing the entry to the Phase 4 temple at Tell el-Hayyat, facing southwest. Brickwork shows lower, original construction and subsequent remodeling, both Phase 4 (photo by Karen Scholz). 90

FIGURE 6.13 Stepped mudbrick platform or "altar" in northeast corner of Phase 4 temple at Tell el-Hayyat (photo by Karen Scholz). 90

FIGURE 6.14 Painted jar set into altar in northeast corner of Phase 4 temple at Tell el-Hayyat (photo by Karen Scholz). 91

FIGURE 6.15 Carnelian beads found in Phase 4 temple altar at Tell el-Hayyat (photo by Karen Scholz). 91

FIGURE 6.16 Standing stones and associated flat-lying stones around north buttress of the Tell el-Hayyat Phase 4 temple shown after excavation to its founding level, facing northwest. Level of chinking stones around bases of the standing stones indicate the stones were added after the initial construction of the northern *anta* and before the subsequent enlargement of the *anta* (photo by Karen Scholz). 92

FIGURE 6.17 Mudbrick steps just outside the temple entrance added late in Phase 4 at Tell el-Hayyat, facing northwest; Pat Fall at corner of altar (photo by Karen Scholz). 92

FIGURE 6.18 Zoomorphic figurines from surface of Phase 4 temple interior at Tell el-Hayyat; upper figurine has perforated base, presumably for hafting (drawings by Jonathan Mabry and Ronald Beckwith). 93

FIGURE 6.19 Copper alloy zoomorphic figurine, possibly bovine, from surface in Phase 4 temple interior at Tell el-Hayyat (photo by Karen Scholz). 93

FIGURE 6.20 Copper alloy zoomorphic figurine from surface deposits (Phase 0) in Area N at Tell el-Hayyat. 93

FIGURE 6.21 Large ceramic krater with two appended anthropomorphic figures recovered from an interior surface in the Phase 4 temple at Tell el-Hayyat (photo by Karen Scholz). 93

FIGURE 6.22 Kernos fragments from courtyard surfaces associated with the Phase 4 and Phase 3 temples at Tell el-Hayyat (photo by Karen Scholz). 94

FIGURE 6.23 Kernos fragment from Phase 4 temple courtyard at Tell el-Hayyat (photo by Karen Scholz). 94

FIGURE 6.24 Well-preserved copper alloy spear points from the courtyard of the Phase 4 temple at Tell el-Hayyat (photo by Karen Scholz). 94

FIGURE 6.25 Copper alloy spear points from the courtyard of the Phase 4 temple at Tell el-Hayyat (drawing by Jonathan Mabry). 94

FIGURE 6.26 Copper alloy tongs, tangs and points from Phase 4 temple courtyard and interior surfaces at Tell el-Hayyat (photo by Karen Scholz). 95

FIGURE 6.27 Carved limestone molds for casting metal anthropomorphic figurines (mold from Phase 3 Temple Forecourt) and tanged tools (mold from Phase 4 East Alley) at Tell el-Hayyat (photo by Karen Scholz). 95

FIGURE 6.28 Fragments of a ceramic ladle with solidified copper in its cracks, suggesting its use for pouring molten copper to cast tools or figurines; found in Phase 4 surface in the East Alley at Tell el-Hayyat (photo by Karen Scholz). 95

FIGURE 6.29 Tell el-Hayyat Phase 3 temple, facing west. Note asymmetrical *antae* and temple interior with central depression for pedestal. Some foundation stones for south wall were removed by Phase 2 foundation trench; Jonathan Mabry at left, John Meloy at right (photo by Karen Scholz). 96

FIGURE 6.30 Isometric reconstruction of Phase 3 (Middle Bronze IIA-B) temple and domestic structures at Tell el-Hayyat (drafting by Chuck Sternberg). 96

FIGURE 6.31 Tell el-Hayyat Phase 3 temple with accompanying standing stones arrayed in a shallow arc outside the temple entrance, facing east; Jonathan Mabry in foreground, John Meloy by standing stones (photo by Karen Scholz). 97

FIGURE 6.32 Group of standing stones and their accompanying flat-lying stones in forecourt of Phase 3 temple at Tell el-Hayyat, facing east. Note that the stones are founded at different levels, suggesting they were installed at different times (photo by Karen Scholz). 97

FIGURE 6.33 Group of standing stones, including stacked stones, and accompanying flat-lying stones in the forecourt of the Phase 3 temple at Tell el-Hayyat, facing east (photo by Karen Scholz). 97

FIGURE 6.34 Portion of collapsed Phase 3 temple enclosure wall at Tell el-Hayyat with its excavator, Area U supervisor Susan Morton, facing northwest. Note diagonal coursing of fallen bricks in north balk (photo by Karen Scholz). 98

FIGURE 6.35 Area P at Tell el-Hayyat, showing collapsed mudbrick wall from Phase 3 temple (directly in front of Area Supervisor Glen Peterman) lying under preserved portions of Phase 2 temple interior plaster floor (behind Peterman and under hand picks at right), facing southwest (photo by Karen Scholz). 98

FIGURE 6.36 Fragment of ceramic anthropomorphic figurine, possibly a depiction of Astarte, from a surface in the Phase 3 East Courtyard at Tell el-Hayyat (photo by Karen Scholz). 99

FIGURE 6.37 Miniature ceramic cart wheel fragments from the Phase 3 temple forecourt at Tell el-Hayyat (photo by Karen Scholz). 99

FIGURE 6.38 Middle Bronze Age temples *in antis* from towns and villages in the southern Levant. a. Megiddo, Temple 2048 (Dunayevsky and Kempinski 1973: fig. 2), b. Kfar Rupin (Gophna 1979: fig. 2), c. Nahariyeh (Mazar 1992: 162), d. Tell Kitan, Stratum V (Eisenberg 1977: 80), e. Shechem, Temple 1a (Wright 1965: fig. 41) (drafting by Barbara Trapido-Lurie). 99

FIGURE 6.39 Tell el-Hayyat Phase 2 temple, facing west. Pat Fall in foreground, Susan Morton at back left. Note portions of two white plaster temple interior floors shown in section at back right. Two superimposed exterior plaster surfaces are preserved in the north balk face behind Pat Fall. Some foundation stones in south wall were removed by Byzantine and later pits and burials (photo by Karen Scholz). 100

FIGURE 6.40 Isometric reconstruction of Phase 2 (Middle Bronze IIB-C) temple and domestic structures at Tell el-Hayyat (drafting by Chuck Sternberg). 100

FIGURE 6.41 Section view of stratified white plaster floors in the interior of the Phase 2 temple at Tell el-Hayyat, facing south (photo by Karen Scholz). 101

FIGURE 6.42 Basalt pedestal shown *in situ* in forecourt of Phase 2 temple at Tell el-Hayyat, facing south. Note foundation stones under the pedestal, and portion of hard-packed surface cut by a burial (photo by Karen Scholz). 101

FIGURE 6.43 Basalt pedestal from the Tell el-Hayyat Phase 2 temple forecourt, and two basalt steps probably related to the Phase 2 temple entrance shown after excavation (photo by Karen Scholz). 102

FIGURE 6.44 Gaetano Palumbo (l, holding miniature carinated bowl) and Steve Falconer (r) excavate a cache of Middle Bronze IIB-C votive bowls and lamps buried under two stratified plaster surfaces in the Phase 2 temple forecourt at Tell el-Hayyat, facing north. East temple wall is behind Palumbo (photo by Karen Scholz). 103

FIGURE 6.45 Temples *in antis* from towns and cities in Syria. a. Mari, Temple of Dagan (Margueron 1984: 48), b. Ugarit, Temple of Ba'al (Yon 1984: fig. 2), c. Emar, Temple of the Diviner (Margueron 1984a: fig. 7), d. Ebla, Temple P2 (Matthiae 1989: fig. 5) (drafting by Barbara Trapido-Lurie). 103

FIGURE 6.46 Relative bone frequencies for major domesticated animal taxa in temple interiors, courtyards and domestic areas at Tell el-Hayyat, Phases 5-3, expressed as percentages of total number of identified specimens (NISP; here NISP excludes other domesticates and wild taxa) (drafting by Barbara Trapido-Lurie). Tests of null hypothesis: a. Temple interiors: $\chi^2 = 21.989$, df = 4, p < .001; Temple courtyards: $\chi^2 = 120.463$, df = 4, p < .001; Domestic areas: $\chi^2 = 86.686$, df = 4, p < .001. 104

FIGURE 6.47 Frequencies of ovicaprid bone elements in temple interiors, temple courtyards and domestic areas at Tell el-Hayyat, Phases 5-3, expressed as percentages of NISP (drafting by Barbara Trapido-Lurie). Tests of null hypothesis: Phase 5: $\chi^2 = 45.545$, df = 4, p < .001; Phase 4: $\chi^2 = 157.432$, df = 4, p < .001; Phase 3: $\chi^2 = 34.295$, df = 4, p < .001. 105

FIGURE 6.48 Relative frequencies of cultivated plant macrofossils in temple compounds and domestic areas at Tell el-Hayyat, Phases 5-3, expressed as percentages of total identified fragments (drafting by Barbara Trapido-Lurie). Tests of null hypothesis: Temple compounds: $\chi^2 = 114.664$, df = 4, p < .001; Domestic areas: $\chi^2 = 31.376$, df = 4, p < .001. 106

FIGURE 6.49 Frequencies of rim types by functional categories in temple interiors, temple courtyards and domestic areas at Tell el-Hayyat, Phases 5-3, expressed as percentages of total identified rims. (drafting by Barbara Trapido-Lurie). Tests of null hypothesis: a. Temple interiors: $\chi^2 = 44.914$, df = 4, p < .001; Temple courtyards: $\chi^2 = 61.279$, df = 4, p < .001; Domestic areas: $\chi^2 = 48.243$, df = 4, p < .001. 107

FIGURE 7.1 Rural mudbrick farmstead and agricultural fields in the *ghor*, looking northwest to the *zor*, or active floodplain of the Jordan River, 1985 (photo by Bob Erskine). 112

FIGURE 7.2 Mudbrick "bee hive" houses at the Deir 'Alla Agricultural Station, 1983 (photo by Steve Falconer). 112

FIGURE 7.3 Excavation of Phase 2 architecture at Tell el-Hayyat, 1983, facing southwest. Stone foundation for temple enclosure wall at right; room in Sector EB1 at left; room in Sector WB2 in background (photo by Jon Kline). 114

FIGURE 7.4 Excavation of Phase 2 architecture at Tell el-Hayyat, 1983, facing south. Stone foundation for southeast temple corner in foreground with two abutting tower foundation walls. Room in Sector EB1 in background (photo by Jon Kline). 114

FIGURE 7.5 Relative bone frequencies for major domesticated animal taxa at Tell el-Hayyat, Phases 5-3, expressed as percentages of total number of identified specimens (NISP), excluding other domesticates (equids) and wild taxa. **A.** All architectural settings, $\chi^2 = 183.21$, df = 4, p < 0.001; NISP: Phase 5 = 2427, Phase 4 = 2802, Phase 3 = 1822. **B.** Domestic areas, $\chi^2 = 86.69$, df = 4, p < 0.001; NISP: Phase 5 = 832, Phase 4 = 882, Phase 3 = 703 (drafting by Barbara Trapido-Lurie). 115

FIGURE 7.6 Faunal survivorship curves at Tell el-Hayyat, Phases 5-3; data from all architectural settings expressed in percentages of NISP that could be aged by bone fusion or tooth eruption. **A.** *Bos taurus* (cattle), NISP: Phase 5 = 137, Phase 4 = 109, Phase 3 = 44. **B.** *Sus scrofa* (pig); NISP: Phase 5 = 60, Phase 4 = 67, Phase 3 = 51 (drafting by Barbara Trapido-Lurie). 116

FIGURE 7.7 Relative frequencies of cultivated plant macrofossils from all architectural settings at Tell el-Hayyat, Phases 5-3, expressed as percentages of total identified seeds. $\chi^2 = 150.08$, df = 4, p < 0.001; number: Phase 5 = 1170, Phase 4 = 707, Phase 3 = 849 (drafting by Barbara Trapido-Lurie). 117

FIGURE 7.8 Relative rim frequencies for major functional categories of pottery at Tell el-Hayyat, Phases 5-3, expressed as percentages of total identified rims, corrected for multiple sherds from the same vessel. **A.** All architectural settings, $\chi^2 = 156.17$, df = 4, p < 0.001; number: Phase 5 = 833, Phase 4 = 1685, Phase 3 = 1449. **B.** Domestic areas, $\chi^2 = 48.24$, df = 4, p < 0.001;

	number: Phase 5 = 644, Phase 4 = 1213, Phase 3 = 902. **C.** Temple compounds, χ^2 = 166.16, df = 4, p < 0.001; number: Phase 5 = 189, Phase 4 = 472, Phase 3 = 547 (drafting by Barbara Trapido-Lurie). 119
FIGURE 7.9	Ron Gardiner and Bonnie Magness-Gardiner excavate mudbrick walls in the southwest corner of the Phase 4 temple at Tell el-Hayyat, facing southwest (photo by Karen Scholz). A pick and shovel rest against the Phase 4 temple southern enclosure wall to the left; the brick coursing of the Phase 3 western enclosure wall is clearly visible in the balk face to the right... 120
FIGURE 7.10	Smashed jars, a juglet and grinding stone lie in Phase 2 occupational debris (Locus T022) just above an earthen surface in the East Building (Sector EB) at Tell el-Hayyat, facing east (photo by Karen Scholz). 120
FIGURE 7.11	Clay pinch pot with clay marbles from a shallow Phase 4 pit (Locus K064) in the East Building (Sector EB) at Tell el-Hayyat. 121
FIGURE 7.12	Clay jar stopper from a shallow Phase 4 pit (Locus K064) in the East Building (Sector EB) at Tell el-Hayyat. 121
FIGURE 7.13	Basalt bowl from a Phase 4 surface (Locus J059) in the East Alley (Sector EA) at Tell el-Hayyat. 121
FIGURE 7.14	Polished porphery bowl fragment, probably Middle Bronze Age, but found in mixed Phase 0 deposits in Area H at Tell el-Hayyat. 121
FIGURE 7.15	Examples of the ground stone industry from domestic contexts at Tell el-Hayyat, including a large stone mortar, basalt grinding stones, and drilled and perforated cobbles. 121
FIGURE 7.16	Examples of domestic ground stone from Tell el-Hayyat, including basalt grinders, a perforated stone weight and worked limestone cobbles. 121
FIGURE 7.17	Perforated ceramic (center top) and stone disks from domestic contexts at Tell el-Hayyat. 121
FIGURE 7.18	Worked animal bone tools from households at Tell el-Hayyat, including scrapers, awls and shuttles. 122
FIGURE 7.19	Finely sharpened animal bone awl or needle fragments from domestic contexts at Tell el-Hayyat. 122
FIGURE 7.20	Hollowed sheep/goat long bones found amid Phase 3 and Phase 4 household remains at Tell el-Hayyat. 122
FIGURE 7.21	Hollowed and perforated sheep/goat tibiae from Phase 3 and Phase 4 domestic contexts at Tell el-Hayyat. 122
FIGURE 7.22	Marine shell amulet from fill in the Central Alley, Phase 4 at Tell el-Hayyat. 122
FIGURE 7.23	Scarab from fill in the East Building, Room 1, Phase 2 at Tell el-Hayyat................................... 122
FIGURE 7.24	Seal impression on a clay fragment from a surface in the West Building, Room 1, Phase 2 at Tell el-Hayyat. Arrow indicates 1 cm.. 123
FIGURE 8.1	Archaeological sites and paleoenvironmental localities in the southern Levant, including Bab edh-Dhra' and Wadi Fidan 4 near the Dead Sea. Inset specifies locations of Tell el-Hayyat and Tell Abu en-Ni'aj in the northern Jordan Valley (drafting by Barbara Trapido-Lurie). 125
FIGURE 8.2	Pat Fall and Steve Falconer at Tell Abu en-Ni`aj, view facing southwest and the edge of the *ghor*, 1985 (photo by Karen Scholtz). 125
FIGURE 8.3	Relative frequencies of barley and wheat macrofossils recovered from Bronze Age archaeological sites along the Jordan Rift (drafting by Barbara Trapido-Lurie). Data from McCreery (1980), Lines (1995), Meadows (1996), Fall et al. (1998). 126
FIGURE 8.4	Relative frequencies of grape and olive macrofossils recovered from Bronze Age archaeological sites along the Jordan Rift (drafting by Barbara Trapido-Lurie). Data from McCreery (1980), Lines (1995), Meadows (1996), Fall et al. (1998). 127
FIGURE 8.5	Relative frequencies of fig macrofossils recovered from Bronze Age archaeological sites along the Jordan Rift (drafting by Barbara Trapido-Lurie). Data from McCreery (1980), Lines (1995), Meadows (1996), Fall et al. (1998). 127
FIGURE 8.6	Tell el-Hayyat during excavation, 1983; Christ-thorn (*Ziziphus spina-christii*) tree in fields in the foreground; hills rise to the east from the Jordan Rift Valley in the background, 1983 (photo by Jon Kline). 129

LIST OF TABLES

TABLE 1.1	Archaeological and historical chronology for the southern Levant (following Levy and Bar-Yosef 1995: figs. 2 and 3)	5
TABLE 2.1	Archaeological chronology for the southern Levant, incorporating the settlement sequence at Tell el-Hayyat (following Levy and Bar-Yosef 1995: figs. 2 and 3)	23
TABLE 2.2	Classification of loci and associated locus codes for Tell el-Hayyat (see Appendices)	26
TABLE 3.1	Phases of occupation and associated architecture at Tell el-Hayyat	33
TABLE 4.1	Chronological table for phases of occupation at Tell el-Hayyat. Absolute dates derived from comparative pottery typologies and radiocarbon determinations (see Table 4.2)	44
TABLE 4.2	Results of AMS ^{14}C on samples from Tell el-Hayyat calibrated in November 2005 with Calib 5.0 on the basis of Stuiver, M., and Reimer, P.J., 1993 (VERA and OxA dates were analyzed and compiled by Ezra Marcus for the MB chronology project, a sub-project of SCIEM2000, funded by the Jubily Fund of the City of Vienna, Austrian Academy of Sciences. SCIEM2000 is a special program of the Austrian Academy of Sciences, headed by Professor Manfred Bietak)	63
TABLE 5.1	Seeds identified from Tell el-Hayyat; summarized by crop categories; data presented as numbers of seeds (and % of total seeds)	71
TABLE 5.2	Floral taxa recovered from Tell el-Hayyat presented as seed densities (number of seeds per kiloliter of sediment); summarized by crop categories	71
TABLE 5.3	Animal taxa from Tell el-Hayyat presented as number of identified specimens (NISP)	73
TABLE 5.4	Bone counts (n = NISP) and relative frequencies (%) of domesticated animal taxa at Tell el-Hayyat, Phases 0-6	74
TABLE 5.5	Bone counts (n = NISP) and relative frequencies (%) of sheep/goat, pig and cattle at Tell el-Hayyat by excavation area	74
TABLE 5.6	Domesticated animal taxa at Tell el-Hayyat presented as minimum number of individuals (MNI), Phases 2-5	75
TABLE 5.7	Sheep/Goat survivorship (% survival) at Tell el-Hayyat based on tooth wear, Phases 2-5	76
TABLE 5.8	Sheep/Goat survivorship at Tell el-Hayyat based on bone fusion, Phases 2-5	76
TABLE 5.9	Sheep/Goat survivorship at Tell el-Hayyat based on bone fusion groupings (% fused), Phases 2-5	77
TABLE 5.10	Pig survivorship at Tell el-Hayyat based on tooth eruption and wear, Phases 2-5	77
TABLE 5.11	Pig survivorship at Tell el-Hayyat based on bone fusion, Phases 2-5	77
TABLE 5.12	Pig survivorship at Tell el-Hayyat based on bone fusion groupings (% fused), Phases 2-5	78
TABLE 5.13	Cattle survivorship at Tell el-Hayyat based on tooth eruption and wear, Phases 2-5	78
TABLE 5.14	Cattle survivorship at Tell el-Hayyat based on bone fusion, Phases 2-5	78
TABLE 5.15	Cattle survivorship at Tell el-Hayyat based on bone fusion groupings (% fused), Phases 2-5	80
TABLE 6.1	Chi-square statistics for comparisons of domesticated animal taxa in temple interiors, temple courtyards and domestic areas at Tell el-Hayyat, Phases 3-5	104
TABLE 6.2	Sheep:goat ratios based on NISP identifiable as *Ovis* or *Capra* in temple vs. domestic contexts at Tell el-Hayyat, Phases 3-5: a. Ratios; b. Bone Counts	104
TABLE 6.3	Chi-square statistics for comparisons of taxonomic frequencies for seeds in temple vs. domestic contexts at Tell el-Hayyat, Phases 3-5	106
TABLE 6.4	Relative frequencies of domesticated fruit taxa in temple vs. domestic contexts at Tell el-Hayyat, Phases 3-5: a. Temple Compounds; b. Domestic Areas	106
TABLE 6.5	Chi-square statistics for comparisons between functional categories of ceramic vessels in temple interiors, temple courtyards and domestic areas at Tell el-Hayyat, Phases 3-5	107
TABLE 6.6	Ratios of flat-bottomed to ovoid cooking pots in temple interiors, temple courtyards and domestic areas at Tell el-Hayyat, Phases 3-5: a. Ratios; b. Rim Counts	108
TABLE 6.7	Ratios of long-term to short-term storage vessels in temple interiors, temple courtyards and domestic areas at Tell el-Hayyat, Phases 3-5: a. Ratios; b. Rim Counts	108
TABLE 6.8	Distribution of manufactured objects in temple and domestic sectors at Tell el-Hayyat categorized by material (unidentifiable fragments and production debris excluded)	109

TABLE 7.1	Sheep: goat ratios at Tell el-Hayyat, Phases 3-5 based on NISP*	115
TABLE 7.2	Frequencies of pig bone elements in domestic areas at Tell el-Hayyat, Phases 4 and 3 presented as percentages of NISP*	116
TABLE 7.3	Frequencies of ovicaprid bone elements in domestic areas at Tell el-Hayyat, Phases 4 and 3 presented as percentages of NISP*	116
TABLE 7.4	Ratios of annual to perennial plant macrofossils at Tell el-Hayyat, Phases 3-5 based on number of identified seeds*	118
TABLE 7.5	Ratios of annual to perennial plant macrofossils at Tell el-Hayyat, Phases 4 and 3 based on number of identified seeds*	118
TABLE 7.6	Ratios of flat-bottomed to ovoid cooking vessels at Tell el-Hayyat, Phases 3-5 based on rim counts corrected for joins*	119
TABLE 7.7	Ratios of long-term to short-term storage vessels at Tell el-Hayyat, Phases 3-5 based on rim counts corrected for joins*	119
TABLE 8.1	Macrobotanical samples and barley:wheat ratios from Bronze Age sites along the Jordan Rift. Data from McCreery (1980); Lines (1995); Meadows (1996); Fall, et al. (1998)	127

LIST OF APPENDICES

APPENDIX A Codes for Tell el-Hayyat databases

APPENDIX B Tell el-Hayyat excavated loci (filename: "TH LOCUS")

APPENDIX C Tell el-Hayyat registered objects (filename: "TH REGISTERED OBJECTS")

APPENDIX D Tell el-Hayyat registered object descriptions (filename: "TH REGISTERED OBJECTS DESCRIPTION")

APPENDIX E Tell el-Hayyat seed counts (filename: "TH FLORA SUMMARY")

APPENDIX F Tell el-Hayyat seed densities (filename: "TH FLORA DENSITY")

APPENDIX G Tell el-Hayyat flotation samples and seed identifications (filename: "TH FLORA ALL PHASES")

APPENDIX H Tell el-Hayyat sheep/goat identifications (filename: "TH FAUNA SHEEP/GOAT")

APPENDIX I Tell el-Hayyat pig bone identifications (filename: "TH FAUNA PIG")

APPENDIX J Tell el-Hayyat cattle bone identifications (filename: "TH FAUNA CATTLE")

APPENDIX K Tell el-Hayyat wild animal identifications (filename: "TH FAUNA WILD")

APPENDIX L Tell el-Hayyat analyzed Phase 5 ceramics (filename: "TH CERAMICS PHASE 5")

APPENDIX M Tell el-Hayyat comments on analyzed Phase 5 ceramics (filename: "TH CERAMICS PHASE 5 COMMENTS")

APPENDIX N Tell el-Hayyat analyzed Phase 4 ceramics (filename: "TH CERAMICS PHASE 4")

APPENDIX O Tell el-Hayyat comments on analyzed Phase 4 ceramics (filename: "TH CERAMICS PHASE 4 COMMENTS")

APPENDIX P Tell el-Hayyat analyzed Phase 3 ceramics (filename: "TH CERAMICS PHASE 3")

APPENDIX Q Tell el-Hayyat comments on analyzed Phase 3 ceramics (filename: "TH CERAMICS PHASE 3 COMMENTS")

APPENDIX R Tell el-Hayyat analyzed Phase 2 ceramics (filename: "TH CERAMICS PHASE 2")

APPENDIX S Tell el-Hayyat comments on analyzed Phase 2 ceramics (filename: "TH CERAMICS PHASE 2 COMMENTS")

PREFACE AND ACKNOWLEDGMENTS

We are grateful to the Department of Antiquities of Jordan and the people of Jordan who made our investigations into Bronze Age life at Tell el-Hayyat so enjoyable and who helped us not only in all aspects of the research, but shared their hospitality and culture with us. The success of the excavations at Tell el-Hayyat was made possible through the professional cooperation of the Department of Antiquities of Jordan, particularly by Director-General Dr. Adnan Hadidi, and the American Center of Oriental Research (ACOR), Amman, and Director Dr. David McCreery. In 1980 Dr. Hadidi brought Tell el-Hayyat to the attention of then ACOR Director Dr. James Sauer, and to Dr. William Dever who promoted the excavation of Tell el-Hayyat in 1982, 1983 and 1985 under the Co-Direction of Steven Falconer and Bonnie Magness-Gardiner. We are indebted, in particular, to both Drs. Hadidi and Dever who supported and encouraged the Tell el-Hayyat project from its inception, including providing financial support for the 1982 and 1983 field seasons (Figure A.1). We thank David and Linda McCreery, staff and fellows at the "old ACOR," the American Center of Oriental Research in Amman, who provided hospitality and helped with logistical support.

Skilled technical support in the field was provided by representatives from the Department of Antiquities and the "Jericho Men" who taught us the finer points of excavating mudbrick architecture (Figure A.2). We thank the villagers from Mashara who worked with us all three seasons; laborers from Egypt (1983) and Wadi Yabis (1985) also assisted us in the field. We especially are grateful to our colleagues and specialists who lived with and worked along side us and provided many happy memories during the three excavation seasons at Tell el-Hayyat:

1982 field season: Department of Antiquities representatives – Mohammed Darwish and Mohammed Jumrah; Fuad Awadd and the "Jericho Men" – Ali Abdul Rusool (Abu Said), "Sheikh" Sadek Abdullah and Khamis Fahid; Bonnie Magness-Gardiner (Co-Director), Thomas Davis, Robert Erskine, Ron Gardiner, Katherine Kamp, Mary Metzger, and John Whittaker (Figure A.3).

1983 field season: Department of Antiquities representatives – Mohammed Darwish and Mohammed Jumrah; Fuad Awadd; the "Jericho Men" – Ali Abdul Rusool (Abu Said) and "Sheikh" Sadek Abdullah; Bonnie Magness-Gardiner (Co-Director), Risa Carlson, Jenny Davis, Thomas Davis, Robert Erskine, Ron Gardiner, Jon Kline, Mary Metzger, Charles Mobley, and Bonnie Wistoff (Figure A.4).

1985 field season: Department of Antiquities representatives – Mohammed Darwish and Saad Hadidi; the "Jericho Men" – Ali Abdul Rusool (Abu Said) and "Sheikh" Sadek Abdullah. Bonnie Magness-Gardiner (Co-Director), Barbara Fall (volunteer), Sam Fall (volunteer), Robert Erskine, Ron Gardiner, Lynn Grant, Mary Metzger, Jonathan Mabry, Paula Marcoux, John Meloy, Susan Morton, Gaetano Palumbo, Glen Peterman, and Karen Scholz (Figure A.5).

In 1982 we rented a house in Meshara (Figure Figure A.6). During the 1983 and 1985 field seasons we lived at the Deir Alla Dighouse, which is supported by a consortium between the Department of Antiquities, Jordan (Dr. Adnan Hadidi), Yarmouk University (Dr. Moawiyah Ibrahim), and Leiden University (Dr Gerrit van der Kooji) (Figure A.7). We are indebted to the staff in Deir Alla, including Mohammed Jumrah (manager), Umm Salem (cook), Fatmeh Umm Mahmoud (housekeeper), Haj Faris Joudeh (caretaker) and several village women who washed pottery and our clothes, and provided companionship while we worked in Jordan (Figure A.8).

We especially appreciate the skilled assistance of many people during the excavations, particularly Mary Metzger (faunal analyst), Robert Erskine (photographer, surveyor and draftsperson), Jenny Davis (registrar), Ron Gardiner (artist), Lynn Grant (registrar and conservator), Katherine Kamp (lithic analyst), Jon Kline (photographer), Jonathan Mabry (draftsperson), Paula Marcoux (dessert and specialty chef), Karen Scholz (photographer), and John Whittaker (lithic analyst). Excavation supervisors include Risa Carlson, Mohammed Darwish, Tom Davis, Robert Erskine, Ron Gardiner, Mohammed Jumrah, Jonathan Mabry, Paula Marcoux, John Meloy, Charles Mobley, Susan Morton, Gaetano Palumbo, Glen Peterman, Bonnie Wistoff.

We gratefully acknowledge the following funding sources for supporting the field work:

1982: The University of Arizona Foundation through William G. Dever of the Department of Oriental Studies, the Department of Antiquities of Jordan through Dr. Adnan Hadidi, Ali Ghandour, President of Alia, the Royal Jordanian Airline, and travel grants from a William Shirley Fulton Scholarship and the Endowment for Biblical Research.

1983: The National Geographic Society, the Wenner-Gren Foundation for Anthropological Research, the University of Arizona Foundation through William Dever of the Department of Oriental Studies, and Ali Ghandour, President of Alia, the Royal Jordanian Airline.

1985: The National Endowment for the Humanities, the National Geographic Society, Ali Ghandour, President of Alia, the Royal Jordanian Airline, and Robert and Judith Falconer.

Funding for analyses was provided by The National Endowment for the Humanities and three Arizona State University Faculty Grants-in-Aid. The University of Arizona provided institutional support during the three field seasons. Arizona State University was the institutional sponsor during the analysis and write-up of the research. After the field work was completed, subsequent analysis was provided by students at Arizona State University and Bryn Mawr College. Tell el-Hayyat provided materials for a number of graduate Master's theses and Doctoral dissertations. The following theses and dissertations were based wholly or in part on data from Tell el-Hayyat: Master's theses – Mary Metzger (University of Alabama, Birmingham), Dennis Hurlbut (Arizona State University), Henry George (ASU), Angie Staples (ASU), Cathryn Meegan (ASU), Cynthia Keller (ASU); Ph.D. Dissertations – Lee Lines (Geography, ASU), and Jennifer Jones (Anthropology, ASU).

We thank the many individuals who aided in the analyses of materials from Tell el-Hayyat. Robert Erskine and Chuck Sternberg drafted the early site maps and architectural diagrams; Barbara Trapido-Lurie produced most of the final figures for this volume. Beth Alpert-Nakhai, Ilya Berelov, Jennifer Jones, Bonnie Magness-Gardiner and Glen Peterman drew the pottery. Tom Chadderton, C. Darby, S. Herr, Jennifer Jones, Samantha Ruscavage, J. Smith and Erik Steinbach entered the pottery data into the Hayyat database. Drawings of metal and stone artifacts were done by Jonathan Mabry and Ronald Beckwith. Bonnie Magness-Gardiner, Ilya Berelov, Henry George and Jennifer Jones analyzed the pottery; stone tools were analyzed by John Whittaker, Katherine Kamp, and Dennis Hurlbut. William Boynton and his staff at the University of Arizona's NSF Planetary and Space Sciences Laboratory provided results for neutron-activation analysis of ceramics. Radiocarbon analyses were provided courtesy of the National Science Foundation Regional Accelerator Facility for Isotope Dating at the University of Arizona, the Oxford University Radiocarbon Laboratory and the Vienna Environmental Research Accelerator. The dates from Oxford and VERA were compiled by Ezra Marcus for the MB Chronology Project, a subproject of SCIEM2000, funded by the Jubily Fund of the City of Vienna, Austrian Academy of Sciences. SCIEM2000 is a special program of the Austrian Academy of Sciences headed by Professor Manfred Bietak. Kimberly Fuqua and student workers in the Department of Geography, Arizona State University assisted in transferring old files into digital formats.

We thank Mary Metzger for her years of collaboration in analyzing and interpreting the animal bones from Tell el-Hayyat and several other Bronze Age villages along the Jordan Rift (Figure A.9). The animal bones from Tell el-Hayyat were identified using comparative collections at the Smithsonian Museum of Natural History in Washington, D.C. and at the Field Museum in Chicago. Additional identifications were made by Wim Van Neer of the Royal Museum of Central Africa in Tervuren, Belgium (fish) and by David Reese (shells). We are grateful to Lee Lines who undertook the analyses of carbonized plant remains from Hayyat. Naomi Miller, Charles Miksicek, and Karen Adams assisted with difficult plant macrofossil identifications. Juerena Hoffman analyzed the human skeletal remains from the Phase 4 pottery kiln. Moawiyah Ibrahim, James Sauer and Khair Yassine kindly provided access to the field notes and ceramic collections of the East Jordan Valley Survey.

We are grateful to the many individuals who have influenced and encouraged us over the years including: Ted Banning, Ilya Berelov, Ghazi Bisheh, Steven Burke, Karl Butzer, George Cowgill, Carole Crumley, William Dever, Phillip Edwards, Margaret Glass, Basil Hennessy, Moawiyeh Ibrahim, Keith Kintigh, Carol Kramer, Kenneth Kvamme, Tom Levy, Lee Lines, Bonnie Magness-Gardiner, Dave McCreery, Tony McNicoll, Charles Redman, Gary Rollefson, James Sauer, Steven Savage, Glenn Schwartz, Alan Simmons, Kate Spielmann, Barbara Stark, Gerrit van der Kooij, Pam Watson, Khair Yassine, and Norman Yoffee.

We especially wish to thank Bonnie Magness-Gardiner, original project Co-Director, for her enthusiasm in launching the Tell el-Hayyat project. Bonnie's help in the original project design and her intellectual contributions throughout the field work and initial stages of analyses and write-up were invaluable in the completion of this research.

Erik Steinbach, Ilya Berelov, and Barbara Trapido-Lurie were instrumental in the completion of this volume. Erik Steinbach digitized and compiled all the photos, completed the data entry, and compiled all the project databases into a standard format. Ilya Berelov compiled and edited all the chapters, including reworking and rewriting substantial sections of Chapter 4 on the site pottery and chronology, and did the final copy editing for the volume. Mariela Soto produced the Bronze Age settlement maps based on data provided by Steve Savage. Barbara Trapido-Lurie drafted most of the final figures and aided in their production in the final Tell el-Hayyat volume.

The research and compilation of the manuscript for this final publication were made possible through a generous grant from The Shelby White - Leon Levy Program for Archaeological Publications.

Figure A.1 Tell el-Hayyat Project Co-Director Bonnie Magness-Gardiner and William Dever, professor at the University of Arizona, at the Deir Alla dighouse, 1983 (photo by Jon Kline).

Figure A.2 Khamis Fahid, Fuad Awadd, "Sheikh" Sadek Abdullah, Mohammed Jumrah, Ali Abdul Rusool (Abu Said) and Mohammed Darwish at the Meshara "dighouse," 1982 (l-r; photo by Bob Erskine).

Figure A.3 Field staff for Tell el-Hayyat excavations, 1982. Land Rover roof (l-r): Ghazi Meisin, Steve Falconer, Pat Fall, Fuad Awadd, workman from Meshara. Standing (l-r) John Whittaker, Khamis Fahid, Tom Davis, Abu Jamal, Ron Gardiner, "Sheikh" Sadek Abdullah, Bonnie Magness-Gardiner, workman from Meshara, Mohammed Darwish, Mary Metzger, Mohammed Jumrah, Bob Erskine; Front Row: workman from Meshara, Kathy Kamp, two boys from Meshara, Ali Abdul Rusool (Abu Said), workmen from Meshara (photo by Bob Erskine).

Figure A.4 Field staff for Tell el-Hayyat excavations, 1983. Standing (l-r) "Sheikh" Sadek Abdullah, Bonnie Wistoff, Tom Davis, Ron Gardiner, Bob Erskine, Risa Carlson, Chuck Mobley, Fuad Awadd, Ali Abdul Rusool (Abu Said); Seated (l-r) Glen Peterman, Jenny Davis, Bonnie Magness-Gardiner, Steve Falconer, Pat Fall, Mary Metzger, Mohammed Darwish (photo by Jon Kline).

Figure A.5 Full field crew for Tell el-Hayyat excavations, 1985; photo taken at Tell Abu en-Niʻaj (photo by Karen Scholz).

Figure A.6 Meshara "dighouse" at the end of the 1982 season at Tell el-Hayyat; Mary Metzger (l) and Bonnie Magness-Gardiner (r) (photo by Bob Erskine).

Figure A.7. Tell Deir ʻAlla at sunset, as seen from the roof of the Deir ʻAlla dighouse, 1983 (photo by Karen Scholz).

Figure A.8 Tell el-Hayyat field and house staff, 1985; photo taken at Deir ʻAlla dighouse. Back row (l-r) Karen Scholz, Mohammed Jumrah, Mary Metzger, Steve Falconer, Pat Fall, Glen Peterman, John Meloy, Ron Gardiner, Gaetano Palumbo. Front row (l-r) Saad Hadidi, Haj Faris Joudeh, Jalal Jumrah, Rima Jumrah, Susan Morton, Lynn Grant, Paula Marcoux, Jonathan Mabry, Bonnie Magness-Gardiner, Umm Salem (photo by Karen Scholz).

Figure A.9 Mary Metzger excavating at Tell el-Hayyat, 1983 (photo by Jon Kline).

CHAPTER 1: VILLAGE COMMUNITIES IN THE BRONZE AGE LEVANT: ECOLOGY AND HISTORY

INTRODUCTION

The ancient Near East has been characterized aptly as a heartland of ancient urbanized civilization (e.g., Adams 1981). Archaeological and historical evidence from this region has engendered a wide range of interpretive studies that emphasize the central roles of state-level political organization and urban-based social authority in the rise and collapse of early complex societies. These central facets of early civilization developed on a rich foundation of small agrarian communities, where the vast majority of pre-industrialized populations worldwide lived and worked the land (Mann 1986). Never the less, the course of rural agriculture and village life has attracted only modest attention as part of the fabric of early urbanized societies (see Eickelmann 1989: 55; Schwartz and Falconer 1994a: 1). Understandably, a broad literature on early civilization tends to highlight the highly visible structure and influences of large communities and the central integrative institutions they housed. In contrast, the comparatively under-studied villages in which most early farmers lived tend to be characterized less rigorously as the antitheses of early cities: relatively homogeneous settlements subject to the influences and dictates of cities and their bureaucrats, merchants and elites. As such, rural communities may be too readily portrayed as largely dependent entities that provided the agricultural surpluses, tax revenues, corvee labor, and military conscripts prescribed by cities. Moreover the small size of early villages may lead us to portray them as minor elements on a larger anthropogenic landscape that evolved as a consequence of economic and political forces beyond their control.

This focus on central institutions and their urban settings sheds insufficient light on village economies and their fundamental roles in the coalescence or collapse of early civilizations (Schwartz and Falconer 1994a). This analytical gap is particularly significant for a comprehensive interpretation of early civilization in the southern Levant (i.e., the region of modern Israel, Palestine, and Jordan), which featured greater long-term continuity in rural settlement and land use than in urban development (Falconer 1994a; Falconer and Savage 1995). In this region, and others like it with discontinuous or small-scale urbanism, villages may provide our best evidence of long-term economic organization. Analyses founded in economic geography exemplify the benefits of detailed attention to rural agrarian systems within larger political economies (e.g., Bassett 1988; Zimmerer 1991, 1993). For example, societies with highly dynamic mixes of subsistence farming and surplus production, most notably in the New World tropics (Whitmore and Turner 1992; Denevan 1996), illustrate the wide variety of forms agrarian civilization may adopt. Thus, explicitly rural investigations of early farmers and farming communities provide an avenue of inquiry that is both particularly appropriate for the ancient southern Levant and more widely applicable to a variety of geographic research settings in both the past and present (Butzer 1996).

This volume details our investigations of agrarian economy and ecology as they illuminate the roles of rural communities in the larger context of the first urbanized civilizations. We explore the ways in which small farming villages like Tell el-Hayyat contributed and responded to the rise and fall of Bronze Age town life in the southern Levant. A rural perspective is particularly appropriate for this region amid its long legacy of sedentary agriculture, dynamic urban-rural relations, and their ecological consequences.

PHYSICAL GEOGRAPHY

The natural environment of the southern Levant provides a backdrop for the cultural landscape overprinted on it. The physical geography of the southern Levant varies from the mountains of Lebanon and the Central Hills of Israel and Palestine to the deserts in the Negev, Sinai and Jordan Rift Valley (Figure 1.1). Due to its tectonic history, the geomorphology of the southern Levant forms a series of north-south landscape features on either side of the Rift System which runs from the Gulf of Aqaba north through Lebanon. The Mediterranean Coastal Plain provides a relatively even, fertile lowland that extends inland from the Mediterranean Sea about 50 km before it rises into the Central Hill country with a series of north-south mountain ranges up to just over 1000 masl (meters above mean sea level). The Central Hills cover most of inland Israel and Palestine between the Galilee in the north and the Negev Desert in the south. The higher elevations to the north in the Lebanon and Anti-Lebanon Mountains (up to 3088 masl) and the Golan Heights (1187masl) provide snowmelt and stream runoff to the Jordan River, flowing between the Sea of Galilee (Lake Kinneret) and the Dead Sea, which occupies the lowest elevation on earth at 400 mbsl (meters below mean sea level). The uplifted Jordanian Plateau to the east of the Jordan River and the mountains of southern Jordan (up to 1736 masl) also provide runoff to the Dead Sea and the Wadi Araba through drainages and springs along the eastern side of the Rift Valley. Farther to the east lie the Eastern Deserts of Jordan and Syria that eventually give way to the Tigris/Euphrates basin. Tell el-Hayyat, the focus of this volume, is situated in the Jordan Rift Valley approximately two kilometers east of the Jordan River on the first terrace above the present floodplain, at an elevation of 240 mbsl (Figure 1.2).

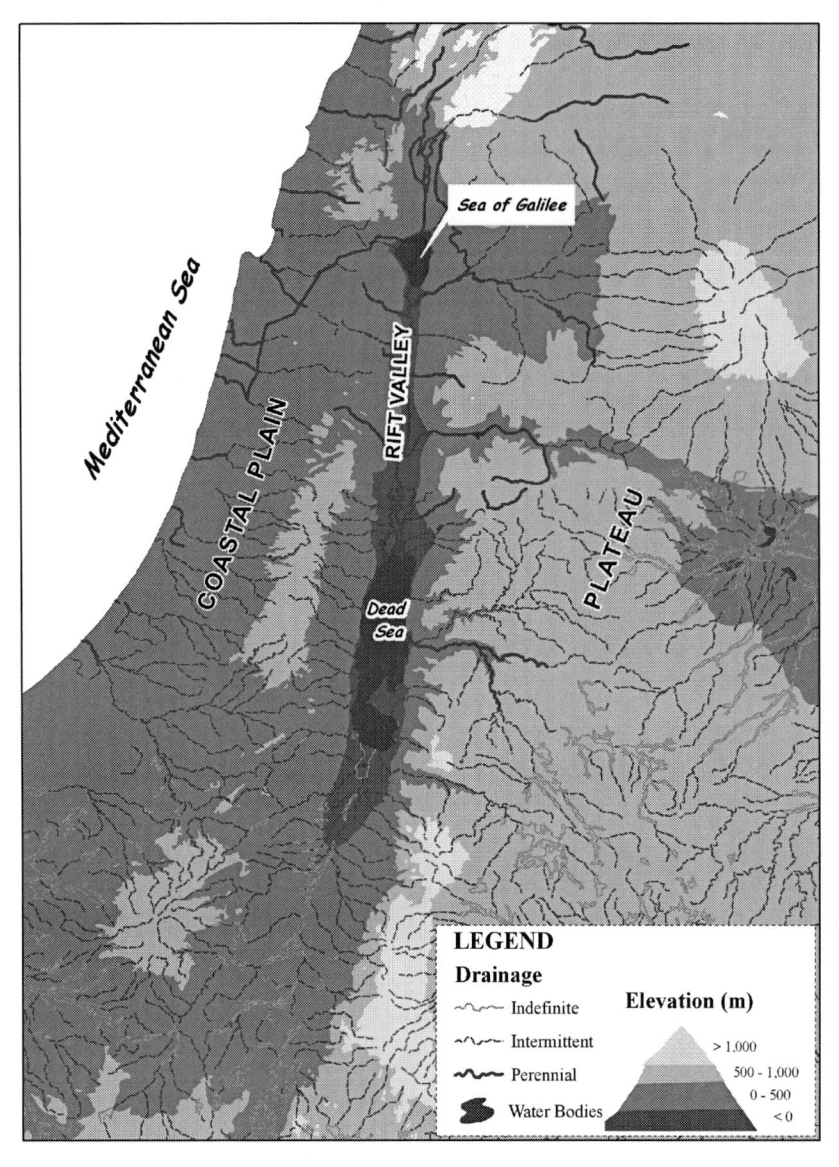

Figure 1.1 Physical geography of the southern Levant showing the Coastal Plain, the Rift Valley and the Jordan Plateau (map produced by Mariela Soto).

The southern Levant has a Mediterranean climate with cool, mild winters and hot, dry summers. Precipitation is seasonal and highly variable throughout the region. Westerly winds bring winter storms from the North Atlantic into southern Europe and across the Mediterranean Basin, providing precipitation as rainfall at lower elevations and snowfall in the mountains. There is a strong precipitation gradient from the Mediterranean Sea inland. Precipitation decreases to the east so that the Coastal Plain and the higher elevation Central Hills receive greater amounts of precipitation than does the Jordan Valley. The Jordanian Plateau further acts as a rain shadow to the Eastern Deserts. In addition, there is a strong gradient in precipitation from northern to southern Jordan. Modern precipitation in the Jordan Valley ranges between about 400 mm in the north to less than 200 mm in the south per year (Horowitz 1979: fig. 2.31; Wilkinson 2003: fig. 2.1), within the range sufficient for rain fed agriculture, especially in the northern Jordan Valley. In contrast, annual precipitation values can drop to only 50-100 mm in parts of southern Jordan.

During the summer months when the moisture bearing westerlies shift north, subtropical air masses dominate in the region, bringing very hot and dry conditions. While there are still temperature gradients across the region due to elevational differences, the domination of the subtropical air masses keeps the region very dry. These subtropical high pressure cells can produce rainfall in parts of the southern Arabian Peninsula as summer monsoons. The location of the southern Levant in one of the world's subtropical high-pressure belts produces extensive desert landscapes across the Sinai, the Negev, southern and eastern Jordan, eastern Syria and the Arabian Peninsula.

In response to the variability in topographic and climatic conditions of the region, the vegetation ranges from

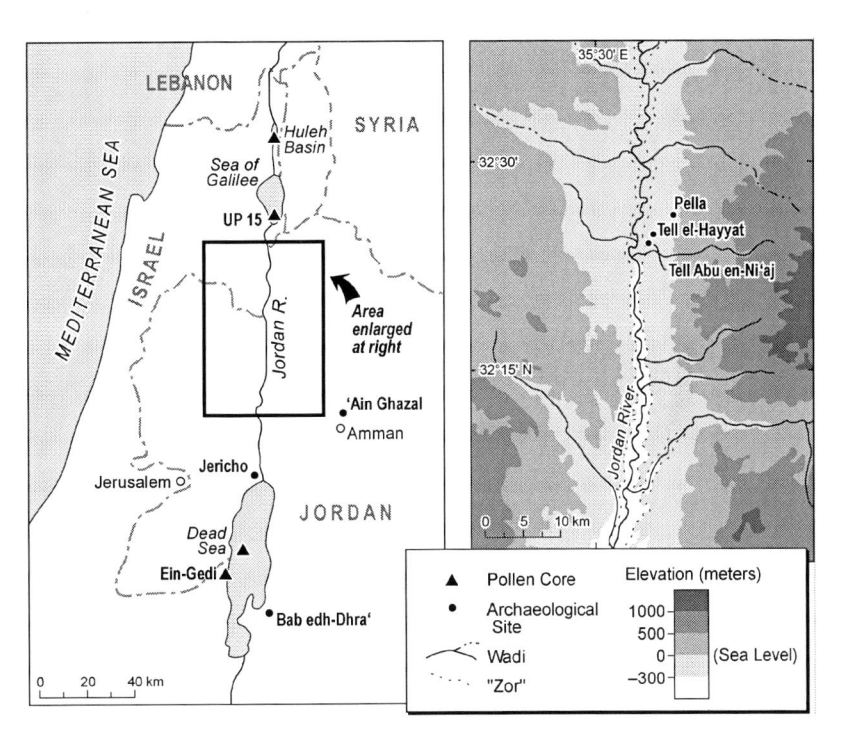

Figure 1.2 Archaeological sites and coring localities along the Jordan Rift.
Inset shows location of Tell el-Hayyat on the *ghor*, the fertile alluvial terrace of the Jordan River
(drafting by Barbara Trapido-Lurie).

forests and woodlands in the wetter, higher elevations to steppe lands and deserts in the drier, lower elevations and in areas inland from the Mediterranean Sea. The complexity of the plant geography of the Southern Levant reflects not only elevation, climate and geology, but also the region's location at the juncture of the African, Asian and European continental plates. Due to its position, four distinct floras converge in the southern Levant: Mediterranean, Irano-Turanian, Saharo-Arabian, and Sudanian (Zohary 1973). The Jordan Rift Valley and Tell el-Hayyat are situated at the intersection of these floral regions and the modern vegetation reflects the history of this mixture. In addition, the resulting plant communities have been changed considerably in the face of human agriculture and landscape modifications over the past 10,000 years.

The Mediterranean floral elements, characterized by sclerophyllous evergreen trees and shrubs, occupy elevations above about 400 m, where annual rainfall varies between 300 and 1000 mm (Wilkinson 2003). Remnants of Mediterranean forests and woodlands are most prevalent today in the Central Hills and in the mountains of Lebanon. In the eastern Mediterranean region the Mediterranean flora generally is defined by the modern geographical extent of the olive tree (*Olea europaea*). On the eastern escarpment above the Jordan River the flora is impoverished and the thermophilous Mediterranean floral elements are mixed with the deciduous shrubs and trees of the Irano-Turanian floral region to the east and northeast (Zohary 1973). The southernmost extent of the Mediterranean forest lies in southern Jordan in the Jebel esh-Shara and is represented by a remnant evergreen forest of oak (*Quercus calliprinos*) and the occasional Palestine terebinth tree (*Pistacia palestina*), an Irano-Turanian species (Davies and Fall 2001).

The steppe lands of the Irano-Turanian floral region are subject to extreme annual and diurnal temperatures and very low amounts of precipitation due to their continental position. Plants characteristic of the Irano-Turanian region are adapted to relatively long periods of dormancy in both the hot summers and cold winters. Plants in the northern Jordan Valley, the eastern edge of the Rift and the Jordanian Plateau have many characteristic Irano-Turanian shrubs, including white wormwood (*Artemisia herba-alba*), thorny saltwort (*Noaea mucronata*), black hammada (*Hammada scoparia*), Syrian anabasis (*Anabasis syriaca*), saltwort (*Salsola vermiculata*), and the Palestine terebinth tree (*Pistacia palestina*).

The Saharo-Arabian flora extends across North Africa and the Arabian Peninsula, regions with short, cool winters and very long, hot summers. Annuals are abundant in wet years. Perennial species of the Saharo-Arabian floral region in southern Jordan and along the Jordan Rift include jointed anabasis (*Anabasis articulata*), bean caper (*Zygophyllum dumosum*), saltwort (*Salsola tetranda*), white broom (*Retama raetan*) and several species each of sea blite (*Suaeda* spp.) and tamarisk (*Tamarix* spp.). The Sudanian floral region, marked by the northern limit of the distribution of acacia trees (*Acacia* spp.), lies at the northern latitudinal limit of

Figure 1.3 View of the *zor* from the edge of the *ghor* at Tell Abu en-Ni'aj, facing west (photo by Karen Scholz). The edge of the riparian trees indicates the position of the Jordan River as it flows through the middle of the *zor*.

the Palaeotropic flora of Africa, and depends upon a tropical climate with warm temperatures year-round. The extreme high temperatures of the Jordan Rift allow for these tropical species to extend north along the Wadi Araba, the Dead Sea and the Jordan River (Zohary 1973). Common Sudanian species along the Jordan Rift Valley are white hammada (*Hammada salicornica*), Christ-thorn (*Ziziphus spina-christi*) and multiple species of acacia trees. Elements of all four of these floral regions are found in the Jordan Valley and its adjacent slopes near Tell el-Hayyat.

Local Environmental Conditions at Tell el-Hayyat

Tell el-Hayyat lies in the Jordan Valley on the broad agricultural terrace called the *ghor*, above the active stream channel, or the *zor*, of the Jordan River (Fall et al. 1998; Figure 1.3). The Jordan River marks the present-day political boundary that separates Jordan from Israel and the occupied territories of the West Bank. The Jordan River flows southward through the Rift Valley, reaching base level at the Dead Sea (van Zeist 1985). The fertile Holocene alluvial sediments of the ghor overlie lake bed deposits exposed along the zor. These lacustrine sediments were deposited at the bottom of Pleistocene Lake Lisan; the Dead Sea is the modern remnant of Lake Lisan. The Jordan Valley provides the most fertile soil in the Levant (Zohary 1982) and for this reason has been intensively cultivated throughout the history of the region. Tell el-Hayyat, a 4.5 m high *tell* (or archaeological ruin mound), is surrounded by Holocene sediments, which have built up approximately one-half meter around the base of the site, providing a highly fertile modern and ancient agricultural setting (Figure 1.4). The northern Jordan Valley in the vicinity of Tell el-Hayyat receives about 300 mm of precipitation (Horowitz 1979: fig. 2.31), with most falling in the winter months, an amount sufficient for rain fed agriculture. The average annual temperature in the vicinity of Hayyat is above $20°$ C (Horowitz 1979: 22), which allows year-round cultivation.

The fields around Tell el-Hayyat today contain a mix of crops, including rain fed cereals, notably wheat, accompanied by other fields and orchards that are irrigated from the King Abdullah Canal, which draws water from the Yarmouk River, a tributary of the Jordan River (Fall et al. 1998). Although there is no direct evidence for local Bronze Age canals, irrigation water could have been obtained from the Jordan River (two kilometers to the west) to supply fields near the river, or from springs along the hills to the east, including a permanent source on the south flank of the ancient town of Pella, about seven kilometers to the northeast of Tell el-Hayyat (see Figure 1.2). Indeed, Glueck reports local irrigation in the 1940s that used waters from the "Qanat er-Rasiyeh" drawn from the Wadi el-Malawi (1951: 259, 361-363, fig. 109). However, modern average annual rainfall would suggest a productive farming environment

Figure 1.4 Tell el-Hayyat in the Jordan Valley during excavation in 1985; village of Mashara in background. Photo taken from Tell Abu en-Ni'aj looking northeast to the eastern escarpment of the Jordan Rift (photo by Karen Scholz).

in the vicinity of Tell el-Hayyat with or without the benefit of irrigation.

The Jordan Valley once supported extensive riparian forests of poplar (*Populus euphratia*) and tamarisk (*Tamarix jordanensis*), while the surrounding highlands sustained an open, diverse forest or woodland community with carob (*Ceratonia siliqua*), almond (*Amygdalus communis*), Aleppo pine (*Pinus halapensis*), pistachio (*Pistacia atlantica*), and olive (*Olea europaea*) (Zohary 1973). Only remnants of this natural vegetation exist today. Human activity, particularly the intensification of agriculture in the Jordan Valley over the past 5000 years, has greatly altered the landscapes along the Rift Valley (van Zeist 1985).

AGRARIAN SOCIETY IN THE SOUTHERN LEVANT

Levantine society adopted agriculture as its economic mainstay over the course of the Pre-Pottery Neolithic, during which the first aggregated settlements arose after ca. 8000 B.C. (e.g., Bar-Yosef 1986; 1995; Gebel et al. 1988; Rollefson and Kohler-Rollefson 1989;). These "proto-towns" eventually were abandoned, leading to more modest village-level society and settlement in the Pottery Neolithic, Chalcolithic and Early Bronze I periods (Gopher 1995; Joffe 1993; Levy 1995) (Table 1.1).

Table 1.1 Archaeological and historical chronology for the southern Levant (following Levy and Bar-Yosef 1995: figs. 2 and 3)

Cultural Period	Duration
Modern*	A.D. 1948 to present
British Mandate	A.D. 1917 to 1948
Ottoman	A.D. 1516 to 1917
Islamic (Umayyad-Mameluke)	A.D. 638 to 1516
Byzantine*	A.D. 324 to 638
Roman	37 B.C. to A.D. 324
Hellenistic	332 to 37 B.C.
Persian	586 to 332 B.C.
Iron Age	1200 to 586 B.C.
Late Bronze Age	1500 to 1200 B.C.
Middle Bronze Age*	2000 to 1500 B.C.
Early Bronze IV	2300 to 2000 B.C.
Early Bronze I-III	3500 to 2300 B.C.
Chalcolithic	4500 to 3500 B.C.
Pottery Neolithic	5500 to 4500 B.C.
Pre-Pottery Neolithic*	8300 to 5500 B.C.

* Periods of most pronounced population aggregation

Town life developed across the region during the Early Bronze II-III periods, marked by the appearance of aggregated communities atop the tells of the southern Levant. This incipient urbanism, in turn, was abandoned in favor of village life and non-sedentary pastoralism during Early Bronze IV (e.g., Dever 1995). Levantine towns and cities were reestablished in the subsequent Middle Bronze Age, during which regional population grew to levels not attained again until the Roman and Byzantine periods (Broshi 1979; Broshi and Gophna 1986). The Late Bronze Age, the first historically well-attested era, experienced a general decline in urbanism and regional population. The ensuing Iron Age is most noteworthy for the rise of the Israelite kingdoms, which never developed the population densities or urban centers of the Bronze Age (Broshi 1979; Fritz 1987; Finkelstein 1995; Holladay 1995).

Following foreign political domination during the Persian and Hellenistic periods, population growth and economic development were renewed on an unprecedented scale with the annexation of the southern Levant into the Roman Empire (Broshi 1979; Anderson 1995; Patrich 1995). After the collapse of Byzantine authority and the introduction of Islam, a series of Muslim dynasties (through the Ottoman Empire) tended to invest only modestly in the southern Levant. The region's population declined drastically and commonly became economically marginalized as mobile pastoralists, especially under Ottoman Turkish rule (Rosen-Ayalon 1995). Only over the last century, following the First World War and the establishment of independent states, have regional population levels surpassed those of the Roman/Byzantine era (Broshi 1979). This long and varied settlement history outlines the changing cultural influences on the molding of agrarian landscapes across the southern Levant.

PAST ENVIRONMENT OF THE JORDAN RIFT

Palynological data from the eastern Mediterranean region can be used to infer long-term *regional* vegetation dynamics that reflect both natural and cultural changes to the landscape, while biological data from archaeological deposits (discussed in Chapters 5 and 8) offer more *local* points of reference. While palynological interpretations of past vegetation must incorporate different rates of pollen production, distribution and deposition when comparing species, variations in pollen data through time within a species are useful in reflecting relative changes in vegetation. For example, the relative amount of pollen produced by each of the three main orchard taxa of the Levant, olive, grape and fig, vary greatly. Olive (*Olea*) produces abundant pollen that is dispersed widely. Large amounts of olive pollen (5-15 %) are found across the southern Levant, even tens of kilometers from where the trees grow (Davies and Fall 2001). In contrast, grape vines (*Vitis*) produce little pollen, so the presence of grape pollen in a pollen diagram is very significant. Even 1 % or less grape pollen signals the presence of nearby orchards. Fig (*Ficus*) is pollinated internally (Zohary and Spiegel-Roy 1975), therefore leaving no pollen fingerprint in the Levant. Thus, the signal provided by olive pollen often is used as a primary indicator of orchard expansion or contraction in the region. In light of these considerations, archaeological data are crucial for inferring chronological trends and spatial distributions of ancient arboriculture for olive, and especially for grape and fig.

The Neolithic development of agriculture and aggregated villages led to revolutionary social and economic changes linked to localized resource exploitation that are reflected in palynological records. The later rise of cities and regional exchange networks in the Bronze Age left an indelible stamp on the landscape with the intensification of agriculture, particularly through forest clearance and orchard cultivation. Thus, agricultural intensification beginning in the Bronze Age broadened the impacts on the landscape that can be sensed by pollen data. Pollen spectra from sediment cores collected along the Rift Valley have been used to assess agricultural and pastoral developments, as well as broad scale changes in vegetation, resulting from deforestation and regeneration following human disturbance (e.g., Bottema and Woldring 1990), and the creation of anthropogenic forests. The vegetation history of the southern Levant is best documented by a series of lake cores collected from three basins along the Jordan Rift: the Huleh Basin, the Sea of Galilee (Lake Kinneret) and the Dead Sea. We discuss these pollen data according to two temporal periods: (1) the latest Pleistocene to early Holocene (especially during the Neolithic and Chalcolithic periods) represented in the Huleh Basin, and the Ein Gedi core near the Dead Sea; (2) the middle and later Holocene (particularly the Bronze Age and continuing into the Classical periods) represented by cores from the Huleh Basin, the Sea of Galilee, and two records from the Dead Sea (see Figure 1.2 for core localities).

Palynological Records for the Late Pleistocene and Early Holocene

Subtle pollen signatures of localized human impacts during the early Holocene may be difficult to separate from climatically-induced vegetation changes that become most obvious in the middle and later Holocene. However, a number of plant taxa serve as "anthropogenic indicators" (Behre 1981; 1990; Bottema 1982[1985]; Bottema and Woldring 1990) since they flourish in the wake of human disturbance of soils and competing flora. The main pollen indicators of disturbance in the southern Levant are *Plantago lanceolata* and *Sarcopoterium*. However, their pollen signals are not readily apparent until at least the Bronze Age or later (see discussion in next section). Earlier disturbances may be seen in changes in sagebrush (*Artemisia*) pollen, a common element of open steppe vegetation of the Eastern Deserts across Southwestern Asia as far east as the steppes of Iran. *Artemisia* may follow human intervention, although its presence also may reflect drier climatic conditions than would support forests. Sediment cores collected from the Huleh Basin and the western shore of the Dead Sea near Ein Gedi document changes in the vegetation of the southern Levant from the late Pleistocene into the

Holocene that are most indicative of climatic shifts, but may hint at landscape modifications coincident with Neolithic village aggregation and agriculture.

The Huleh Basin has yielded several pollen cores, two of which illuminate the late Pleistocene and early Holocene. One core, measuring 54 m in depth and covering the last 30,000 years, has been analyzed by Tsukada, but remains published only as a summary diagram (van Zeist and Bottema 1991). A second record from the Huleh Basin is a 16.25 m core for which data from the lower 6.25 m, covering ca. 15,000-7000 B.C., are published (Baruch and Bottema 1991). The Ein Gedi core spans approximately the last 9000 years of the Holocene, as indicated by two radiocarbon dates toward the core's base (Baruch 1990). Since the uppermost meter of the core was truncated during recovery, and remains unpublished, we present a summary diagram of the main pollen taxa from the lower five meters of the Ein Gedi core (Figure 1.5).

The Huleh Basin records reveal that the late Pleistocene landscape was a mosaic of low elevation desert, steppe and forest-steppe vegetation, with extensive highland forests and woodlands dominated by deciduous oak (*Quercus boissierii*) trees. These cores show a substantial increase in oak pollen between ca. 13,000 and 9500 B.C. (Baruch and Bottema 1991: fig. 3; van Zeist and Bottema 1991: fig. 37), most likely in response to greater summer precipitation induced by increased monsoonal flow into the region (Wright 1993). Between ca. 9500 and 7200 B.C. both cores show a thinning of deciduous oak forests, coupled with increased olive (*Olea*) and pistachio (*Pistacia*) pollen (Baruch 1990; Baruch and Bottema 1991). Wright (1993) hypothesizes a shift to a Mediterranean climate with dry summers that favored annual grasses and the Mediterranean trees and vines (olive, evergreen oak, pistachio, and grape) at the expense of deciduous oaks. This climatic shift may have compounded the human decimation of oak woodlands around Neolithic farming communities (e.g., as seen at 'Ain Ghazal; e.g., Rollefson and Kohler-Rollefson 1992). However, despite the *localized* impacts of the Neolithic Period, the oak-pistachio forests of the southern Levant remained relatively undisturbed until the Chalcolithic and Bronze ages.

While anthropogenic indicators become sharply pronounced throughout the eastern Mediterranean by the mid-Holocene (Bottema and Woldring 1990; Baruch 1990; Behre 1990), evidence from Ein Gedi may indicate earlier human environmental impacts in the southern Levant on a supra-local scale. The Ein Gedi core (Baruch, 1990) documents forests during the Pre-Pottery Neolithic dominated by deciduous oak (*Q. boissierii*-type), with a modest amount of pistachio. Unexpectedly high frequencies of *Artemisia* through the Pre-Pottery and Pottery Neolithic do not seem to reflect forest clearance, since there is little change in arboreal taxa. Instead, this abundance of *Artemisia* may be an early Holocene remnant of late Pleistocene steppe vegetation or, more interestingly, it may reflect the impact of grazing following the inception of Neolithic pastoralism. Pollen frequencies and counts of charcoal particles in a core from the Ghab Valley of northwestern Syria are interpreted to document the earliest clearance of deciduous oak forests in the Levant by about 9000 years ago (Yasuda et al. 2000). The palynological records for subsequent periods in the southern Levant display more pronounced and less equivocal anthropogenic patterns that betray the oscillations of urbanism and the environmental impacts of the secondary products revolution.

Palynological Records for the Bronze Age and Subsequent Periods

The characteristic anthropogenic vegetation of the Eastern Mediterranean today is derived in large measure from the effects of orchard expansion and the production of trade commodities -- especially wine, olive oil, and dried fruit -- to serve emerging Bronze Age urban markets (Stager 1985; Ben-Tor 1986). While the Neolithic development of agriculture signaled revolutionary social and economic changes tied to newly aggregated communities and localized resource depletion (e.g., Rollefson and Kohler-Rollefson 1992), the much later emergence of orchard intensification intimately involved expanded regional commerce and a variety of correspondingly broadened environmental impacts on the countryside. The regional environmental effects of the expansion of Bronze Age markets are reflected in pollen spectra from sediment cores recovered near Ein Gedi, the Dead Sea, the Huleh Basin, and the Sea of Galilee.

Pollen Spectra from the Dead Sea Area

The late Neolithic oak-pistachio forest represented in the Ein Gedi core continues into the Chalcolithic and Bronze ages (Baruch 1990) (see Figure 1.5). High olive pollen values support the argument of Zohary and Spiegel-Roy (1975) and Neef (1990) that olive cultivation began by the Chalcolithic Period. The Ein Gedi data suggest that olive cultivation was well established by the Early Bronze Age, but did not immediately entail major forest clearance. Interestingly, arboreal pollen values *rise* between the Neolithic and Middle Bronze Age, primarily due to a prolonged increase in olive. Continued high frequencies of upper elevation deciduous oak (Quercus boissieri) lead Baruch (1990) to propose that olive cultivation prior to the Roman/Byzantine era was concentrated in lower forest areas.

Olive pollen frequencies remain at about 10-15 % between the rise of the Israelite kingdoms in the Iron Age and the collapse of Byzantine imperial control of the

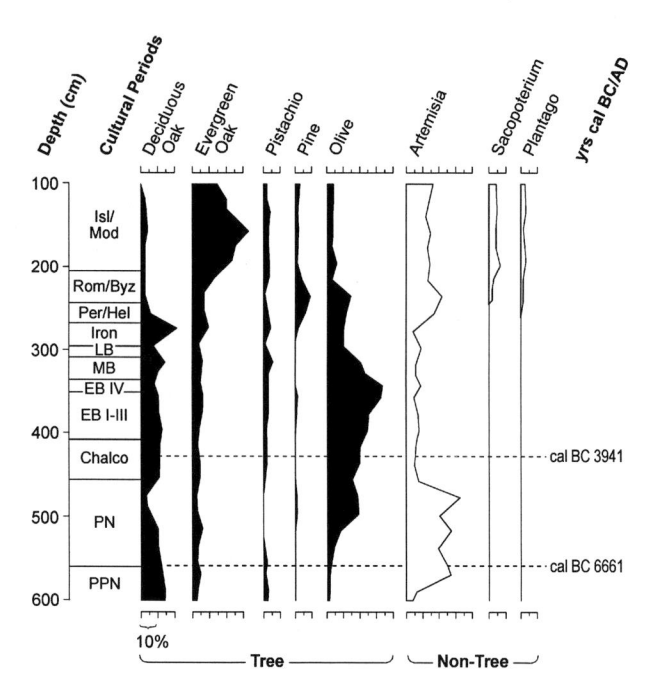

Figure 1.5 Pollen diagram from Ein Gedi, Dead Sea (data from Baruch 1990; drafting by Barbara Trapido-Lurie).

Levant in the 7th century A.D. These olive pollen values are more modest than those shown in the Chalcolithic/Bronze Age peak, but they occur amid several significant new trends. First, a sharp decline in deciduous oak values after the Iron Age marks a major shift in forest composition. This drop is followed by an immediate spike in pine values. Baruch (1990) notes that pine (*Pinus halepensis*) thrives with the removal of competition from other arboreal taxa. The short-lived rise in pine is followed by the emergence of evergreen oak (*Q. calliprinos*-type) as the dominant tree type. Intriguingly, this fundamental shift in forest composition lags behind the earlier olive peak. This forest transition implies that olive orchards expanded upslope, where they displaced natural stands of deciduous oak.

The period following the Iron Age also features heightened *Artemisia* values and the first appearance of *Sarcopoterium*-type and *Plantago lanceolata*-type pollen in significant frequencies. *Plantago lanceolata* is a hallmark component of vegetation in disturbed soils, including heavily grazed areas (Behre 1990). Likewise, the successional shrub *Sarcopoterium* spreads after degradation or destruction of forests or shrublands. Animals dislike its taste, and it commonly thrives in abandoned fields or orchards in the Near East. Thus, heightened frequencies of these taxa indicate significant impacts of agricultural intensification.

Following the Muslim conquest of the southern Levant, evergreen oak forest became the dominant element of arboreal vegetation. Evergreen oak tended to displace deciduous oak following the abandonment of widespread olive cultivation, which is indicated by dwindling olive pollen deposition. This transition is best explained as a result of cultural impacts, since the multiple stemmed evergreen oak withstands wood cutting and animal browsing better than the single trunk deciduous form (Shmida 1980; Baruch 1990). Olive cultivation appears to have been reduced drastically, and continued human disturbance is signaled by high *Artemisia* values and considerably accentuated values for *Sarcopoterium*-type and *Plantago lanceolata*-type pollen. This pattern suggests the recovery of natural vegetation following orchard abandonment, and probably a greater reliance on pastoralism by Levantine populations. These data also reveal an intriguing parallel to our earlier suggestion of elevated *Artemisia* as an anthropogenic indicator of Neolithic pastoralism.

Evidence from a Dead Sea sediment core (Heim et al. 1997) reinforces some of the results from Ein Gedi. This core, recovered from a depth of 320 m roughly five kilometers offshore of Ein Gedi (see Figure 1.2 for location), provides well-dated deposits covering 3.6 m and approximately the past 2500 years. The pollen spectra reveal maximum olive percentages during the Hellenistic, Roman, and Byzantine periods (Figure 1.6). Relatively high frequencies of cereal (*Cerealia*), walnut (*Juglans*), and grape (*Vitis*) pollen, as well as olive, document broadly intensified orchard cultivation during this era (Heim et al. 1997: 399). Increased grape pollen, while modest compared to that of olive, is particularly noteworthy, because of grape's low pollen production, as noted above. Orchard abandonment is apparent after the Byzantine collapse, as reflected by a drop in olive, regeneration of pine (*Pinus*) and evergreen oak (*Quercus ilex*-type), and the spread of more arid steppe vegetation (Heim et al. 1997: 399).

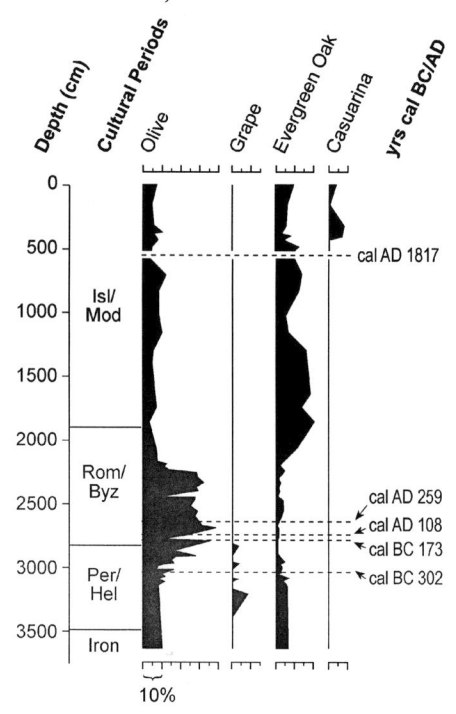

Figure 1.6 Pollen diagram from Dead Sea (after Heim et al. 1997: fig. 3; drafting by Barbara Trapido-Lurie).

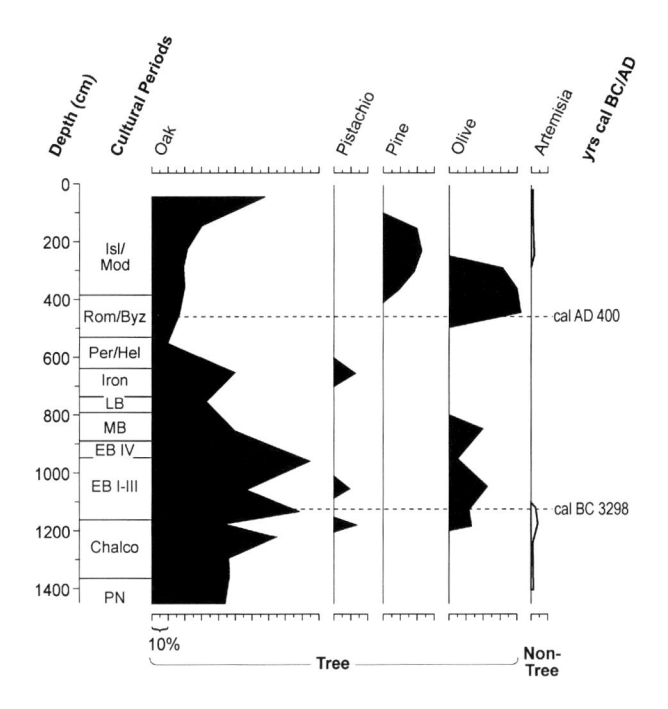

Figure 1.7 Pollen diagram from borehole U.P. 15 in the Huleh Basin (data from Horowitz 1971; 1979: fig. 6.20; drafting by Barbara Trapido-Lurie).

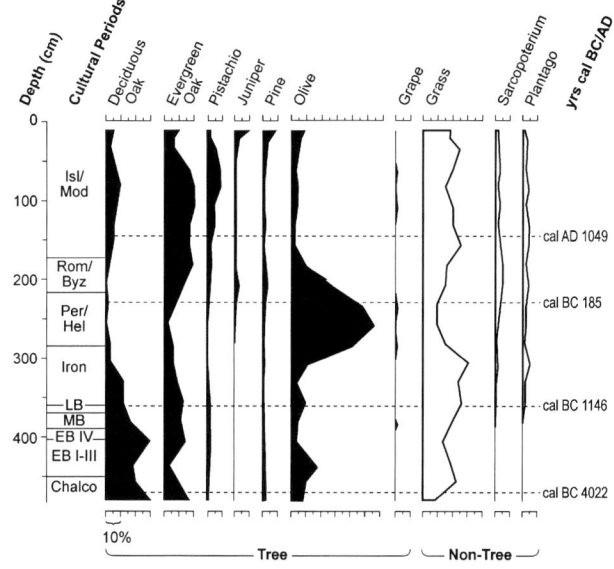

Figure 1.8 Pollen diagram from the Sea of Galilee (Lake Kinneret) (data from Baruch 1990; drafting by Barbara Trapido-Lurie).

Pollen Spectra from the Sea of Galilee

In combination, borehole U.P. 15 in the Huleh Basin (Horowitz 1971; 1979: 222-230) (Figure 1.7) and the Sea of Galilee core (Baruch 1986, 1990) (Figure 1.8) reveal vegetation change over the latter half of the Holocene. As seen in the record from borehole U.P. 15, *Artemisia* persists into the Chalcolithic in the Huleh Basin, once more suggesting remnant Pleistocene vegetation or the disruptive effects of pastoralism on the landscape. In subsequent periods, both cores show modest olive peaks and an aggregate trend of decreased arboreal pollen.

The beginnings of orchard cultivation are marked by the abrupt appearance of olive in the Huleh Basin in the late Chalcolithic and its persistence at significant levels through the Bronze Age. The Huleh Basin also reveals pistachio pollen and intermittent peaks in oak pollen (not differentiated by type, but attributed primarily to deciduous oak; Horowitz 1979: 223), during the late Chalcolithic and into the Bronze Age. These patterns parallel those in the Ein Gedi core, again suggesting that Bronze Age olive orchards did not encroach pervasively into higher elevation stands of deciduous oak-pistachio forests.

Evidence from the base of the Sea of Galilee core suggests that the dense oak forest receded while olive increased during the beginnings of population growth and early urbanism in the Early Bronze Age. This core reveals that oak forest regenerated sharply (especially deciduous oak), while olive values declined about at the time of the urban collapse at the end of the Early Bronze Age. Renewed forest clearance and orchard expansion in the Middle Bronze, Late Bronze and Iron Age are implicated by a long-term decline in both deciduous and evergreen oak, a second rise in olive and the first appearance of grape pollen. Significant agricultural disturbance also is indicated by the first appearances of *Sarcopoterium*-type and *Plantago lanceolata*-type pollen in the Late Bronze and Iron ages. This suite of trends then leads to the most dramatic palynological illustration of human environmental intervention in the eastern Mediterranean.

Olive frequencies following the Iron Age in the Sea of Galilee core quickly approach 60 % of the pollen sum, while oak frequencies recede to roughly 5 %. Anthropogenic impacts are revealed by the simultaneous reappearance of grape pollen. *Sarcopoterium*-type and *Plantago lanceolata*-type jump to higher values (ca. 5 %) during and after this peak. Contemporaneously, olive soars to over 40 % in the Huleh Basin, as oak drops to half this frequency. These data describe a pattern of long-term intensive olive oil production, particularly during the Hellenistic, Roman, and Byzantine periods. Latin texts provide corroborating historical documentation of olives, grapes and figs as the three major crops of the region (Felix 1982; Baruch 1990). The success of this arboriculture is attested by the widespread marketing of Levantine olive oil and wine throughout the eastern Mediterranean, just as must have been true during the Bronze Age as well.

Following the advent of Muslim rule in the Levant, olive pollen percentages dwindle to new lows (disappearing altogether in the Huleh Basin), and arboreal pollen frequencies suggest the growth of new forest communities. Pine pollen peaks in the Huleh Basin, then leads to renewed oak forest during the modern era. Around the Sea of Galilee increased evergreen oak and pistachio become mixed with diminished deciduous oak. Substantial frequencies of *Sarcopoterium*-type and *Plantago lanceolata*-type pollen suggest a constant backdrop of disturbance vegetation around this lake throughout the Classical era orchard intensification and its subsequent abandonment.

Temporal and Spatial Vegetation Dynamics along the Levantine Rift

The changing landscapes of the southern Levant are particularly well documented by palynological evidence along the Jordan Rift. These records attest long-term variations in both natural and human impacts on the region's vegetation. The legacy of human intervention is particularly noteworthy during the rise of urbanism in the Bronze Age. The most pronounced anthropogenic indicators of altered landscapes are the unmistakable imprints of olive cultivation, and a shifting woodland balance between deciduous oak, evergreen oak, pistachio and pine forests. The palynological evidence from sediment cores along the Rift Valley demonstrates that agricultural disruption and the rise and fall of forests on the Levantine landscape has unfolded according to a variety of scenarios at different times and in different locales. Olive arboriculture emerges as the clearest palynological footprint of human intervention. However, despite its contemporaneous inception throughout the southern Levant, its intensification and consequences followed strikingly different schedules and different spatial patterns. The greatest development of olive orchards, as reflected in the Ein Gedi and Dead Sea cores, resulted from the secondary products revolution of the Bronze Age, which held consequences for natural vegetation communities that unfolded over the balance of their histories, including the systematic transition from deciduous to evergreen oak in the Roman and Byzantine periods. The less pronounced evidence of Bronze Age olive cultivation around the Sea of Galilee serves as a prelude to the striking proliferation of Classical Period arboriculture, and the subsequent, more subtle changes in natural vegetation that followed.

Perhaps counterintuitively, peaks in anthropogenic shrubs and herbs, which could result from overgrazing by sheep and goats, are well pronounced in the late Neolithic at Ein Gedi and the Huleh Basin, but do not reappear until the Classic Period olive maxima in the pollen cores. Mobile pastoralists constitute a particularly fluid component of traditional societies, both ancient and modern, in southwestern Asia. They are especially noteworthy for their resilience in the face of political and economic pressures (Adams 1978). Eras of instability or excessive urban demands (e.g., taxes, corvee labor, military conscription) may induce families to change their lifeways from settled farming to mobile pastoralism. Strikingly, the Levantine pollen data suggest that pastoral impacts may be more pronounced in the face of pronounced state bureaucracies (e.g., during the Roman, Byzantine, and Ottoman empires) than in the wake of their collapse (e.g., during Early Bronze IV or following the destruction of the Israelite kingdoms).

When multiple data sources are coordinated, the pollen record makes it clear that the characteristic modern mosaic of decidedly anthropogenic vegetation communities in the southern Levant should come as no surprise. This configuration was achieved, in no small part, by a suite of agricultural influences, most notably orchard and vineyard cultivation conditioned by the regional exchange of secondary products.

Evidence for Climatic Change during the Bronze Age

Although much of the paleoenvironmental data for the middle and late Holocene can be interpreted in terms of land-use change related to the waxing and waning of towns and markets in the southern Levant, there are strong climatic signals represented in the record as well. Significantly lowered Nile River water levels are inferred by Bell (1971) from historic records relating to the First Intermediate Period (ca. 2160 to 2040 B.C.), during a collapse of central authority in Egypt roughly contemporaneous with Early Bronze IV in the southern Levant. Similarly, the collapse of the Akkadian Empire (ca. 2350 to 2150 B.C.) in Mesopotamia has been attributed to drier climatic conditions leading to the abandonment of towns and villages in the rain fed plains of northern Mesopotamia and an influx of people into towns on the irrigated plains of southern Mesopotamia (Weiss et al. 1993). Tell sites, like Tell Leilan in northeastern Syria, collapse abruptly ca. 4170 ± 150 cal yr B.P. in response to a several hundred year period of lower rainfall (Weiss et al. 1993; deMenocal 2001). Approximately 300 years after the collapse, the northern plains of Mesopotamia were resettled (Courty and Weiss 1997). Some have questioned this climatic interpretation for the collapse of towns in northern Mesopotamia starting late in the Akkadian period and continuing through the Third Dynasty of Ur (ca. 2100-2000 B.C.). However, the interpretations by Weiss et al. (1993) based on the deposition of aeolian silts following abandonment of tells like Leilan have been corroborated by sediment analysis of cores from the Gulf of Oman (deMenocal 2001). Cullen and de Menocal (2000) interpret variation in mineral and geochemical signals in deep sea core sediments to reflect regional aridity in the Mesopotamian basin for a 300 year period dated to begin at 4025 ± 125 cal yr B.P. (deMenocal 2001). Indeed, similar chemical analyses of tephra shards in the deep sea cores and Tell Leilan further suggest the synchronicity of this collapse and climate change (Cullen et al. 1997). The reinterpretation of sediment cores from Lake Van in

Turkey also indicates regional aridity in the middle Holocene (Landmann et al. 1996). This arid period in greater Mesopotamia beginning about 4100 cal yr B.P. coincides with cooler sea surface temperatures in the North Atlantic (deMenocal et al. 2000) which would have reduced winter precipitation throughout the Mediterranean region.

One reflection of this hypothesized period of lower rainfall during Early Bronze IV in the southern Levant can be demonstrated in fluctuating barley to wheat ratios in archaeological settlements. Barley generally requires less water, is more tolerant to soil salinity, and is less susceptible to insect infestations than is wheat (McCreery 1980; Zohary 1982; Hopf 1983; Zohary and Hopf 1988). Barley frequencies are high at Bronze Age sites along the Jordan Rift, peaking in Early Bronze IV (ca. 2300-2000 B.C.) (Fall et all. 2002). A concurrent drop in relative frequencies of wheat seeds may reflect a decrease in available water. Wheat, particularly bread wheat, requires more water than barley, thus significant increases in the barley to wheat ratios along the Rift Valley during the Early Bronze IV (Fall et al. 2002; table II) may be a response to regional aridity. Anomalously high concentrations of boron in wheat and barley grains have been attributed to increased soil salinity around Bab adh-Dhra', near the Dead Sea (McCreery 1980), presumably in response to intensification of irrigated agriculture spurred by deteriorating environmental conditions. Thus, patterns of increased soil salinity and implied lower rainfall along the Jordan Rift in the Early Bronze IV Period coincides with the timing for lower Nile River flows (Bell 1971) and abandonment of the rain fed agricultural system of the northern reaches of the Tigris and Euphrates rivers (e.g., Courty and Weiss 1997). These inferences point out the potential significance of climatic oscillations, as well as cultural influences, on long-term patterns of Bronze Age settlement and land use in the southern Levant.

THE LEVANTINE BRONZE AGE

The first large towns in the southern Levant developed during the Early Bronze Age, especially during the periods of Early Bronze II-III (ca. 2900-2300 B.C.) (Table 1.1). The subsequent period, ca. 2300-2000 B.C., has been characterized as an interval of urban abandonment between the town life of the Early Bronze Age and the Middle Bronze Age (ca. 2000-1500 B.C.). The provocative nature of this transitional era has inspired a variety of nomenclature and interpretive schemes, including the archaeological periods originally labeled "Early Bronze IV" and "Middle Bronze I" by W. F. Albright (1949, 1962, 1966). Subsequently, "Early Bronze IV," "Intermediate EB-MB," or "Intermediate Bronze Age" terminology has been suggested for the whole of Albright's old Early Bronze IV and Middle Bronze I (e.g., Olavarri 1969; Lapp 1970; Wright 1971;

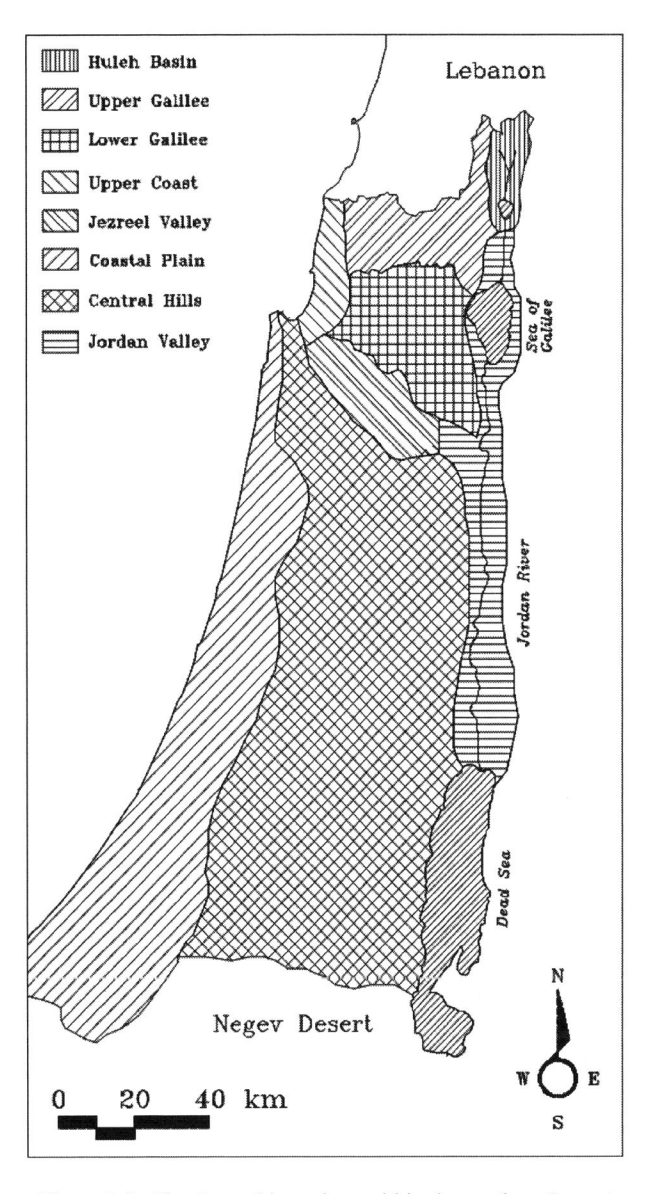

Figure 1.9 Physiographic regions within the southern Levant from the Mediterranean Sea east to the Jordan Rift Valley (map created by Steve Savage).

Oren 1973; and Dever 1973, 1980). A basic tenet of this discussion maintains that the Middle Bronze I material culture really derives from Early Bronze traditions and that the "Middle Bronze" terminology is both inappropriate and misleading. This volume will utilize "Early Bronze IV" terminology for the non-urban archaeological interval between the end of Early Bronze III and the beginning of the Middle Bronze Age.

The Early Bronze IV Period (ca. 2300-2000 BC) has left little archaeological evidence of permanent settlements and major tells. The wide-ranging explorations of Nelson Glueck (1934, 1935, 1939, 1951) first revealed Early Bronze IV settlement systems with extensive use of land outside the present limits of dry farming (see also Evenari et al. 1961: 982; 1971: 97). In contrast, Early Bronze II-III tell sites were usually restricted to areas with more than 300 mm annual rainfall, and Middle Bronze II sites

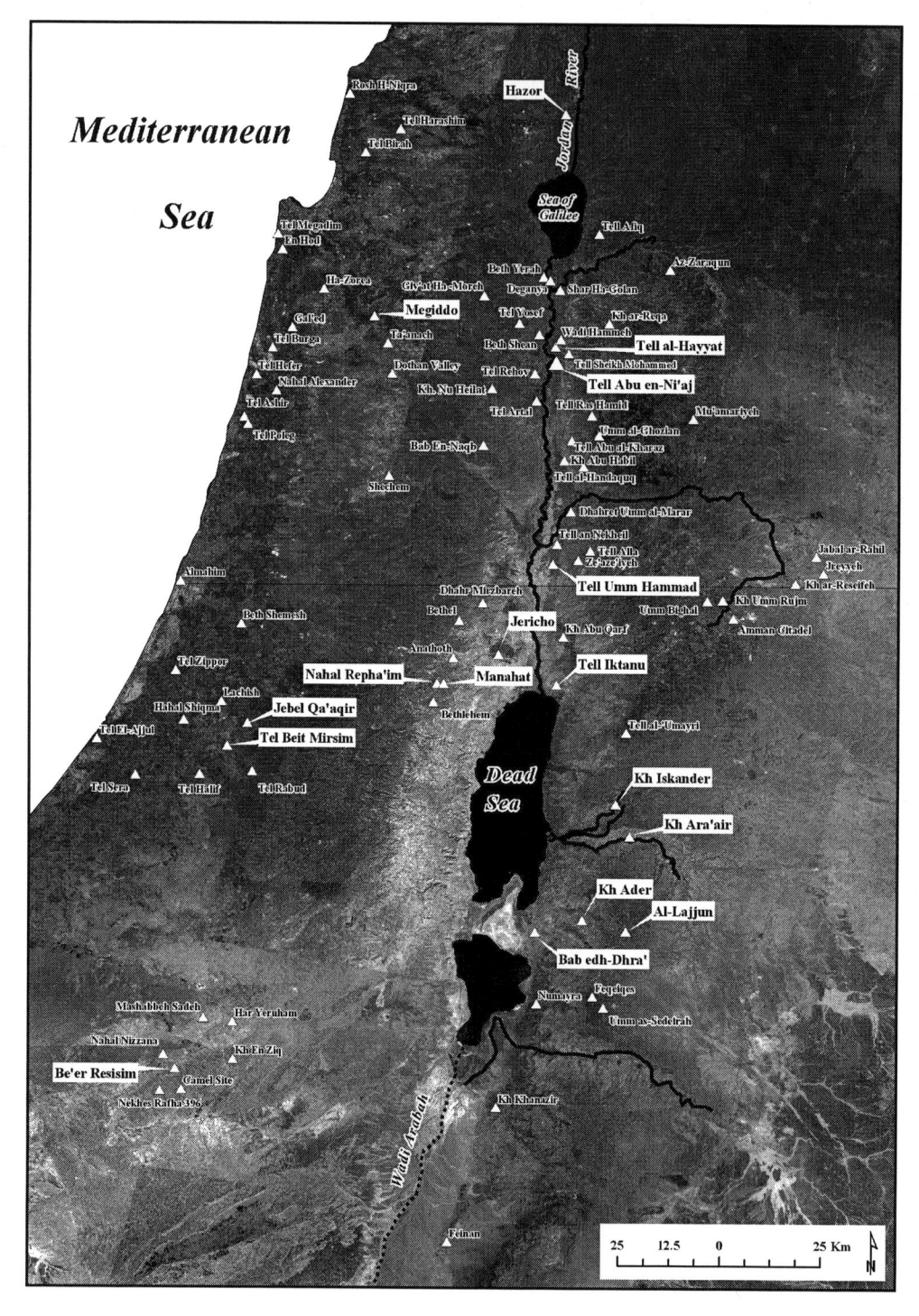

Figure 1.10 Digital image 10m resolution (CNES/SPOT Image 1992-1994) showing locations of Early Bronze IV sites in the southern Levant, with sites mentioned in the text highlighted (data from Steve Savage; map created by Mariela Soto).

generally received 400 mm or more (Prag 1974: 69-77; Raikes 1967). Excavation of Early Bronze IV evidence has been carried out largely at seasonal encampments (e.g., in the Negev) or high country cemeteries in the Levantine Central Hills, with a particular emphasis on evidence from burials (e.g., Palumbo 1987, 1991; see Figures 1.9 and 1.10). As a result, the most generally accepted interpretation of Early Bronze IV society emphasizes pastoral nomadism at the expense of the sedentary agrarian populations that certainly also existed (Dever 1995). The investigations at Tell el-Hayyat synthesized in this volume illuminate village life from the end of Early Bronze IV non-urban society through the subsequent reurbanization of the Middle Bronze Age.

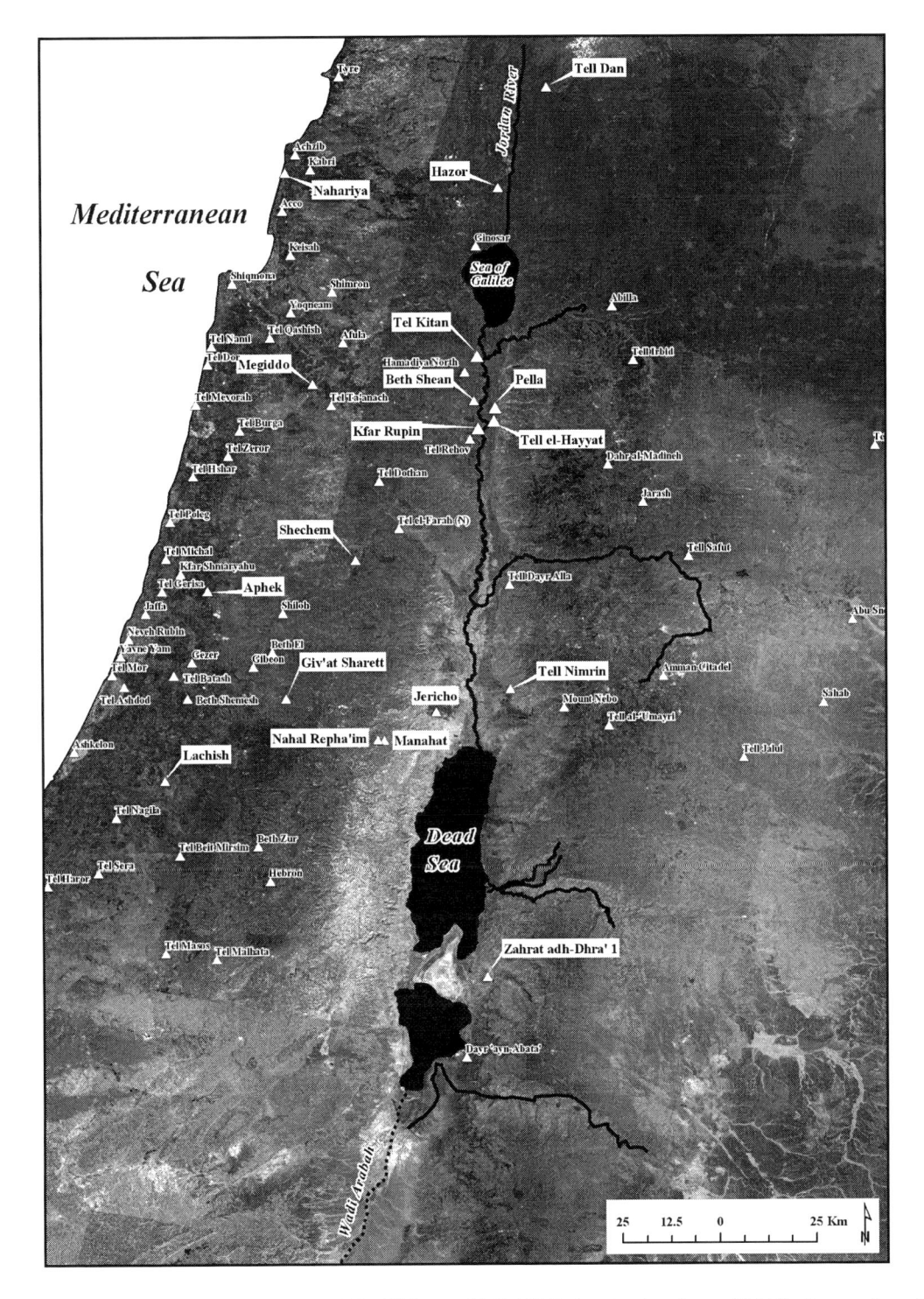

Figure 1.11 Digital image 10m resolution (CNES/SPOT Image 1992-1994) showing locations of Middle Bronze Age sites in the southern Levant, with sites mentioned in the text highlighted (data from Steve Savage; map created by Mariela Soto).

MIDDLE BRONZE AGE URBANISM AND RURALISM

The beginning and end dates traditionally assigned to the Middle Bronze Age derive, in large part, from the dynastic history of ancient Egypt. The beginning of the Middle Bronze Age is correlated axiomatically with the end of the First Intermediate Period and the ascension of Egypt's Twelfth Dynasty ca. 1991 B.C. Most chronologies argue that the Middle Bronze Age spanned roughly the time range of Egypt's Middle Kingdom and "Second Intermediate Period." This era's last interval, Middle Bronze IIC, coincided with an era of political turmoil in Egypt during which the Fifteenth Dynasty of "Asiatic" or "Hyksos" kings ruled much of Lower Egypt. Military disruptions associated with the collapse of

Hyksos power, and possibly their expulsion into the southern Levant, provide an end point for the Middle Bronze Age that is marked archaeologically by the destruction of many Canaanite cities (Weinstein 1991). A variety of syntheses propose revised Middle Bronze Age chronologies (e.g., Kenyon 1973; Gerstenblith 1983: 2-3; Dever 1987). For example, Gerstenblith (1983) and Dever (1987) propose substituting "Middle Bronze I, II and III" for Albright's "Middle Bronze IIA, B and C." Some recent overviews (e.g., Ilan 1995: 229; Marcus 2003) call for an independent, radiocarbon-based chronology in light of the scarcity of chronologically sensitive Egyptian material in the Levant and the poorly understood geographical variability that marks some Middle Bronze Age evidence. This volume utilizes "Middle Bronze IIA," "IIB" and "IIC," which remains the most common nomenclature, and provides an unambiguous definition for the term "Middle Bronze II."

Significantly, the best evidence for Middle Bronze Age society comes from reoccupied Early Bronze II-III tell sites that had been abandoned by Early Bronze IV, (or even by the end of Early Bronze II at some sites; Richard 1980). The rebirth of Levantine towns in Middle Bronze IIA was followed by their expansion into fortified cities in Middle Bronze IIB-C, culminating with the apex of Canaanite urban development ca. 1500 B.C. By the end of the period, a variety of sites provide evidence ranging from small forts (e.g. Mevorakh, one hectare) to substantial towns (e.g. Shechem, five hectares; Gezer 13 ha) and sizable urban centers (e.g. Hazor, 80 ha) (see Figure 1.11). The Middle Bronze Age covered a span of five centuries for which we have sufficient evidence to posit long-term population increase (see Broshi and Gophna 1986; Falconer and Savage 1995), and economic and political development (Mazar 1968; Kenyon 1966; Dever 1987; Ilan 1995). In this larger cultural context, the village of Tell el-Hayyat, Jordan exemplifies the small agrarian communities that lay at the foundation of Middle Bronze Age urbanized society in the Jordan Valley and the southern Levant generally during the early second millennium B.C.

Agricultural surpluses generated by rural farmers and herders provided much of the capital underlying the development of early Near Eastern cities. In return, social institutions, including managerial elites, seats of religion, professional bureaucrats and mercantile specialists provided the decidedly mixed blessings of urban authority. Hierarchical urban-rural relations featured a variety of ways in which broad decisions and directives were issued from larger communities. A material manifestation of this relationship is seen in relative settlement sizes that often reflect the hierarchical interactions between communities in ancient regional economic systems (e.g., Johnson 1977; 1980).

Rank-size analyses provide empirically based descriptive portraits of settlement hierarchies like those of the southern Levant (see Falconer and Savage 1995).

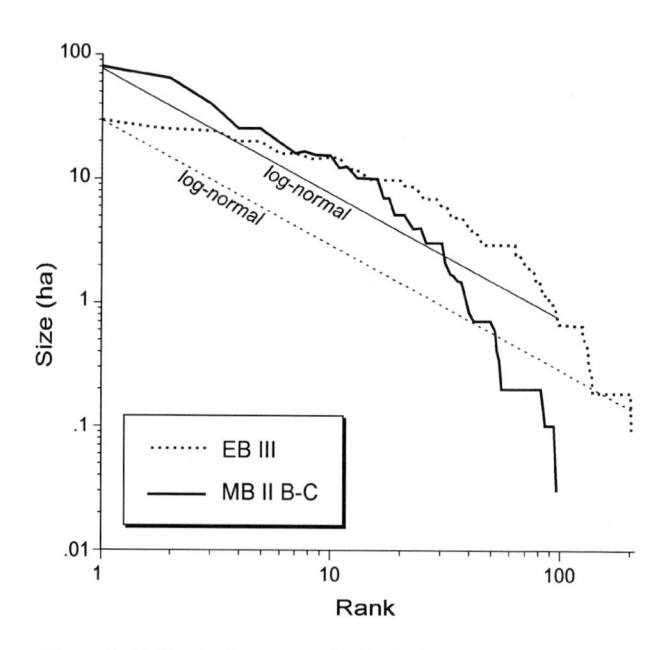

Figure 1.12 Rank-size curves for Early Bronze III and Middle Bronze IIB-C settlements in the southern Levant (see discussion in Falconer and Savage 1995; drafting by Barbara Trapido-Lurie).

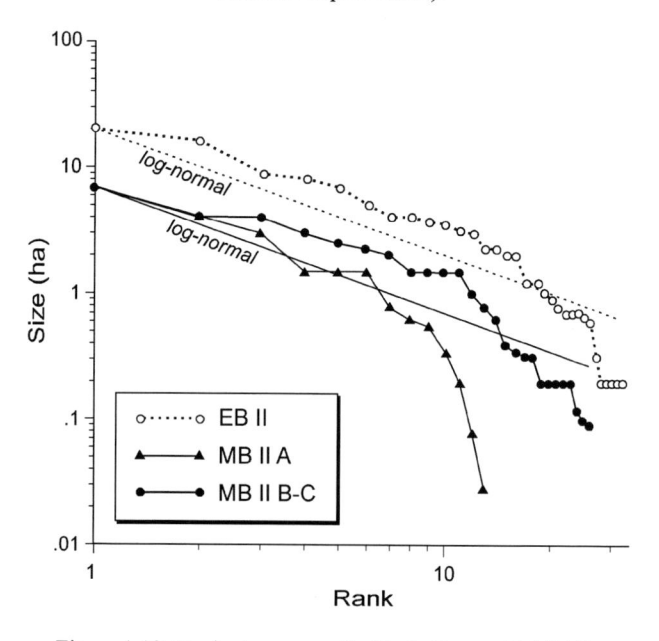

Figure 1.13 Rank-size curves for Early Bronze II, Middle Bronze IIA and Middle Bronze IIB-C settlements in the Jordan Valley (see discussion in Falconer and Savage 1995; drafting by Barbara Trapido-Lurie).

According to the "rank-size rule," the size of any nth-ranked place in a settlement system may be predicted by dividing the size of the largest place by n, such that a plot of the rank and size of all places in the system describes a log-normal distribution when plotted logarithmically (Zipf 1949; see straight log-normal lines plotted in Figures 1.12 and 1.13). Log-normal rank-size distributions "appear to be typical of larger countries with a long tradition of urbanism, which are politically and economically complex" (Berry 1961: 582). However, the structural implications of pre-industrial settlement systems appear most commonly in their departures from log-normal rank-size distributions (e.g., Johnson 1977; 1980; Adams 1981; Paynter 1983; Falconer and Savage 1995). A variety of factors regarding community interactions mold these departures, including the "closure" of the settlement system (i.e., the degree to which interactions are bounded within a system) and the "interdependence" or "integration" of communities (i.e., the relative frequency of interaction between communities in a system) (Vapnarsky 1968; Johnson 1980).

Interestingly, analysis of the Levantine Bronze Age settlement, using data from a variety of regional surveys (e.g., Ibrahim, et al. 1976; 1988; Broshi and Gophna 1986; Gophna and Portugali 1988) (see Figure 1.9), reveals stark contrasts with early urbanized settlement systems elsewhere in the ancient Near East, most notably in lower Mesopotamia (Adams 1981; Falconer and Savage 1995). Unlike Mesopotamian metropoli, even large Levantine Bronze Age cities had populations rarely exceeding a few thousand inhabitants (Falconer 1987b; 1994a). Levantine rank-size distributions predominantly describe "convex" curves in which large settlements are smaller, and small settlements are larger, than predicted for a log-normal distribution (Johnson 1977: 497). Even the urban apogees of Early Bronze III and Middle Bronze IIB-C reveal clearly convex rank-size distributions (see Figure 1.12). Intriguingly, convex patterns like these are increasingly rare in the modern world, occurring most often in underdeveloped countries with high closure and low interdependence (Vapnarsky 1968; Johnson 1980). Period-by-period settlement patterns for the southern Levant produce consistently convex rank-size distributions, reflecting only modest regional integration and the influences of multiple local settlement systems through the Bronze Age (Falconer and Savage 1995).

Settlement data from the Coastal Plain suggest the superimposition of a few Middle Bronze Age cities and towns on a convex lower rank-size curve that closely resembles the patterning of Early Bronze IV villages (Falconer and Savage 1995: fig. 10). This result implies the persistence of rural settlement through the collapse and rejuvenation of Levantine urbanism. The coastal cities atop the Middle Bronze IIB-C curve apparently developed in response to the external stimulus of Mediterranean maritime commerce (e.g., between Egypt and the cities of coastal Syria), which had disappeared during Early Bronze IV, but recovered during the Middle Bronze Age (Gerstenblith 1983; Falconer 1987b; 1994a; Falconer and Savage 1995). In the Jordan Valley, Bronze Age settlement data produce generally log-normal patterns (see Figure 1.13), reflecting the clearly bounded and more closed nature of the settlement pattern of Rift Valley. The Middle Bronze Age curves portray moderately integrated settlement systems incorporating modestly-sized towns (all less than 10 ha). These rank-size analyses highlight the development of urbanism in the southern Levant on a tightly defined stage, a relatively small scale, and with generally modest interdependence between central and peripheral communities. Tell el-Hayyat, lying close to Middle Bronze Age towns like Pella, provides an incomparable rural vantage point for investigating the nature of Levantine Bronze Age settlement, society and urban-rural relations.

LATE THIRD AND EARLY SECOND MILLENNIUM SETTLEMENT IN THE JORDAN VALLEY

An overview of Bronze Age settlement in the Jordan Valley helps place Tell el-Hayyat in a larger context of social and economic development during the redevelopment of early urbanism. During Early Bronze I and II, the Jordan Valley experienced a drop in population and settlement frequency similar to that of the southern Levant generally (Joffe 1991: table 18; Falconer 1994a). While valley-wide population leveled off in Early Bronze III, the settlement system became significantly less integrated as suggested by its convex rank-size distribution (Falconer and Savage 1995: fig. 12). During the Middle Bronze Age, sedentary settlement redeveloped in the Jordan Valley on a more modest scale. The valley's population grew slightly, while the number of settlements roughly doubled (Broshi and Gophna 1986; Falconer 1994a). Settlement data produce log-normal curves, suggesting that local inhabitants were distributed in a moderately integrated hinterland network of modest towns and villages. The archaeological evidence for Bronze Age settlement and society in the Jordan Valley stems from excavations at an array of Early Bronze IV and Middle Bronze II villages and towns.

Early Bronze IV Settlements

Sedentary Early Bronze IV settlements are documented at the Jordanian sites of Khirbet Iskander (Parr 1960; Richard 1983), 'Aro'er (Olavarri 1965, 1969), Iktanu (Prag 1974), Ader (Cleveland 1960), and Bab edh-Dhra' (Rast and Schaub 1974, 1978, 2003), all of which have at least two phases of occupation (see also Cohen 1999 for sites in the Negev). The discovery of Early Bronze IV material at Tell el-Hayyat (Falconer and Magness-Gardiner 1984), and seven Early Bronze IV strata at nearby Tell Abu en-Ni'aj (Falconer and Magness-Gardiner 1989; Falconer et al. 2004) provide complementary data for the sites mentioned above.

Middle Bronze II Settlements

Middle Bronze IIA sites in the Jordan Valley have been elusive, but provide evidence for agriculturally prosperous settlement, ranging from large towns to small villages. Archaeological data related to early Middle Bronze II occupation until recently consisted of ceramic collections from the cemetery at Pella (Smith 1973; McNicoll and Smith 1980; Smith et al. 1981), and the domestic deposits, fortifications, and tomb groups from Jericho (Kenyon 1965). These have now been augmented to include excavated settlements.

Only a handful of Middle Bronze Age sites in the Jordan Valley have been excavated to a significant extent, with many other sites showing an apparent hiatus in occupation during this period (e.g. Tell Abu Kharaz, Tell es-Saidiyyeh). Ancient communities east of the Jordan River, like Tell Deir 'Alla and Tell Nimrin lie in the *ghor*, while Pella lies in the first line of foothills to the east immediately overlooking the *ghor*. Pella's role as a major town early in the Middle Bronze Age is attested by a massive mudbrick town wall in the East Cut (Area III, plots D and F) (Smith and Potts 1992: 35, 40-44, fig. 7). Currently available pottery assemblages suggest a building date in Middle Bronze IIA (Smith 1993: 1176) and continued occupation into Middle Bronze IIB and IIC (Smith and Potts 1992: 44-47). The main mound at Pella covers an area of perhaps eight hectares, representing a settlement of about 2000 people. The likelihood that Pella was a fortified town early in the Middle Bronze Age is strengthened by its inclusion (as *Pihilum*) among the ritually cursed cities of the Egyptian Execration Texts (Smith 1973: 23).

Tell Deir 'Alla, which lies near the confluence of the Zarqa and Jordan rivers, provides another example of a Middle Bronze II town. The earliest known Middle Bronze Age remains at the site include a substantial mudbrick town wall preserved to a height of two and one-half meters at the southeast foot of the tell (van der Kooij and Ibrahim 1989: 75-76). This wall in Deir 'Alla's Phase IV dates no earlier than Middle Bronze IIB, based on associated Tell el-Yehudiyeh Ware. Domestic architecture, including mudbrick walls and courtyards, also are found in Phase IV and the subsequent Phase V. Thus, Tell Deir 'Alla represents a small fortified community a few hectares in size with a population on the order of 1000 inhabitants.

Tell Nimrin, lying near the mouth of the Wadi Shueib in the modern town of South Shuna, contains nearly six meters of stratified remains from the Middle Bronze Age. Unlike Tell Deir 'Alla, Nimrin provides domestic architecture and material culture dating to Middle Bronze IIA, apparently reflecting an unfortified village. Massive stone-founded mudbrick fortification walls date later in the Middle Bronze Age, and remain preserved up to four meters in height, with a *glacis* along their exterior. This monumental architecture was constructed in two phases, the first in late Middle Bronze IIB and the second in Middle Bronze IIC (Flanagan et al. 1994: 217-218). Interestingly, this massive wall system may have protected a village perhaps only one hectare in size (200-300 inhabitants), which was abandoned abruptly in the 16th or early 15th century B.C. (Flanagan et al. 1994: 217-219).

On the western side of the Jordan River, Middle Bronze II occupation of the Jordan Valley was dominated by the towns of Jericho and Tell Beit She'an (west of Pella across the Jordan River; see Figure 1.2). The excavations at Beit She'an revealed up to three strata of Middle Bronze II occupation composed of courtyard architecture with surrounding rooms. Middle Bronze II tombs produced Syrian luxury objects and weapons, and Egyptian imports are reported in abundance. Public architecture consisted of a street that was maintained through multiple phases, while the presence of a temple or cult area was deduced from ritual objects found in association with a central courtyard. As with other Middle Bronze II sites, such as Jericho and Tell el-'Ajjul, the build up of domestic architecture around a temple precinct suggests an element of town planning (Maeir 1997a). While some of the tombs at Tell Beit She'an may date to late Middle Bronze IIA or early Middle Bronze IIB, evidence for settlement during this time is limited. The major occupation at Beit She'an dates to late Middle Bronze IIB/early Middle Bronze IIC.

The Middle Bronze Age settlement at Jericho seems to have started in Middle Bronze IIA, and was not fortified until Middle Bronze IIB (cf. Marchetti 2003). During its Middle Bronze IIB-C occupation, Jericho became a fortified center characterized by shop-lined streets, storage facilities and public buildings. The settlement included rectilinear mud-brick courtyard architecture, which occasionally showed evidence for second story construction, conforming to a town-house plan common to urban Middle Bronze II settlements (Wright 1985). Silos and *tabun* ovens were found in both house interiors and courtyards (Kenyon 1981). Jericho is unusual in providing systematic data on annual and perennial crop cultivation (Hopf 1969), livestock husbandry dominated by sheep/goat and cattle (Clutton-Brock 1971), and participation in the regional trade of the Middle Bronze II world.

Excavated evidence for small agrarian communities along the Jordan Valley is currently limited to a few sites: Tell Kitan, Kfar Rupin, Hamadiya-North, Zahrat adh-Dhra' 1, and of course Tell el-Hayyat. Tell Kitan, located 12 km north of Beit She'an represents an example of a rural village with its own temple complex. During Middle Bronze IIA, Tell Kitan was an open village covering an area of less than one hectare. Domestic areas, though preserved poorly, produced evidence of rectilinear architecture with specialized refuse pits containing predominantly cooking vessels, jars and kraters. During Middle Bronze IIB, the site was fortified and a mudbrick temple was erected. Residential areas, again preserved poorly, included frequent intramural infant jar burials in residential housing (Eisenberg 1976, 1993). Tell Kitan's temple is centrally located and surrounded by residential architecture in a manner similar to Tell el-Hayyat (see discussion in subsequent chapters).

Middle Bronze IIA-B Kfar Rupin, located only a few kilometers to the west of Tell el-Hayyat across the Jordan River, was characterized by densely built rectilinear multi-cellular architecture revealed at the bottom of a fish pond. Evidence of a small temple, similar in design to those uncovered at Tell Kitan and Tell el-Hayyat, also came to light during the brief investigations. The ceramic repertoire included bowls, kraters, flat-bottomed cooking pots and storage jars as material components of a sedentary agricultural community (Gophna 1979).

Hamadiya-North exemplifies a poorly preserved Middle Bronze IIB settlement defined by a few stone houses conforming to a rectilinear broad room plan. Excavated material culture shows an absence of painted wares and luxury goods (Maeir 2000). Courtyard architecture features *tabun* ovens and flat-bottomed cooking pots. The remains of a *tournette*-type potter's wheel provide evidence for village pottery production. Although the site has suffered extensively from modern disturbance, the limited evidence is interpreted to represent a sedentary agrarian community.

In the extreme south of the Jordan Valley, on the Dead Sea Plain, recent excavations have uncovered the remains of a Middle Bronze IIA/B settlement at Zahrat adh-Dhra' 1 (Berelov 2001; Berelov and Falcon 2001; Edwards et al. 2001, 2002, 2004). The site is marked by exposed stone architecture along a northwest-southeast trending ridge in the Plain of Dhra', east of the ancient community of Bab edh-Dhra'. The remains of numerous rectangular structures and curved enclosures are spread widely over an area that originally may have covered approximately 12 ha. Excavations suggest intermittent occupations in Middle Bronze IIA and early Middle Bronze IIB (Berelov 2006). Severe downcutting followed this occupation (or may have ended it), as shown by the erosion of Middle Bronze Age structures into the steep-sided *wadi*s to the northeast and southwest, leaving a preserved site of only about six hectares.

This brief survey indicates that sedentary agrarian communities dotted the landscape of the Jordan Valley during the Early Bronze IV and Middle Bronze II periods from south of the Sea of Galilee to the southern edge of the Dead Sea. Characterized by low levels of integration despite the burgeoning trade networks of Middle Bronze II, the agricultural communities of the *ghor* seem to reflect a persistent yet highly diverse and ever-changing socioeconomic landscape. Elucidation of the roles of agrarian communities in Bronze Age settlement systems and society calls for in depth study of the social and economic dynamics of Bronze Age farming villages. Thus, the evidence from Tell el-Hayyat provides the basis for a detailed archaeological perspective on Bronze Age agricultural village life in the Jordan Valley (Falconer and Magness-Gardiner 1984; 1989).

CHAPTER 2: INTERPRETATIVE FRAMEWORK FOR EXPLORING BRONZE AGE RURALISM

INTRODUCTION

The settlement of Tell el-Hayyat provides a rare, intimate portrait of agrarian ecology on an increasingly anthropogenic landscape during the collapse and development of early towns and cities in the southern Levant. Amid relatively long-term trajectories of agrarian and environmental change, rural communities often demonstrate remarkable resilience (e.g., Adams 1978; Butzer 1996), making them ideal vantage points for detailed reconstructions of the economy and ecology that lay at the root of early civilizations. Tell el-Hayyat therefore offers a challenging opportunity to assess village life during the development of "reurbanized" society in the Middle Bronze Age. Building on previous Early and Middle Bronze Age investigations in the Jordan Valley, and in the southern Levant generally, our research explores the cultural and economic interactions between large towns and small villages that lay at the heart of Bronze Age civilization. Our interpretations of the village of Tell el-Hayyat derive from analyses of a wide range of evidence, including crop cultivation, animal management, private and public architecture, and pottery production and consumption. We are particularly interested in portraying sedentary agrarian life in small rural communities, which often eludes larger studies focused on urban centers and general questions of culture history.

TELL EL-HAYYAT: DISCOVERY AND PREVIOUS RESEARCH

Archaeological surveys in the Jordan Valley, notably those published by Glueck (1951), Mellaart (1962), and Ibrahim, Sauer and Yassine (1976), indicated several characteristics that made Tell el-Hayyat a particularly appropriate setting for the research detailed in this volume. Glueck's report of his surveys between 1939 and 1947 noted that "Tell abu Hayet" (his site 154) was used for modern burials and had no visible ancient architectural remains. He continued, "this insignificant looking site must, however, have been of considerable importance in ancient times, to judge from the considerable number of sherds found on and around it. They belong to the Middle Bronze I-II, Late Bronze I-II and Iron Age I-II periods. There are also numerous Roman period fragments" (Glueck 1951: 259). Glueck commented that, due to its diminutive size, Tell el-Hayyat had escaped inclusion on earlier maps, but that it "represents the site of a thriving agricultural settlement, which endured for many centuries (1951: 259)."

Mellaart's three month survey in 1953 for the Jordan Valley irrigation plan briefly identifies "Tell Abu Hayet" (his site 24) as a village marked by a slight rise of only a few meters. Following Glueck, he suggests occupation during the "Early Bronze (?), EB/MB and Iron" ages (Mellaart 1962: 144-145). In many cases Glueck's identification and interpretation of surface remains require serious revision (e.g., see the discussion in Prag 1974: 74-75). He has been taken to task for analyzing surface pottery in Transjordan (lands to the east of the Jordan River) based on misleading analogies with ceramics from west of the Jordan River (Parr 1972). In all fairness, Glueck and other early surveyors managed with the limited comparative samples available to them. As the archaeological record of Jordan has become better known, more systematic archaeological surveys have revised our appreciation of settlement in the Jordan Valley.

The major impetus for excavation at Tell el-Hayyat came from the results of the 1975 fieldwork of the East Jordan Valley Survey directed by Ibrahim, Sauer and Yassine. They analyzed their surface collections from "Tell el-Hayyat" (their site 56) as including "EB-MB, MB IIA, MB IIB-C and Persian" pottery (Ibrahim, Sauer and Yassine 1976: 49). The surveyors noted that their revision of Glueck's suggested periods of occupation meant that Hayyat could provide a readily accessible, "controlled sequence from EB-MB to MB IIB-C" (Ibrahim, Sauer and Yassine 1976: 54). They list Hayyat among those sites in the Jordan Valley with the greatest potential for future excavation and most "threatened with damage in the near future" (Ibrahim, Sauer and Yassine 1976: 64-65). This threat was demonstrated to us rather forcibly when we arrived at the tell in 1982 to find that a corner of the site had been bulldozed to enlarge an adjacent irrigated field. The Tell el-Hayyat Project was conceived in 1980 and conducted excavations in 1982, 1983 and 1985. The results of those excavations portray village life as it unfolded amid the reurbanization of the southern Levant and the growth of modestly-sized towns in the Jordan Valley during the Middle Bronze Age.

EXCAVATIONS AT TELL EL-HAYYAT

The excavation of Tell el-Hayyat began with a four-week investigation of its archaeological sequence between mid-January and mid-February, 1982 (Figures 2.1 and 2.2). In 1983 and 1985 our excavations were enlarged to explore broadened horizontal exposures and retrieve more representative samples of material remains and village architecture. We began the 1982 season by preparing a topographic plan of the 0.5 hectare site, superimposing a 5 x 5 m grid that delineated 4 x 4 m excavation units separated by one meter balks (Figure

2.3). In 1982 we laid out six 2 x 4 m "half squares" (lettered A-F) for excavation on the western and southern slopes of the tell. The southern units (A and B) were intended to probe village middens on the site's periphery (Figure 2.4). The western units (C-F) were situated on the steepest slope of the tell to provide rapid exposure of the site's stratification (Figure 2.5).

Through careful, but relatively expedient excavation of our six "half squares" in 1982 we were able to meet our initial objectives: (1) recovery of a stratified ceramic sequence that confirmed Early Bronze IV through Middle Bronze IIC occupation as interpreted by Ibrahim, Sauer, and Yassine (1976); (2) recovery of detailed information

Figure 2.1 The first day of excavation in Area A at Tell el-Hayyat, January 1982, facing north; Ron Gardiner (l) and Pat Fall (r) (photo by Bob Erskine).

Figure 2.2 Excavation of Areas C and D early in the 1982 season at Tell el-Hayyat, facing southwest (photo by Bob Erskine).

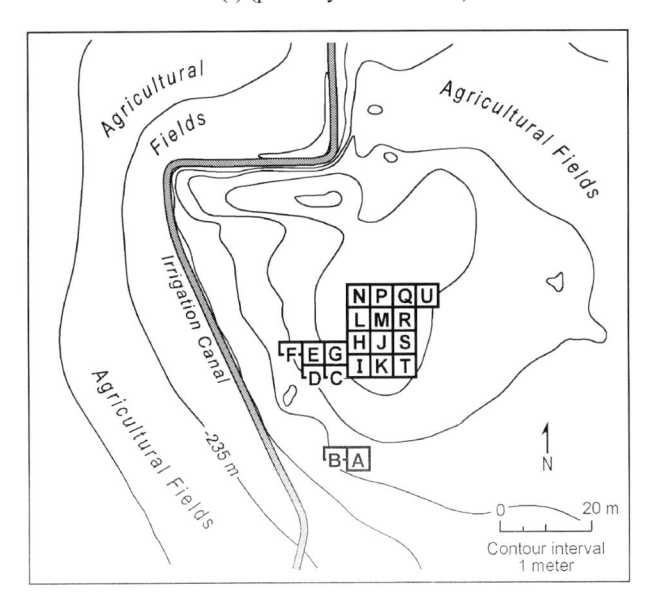

Figure 2.3 Topographic map of Tell-el-Hayyat showing the *tell*'s setting among agricultural fields. Excavation areas shown: Areas A and B (domestic trash and Phase 4 pottery kiln); Areas C, D, E, F, G, H, I, J, K, S and T (domestic architecture); Areas L, M, N, P, Q and R (temples); Area U (Phase 2 temple enclosure wall) (drafting by Barbara Trapido-Lurie).

Figure 2.4 Excavation of Areas B (foreground; supervisor Kathy Kamp) and A (background; supervisor Ron Gardiner) at Tell el-Hayyat, 1982, facing east (photo by Bob Erskine).

Figure 2.5 Sheikh Sadek, Bonnie Magness-Gardiner and Abu Said (l to r) excavating Areas C and D after removal of intervening balk at Tell el-Hayyat, 1982, facing east (photo by Bob Erskine).

Figure 2.6 Excavation of Areas D (foreground; supervisor Bonnie Magness-Gardiner with notebook) and C at Tell el-Hayyat, showing domestic household features, 1982, facing east (photo by Bob Erskine).

on other material culture, particularly floral and faunal remains, and stone tools; and (3) identification of areas with domestic architecture and floor levels for extended examination in subsequent seasons. The 1982 excavations revealed mudbrick domestic architecture associated with a predominantly Middle Bronze Age ceramic assemblage. Areas A and B produced extramural trash deposits and exposed half of the standing remains of a pottery kiln (Area A). Areas C-F revealed portions of house interiors and exterior alleyways (Figure 2.6). In three of the probes (A, B, and F) we reached sterile soil, approximately 0.5 meters below the level of the surrounding modern agricultural fields, thereby providing initial exposures of the site's stratification. The contexts excavated in 1982 produced small amounts of Early Bronze IV pottery, but no levels with entirely Early Bronze IV evidence. Having completed a successful initial field season, the 1982 project staff and field crew looked forward to renewed excavations the following year (Figures 2.7 and 2.8).

During an eight-week season in spring 1983 we continued and completed the excavations of our 1982 areas down to sterile soil, and broadened our operations in seven new areas (Figures 2.9 and 2.10). We enlarged Area A to the south, making it a full 4 x 4 meter square that captured the entire structure of the pottery kiln (Figure 2.11). Area E likewise was expanded to 4 x 4 m, making it contiguous with areas D and F. Excavations in areas B-D and F continued in their 2 x 4 m configurations. Since the 1982 excavations appeared to reveal the peripheries of the village at Tell el-Hayyat, our new 1983 operations extended toward the center of the site, where we expected more household architecture. At the beginning of the 1983 season we opened 4 x 4 m areas G-K, and at mid-season we added areas L and M. Excavations in areas L and M finished the season by exposing broad stone-founded walls for a structure in Phase 2 that was larger than the houses revealed previously at Tell el-Hayyat (Figure 2.12). In addition, small exposures just above sterile soil in areas H and J unearthed a thin stratum (Phase 6) with unmixed Early Bronze IV ceramics, but no architectural remains.

During the twelve-week field season between mid-September and mid-December 1985 we resettled into our home at the Deir Alla dighouse (Figures 2.13 and 2.14) during renewed and lengthened excavations at Tell el-Hayyat. We continued operations at the base of areas H and J, and resumed work in areas L and M (Figure 2.15). New excavations were opened in adjoining areas N-U (see Figure 2.3). This sampling strategy provided a particularly broad exposure at the heart of Tell el-Hayyat enabling us to explore the larger-scale architecture of Phase 2 and the Early Bronze IV deposition of Phase 6, as well as the development of the village through the intervening phases. The exposure resulting from all three seasons totaled approximately 400 m^2 (roughly 8 % of the site's area) through 4.5 meters of cultural debris (Figure

Figure 2.7 Teatime on the southern slope of Tell el-Hayyat, 1982, facing west;
(photo by Bob Erskine).

Figure 2.8 Mansaf lunch outside Meshara "dighouse" during visit by Bill Dever, 1982;
Khamis Fahid, Ali Abdul Rusool (behind Khamis), Fuad Awadd, "Sheikh" Sadek Abdullah, Bill Dever,
Mohammed Jumrah, Bonnie Magness-Gardiner (l-r) (photo by Bob Erskine).

Figure 2.9 Excavation of Areas C-E and G-K at Tell el-Hayyat, 1983, with Areas H-K shown to the right, facing north
(photo by Jon Kline).

Figure 2.10 Egyptian workmen during breakfast on the western slope of Tell el-Hayyat, 1983; facing north (photo by Jon Kline).

Figure 2.11 Tom Davis (on balk) and Ron Gardiner (below) excavating the Phase 4 pottery kiln in Area A at Tell el-Hayyat, 1983, facing southeast (photo by Jon Kline).

Figure 2.12 Excavation showing the discovery of the Phase 2 south temple wall in Areas L and M at Tell el-Hayyat, 1983; Steve Falconer cleaning pit dug into temple wall; facing east (photo by Jon Kline).

Figure 2.13 Bonnie Magness-Gardiner and Paula Marcoux shop for vegetables in Deir 'Alla, 1985 (photo by Karen Scholz).

Figure 2.14 John Meloy and Glen Peterman tend to yet another flat tire and other mechanical challenges of our trusty pickup truck at the Deir 'Alla dighouse, 1985; Haj Faris (dighouse caretaker) and Gaetano Palumbo supervise (photo by Karen Scholz).

Figure 2.15 Early in the 1985 excavations at Tell el-Hayyat; (l-r) Jake Jacobson (visitor), David McCreery (visitor), Steve Falconer, Bonnie Magness-Gardiner, Don Whitcomb (visitor), Linda McCreery (visitor) and John Meloy (in excavation unit) (l to r) (photo by Karen Scholz).

TABLE 2.1 Archaeological chronology for the southern Levant, incorporating the settlement sequence at Tell el-Hayyat (following Levy and Bar-Yosef 1995: figs. 2 and 3)

Cultural Period	Duration (yrs. B.C.)	Regional Settlement	Settlement Phases
Late Bronze	1500 to 1200	Urban recession	
Middle Bronze IIC	1650-1500	Height of urbanism	Phases 2-1
Middle Bronze IIB	1800-1650	Height of urbanism	Phase 3
Middle Bronze IIA	1900-1800	Cities redevelop	Phase 4
Middle Bronze IIA	2000-1900	Cities reappear	Phase 5
Early Bronze IV	2300-2000	Urban collapse	Phase 6
Early Bronze II-III	2900-2300	First cities	
Early Bronze I	3500-2900	Village-level farming	
Chalcolithic	4500 to 3500	Village-level farming	
Pottery Neolithic	5500 to 4500	Village-level farming	
Pre-Pottery Neolithic*	8300 to 5500	First farming towns	

2.16 and 2.17). Ultimately, Phase 6 remains, containing stratified Early Bronze IV ceramics with no associated architecture, were limited to thin deposits in areas H, J and S. Our most robust data, including a wide variety of material evidence and well-preserved architecture, document the course of the Middle Bronze Age village life at Tell el-Hayyat through phases 5-2. Hayyat's final occupation is reflected by the very limited remains of Phase 1, recovered primarily in 1985 (Table 2.1).

The 1985 season featured the excavation of a stratified sequence of four mudbrick temples, each surrounded by an enclosure wall, in phases 5-2 on the central high ground of Tell el-Hayyat. The stone-founded wall excavated in areas L and M in 1983 emerged as the south wall of the Phase 2 temple (see Figure 2.12). Our interpretation of this farming hamlet expanded to include the pivotal role of these temples, which formed a focus for community-wide behavior over four phases of occupation. Household activities were reflected in the evidence from houses, courtyards and alleyways in phases 5-2. Although our excavated sample from Phase 5 includes no domestic structures, the evidence recovered outside the Phase 5 temple suggests household activities similar to those documented outside the temples of phases 4-2. Phase 1 evidence is limited to fragmentary remains of wall foundations and small portions of surfaces dating to the end of Middle Bronze IIC. Phase 0 is used to designate any artifacts that postdate Phase I, including possible Byzantine pits and modern burials. Following the 1985 season, all excavation areas at Tell

Figure 2.16 Excavations at Tell el-Hayyat in 1985 after removal of balks. Domestic architecture in foreground; temple enclosure wall running across the middle of the excavated area; beginning of exposure of Phase 4 temple in background, facing northwest (photo by Karen Scholz).

Figure 2.17 Large-scale balk removal to expose Phase 2 temple architecture at Tell el-Hayyat, 1985 (photo by Karen Scholz).

el-Hayyat were backfilled. In sum, three seasons of excavation provided data illuminating agrarian village life in the Jordan Valley from the very end of the Early Bronze IV abandonment of towns through the redevelopment of urbanized society in the Middle Bronze Age. In this manner, Tell el-Hayyat provides a detailed rural perspective on the rise of townlife and its impacts on surrounding communities and their environments.

EXCAVATION METHODS, CONCEPTS AND TERMINOLOGY

The Tell el-Hayyat excavations adopted a 5 x 5 m grid, first laid out in 1982, and expanded in 1983 and 1985. Each grid square, usually termed an "excavation area" was assigned an alphabetic designation, generally according to the sequence in which their excavation was begun. Each area was excavated in "loci;" each "locus" being a three-dimensional context defined by the excavation supervisor (e.g., a wall, pit, surface, etc.). Each locus was numbered sequentially, in order of identification by the Area Supervisor, using a three-digit designation beginning with "001." In the course of excavating each locus the field crews collected bags of pottery, chipped stone, animal bones, sediment for botanical flotation, and other remains. These bags were numbered sequentially, beginning with "1." Thus, the most specific context for any evidence from Tell el-Hayyat is reflected hierarchically by its excavation area, locus number and bag number, with the locus and bag numbers separated by a period (e.g., P.012.054 or P012.054) (see Figure 2.18).

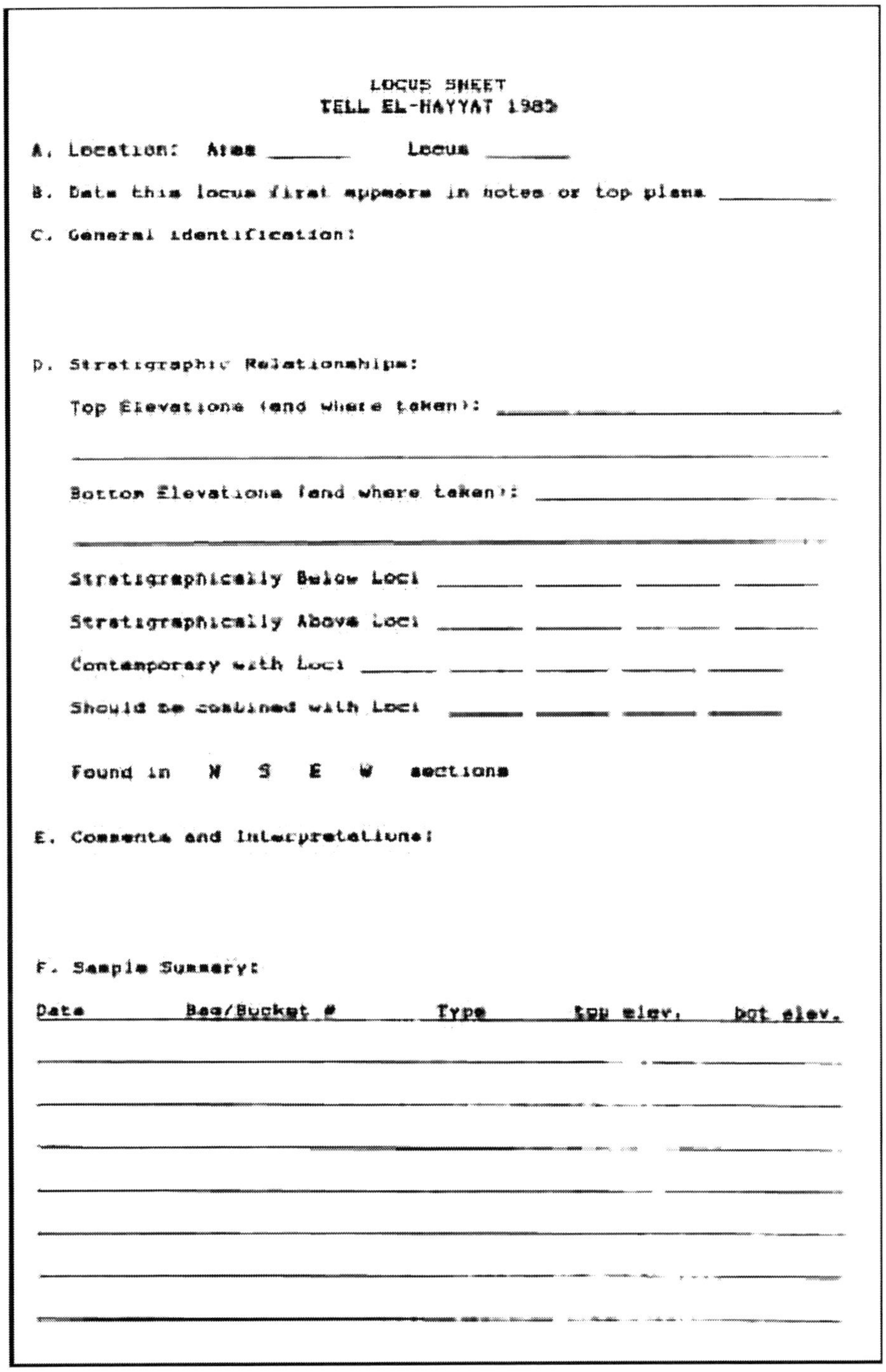

LOCUS SHEET
TELL EL-HAYYAT 1985

A. Location: Area ______ Locus ______

B. Date this locus first appears in notes or top plans ______

C. General identification:

D. Stratigraphic Relationships:

Top Elevations (and where taken): ______

Bottom Elevations (and where taken): ______

Stratigraphically Below Loci ______ ______ ______ ______

Stratigraphically Above Loci ______ ______ ______ ______

Contemporary with Loci ______ ______ ______ ______ ______

Should be combined with Loci ______ ______ ______ ______

Found in N S E W sections

E. Comments and Interpretations:

F. Sample Summary:

Date	Bag/Bucket #	Type	top elev.	bot elev.

Figure 2.18 Example of locus sheet used during the excavation of Tell el-Hayyat.

The sediments from all loci within the excavation areas, as well as selected loci in balks, were sieved through 1 x 1 cm mesh in the field (the thickness of sieve wire left openings approximately 0.75 x 0.75 cm) (Figure 2.19). All material remains collected during excavation or through sieving (e.g., stone, bone, ceramic and other artifacts) were washed, counted and examined in camp (Figure 2.20), where samples were selected for further analysis. Sediment samples also were taken from selected loci for flotation and retrieval of macrobotanical remains.

After we completed the field work, a relational database was constructed (first in Dbase, then in Paradox, finally in Access) to curate information on ceramics, stone tools, animal bones, botanical remains, and stone, shell and metal objects. The locus number (usually in the form of a combined area and locus designation; e.g., C019) serves as the key field in each file, allowing us to relate the files to each other so that different types of artifacts and ecofacts can be quantified and correlated with each other spatially and temporally across Tell el-Hayyat.

Figure 2.19 Jenny Davis sieving sediment at Tell el-Hayyat, 1983 (photo by Jon Kline).

Figure 2.20 Lynn Grant, Bonnie Magness-Gardiner, Steve Falconer and Gaetano Palumbo (l to r) analyzing pottery from Tell el-Hayyat on the roof of the Deir 'Alla dighouse, 1985 (photo by Karen Scholz).

UNITS OF SPATIAL ANALYSIS

Each locus, the smallest unit of excavation, has a unique spatial definition that reflects its depositional history and spatial context. After completing the excavation, each locus was assessed according to its location, description, contents and relationship to architecture, then assigned to a stratigraphic phase and a "locus code" based on its depositional character. The "TH Locus" database (see Appendix B) lists each locus with its Phase and Locus Code. The locus codes classify the loci according to one- and two-letter abbreviations (see Table 2.2). Loci that indicate village activities most directly include those with "primary refuse" deposited in original use areas and "de facto refuse" left behind when a structure was abandoned (Schiffer 1987). These forms of refuse are found at Tell el-Hayyat on use surfaces (usually earthen, sometimes stone-paved; locus code "S"), build-up immediately above surfaces (usually roughly 10 cm deep; locus code "Do"), and shallow ash lenses and pits embedded in surfaces (locus code "P").

Table 2.2 Classification of loci and associated locus codes for Tell el-Hayyat (see Appendices)

Codes:

A = Ash lens (usually embedded in a surface)
B = Burial (i.e., modern)
DO = Occupational debris (i.e., buildup on surface)
DM = Mudbrick debris
DF = Fill debris
H = Posthole
I = Installation (unidentified industrial or architectural feature)
K = Kiln
M = Modern *tell* surface
P = Pit (usually shallow, embedded in surface)
R = Rodent burrow
S = Surface (earthen)
SP = Plaster surface
T = Tabun (earthen oven)
TF = Tabun fill
V = Virgin soil (i.e., archaeologically sterile deposit)
X = Test trench

Sectors:

TB = Temple backcourt
TF = Temple forecourt
TFE = Temple forecourt exterior
TI = Temple interior
TS = Temple sidecourt
TT = Tower
WA = West alley
WB = West building
WE = West exterior
WR = West room
EA = East alley
EB = East Building
EC = East courtyard
CA = Central alley
CE = Central enclosure
CC = Central courtyard
CR = Central room

Temple Interior – Sector TI only
Temple Courtyard – Sectors TF, TS, TB, and TT
Domestic Interiors – Sectors WR, CR, CE, EB, and WB
Domestic Exteriors – Sectors WA, CA, EA, CC, EC, WE and TFE

A number of ethnoarchaeologists have considered the implications of evidence from variable contexts and we apply many of their insights in our interpretations of Tell el-Hayyat. Using the Human Relations Area Files,

INTERPRETATIVE FRAMEWORK FOR EXPLORING BRONZE AGE RURALIS

CA	Central Alley	T	Temple Walls	WA	West Alley
CE	Central Enclosure	TB	Temple Backcourt	WB	West Building
CR	Central Room	TE	Temple Enclosure Walls	WE	West Enclosure
EA	East Alley	TF	Temple Forecourt	WR	West Room
EB	East Building	TFE	Temple Forecourt Exterior		Mudbrick Walls
EC	East Courtyard	TI	Temple Interior		Stone Walls
		TS	Temple Sidecourt		Reconstructed Walls

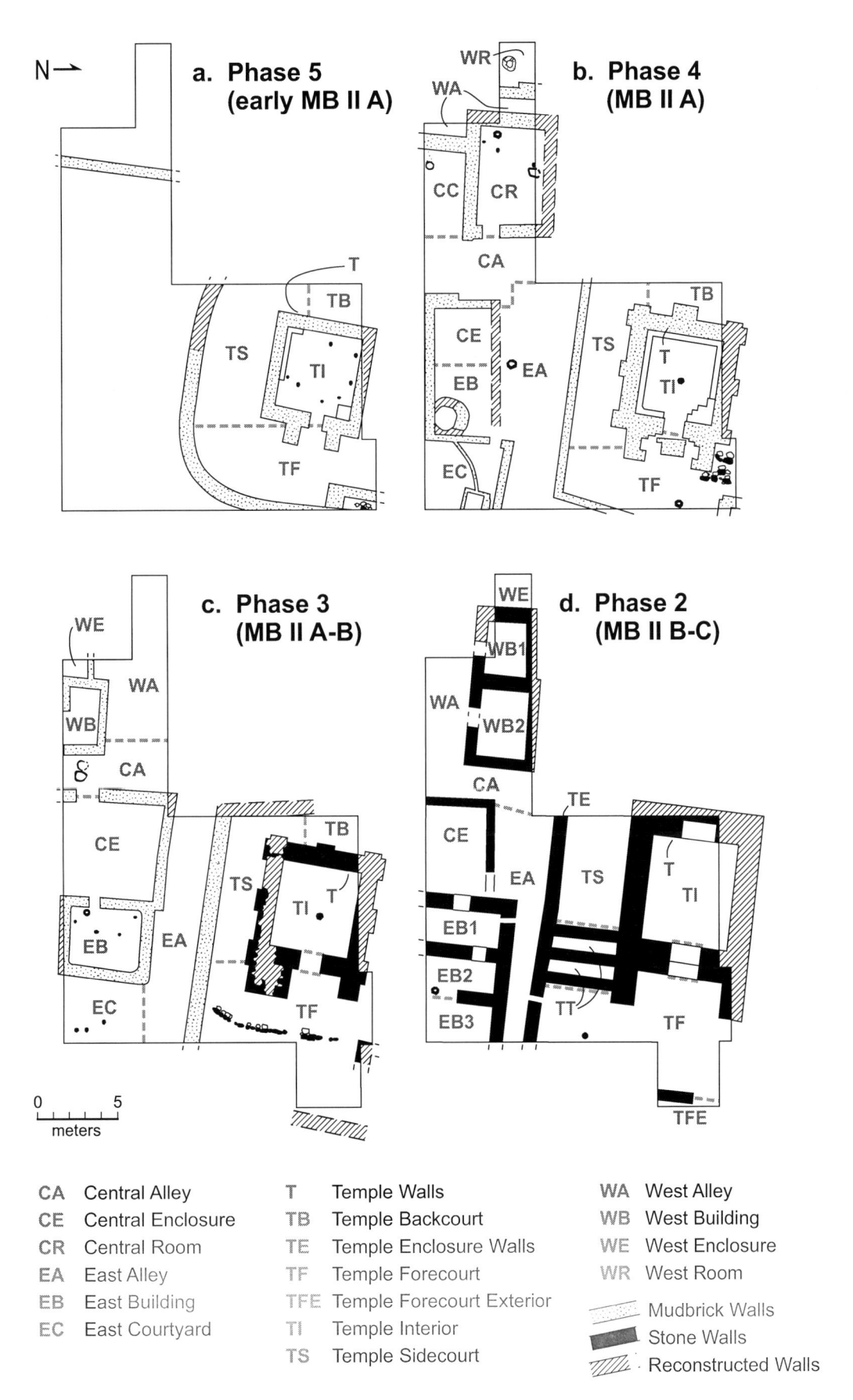

Figure 2.21 Architectural plans for phases 5-2 at Tell el-Hayyat showing sectors used in spatial analyses (drafting by Barbara Trapido-Lurie).

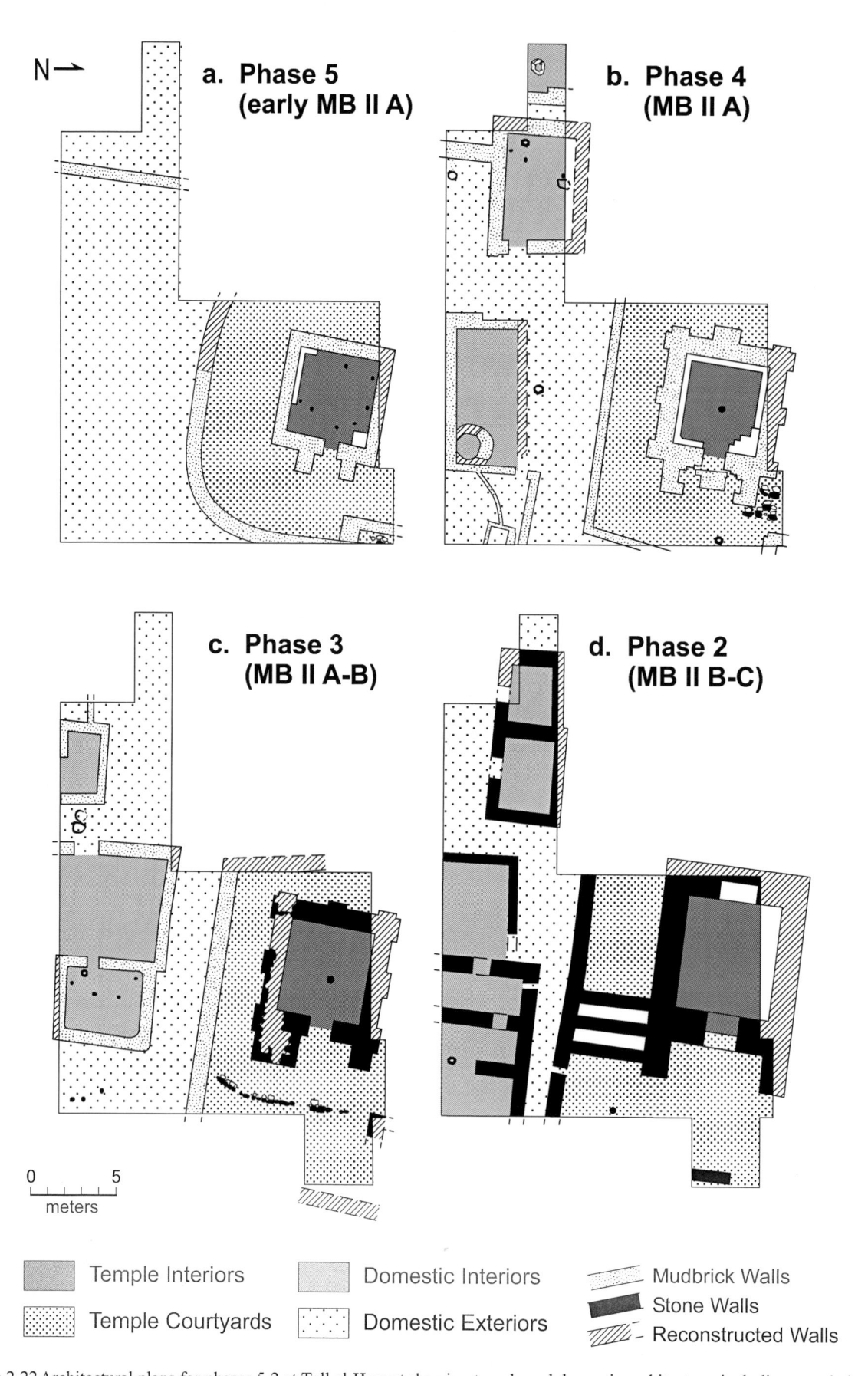

Figure 2.22 Architectural plans for phases 5-2 at Tell el-Hayyat showing temple and domestic architecture, including temple interiors and courtyards and domestic interiors and exteriors (drafting by Barbara Trapido-Lurie).

Murray (1980: 493) found that ethnographically documented societies tended to keep architectural interiors swept and clean, but that discarded material often accumulated outside inhabited architectural units. In examining household pottery disposal in the Maya highlands, Deal (1985: 259-260) observed that sweeping interior and exterior living surfaces did not remove all traces of broken pottery, and that sherds and other debris were simply moved off patio edges and thus deposited very close to living areas. Intentional dumping (as opposed to daily sweeping) took place within Maya household compounds, in neighborhood dump sites or in streets (Deal 1985: 261). By analogy we interpret similar deposits at Tell el-Hayyat as most directly indicative of daily household behavior. These include buildup on surfaces, swept and trampled, but not moved far prior to archaeological deposition, as well as ash deposits from cooking fires or industrial activity, and pits filled with trash very likely from the immediate vicinity. Thus, the loci we interpret as our best indicators of household behavior include surfaces, occupational debris, pits and ash lenses. Other locus types play lesser roles in our interpretations since they reflect household activity patterns less directly. These loci tend to have deposits with "secondary refuse" (especially fill and mudbrick debris) often containing materials redeposited from more distant locations in the village. Likewise, material culture (pottery, lithics and bones) from wall loci (e.g., standing foundations or collapsed mudbrick) are excluded from most of our analyses because mudbricks most likely contain debris quarried elsewhere on or near Tell el-Hayyat.

Following the completion of the Hayyat excavations, loci that shared a common architectural setting in the same phase were grouped into architecturally-defined "sectors" (Figure 2.21). This method brings together data from multiple excavation areas to facilitate spatial analysis of behavioral patterns, since human activities often are bounded and segregated by architecture (Rapoport 1990). Each sector includes a set of primary and secondary loci that are related by their spatial and stratigraphic proximity to each other and bounded by a shared set of walls or other architectural features. For example, space within the temple enclosure wall is divided into temple interior, forecourt, sidecourt, and backcourt sectors. Household remains are grouped into various house interiors, courtyards and alleyways. Our analyses also combine multiple sectors according to "domestic interior," "domestic exterior," "temple interior," and "temple exterior" (Figure 2.22). Our interpretations of Tell el-Hayyat consider several lines of evidence as they illustrate changes through time, especially by comparing data from phases 5-2, and across space, by contrasting patterns of behavior in temple and domestic contexts. These analyses enable multi-faceted inferences of depositional patterns and their behavioral implications for Bronze Age village life at Tell el-Hayyat.

CLASSIFICATION AND ANALYSIS OF MATERIAL REMAINS

Excavation and dry sieving produced large samples of animal bones, ceramics and chipped stone, as well as smaller amounts of metal artifacts, worked bone and shell, and stone and shell beads. Through simple water flotation we recovered abundant plant macrofossils, as well as occasional small animal bones and diminutive artifacts (e.g., beads). We tailored our methods of recovery, sampling and analysis to each of these major lines of evidence. Processing, sampling and preliminary analyses of these archaeological materials were supervised in the field by Steve Falconer and Bonnie-Magness-Gardiner (ceramics), Patricia Fall (botanical remains), Mary Metzger (animal bones), John Whittaker and Kathy Kamp (lithics, 1982), and Ron Gardiner (lithics, 1983 and 1985). Initial analyses of all artifacts and floral and faunal material took place in Jordan in our rented house in Mashara in 1982 and at the Deir 'Alla dighouse during the 1983 and 1985 seasons. Final analyses were undertaken at Bryn Mawr College (pottery), the University of Alabama, Birmingham (animal bones), the University of Arizona (pottery and floral material), and Arizona State University (pottery, lithics and floral material).

Pottery

Our methods for generating ceramic data from Tell el-Hayyat were designed to provide representative samples of pottery vessel types and sizes, decorative motifs and manufacturing methods. These data provide the basis for Tell el-Hayyat's chronology and a variety of interpretations of household and village-wide behaviors. All sherds roughly 1 x 1 cm and larger were collected from every locus, washed, and checked for restorable pieces. If restorable vessels were present, then all the sherds from that locus were saved to facilitate refitting. All sherds were counted, and a sample was selected from each locus for further analysis. The samples selected in the field for further processing consisted of sherds diagnostic of vessel form (rims, bases, handles, spouts and decorated sherds), as well as selected body sherds, and all examples of Early Bronze IV ceramic wares (Figure 2.23). Unsaved sherds were returned to Tell el-Hayyat. The saved sherds were labeled in ink with a site abbreviation (TH), Area letter, Locus number (three digits), and Bag number (one to three digits) (e.g., TH A011.035). The labeled sherds were shipped to the United States for analysis at Bryn Mawr College, University of Arizona and Arizona State University. Descriptive processing at Bryn Mawr and Arizona State involved assigning each sherd its appropriate contextual information (Area, Locus and Bag), and identifying sherd type (rim, handle, body, etc.), vessel form, surface decoration and vessel size (e.g., rim or base diameter, body thickness, largest sherd dimension). This process of sherd description included over 23,000 sherds from all locus types, providing a 10-12% sample of the total collection of sherds excavated during the three seasons.

Figure 2.23 Pottery reading with Steve Falconer, Pat Fall, Bill Dever (visitor) and Bonnie Magness-Gardiner (l to r) at the Deir 'Alla dighouse, 1983 (photo by Jon Kline).

A pilot project of about 5,000 sherds from all locus types showed that primary refuse from surfaces, surface build up, ash lens and shallow pits contained a consistently larger percentage of restorable sherds and fewer EB IV sherds than deposits with secondary refuse (primarily fill and mudbrick debris). Therefore, we judged surface deposits to be less mixed and more reliable as functional and chronological indicators than secondary deposits. As this matched our expectations based on the ethnographic work summarized above, we analyzed ceramic patterns mostly from loci characterized by primary refuse.

Animal Bones

Animal bones were recovered and sampled in an effort to reflect the range of domestic and wild animals characteristic of Tell el-Hayyat and its environmental setting in the Middle Bronze Age. As with pottery sherds, animal bones were recovered over the course of excavation and dry sieving in the field. In field camp all recovered bones and bone fragments were washed, sorted by taxon and bone type, and counted. Identifiable bones were shipped to the United States for detailed analysis. The Tell el-Hayyat excavations produced about 95,000 bones and bone fragments, approximately 27,500 of which could be assigned to rough categories by bone size and type.

Following the excavation seasons, taxonomic identifications were finalized with reference to comparative collections. Wim Van Neer identified the Tell el-Hayyat fish bones alongside comparative specimens from the Royal Museum of Central Africa in Tervuren, Belgium. Shells were identified by David Reese with reference to his own collections. Other reference collections were consulted at the Smithsonian Museum of Natural History in Washington, D.C. and the Field Museum in Chicago. The number of specimens identifiable by taxon totaled 12,586.

Quantified patterns of bone deposition commonly reflect animal management strategies and economic relations within and between communities. The Tell el-Hayyat animal bone data are reported most often as numbers of identified specimens (NISP) following various arguments (e.g., Redding 1992; Crabtree 1990: 159-160) that NISP is preferable to MNI (minimum number of individuals) for estimating relative abundances of taxa (cf. Grayson 1984: 94-96). The common use of NISP in literature pertaining to southwestern Asia (e.g., Meadow and Zeder 1978; Clutton-Brock 1979; Hellwing and Gophna 1984; Horwitz 1989; Zeder 1991; Redding 1992) also recommends its use, particularly for comparative purposes.

Floral Remains

Carbonized remains were recovered to infer the array of plants incorporated in Tell el-Hayyat's Bronze Age agricultural practices and surrounding environment. Carbonized plant fragments were extracted from archaeological sediment samples using simple water flotation (Figure 2.24). We employed a non-random sampling strategy in which most samples were collected from deposits that showed evidence of burning, or contained visible carbonized seeds or wood. Samples were taken from hearths, tabuns (cooking ovens), surfaces (floors), storage pits, trash deposits, and the pottery kiln. Recovery of floral evidence from Tell el-Hayyat entailed processing 151 flotation samples totaling approximately 900 liters of sediment (samples ranged between 4 and 16 liters each). Water flotation takes advantage of contrasting densities of organic and inorganic materials, facilitating the recover of all size classes of carbonized plant material. Each sample was poured into a metal basket with 3.2 mm mesh screen across the bottom. This basket was suspended in a metal tub of water. Each sample was then gently agitated to dissolve the sediment and free the carbonized plant fragments from the soil matrix. Suspended plant material was removed with a large tea strainer (1.6 mm mesh). The smallest seeds were recovered by placing a piece of cheese cloth over the tea strainer. The contents of the metal basket were checked for heavier seeds that may not have floated (e.g., olive stones). Following flotation, plant remains were dried indoors for about 24 hours. Carbonized seeds were separated from other carbonized plant material by sorting each sample with the aid of a microscope (Heergurgg WILD M3Z) at 6 to 10x magnification. Samples were sieved to separate the carbonized material into discrete size categories. Sieving improves sorting efficiency because objects of fixed size do not require constant adjustment of the eyes or microscope (Pearsall 1989).

Figure 2.24 Glen Peterman and Lynn Grant (l to r) processing flotation samples at the Deir 'Alla dighouse, 1985 (photo by Karen Scholz).

Over 8100 carbonized seeds were identified from Tell el-Hayyat. The quantification of paleobotanical evidence presents many of the same challenges inherent in assessing animal bone counts. The Tell el-Hayyat floral analyses use counts of identified plant macrofossils in a manner roughly analogous to the NISP counts utilized for Hayyat's faunal data. Whenever possible, broken olive stones were reassembled and counted as one whole seed. Olive stone fragments that could not be pieced together were counted as representing 0.50 or 0.25 of a seed. Species identification was aided by Patricia Fall's comparative seed collection, and published illustrations (Renfrew 1973; Hopf 1983). Naomi Miller, Karen Adams, and Charles Miksicek aided in the identification of several unknown seeds.

The wide diversity of species represented in the carbonized seed assemblage from Tell el-Hayyat means that there are a number of potential sources of bias affecting interpretation (e.g. the overrepresentation of species with fruit containing large numbers of seeds, such as fig). The carbonization process actually represents an "accidental sampling" of plant usage, a chance occurrence in which misplaced seeds inadvertently become carbonized through incomplete burning or through the burning of animal dung as a fuel source. The absolute numbers of seeds may not always reflect the extent to which a particular species was utilized (Jones 1991). Even the absence of a particular seed from the plant remains of an archaeological site does not necessarily mean that the species was not utilized. For instance, date palm seeds are rarely preserved by carbonization because they are not exposed to heat during crop processing (McCreery 1980).

Pearsall (1989) recommends presence/absence, or ubiquity analysis, as a means of offsetting some of the problems associated with sample bias. Presence/absence utilizes the number of samples containing at least one carbonized seed from a particular species (a species is considered present whether there is one seed or fifty). Presence/absence is often used to avoid the bias and standardization problems associated with absolute counts. However, Kadane (1988) points out that the probability of a species being present in a given sample is still influenced by preservation bias and sample size.

Miller (1988) and Pearsall (1989) discuss the use of density ratios (number of seeds/sample volume) as a means of standardizing paleoethnobotanical samples of unequal size. An assumption underlying the use of density ratios is that the number of carbonized seeds in a given sample increases with increasing sample size (Miller 1988). This appears to be a reasonable assumption, given the random nature of seed carbonization. The botanical analyses in this volume utilize both density ratios expressed as the number of plant fragments for a given taxon per kiloliter of sediment to explore the spatial and temporal patterns of floral deposition at Tell el-Hayyat, and seed frequencies when comparing Tell el-Hayyat to other Bronze Age villages along the Jordan Rift. Density ratios and seed frequencies provide an estimate of plant uses and their implications for Bronze Age agriculture, urban-rural interactions, and effects on the agrarian landscape in the Jordan Valley.

Stone Tool Industries and Other Remains

A variety of other forms of material evidence from Tell el-Hayyat were systematically recovered, processed and sampled for analysis. The remains of stone tools were collected to document the range of raw materials, manufacturing debris, and flake and blade tools at Tell el-Hayyat. Along with ceramics and animal bone, all chipped stone remains greater than approximately 1 x 1 cm were recovered in the course of excavation and dry sieving in the field. These flint or chert chipped stone collections were sorted in camp to segregate cores, blades, flakes and debitage, which were saved for analysis, from naturally-caused shatter and debris, which was returned to Tell el-Hayyat. Ground stone objects were sampled selectively and in limited numbers for descriptive analysis in the field and a subsequent interpretive report by Jane Peterson. Unusual objects excavated from Tell el-Hayyat include metal and ceramic figurines, metal tools, ceramic crucibles, stone metallurgical molds, perforated bones, and stone and shell beads. These objects, mainly recovered in our second and third seasons, were processed by Jenny Davis in 1983, and processed and conserved by Lynn Grant in 1985 at the Deir 'Alla dighouse.

Multiple Lines of Evidence and Analysis

Our interpretations of Bronze Age village life at Tell el-Hayyat derive most fundamentally from patterns of ceramic, floral and faunal evidence. Spatial patterning distinguishes communal behaviors centered on Hayyat's temples from smaller scale household practices reflected by domestic remains. Temporal patterning reveals trends of village agriculture and economy over the course of Middle Bronze Age reurbanization. More specific data, derived from a variety of other remains, flesh out details of Bronze Age village life, including metallurgy, pottery manufacture, and village and household ritual. Jointly, these many lines of evidence and interpretation help portray the development of early urbanized society from the perspective of the rural farmers of the Jordan Valley.

CHAPTER 3: DOMESTIC AND PUBLIC ARCHITECTURE AT TELL EL-HAYYAT

TEMPLES AND HOUSEHOLDS: THE ARCHITECTURAL SEQUENCE

Tell el-Hayyat provides a detailed illustration of rural settlement from the end of the Early Bronze IV Period through the full course of the Middle Bronze Age. The occupational history of Tell el-Hayyat is inferred from the mound's stratification, architecture and associated material culture. The six phases at Hayyat are defined according to major episodes in the building and rebuilding of village temples and houses. The dating of these architecturally defined phases stems primarily from comparative pottery analysis (Table 3.1; see Chapter 4). The earliest archaeological deposition at Hayyat in Phase 6, lying just above sterile soil, incorporates chipped stone and Early Bronze IV ceramics, but no architectural remains. Hayyat's first architecture consists of a small, centrally located, mudbrick shrine in Phase 5, which is the first in a stratified series of mudbrick temples that were enlarged and elaborated in Phases 4 through 2 (Figure 3.1). Outside the temple compounds of Phases 4-2 lie domestic structures, walled courtyards, and alleyways. Phase 1 (Middle Bronze IIC) includes only fragments of domestic architecture and no evidence of a temple. Phase 0 provides a stratigraphic designation for a variety of material from Tell el-Hayyat that post-dates Phase 1, including possible Byzantine pits, post-Byzantine burials, and surface remains. The sequence of archaeological deposition at Tell el-Hayyat is reflected particularly well in the north balk face of Areas N, P and Q that cross-cuts the stratified village temples (Figure 3.2). The successive rebuilding of Hayyat's temples is revealed graphically by a cross-section across this north balk face (Figure 3.3). A series of stratigraphic cross-section drawings represent the successive reconstructions of temples and houses, along with their associated sediment loci (Figure 3.4). These cross-sections capture Hayyat's stratification in a series of strategic locations across the site. The history of household structures and their associated sediments is reflected by cross-sections across the south balk face of Areas K and I (Figure 3.5) and the north balk face of Area F (Figure 3.6). The sedimentation associated with Hayyat's village periphery and pottery kiln (located in the middle of Area A) is illustrated by a cross-section through the kiln facing south (Figure 3.7).

Table 3.1 Phases of occupation and associated architecture at Tell el-Hayyat

Cultural Period	Regional Settlement	Phase	Architecture
Post-MBA		Phase 0	No architecture
MB IIC	Height of urbanism	Phase 1	Domestic Architecture
MB IIB/C	Height of urbanism	Phase 2	Temple/Domestic Architecture
MB IIA/B	Height of urbanism	Phase 3	Temple/Domestic Architecture
MB IIA	Cities redevelop	Phase 4	Temple/Domestic Architecture/Kiln
MB IIA	Cities reappear	Phase 5	First temple
EB IV	Urban collapse	Phase 6	No architecture

of vessel form. Although Early Bronze IV ceramics were mixed into some later deposits at Hayyat, unmixed Phase 6 Early Bronze IV material was limited to a modest selection of loci at the bottom of Areas H, J and S, lying just south of the Phase 5 temple enclosure wall. In light of the limited distribution and apparently reworked nature of these basal deposits, as well as the repeated leveling and rebuilding of later temples, Phase 6 probably represents merely a remnant of Early Bronze IV deposition pushed aside just prior to the construction of the Phase 5 temple.

Phase 5 (early Middle Bronze IIA)

The only building recovered from Phase 5 is a small, nearly square temple near the center of Tell el-Hayyat. It was razed and replaced in precisely the same location and orientation by new temples in each of three successive phases. The Phase 5 temple corresponds to Hayyat's later temples in overall form, orientation, and physical separation from domestic structures. The Phase 5 temple foundation is constructed very simply of compacted earth (*terre pise*) resting directly on sterile soil (see the northwest corner and most of the northern wall of *terre pise* temple foundations in Figure 3.2). Remnants of brick on top of this foundation hint at mudbrick walls, in keeping with subsequent Hayyat temples. The Phase 5 temple is encircled by an enclosure wall, which was exposed by excavation to the south and east of this structure. The evidence excavated in association with the Phase 5 temple may be segregated into sectors pertaining to the temple interior (Sector TI; see Figure 2.21) and various portions of the temple courtyard (Sectors TB, TF and TS). All evidence from outside the temple enclosure is aggregated into a common domestic sector.

Phase 6 (late Early Bronze IV)

The earliest stratified material from Tell el-Hayyat includes a thin layer of sediments with Early Bronze IV ceramics and lithics lying on sterile soil at the base of the mound. This phase revealed no architectural remains and only very fragmentary pottery with few sherds indicative

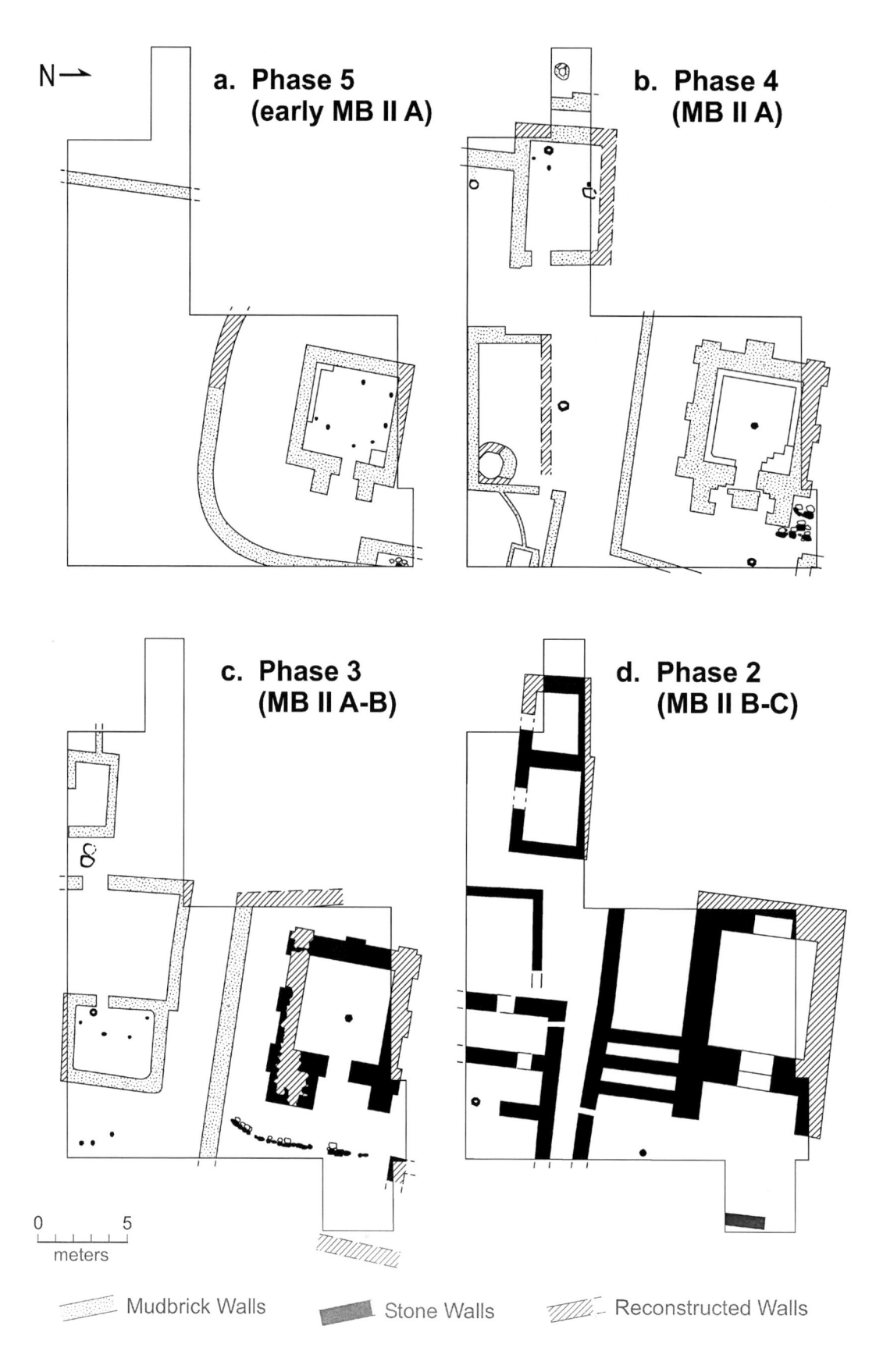

Figure 3.1 Plan views of phases 5-2 at Tell el-Hayyat detailing architectural features in households and temples. Excavated foundations are stone (dark), mudbrick (stippled) and reconstructed (lined). Note depressions for postands in Phase 5 temple, pedestal bases in center of Phase 4 and 3 temples, and in forecourt of Phase 2 temple. In temple forecourts standing stones are shown as dark; flat-lying stones shown in outline. Domestic features include small postholes, circular tabuns; in Phase 4 a rectangular basin drains west into a deep circular pit (drafting by B. Trapido-Lurie).

DOMESTIC AND PUBLIC ARCHITECTURE AT TELL EL-HAYYAT

Figure 3.2 View across the Phase 5 temple at Tell el-Hayyat showing the stratification of all four temples in the north balk face of Areas N, P and Q. Conclusion of excavations, 1985, facing north, Glen Peterman (l), Steve Falconer (r). Note stratified remains of Phase 4, 3 and 2 temples in north and west balks. Phase 4 standing stone in north balk; Phase 5 structure in northeast corner (photo by Karen Scholz).

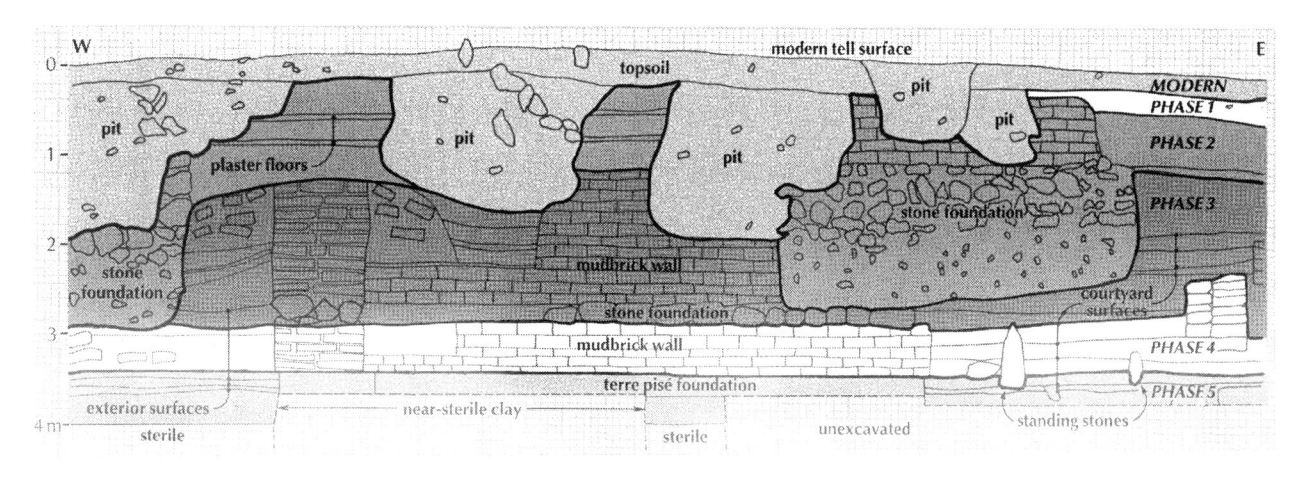

Figure 3.3 Stratigraphic cross-section across the north balk face of Areas N, P and Q, Tell el-Hayyat; drawn at the conclusion of the 1985 excavation season.

Figure 3.4 Drawing stratigraphic cross-sections at Tell el-Hayyat, 1985, facing southeast. Left to right: Pat Fall drawing south balk face of Area R; Bonnie Magness-Gardiner drawing north balk face of Area S; Ron Gardiner taking notes in Area T (photo by Karen Scholz).

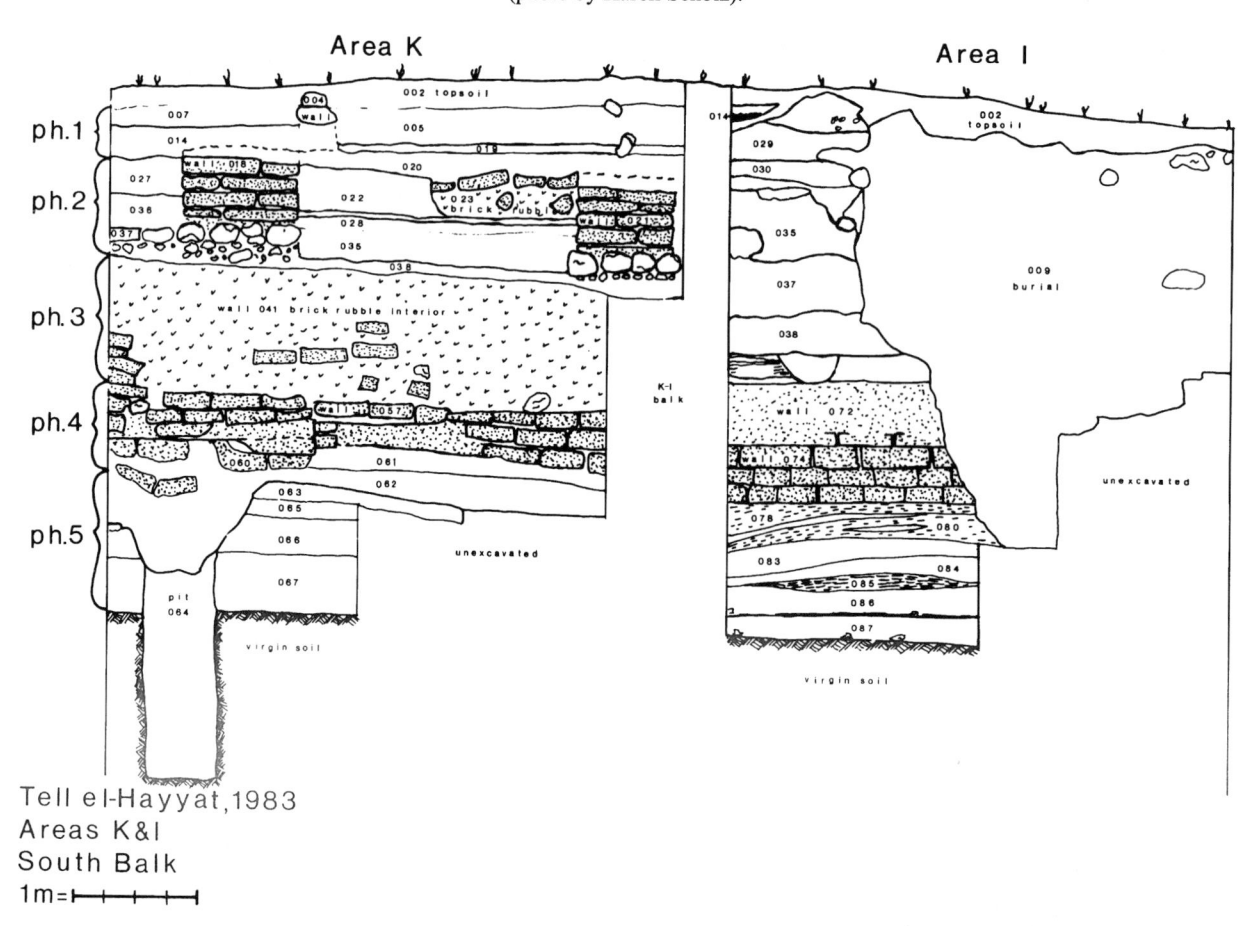

Figure 3.5 Stratigraphic cross-section across the south balk face of Areas K and I at Tell el-Hayyat;

DOMESTIC AND PUBLIC ARCHITECTURE AT TELL EL-HAYYAT

drawn at the conclusion of the 1983 excavation season.

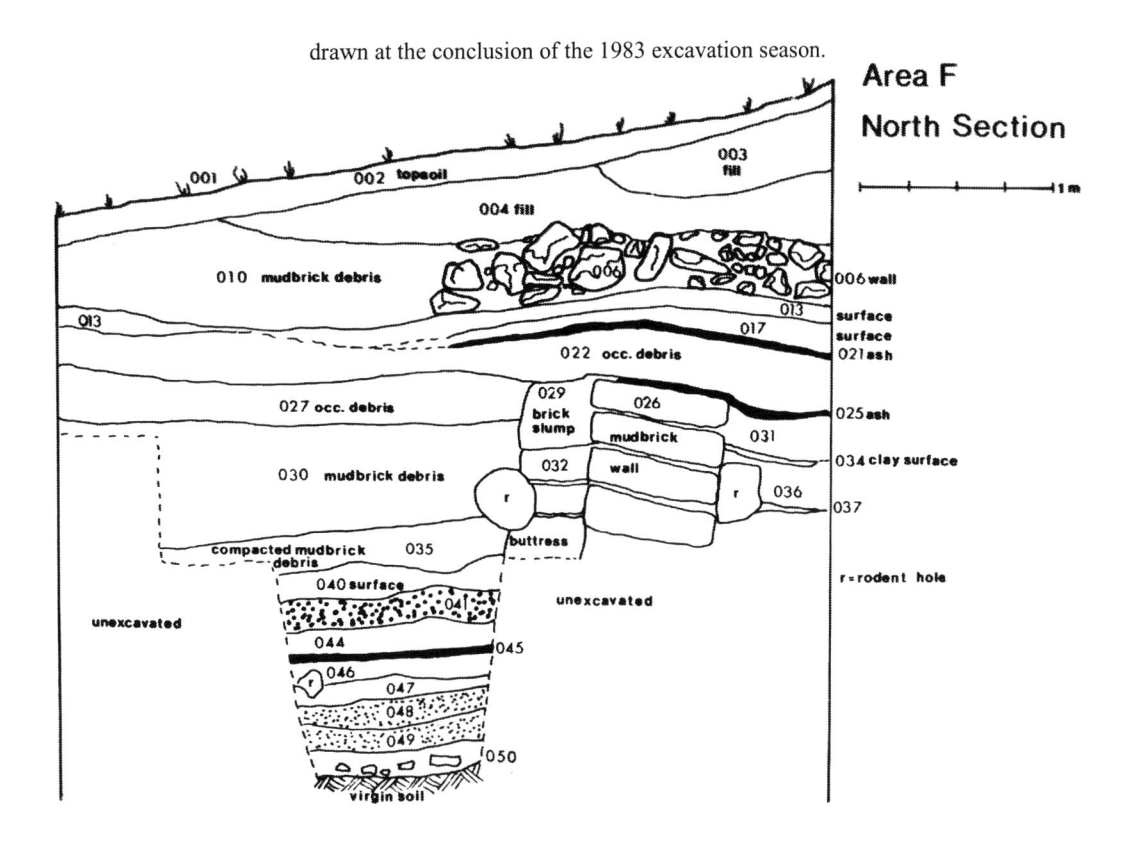

Figure 3.6 Stratigraphic cross-section across the north balk face of Area F at Tell el-Hayyat; drawn at the conclusion of the 1982 excavation season.

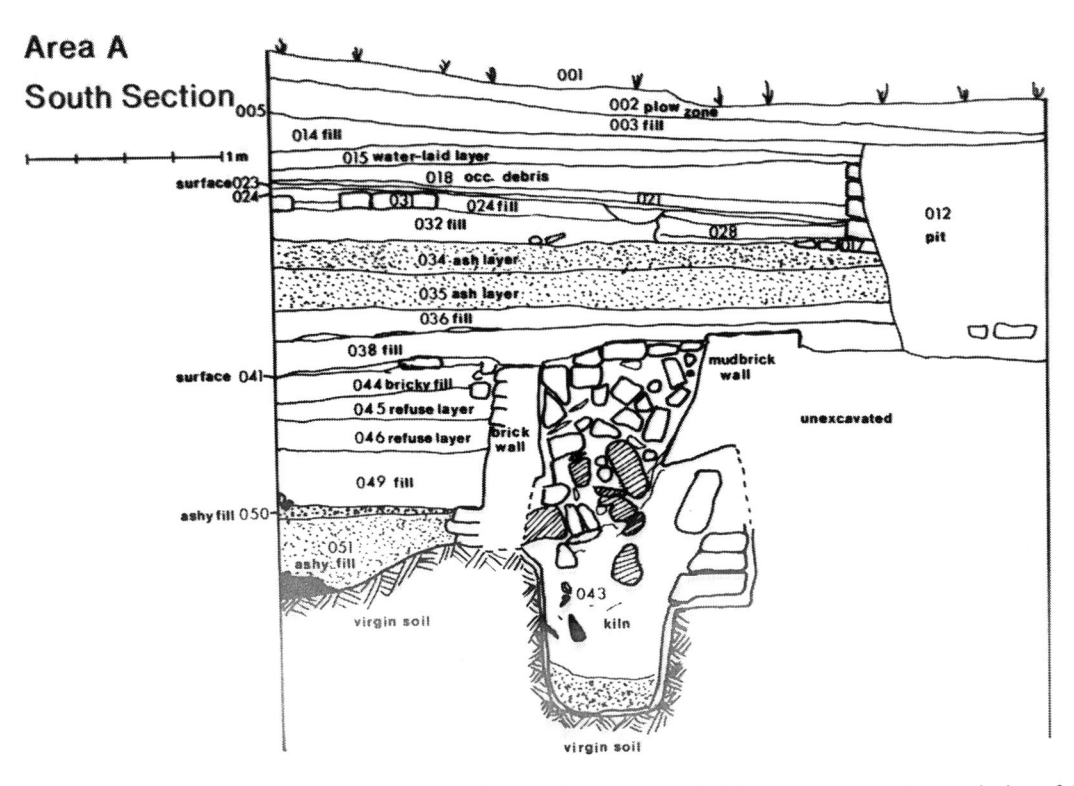

Figure 3.7 Stratigraphic cross-section across the south balk face of Area A at Tell el-Hayyat; drawn at the conclusion of the 1982 excavation season. The northern half of Area A was excavated in 1982, exposing the northern half of the Phase 4 kiln. Excavation of the southern half of Area A in 1983 revealed the remaining portion of Tell el-Hayyat's kiln.

Figure 3.8 Excavation of the Phase 4 temple at Tell el-Hayyat, 1985, facing northwest. Note clear Phase 4 mudbricks and standing stones in temple forecourt to the right. Single course stone foundation for Phase 3 temple shown directly on top of remains of Phase 4 temple north wall. Stone foundations and foundation trench for Phase 2 temple revealed in north and west balk faces. Two stratified Phase 2 temple plaster floors shown in north balk face (photo by Karen Scholz).

Aside from the lowermost remains of a single mudbrick wall running across Areas D and E on the western edge of the village, domestic architecture was not exposed in Phase 5. The ceramic, floral and faunal evidence excavated outside the temple enclosure walls resembles the household refuse of later phases, rather than the distinctly different temple assemblages from Tell el-Hayyat (see Chapters 6 and 7). Therefore, we suggest that Phase 5 domestic architecture probably lies in the unexcavated portions of the mound. The domestic deposits south of the temple enclosure consist of exterior surfaces and fill (e.g., Figure 3.5: Loci K063, K065-067, I078, I080, I083-087). Down Hayyat's western slope and outside the lone Phase 5 domestic wall, similar buildup of successive Phase 5 surfaces is apparent in Area F (e.g., Figure 3.6: Loci F044-050). At the southern periphery of the village, the lowermost deposits in Area A (Figure 3.7: Loci A050-051), into which the Phase 4 kiln was built, include ashy fill dating to Phase 5.

Phase 4 (Middle Bronze IIA).

The central architectural structure of Phase 4 is a slightly enlarged and thoroughly elaborated mudbrick temple built directly over the remains of the Phase 5 temple (Figure 3.8). The northwestern corner and much of the northern mudbrick wall of the Phase 4 temple appear clearly in Figures 3.2 and 3.3. As in Phase 5, the temple is surrounded by an enclosure wall, which clearly separates the temple interior (Sector TI) and courtyard (Sectors TB, TF and TS) from surrounding village households. Phase 4 domestic architecture includes portions of three structures lying south of the temple enclosure, which are separated by alleyways (Sectors EA, CA and WA). To the southeast of the temple compound lies an exterior area (Sector EC) housing a shallow mudbrick basin (Figure 3.9) feeding into a channel that appears to drain to the west into a deep ash-filled trash pit (Locus K064: Figure 3.10) cut into sterile soil in the East Building (Sector EB).

Figure 3.9 Shallow mudbrick basin with channel draining into a deep trash pit in the East Building, Phase 4 at Tell el-Hayyat, 1985, facing east (photo by Karen Scholz).

Figure 3.10 Deep trash pit excavated by Ron Gardiner (l) and Tom Davis (r) in the East Building, Phase 4 (Locus K064) at Tell el-Hayyat, 1983, facing southeast (photo by Jon Kline).

Figure 3.12 Phase 4 pottery kiln interior at Tell el-Hayyat, 1982, showing brick walls and mud plastered interior wall of firing chamber, plus trash fill post-dating the kiln's use, facing south (photo by Bob Erskine).

Figure 3.11 Mudbrick-encircled trash pit in the West Room, Phase 4 at Tell el-Hayyat, 1982, facing west. Note Phase 4 exterior paved alleyway in the foreground. Small square sounding reveals Phase 5 deposition (photo by Jon Kline).

Figure 3.13 Phase 4 pottery kiln at Tell el-Hayyat following excavation in 1983, facing southeast (photo by Jon Kline). Note brick work for firing chamber that was built back against tell sediments to the left.

The East Building and Central Enclosure (sectors EB and CE), bounded by mudbrick walls on the east, west and south, form a possibly roofed structure. The south wall for sectors EB and CE appears clearly in the Area K/I section drawing (Figure 3.5: Loci K057, I072 and I074). Farther west, portions of western, eastern and southern walls frame a second Phase 4 structure, the Central Room (Sector CR). This house contains the remains of two tabun ovens and three postholes running diagonally across the interior. Just south of this structure a small courtyard (Sector CC) features an exterior tabun. An alleyway comprised of Sectors EA and CA winds between the two houses noted above (i.e., Sectors CR and EB/CE). A house interior (Sector WR) with a stone-paved floor and mudbrick-encircled trash pit (Figure 3.11) lies at the western end of our excavations in Area F. The mudbrick wall on the east of Sector WR stands out in Figure 3.6 (Loci F026, F029 and F032). The walls framing Sectors WR and CR are separated by a narrow stone-paved alleyway (Sector WA).

The primary Phase 4 feature in Area A is an intact updraft pottery kiln. The northern half of Area A was excavated in 1982, exposing the northern half of the kiln (Figure 3.12). The kiln walls and associated interior refuse (Locus A043) and exterior deposits (Loci A041, A044-046, A049) are represented clearly in the Area A cross-section drawn in 1982 (Figure 3.7). Excavation of the southern half of Area A in 1983 revealed the remaining portion of Tell el-Hayyat's kiln (Figure 3.13). Following the 1983 season, the kiln was cut in cross-section to reveal its internal features (Figure 3.14). The Phase 4 villagers constructed the kiln by digging a fuel box into sterile soil, cutting into the south slope of the tell to create a back wall, and building the remaining circular walls of the firing chamber using mudbrick. This installation is a

Figure 3.14 Phase 4 pottery kiln at Tell el-Hayyat cut in cross-section following excavation in 1983, facing northwest (photo by Karen Scholz). Note plastered interior wall of firing chamber, access for stoking fuel from the left, three flues along edge of firing chamber in foreground.

Figure 3.16 Human skeletal remains uncovered amid trash in Phase 4 pottery kiln at Tell el-Hayyat, 1982 (photo by Bob Erskine).

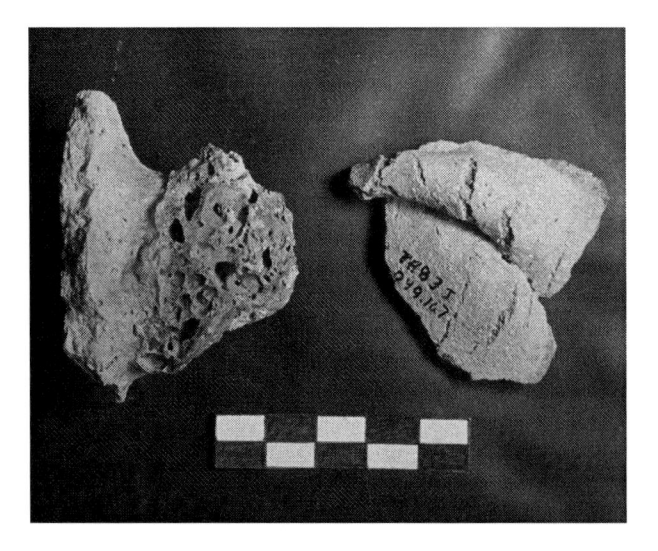

Figure 3.15 Examples of ceramic wasters from Area A kiln debris, Tell el-Hayyat. Storejar handle on left displays the effects of bloating due to trapped gases or liquids; storejar body sherd on right exemplifies slumping due to excessive firing.

simple intermittent updraft kiln in which pottery would have been loaded into the top of the firing chamber prior to firing. The firing chamber was then closed with debris, especially potsherds and wasters from previous firings (Figure 3.15). Fuel was loaded into the fuel box below the firing chamber and ignited, creating an updraft of intensely heated air. Following firing and then cooling, the covering debris would have been removed and the fired pottery unloaded from the opened firing chamber. The Tell el-Hayyat kiln held the remains of burned animal dung, suggesting the use of dung as a primary fuel source.

After the kiln went out of use it was filled with refuse, including the well preserved skeletal remains of one young adult male (Figures 3.16 and 3.17). Analysis of

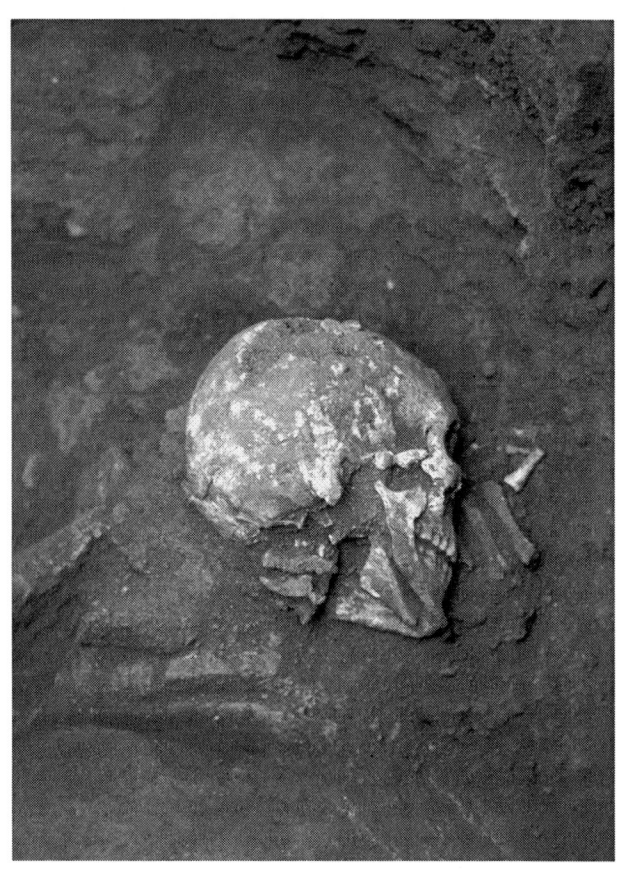

Figure 3.17 Skull, hand and wrist bones of a young adult male found buried in the Phase 4 pottery kiln at Tell el-Hayyat, 1982 (photo by Bob Erskine).

these remains was conducted in the Human Identification Laboratory, Department of Anthropology, University of Arizona. All of the skeletal material was cleaned and preserved in a polyvinyl acetate resin (GELVA) to facilitate restoration and to insure against subsequent damage. Gender and race determinations were based on osseous and dental morphology. No cranial measurements were attempted, due to the fragmented state of the skull.

Figure 3.18 Remains of burned, chaff-plastered Phase 3 house (Sector EB) at Tell el-Hayyat, 1983, facing south (photo by Jon Kline).

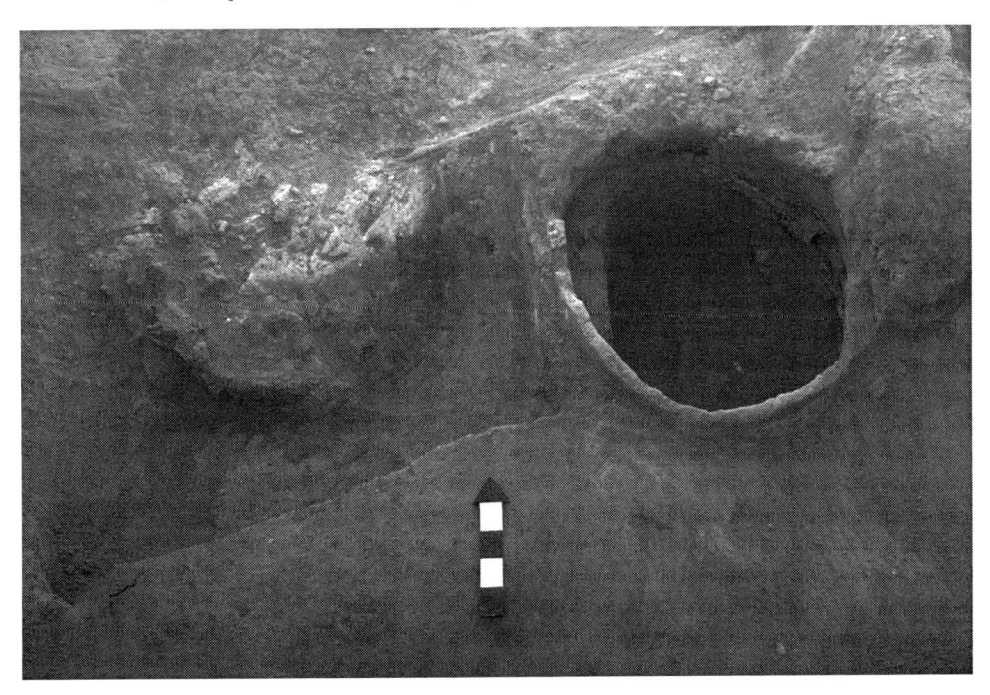

Figure 3.19 Remains of two tabuns excavated in Phase 3 alley (Sector CA) at Tell el-Hayyat, 1983, facing north (photo by Jon Kline).

These remains are from a 25-30 year old male of generally Caucasian affinity. The individual's gender was inferred from the pronounced supraorbital tori of the frontal bone and the nuchal crest of the occipital, with the latter bearing a definite inion hook. The age was estimated from the full eruption and slight wear of all four third molars. A full set of 32 teeth was recovered, though many experienced postmortem breakage. Only the first molars show extensive wear, and none of the teeth show any abnormalities, caries or abscesses. The racial identification stems from the lack of alveolar prognathism of the maxilla, the visibility of the oval window in the external auditory meatus of the left temporal bone, and the bifed root of the first maxillary premolars. These features are not characteristic of non-Caucasian populations.

The skeletal evidence includes a cranium, mandible, four vertebrae, and both left and right carpals, metacarpals and phalanges. Although ossification had begun endrocranially along the lambdoidal and coronal sutures, much of the skull fragmentation occurred along sutures that had not fully closed. Postcranial remains include the first, second, third, and part of the fourth cervical vertebrae. The second cervical vertebra shows three antemortem sharp implement cut marks on the spinous process, and two cuts on the superior surface of the left neural arch just posterior of the superior articular facet.

Two transverse marks are apparent on the anterior of the centrum of the third cervical vertebra. Three cut marks on the lateral surface of the right superior articular process of the fourth cervical vertebra run transversely, with the upper-most continuing on to the mammary process of the third cervical vertebra.

Unlike the cervical vertebrae, the wrist and hand bones show no evidence of cut marks. A fragment of the articular facet of the distal left radius is accompanied by a variety of carpal bones, including the left navicular, lunate, triquetral, greater multangular, capitate and hamate, and the right navicular, lesser multangular and hamate. The recovered left metacarpal bones include the first, second, diaphysis and proximal end of the third, diaphysis and distal end of the fourth, and diaphysis and proximal end of the fifth. The right metacarpals include the proximal and distal ends of the first, the diaphysis and distal and proximal ends of the second, and the complete third, fourth and fifth. Recovered phalanges include seven out of a full complement of 10 distal phalanges, seven (of eight) middle phalanges, and 10 (of 10) proximal phalanges.

Phase 3 (Middle Bronze IIA/B)

The Phase 3 temple is marked by single-course stone foundations that are laid directly on the wall remnants of the Phase 4 temple. The stone foundation and mudbrick coursing for the north and west temple walls are shown distinctly in Figures 3.2 and 3.3. Aside from the temple foundations, all Phase 3 architecture is constructed entirely of mudbrick. Excavation exposed the southern Phase 3 temple enclosure wall, while the face of the western enclosure wall was revealed during the trimming of the western balk of Area L (see the reconstructed western enclosure wall in Figure 3.1). The location of the foundations for the eastern temple enclosure wall is uncertain, however the wall was found collapsed intact where it had fallen into Area U. The estimated location and height (almost 4m) of the enclosure wall are extrapolated from these fallen remains (Figures 3.1 and 6.30).

To the south of the Phase 3 temple, a roofed structure (Sector EB) with stone-paved floor, four postholes and door socket adjoins an enclosed courtyard (Sector CE). The lower walls of the Sector EB house were lined with a chaff plaster that had burned during Phase 3 (Figure 3.18). The south wall of this house is seen in the Area K cross-section (Figure 3.5: Locus K041). Behind the eastern wall of this house is an exterior courtyard (Sector EC) with three postholes. A second, relatively small Phase 3 structure (Sector WB) lies to the west in Areas C and D. Once again, the temple enclosure is clearly set off from domestic architecture by alleyways that run roughly east-west through Sectors WA, CA and EA. The Sector CA alley features the remains of two tabun ovens (Figure 3.19). The Phase 3 sediments in Sector WA are exemplified by a succession of exterior surfaces shown in the Area F cross-section (Figure 3.6: Loci F013, F017, F021, F022). Likewise, exterior sediment build-up marks the site periphery in Area A during phase 3 (Figure 3.7: Loci A034-038).

Phase 2 (Middle Bronze IIB/C)

The Phase 2 temple marks the culmination of the Tell el-Hayyat temple sequence (see Figure 3.1). Massive trenches provided support for multi-course stone foundations that raised the mudbrick superstructure and the interior floor of the temple above the level of its surrounding courtyard and Hayyat's houses. As the temple was expanded from Phase 3 to Phase 2, some of its foundation trenches were dug into the remnants of the Phase 3 temple's mudbrick walls and stone foundations (Figures 3.2 and 3.3). All other Phase 2 walls are made of mudbrick founded on a single course of stone, including three walls that link the temple to its enclosure wall and may have served as the base for a tower.

Outside the temple lie two multi-room compounds (see Figures 2.21 and 3.20). The East Building incorporates three rooms (Sectors EB1-3) that probably were roofed, although Sector EB2 is paved and may have served as a central atrium. The cross walls that bound Sector EB 1 may be seen clearly in the Area K-I section drawing as Loci K018 and K021 (Figure 3.5), along with their associated Phase 2 surfaces. An attached courtyard (Sector CE) is defined by modest, non-load-bearing mudbrick walls on its northern and western sides. Farther west a simple two-room building (Sectors WB1 and 2), which probably was roofed, has doors opening to the south. The north wall of this structure appears as stone foundation wall F006 in the Area F section drawing (Figure 3.6). Phase 2 remains in Area A include the vestiges of a mudbrick wall (Figure 3.7: Locus A017), which is cut by a possible Byzantine pit (Locus A012). A series of associated surfaces and debris layers (Loci A018-032) provide evidence of extramural activities on Hayyat's south slope.

Phase 1 (Middle Bronze IIC)

Phase 1 remains are limited to remnants of stone wall foundations and their associated surfaces in Areas C, G, H, I, J, K, L and S. These fragmentary deposits are distributed generally to the southwest of the center of the mound, where the Phase 5-2 temples once stood. Phase 1 remains characteristically provide minimal remnants of stone wall foundations (e.g., Figure 3.5: Locus K004) and patches of earthen surfaces (e.g., Figure 3.5: Locus I014). These remains are too fragmentary to suggest coherent architectural plans, but they do clearly attest to a final

Figure 3.20 Stone foundations and mudbrick walls for Phase 2 domestic architecture at Tell el-Hayyat, 1983, facing west. Bonnie Wistoff in Phase 2 East Building (foreground left), Bonnie Magness-Gardiner at western end of temple enclosure wall (middle right), and Bob Erskine, Mary Metzger and workers excavating West Building 1 and West Building 2 (background) (photo by Jon Kline).

TELL EL-HAYYAT VILLAGE ARCHITECTURE IN OVERVIEW

The stratified architectural remains exposed at Tell el-Hayyat portray the development of this agricultural village from the end of Early Bronze IV through the Middle Bronze Age. Phases 5-2, in particular, provide a detailed sample of community growth based on several readily discernible characteristics. The architectural history of Tell el-Hayyat clearly is focused on the repeated building and rebuilding of its central temple. This structure and its associated courtyard grow in size, elaboration and investment in construction material through time. Outside the temple enclosures, domestic architecture follows a parallel path of remodeling through the Middle Bronze Age, in which these households are rebuilt and improved (e.g., with the addition of stone foundations in Phase 2) in tandem with each new temple. Thus, the phasing of the Hayyat temples and houses proceeds synchronously. While each Tell el-Hayyat temple is built directly on the remains of its predecessor, the houses tend to be relocated in approximately, but not exactly, the same locations through time. In general, the excavated sample of Tell el-Hayyat reveals two to three domestic compounds in Phases 4-2. In each of these phases, an alleyway rich with domestic refuse runs east-west just outside the temple enclosure wall, before turning south between two domestic compounds. On the southern flank of Tell el-Hayyat, Areas A and B provide valuable evidence of extramural activities and trash deposition to balance the evidence from temple and household settings farther up the mound. In concert, the multi-faceted evidence drawn from these varying locales illustrates the development of Tell el-Hayyat through a variety of analyses that are summarized in the following chapters.

phase of occupation at Tell el-Hayyat, apparently not associated with a temple. Thus, the stratigraphic record of Bronze Age habitation at Tell el-Hayyat ends with very limited material evidence in a manner similar to the ephemeral remains of its earliest occupation in Phase 6.

Phase 0 (Post-Bronze Age)

Phase 0 designates all stratified sediments post-dating the Bronze Age and all unstratified material on the modern surface of the tell. This evidence includes post-Bronze Age ceramics, very large, possibly Byzantine trash pits dug from near modern surface level (e.g., Locus A012; Figure 3.7; also see pits in Figure 3.3) and post-Byzantine burials (e.g., Locus I009; Figure 3.5).

CHAPTER 4: CERAMIC AND RADIOCARBON CHRONOLOGY FOR TELL EL-HAYYAT

Steven E. Falconer and Ilya Berelov

INTRODUCTION

The record of stratified architecture, its repeated construction, leveling and reconstruction provides the structure for inferring the sequence of occupations at Tell el-Hayyat. As related in Chapter 3, the Tell el-Hayyat excavations revealed six stratified phases of architectural remains beginning in Early Bronze IV and continuing through the Middle Bronze Age. The inference of a detailed chronology for these phases of architecture depends primarily on analysis of the stratified ceramic assemblages from Hayyat in comparison to other Early Bronze IV and Middle Bronze Age settlements in the southern Levant (see Figures 1.9-1.11). This comparative ceramic chronology is augmented by a series of radiocarbon dates from Phases 5 and 4 pertaining to the earlier portions of Tell el-Hayyat's history of occupation. The results of these analyses provide a chronology extending from the late third millennium to the mid-second millennium B.C. (see Table 4.1).

Table 4.1 Chronological table for phases of occupation at Tell el-Hayyat. Absolute dates derived from comparative pottery typologies and radiocarbon determinations (see Table 4.2)

Time Range	Phase	Period
ca. 1550 B.C.		
ca. 1600 B.C.	Phase 1	Middle Bronze IIC
ca. 1700 B.C.	Phase 2	Middle Bronze IIB/C
ca. 1800 B.C.	Phase 3	Middle Bronze IIA/B
ca. 1900 B.C.	Phase 4	Middle Bronze IIA
ca. 2000 B.C.	Phase 5	early Middle Bronze IIA
ca. 2100 B.C.	Phase 6	late Early Bronze IV

CERAMIC HISTORY AT TELL EL-HAYYAT

The ceramic typology for Tell el-Hayyat identifies pottery vessel form based on Cole's (1984) typology of Middle Bronze Age ceramics from Shechem (1984). Cole works through a large sample of well-stratified, systematically retrieved pottery from Shechem, dating mostly to Middle Bronze IIB. We adapt this system to accommodate the broader range of ceramic variability from Middle Bronze IIA to IIC at Tell el-Hayyat (Phases 5-1). More substantial modification allows us to apply this system to the Early Bronze IV pottery of Phase 6 at Hayyat. Our application of Cole's typology designates each sherd first according to general morphological and functional classes: cooking pots (abbreviated "C"), jars ("J"), and bowls ("B"). Within each of these vessel types, sherds are classified according to rim, base and handle treatment (Cole 1984:8-10). This system is particularly valuable for functional analysis of sherd material because, with few exceptions, sherds may be assigned unambiguously to a vessel form that indicates general function (see Cole 1984: 33; table 5). Because rim morphology is particularly indicative of vessel form, our analyses often estimate relative amounts of pottery vessel types based on frequencies of various rim forms. We adjust our sherd counts for multiple rim sherds that join or obviously were parts of the same vessel. We do not assume that our rim counts represent the number of vessels from a particular spatial or temporal unit; instead we use these counts to estimate the relative frequency of different vessel classes in these units.

Phase 6 Pottery

Phase 6 sediments at Tell el-Hayyat include exclusively Early Bronze IV pottery forms, including bowls, cooking pots and storage vessels. The Phase 6 sherds come from handbuilt vessels, with a few examples, such as small "trickle-pained" cups (Figure 4.1: a-b), finished on a slow wheel. The relatively small Phase 6 assemblage reflects a limited typological repertoire that, none the less, offers a number of geographic and temporal insights. One bowl form (Cole's form *Bp*) accounts for the entire range of Phase 6 serving vessels (Figure 4.1: a-b). The exterior trickle paint design and incurved pointed and rilled rim at Tell el-Hayyat find parallels within other assemblages of Dever's Family "J" and "N" (Dever 1971, 1980; Helms 1986), although the forms also are found more widely among the "TR" and "CH" families from Tell Iktanu (Prag 1988) to Jebel Qa'aqir (Gitin 1975).

Phase 6 holemouth jars (Figure 4.1: i-k) are characterized by squared rims with examples of piecrust decoration sitting flush on the rim. These forms occur over a very broad geographic range from Be'er Resisim (Cohen and Dever 1981), to Jebel Qa'aqir (Gitin 1975), Tell Iktanu (Prag 1988) and Tell Um Hammad (Helms 1986). Large

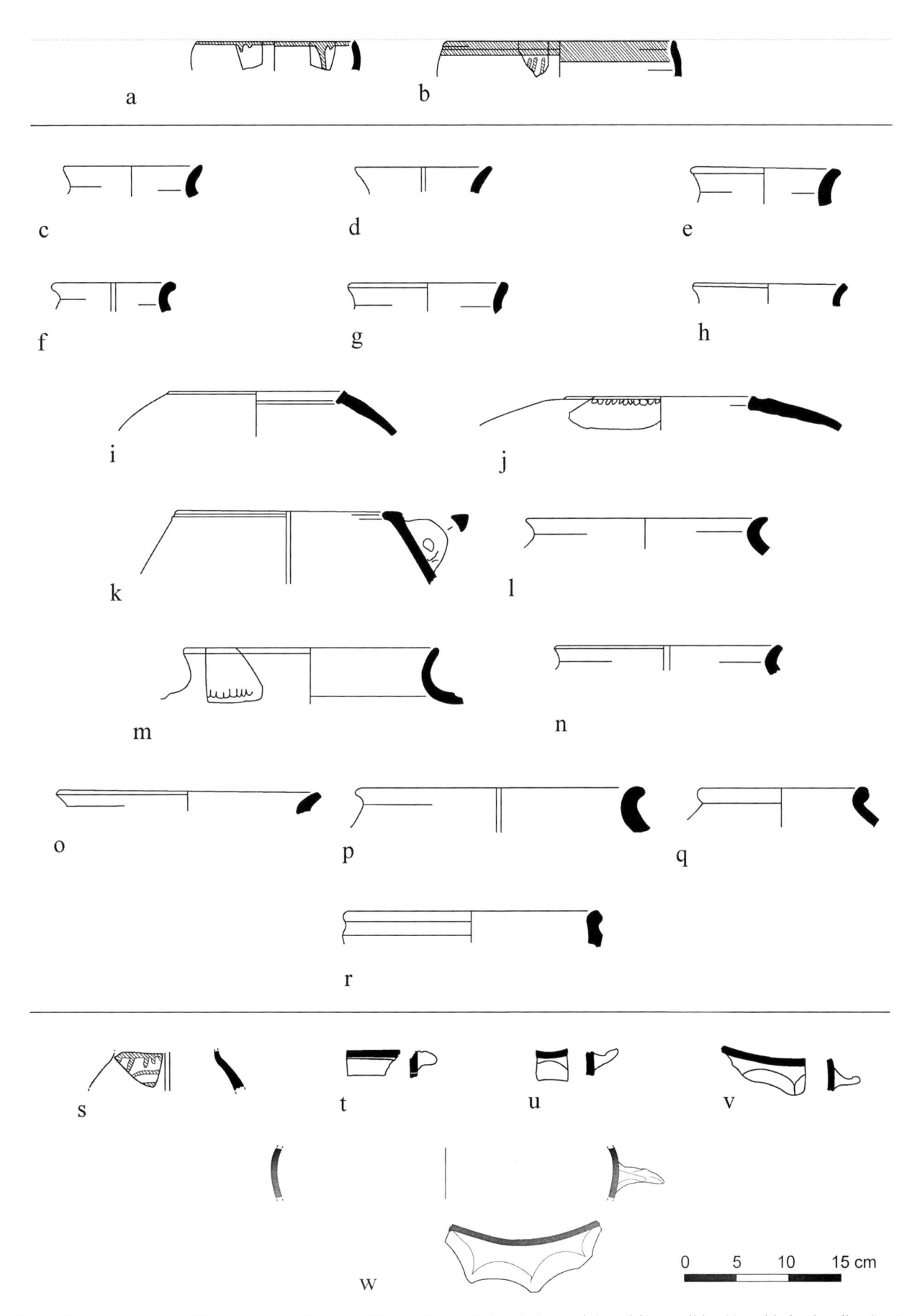

Figure 4.1 Early Bronze IV trickle painted cups (a, b), storejars (c-h, l-r), holemouth jars (i-k), small jar (s) and ledge handles (t-w) from Phase 6 at Tell el-Hayyat. Scale 1:5.

and small necked storejars (Figure 4.1: c-h, l-p) with flaring tapered rims occur in both undecorated and decorated examples, the latter with incision or applique decoration (Figure 4.1: m). Hayyat's Early Bronze IV jars utilize loop handles and folded envelope ledge handles (Figure 4.1: k, t-w). As with other vessel types, these storejar forms are widespread, occurring in all of Dever's "Families," as exemplified at Jericho (Kenyon 1965), Tell Iktanu (Prag 1988), Khirbet Iskander (Richard and Boraas 1984), Tell Um Hammad (Helms 1986), Jebel Qa'aqir (Gitin 1975) and Bab edh-Dhra' (Rast and Schaub 2003: fig. 274).

Most of the Tell el-Hayyat Early Bronze IV ceramic wares are undecorated, a manifestation of later (i.e., EB IVB/C) assemblages. The "trickle-painted" decoration on a few cups and jars is typical of the Jezreel Valley and Transjordanian Plateau ("Family NC," Dever 1971: 201; 1980: 39, 40, 46, 47; also Amiran 1970: pl. 24: 17-19; Harding and Isserlin 1953), and has been dated roughly to the middle of Early Bronze IV (i.e., EB IVB; Dever 1980).

The limited use of rope-molding and thumb-impressed or incised bands at Tell el-Hayyat (Figure 4.1: i, j, m) lends further credence to the regional definition of these decorative schemes. This array of designs is characteristic of Early Bronze IV pottery in the Jordan Valley (Dever's "Family J," 1971: 202; 1974: 35, n. 13; 1980: 41-44, 47-48). A combination of characteristics from families NC and J is precisely what we should expect from Tell el-Hayyat, which lies at the intersection of their regional distributions. Dever (1971: 202) dates families NC and J to the 21st century B.C. However, elements of continuity between the ceramics of phases 6 and 5 suggest that the Early Bronze IV forms at Hayyat evolved directly into those of Middle Bronze IIA without undergoing the typological developments Dever proposes for his later southern "Family S" of Palestine (1971: 203).

A chronological definition of the Phase 6 pottery also should consider what elements are lacking from the Tell el-Hayyat Early Bronze IV assemblage. The absence of red slip and burnish, heavy platter bowls with incurved rims, and large flaring ledge handles is noteworthy because these attributes are associated with early Early Bronze IV (i.e. EB IVA) assemblages in and around the Jordan Valley (Dever 1973; Prag 1988). At Tell Iktanu and Bab edh-Dhra' these features have been dated to the early stages of Early Bronze IV, based on both typological and radiometric evidence (see Prag 1974; Rast and Schaub 2003). On the other hand, the flaring long necked jars so common among the chronologically later southern Early Bronze IV groups (see Cohen 1999) also are lacking. Typologically, the Phase 6 assemblage meshes with families NC and J, which were assigned to Early Bronze IVB more than 25 years ago (Dever 1971; 1973). Given the stratigraphic continuity between phases 6 and 5 at Tell el-Hayyat, as well as the transitional nature of the Phase 5 pottery (see below), we interpret the Phase 6 assemblage as a late manifestation of Early Bronze IV (i.e., EB IVB/C).

Phase 5 Pottery

The Phase 5 pottery represents a very early Middle Bronze IIA assemblage that features unique vessel forms representing transitions between late Early Bronze IV and early Middle Bronze IIA, in the form of cooking vessels, bowls and, to a lesser extent, jars. Phase 5 bowls include four major morphological types: 1) open forms with slightly beveled rims (Figure 4.2: a); 2) deep bowls with slightly incurved, pointed rims (Figure 4.2: b-d); 3) closed, globular vessels with externally thickened rims and exterior rilling (Figure 4.2: e-g); and 4) open carinated bowls (Figure 4.2: h-j). Flat and disc bases predominate among bowls in all our phases of Middle Bronze IIA (Figures 4.4: n-o; Figure 4.6: q-v), including the transitional forms of Phase 5.

Early Bronze IV bowl forms that relate directly to the repertoire of examples seen in Phase 6 include gently incurved deep bowls or cups with trickle-painted decoration (Figure 4.2: b). Middle Bronze Age variations of this form include rims with slight external rilling (Figure 4.2: c) as well as plain, undecorated examples with tapered rims (Figure 4.2: d). The predecessors of these bowls extend far back into the Early Bronze Age, but they become less common by Early Bronze IVC (Dever 1973). They occur with paint at Tell Iktanu (Prag 1988) and Tell Um Hammad (Helms 1986). By comparison, early Middle Bronze IIA examples tend more towards hemispherical shapes (see Beck 2000).

Transitional Early Bronze IV-Middle Bronze II bowls occur in three forms: 1) incurved globular vessels (Figure 4.2: e-g); 2) thick-bodied, slightly carinated types (Figure 4.2: i-j); and 3) platter bowls (Figure 4.2: a). The first of these forms has a closed stance with an externally thickened rim. The rim is finished on a wheel, but the addition of external ribbing, and in one case exterior rim rilling, lends these bowls an Early Bronze IV quality. Cups of this sort are found in Early Bronze IV contexts at Tell Iktanu (Prag 1988) and Jebel Qa'aqir (Gitin 1975), albeit with less pronounced thickening of the rim. The Tell el-Hayyat examples are generally unpainted. One highly unusual example resembling a globular krater with a series of exterior ridges or rills (Figure 4.2: g), incorporates an idiosyncratic combination of decorative schemes on interior and exterior surfaces. This decoration combines painted diagonal lines with wavy horizontal lines, which are themselves overlaid with circles. The wavy line motif is bordered by rows of evenly spaced dark notches. Parallels for this motif are extremely elusive, although similar design elements are seen in the ceramics of Hama J (Thuesen 1988).

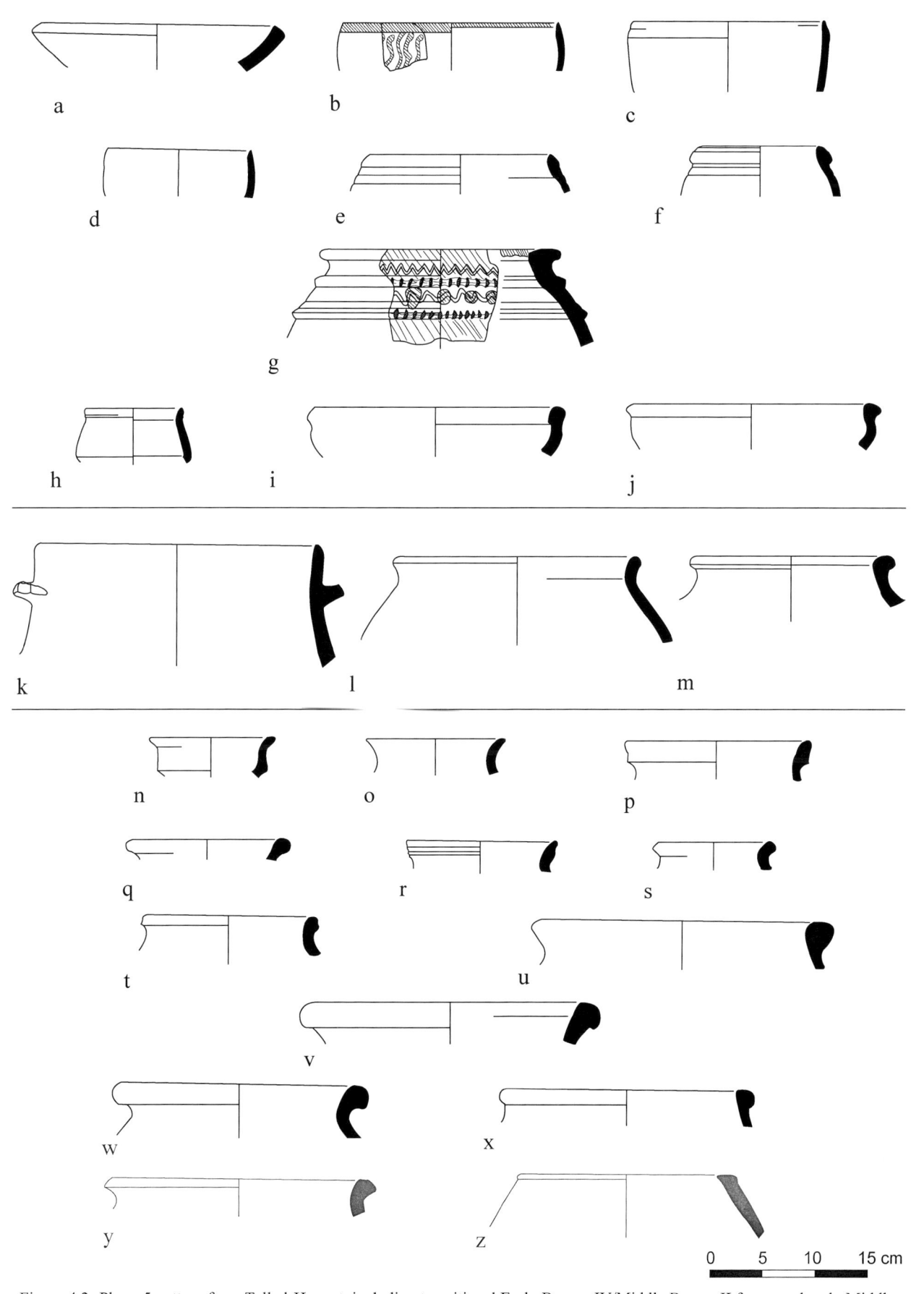

CERAMIC AND RADIOCARBON CHRONOLOGY FOR TELL EL-HAYYAT

Figure 4.2 Phase 5 pottery from Tell el-Hayyat, including transitional Early Bronze IV/Middle Bronze II forms and early Middle Bronze IIA vessels: bowls (a-d, h-j), closed globular vessels (e-g), cooking pots (k-m), storejars (n-y) and holemouth jar (z). Scale 1:5.

Figure 4.3 Early Middle Bronze IIA hand-built carinated bowls found in conjunction with the Phase 5 temple at Tell el-Hayyat. Note the associated fragmentary incense burner found on a surface in the Phase 5 temple interior.

The second transitional bowl type in Phase 5, with heavy carinated body and thick rounded rim, resembles the Early Bronze IV carinated bowls of Dever's "Southern Family" (1971: 203; 1980: 39-43, 48-49), rather than the more pronounced carination of the later Middle Bronze Age. However, one small example (Figure 4.2: h) characterized by a globular shape, gentle carination and out-turned rim is more typical of Middle Bronze IIA vessels (see Beck 2000). Phase 5 transitional forms also include thick-bodied, everted rim forms that are precursors of Middle Bronze II carinated bowls, whose hand-built construction is reminiscent of Early Bronze IV ceramic technology (Figure 4.3). Transitional platter bowls are characterized by an open stance and beveled rim (Figure 4.2: a). This type occurs in both Early Bronze IV contexts, such as Tell Um Hammad (Helms 1986: 32), and Middle Bronze IIA settings like Tel Aphek (Beck 2000: 119)

Two main types of cooking vessels occur in Phase 5: hand-built straight-sided pots (Figure 4.2: k), and necked, wheel-finished globular vessels (Figure 4.2: l-m). The illustrated example of the first form (Figure 4.2: k) is bell-shaped, with two thumb-impressed ledge handles. Its body and rim suggest the classic Middle Bronze II straight-sided cooking pot, but without "steam-holes" and thumb-impressed rope molding (see examples discussed below). This example has clear parallels in Early Bronze IV levels at 'Aro'er (Olavarri 1969: fig. 5:12) and at Tel Halif (Alon 1973), and appears to represent an intermediary form between Early Bronze IV globular shapes and the classic Middle Bronze II flat-bottomed, straight-sided cooking pot (Cole's *Cf* type; 1984: 151).

The second type of cooking pot (Figure 4.2: l-m) conforms to Cole's upright rim (*Cu*) form (Cole 1984: 151) and occurs more commonly throughout Middle Bronze II at Tel Aphek (Beck 2000), Megiddo (Shipton 1938), Tel Dan (Ilan 1996) and Jericho (Kenyon and Holland 1982; 1983). A very early Middle Bronze IIA date for Phase 5 is signaled by the transitional upright (*Cu*) cooking pots and the absence of the classic early Middle Bronze Age flat-bottomed, straight-sided form.

Jar rims (Figure 4.2: n-z) in Phase 5 likewise include clear Early Bronze IV examples, transitional types and definite Middle Bronze Age types. The first category includes an example of the classic Early Bronze IV everted, tapered rim (Figure 4.2: o), as well as a holemouth type with squared rim and slight external ridge (Figure 4.2: z). These vessels find parallels across all geographic Early Bronze IV families, including the purportedly very late Family "S". The everted jar rim occurs extensively in the Negev (Cohen 1999), Jebel Qa'aqir (Gitin 1975), and Bab edh-Dhra' (Rast and Schaub 2003). The holemouth form is similarly widespread, occurring at Jebel Qa'aqir (Gitin 1975), Tell Iktanu (Prag 1988) and Tell Um Hammad (Helms 1986).

Transitional Early Bronze IV-Middle Bronze II storejars have wide mouths, little or no neck, and thickened rounded rims (Figure 4.2: s-t). This type of storejar is not found commonly in Middle Bronze IIA sites, although there is a similar rim from the Pre-Palace phase at Aphek (Beck 1975: fig. 3:6). At Tell el-Hayyat the thickened rim is most common in Phase 5, but it occurs in Phases 4 and 3 as well. The transitional nature of the Phase 5 jar rims, therefore, is characterized by their thickness and roundness (e.g., Figure 4.2: u-y), in direct contrast to the elongated, flared, and "profiled" rims of Phases 4 and 3 (see below) and other Middle Bronze IIA assemblages from Aphek (Beck 2000) and Megiddo (Shipton 1938). More classic Middle Bronze IIA jars are exemplified by everted rims with parallel striations or ridges (e.g., Figure 4.2: r). This form occurs in all phases of Middle Bronze IIA at Tell el-Hayyat. Parallel examples are reported from Nahariya (Ben-Dor 1950: 28), Tomb 7 at Aphek (Beck 1975: fig. 14:4) and the village of Kfar Rupin (Gophna 1979: fig. 3:11).

In general, Phase 5 pottery is especially noteworthy for its unique transitional Early Bronze IV-Middle Bronze IIA vessel forms. These intermediate types fit well chronologically between the distinctly Early Bronze IV repertoire of Phase 6 and the classic Middle Bronze IIA assemblage of Phase 4. Aphek (Beck 2000) or Megiddo (Shipton 1938) might be expected to provide transitional parallels, but their Middle Bronze IIA assemblages show little or no typological connection with preceding strata.

Phase 4 Pottery

Ceramics from Phase 4 are more consistent with the assemblages of kraters, bowls, juglets, jars, storejars, and straight-sided cooking pots published from other excavated sites. For example, open shallow bowls (Cole's *Bp*) with slightly beveled in-turned rims, like those from Hayyat (Figure 4.4: a-c), are common elsewhere. Open bowls with a painted band of red paint on the rim (Figure 4.4: c) are illustrated in the Megiddo tomb groups (Guy 1938) and the collective grave at Munhatta (Ferembach et al.1975: fig. 2:4-6). Undecorated open shallow forms with horizontal flattened and molded rims (Figure 4.4: a-b) provide the most common bowl type at Aphek (Beck 2000: 112). This form occurs widely during Middle Bronze II (Cole 1984), as exemplified at Lachish (Singer-Avitz 2004: 908, fig. 16.4: 7-9) and Jericho (Kenyon and Holland 1982: 297, fig. 106: 24). Once again, externally rilled rims are common at Tell el-Hayyat.

Phase 4 kraters from Tell el-Hayyat (Figure 4.4: i-j) are slightly closed, deep and globular, with horizontally thickened rims. The two examples illustrated from Phase 4 have slightly rilled rims that are square in profile. Plain, rounded, externally molded rims also occur, and these more closely resemble the krater forms from the Pre-Palace phases at Aphek (Beck 1975: 48, fig. 2:7-10; 2000: 183, fig. 10.1: 16-17). These types also are found in the Middle Bronze Age temple at Nahariya (Ben-Dor 1950: fig. 23) and at Jericho (Kenyon and Holland 1982: 310, fig. 113:1-7), indicating their persistence well into Middle Bronze IIB. However, the pronounced rilling on kraters is peculiar to Tell el-Hayyat.

The most common bowls from Tell el-Hayyat Phase 4 (Cole's form *Bd*) differ from the kraters only in the their thinner in-turned rims (Figure 4.4: d-h), although the upper surface of bowl rims also may be rilled or ribbed, as seen in some kraters. Deep bowls with in-turned rims also are reported from Jericho (Kenyon and Holland 1982: 311, fig. 114: 1-10), the Pre-Palace phases at Aphek (Beck 1975: fig. 4:10-11) and the Nahariya temple (Ben-Dor 1950). A small red-slipped bowl with knob decoration (Figure 4.4: k) has parallels in the Megiddo tombs (Amiran 1970: pl. 25:7) and in Stratum II of Ory's excavations at Ras el-'Ain (Ory 1936/37: no. 26 A). An open bowl with external carination and bulbous rim (Figure 4.4: l) seems to be an intermediate form between the heavy carinated open bowls of Phase 5 and the shallow open bowls with external flanges in Phase 3 (see below). One common bowl form at Tell el-Hayyat adheres to the characteristic profile of Middle Bronze IIA carinated bowls (Amiran 1970: pl. 27:1-4). Variations on this bowl form may be undecorated (Figure 4.4: m), painted with horizontal red stripes (Figure 4.4: p), red-slipped but unburnished (Figure 4.4: o) or red-slipped and burnished (Figure 4.4: n). Although painted stripes appear on bowls at Tell el-Hayyat, this motif is more common elsewhere on small juglets (Ory 1936/37: no. 80) and medium-sized jars (Amiran 1970: pl. 31:3). The painted designs and subtle carinations of these bowls at Hayyat are hallmarks of the Middle Bronze IIA assemblage from Aphek (Beck 2000), and are notably lacking at later assemblages as seen at Jericho (Kenyon and Holland 1982). Flat bowl bases (Figure 4.4: n-o) also clearly place the Phase 4 pottery in Middle Bronze IIA.

Phase 4 cooking pots are typified by their coarse tempered ware and flat-bottomed, straight-sided form with applied thumb-impressed decoration (Figure 4.4: q). This standard Middle Bronze IIA hand-built vessel (e.g., Amiran 1970: pl. 30:1) occurs for the first time at Tell el-Hayyat in Phase 4. At most other sites such as Aphek, this cooking vessel (Cole's form *Cf*) ushers in the beginning of the Middle Bronze IIA (Albright 1932; Beck 2000; Cole 1984), whereas at Hayyat this type follows the earlier Middle Bronze Age cooking pots of Phase 5. Punctate or perforated "steam-holes," seen on many early Middle Bronze IIA examples elsewhere, are rare on the Phase 4 cooking pots of Tell el-Hayyat. Although earlier studies (Albright 1932; Cole 1984) place the purported "steam-holes" early in the Middle Bronze II sequence, subsequent analyses show this feature is a poor chronological marker (e.g., Berelov 2006; Maeir 2000). Examples both with and without steam holes are found from widespread Middle Bronze II sites like Beth She'an (Maeir 1997a: pl. 14: 1-6), Aphek (Beck 2000) and Lachish (Singer-Avitz 2004).

Dipper juglet rims (Figure 4.5: b) and red-slipped double-handled juglets (Figure 4.5: a) find their closest parallels in the Middle Bronze IIA collective grave at Munhatta (Ferembach et al. 1975: fig. 8: 6-9, fig. 5:1-4). However, since they persist through the entire Middle Bronze Age,

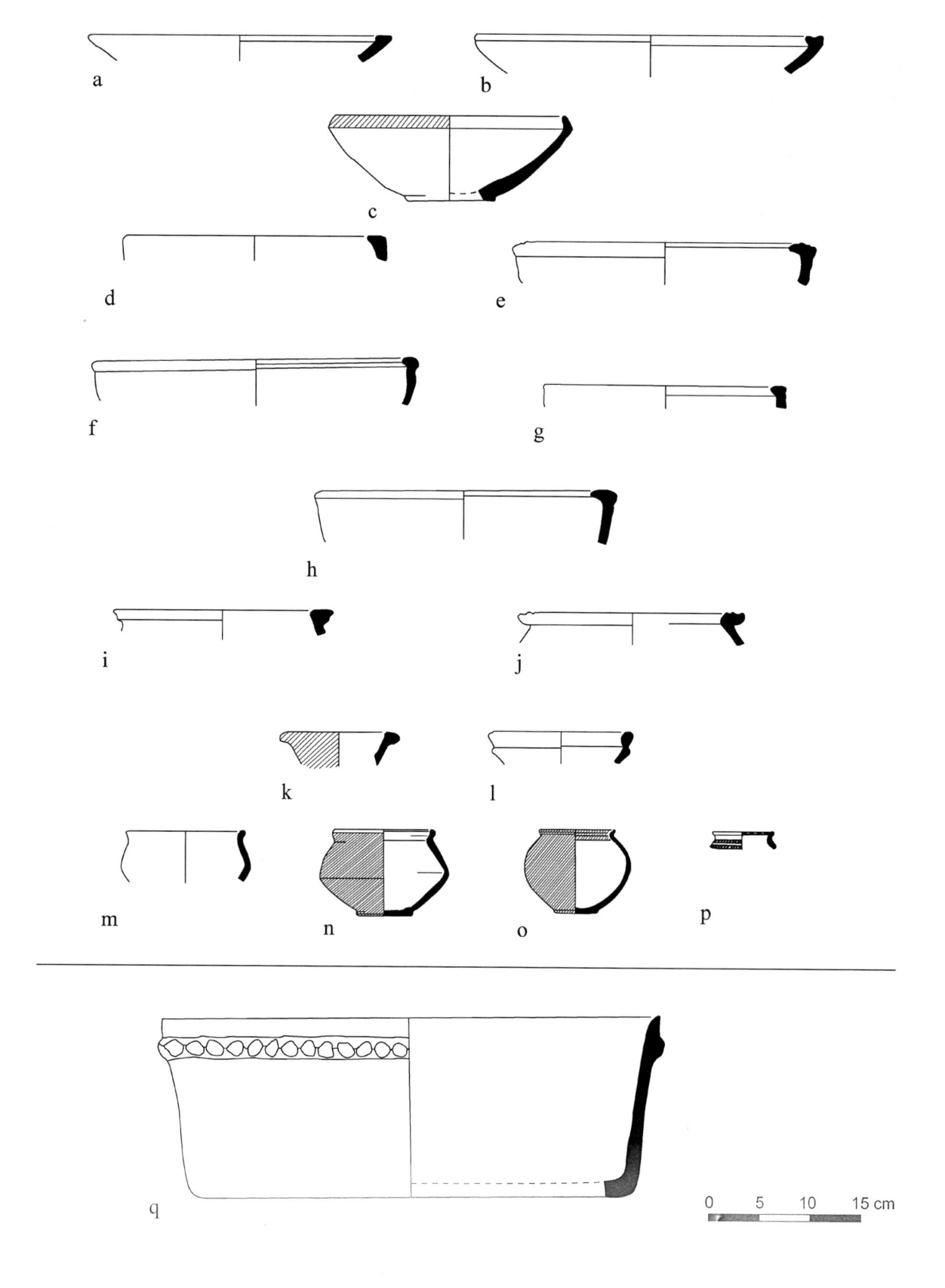

Figure 4.4 Middle Bronze IIA bowls (a-h, k-p), kraters (i-j) and flat-bottomed cooking pot (q) from Phase 4 at Tell el-Hayyat. Scale 1:5.

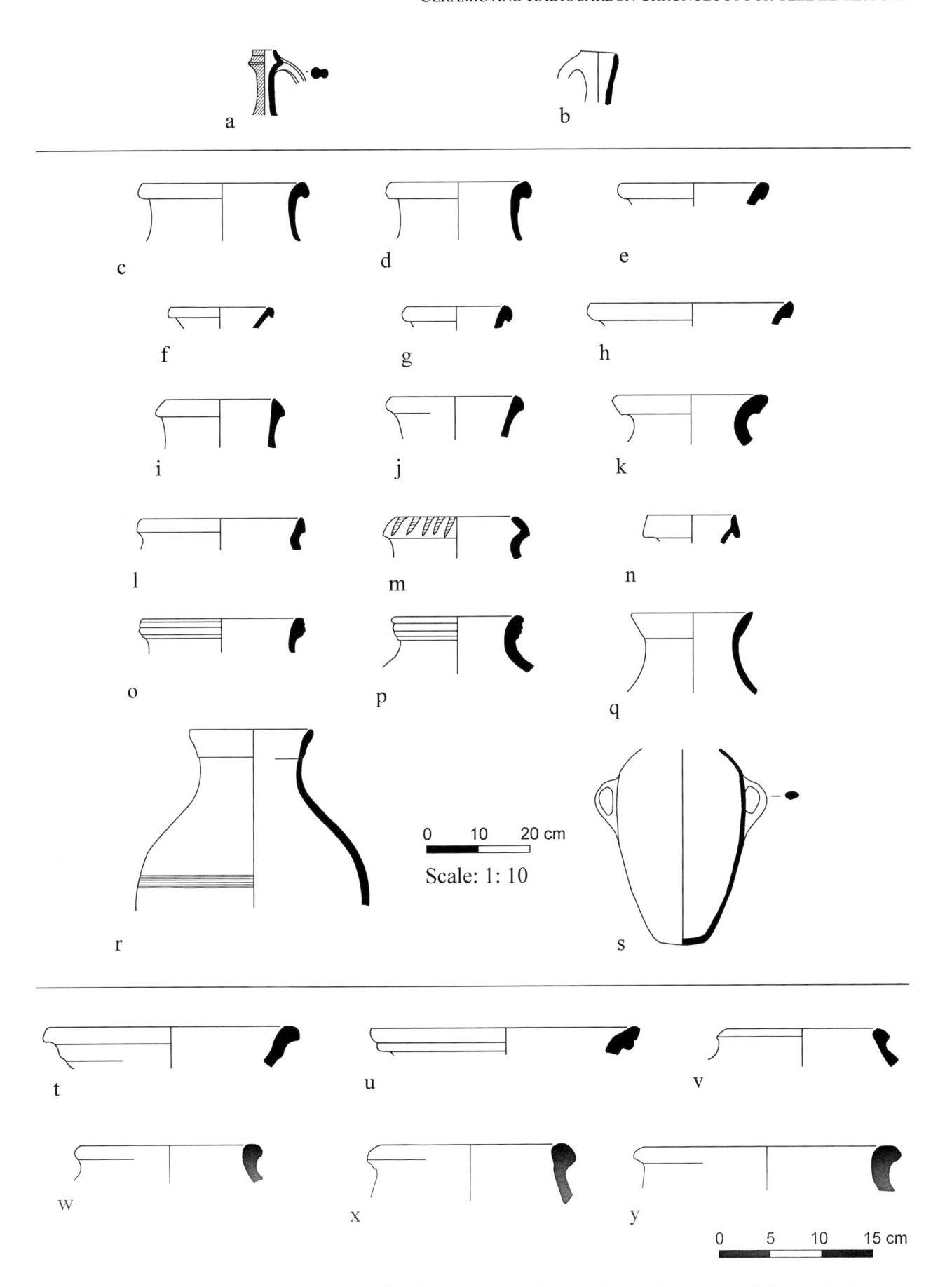

CERAMIC AND RADIOCARBON CHRONOLOGY FOR TELL EL-HAYYAT

Figure 4.5 Middle Bronze IIA juglets (a, b), storejars (c-s) and widemouth jars (t-y) from Phase 4 at Tell el-Hayyat. Scale 1:5, except as noted (s).

they are not precise chronological markers (Cole 1984; Ilan 1996).

Jars in Phase 4 commonly have rims that are simple, flared and roughly triangular in cross section (Figure 4.5: f-j) or elongated and folded (Figure 4.5: q). The flared rims appear in the Pre-Palace phases at Ras el-'Ain (Beck 1975: 53) and Stratum XII at Tell Dan (Ilan 1996), while the elongated form is found in both Pre-Palace (Beck 1975: 52) and Palace (Beck 1975: 58) phases at Ras el-'Ain. At Tell el-Hayyat elongated rims often are found on storejars with parallel incised lines on their upper shoulder (Figure 4.5: r) adhering to the most common form of decoration on storejars in Middle Bronze IIA (Amiran 1970; Beck 1975:58; Gerstenblith 1983).

A smaller jar rim painted with short red strokes (Figure 4.5: m) from Tell el-Hayyat parallels an example from Megiddo whose body is painted with concentric circles in black and red (Guy 1938). At Hayyat, the ridged (Figure 4.5: o-p) and widemouth storejar rims (Figure 4.5: t-y) of Phase 5 also appear in Phase 4. "Profiled" rims (i.e., thickened everted jar rims with square cross sections and external molding) occur for the first time in Phase 4. These profiled rims are most common in the Palace phase at Ras el-'Ain (Beck 1975: 58) and in the Middle Bronze IIA levels at Nahariya (Ben-Dor 1950: fig. 20:a-f). The general lack of rim elaboration on the Tell el-Hayyat jars, together with a very small number of handles, suggesting common handle-less jars, indicates a strictly Middle Bronze IIA date for this phase (see Cole 1984). This chronological interpretation is reinforced by the first appearance of the early Middle Bronze IIA flat-bottomed, straight-sided cooking pots noted above.

Phase 3 Pottery

The Phase 3 pottery shows continuities with many Middle Bronze IIA vessel forms seen in Phase 4. Some of these forms show developments indicative of Middle Bronze IIB, especially in the early portion of this sub-period. Among the stratified assemblages from Tell el-Hayyat, Phase 3 shows the greatest variety and elaboration of rim forms on all types of vessels. The serving vessels from Phase 3 have four basic forms: 1) shallow open bowls with rounded rims, often with a narrow flange below the rim (Figure 4.6: a); 2) open bowls, both shallow and deep, with externally beveled rims (Figure 4.6: d-f; Figure 4.6: f has a spout set into its rim); 3) deep bowls/kraters with wide flattened rims (Figure 4.6: g-l; rims often rilled on top); and 4) carinated and globular bowls with more pronounced necks than seen in Phase 4 (Figure 4.6: m-q). All of these bowl forms have low disc or ring bases (Figure 4.6: r-v) that follow the flat bases of Phase 4 and indicate the retention of some Middle Bronze Age IIA ceramic traits (see Cole 1984) into Phase 3.

Shallow flanged bowls occur also at Ras el'Ain (Ory 1936/37: Grave 2, no. 16), Megiddo (Guy 1938: pl. 28:15-19) and the collective grave at Munhatta (Ferembach et al. 1975: fig. 2:9). However, the bowls from Tell el-Hayyat never are slipped and burnished, as they are at Ras el'Ain. Occasionally they are decorated with a band of red paint, as at Megiddo. These bowls occur infrequently among Middle Bronze IIB-C assemblages, such as those from Shechem (Cole 1984) and Jericho (Kenyon and Holland 1982).

Bowls with beveled rims from Tell el-Hayyat have parallels at Aphek (Beck 2000), Beth She'an (Maeir 1997a), and Megiddo (Amiran 1970: pl. 25: 8-9; Ilan 2000: fig. 9. 4: 11), but have their closest counterparts at Munhatta (Ferembach et al. 1975: fig. 2: 3-8). A particularly enigmatic open bowl from Phase 3 (Figure 4.6: m) displays an everted rim, interior rilling and relatively sharp carination. Generally similar forms may be seen at Jericho (Kenyon and Holland 1982: fig. 109: 34), and at Beth She'an in the form of an open krater (Maeir 1997a: pl. 7: 8).

Tell el-Hayyat's Phase 3 kraters (roughly Cole's form *Bd*) have wide in-turned rims (Figure 4.6: g-l), most often with a slight external ridge. As in Phase 4, similar forms are apparent at Nahariya and in the Pre-Palace and Palace phases at Ras el-'Ain. Although strikingly absent from Dan (Ilan 1996) and Megiddo (Ilan 2000), their closest parallels lie at Beth She'an (Maeir 1997a: pls. 12-13), across the Jordan River from Hayyat. This geographical pattern suggests that the Tell el-Hayyat krater forms may be one facet of a local Jordan Valley late Middle Bronze IIA-early Middle Bronze IIB assemblage.

Necked bowls, such as those from Tell el-Hayyat (Figure 4.6: n-q), are found widely through the Middle Bronze Age (Cole 1984). Chronological development of this type shows a gradual exaggeration of the carination and lengthening of the out-turned neck. The Tell el-Hayyat examples show moderate carination and neck elongation, in keeping with Middle Bronze IIA contexts, such as Pre-Palace Aphek (Beck 2000) and Stratum XII at Tell Dan (Ilan 1996: fig. 4.78). This form also continues into Middle Bronze IIB as indicated by parallels from Beth She'an (Maeir 1997a: pl. 5: 18-19).

Among cooking pots, flat-bottomed, straight-sided vessels continue from Phase 4 into Phase 3 (Figure 4.7: a-l) and are well paralleled in Middle Bronze II contexts such as Beth She'an (Maeir 1997a: pl. 14: 1-6), Aphek (Beck 2000) and Lachish (Singer-Avitz 2004) A few examples (Figure 4.7: c, e) have partially or completely pierced holes above the applied decoration. The Phase 3 flat-bottomed cooking pots become especially diverse in the placement and style of their molded decoration, as well as the presence or absence of perforations. The *Cf* cooking pot type is joined by globular cooking pots with upright rims (Cole's *Cu* form; Figure 4.7: m-p), which becomes the dominant cooking pot form in Phase 3. The

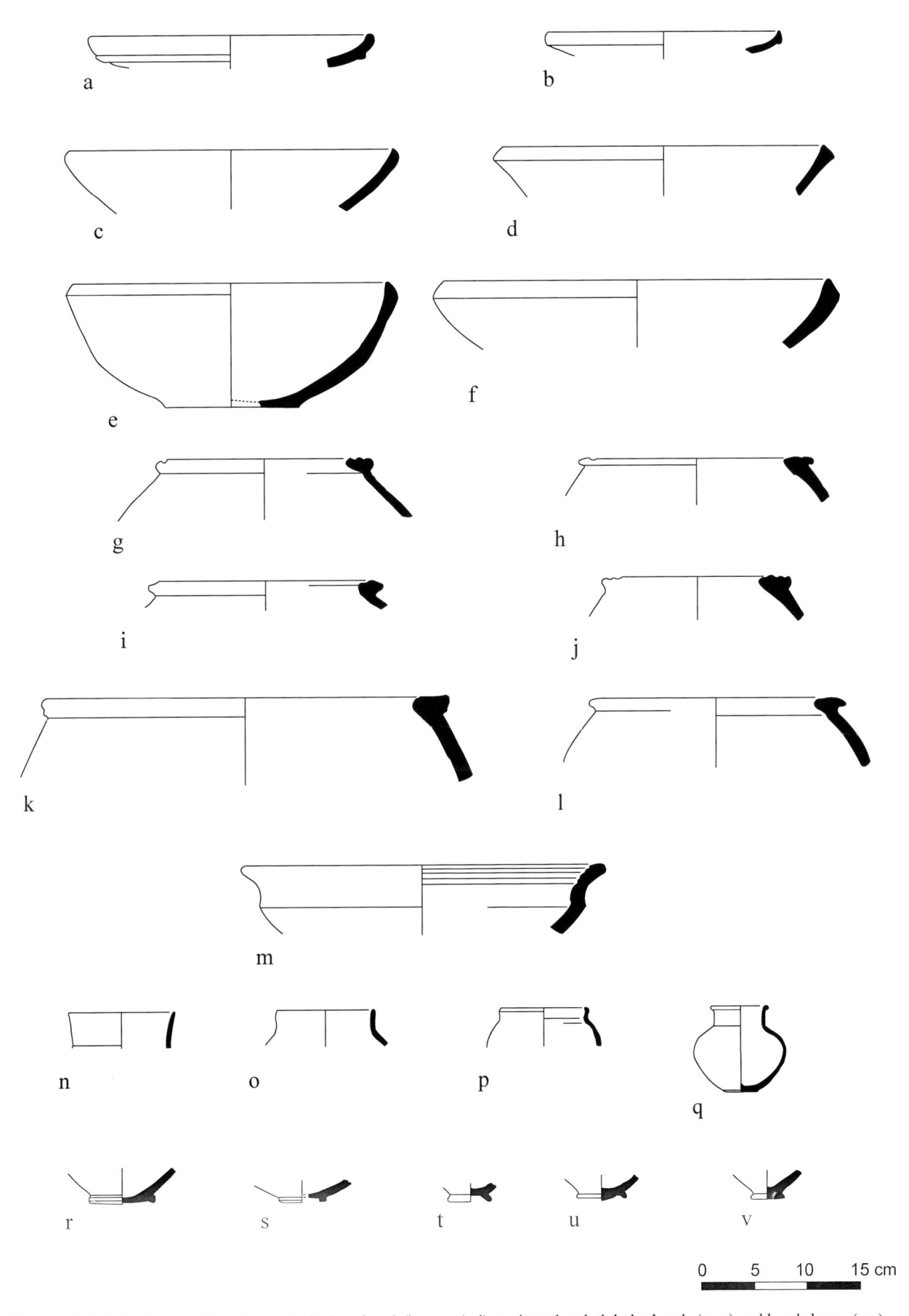

Figure 4.6 Middle Bronze IIA-B bowls (a-f), deep bowls/kraters (g-l), carinated and globular bowls (m-q) and bowls bases (r-v) from Phase 3 at Tell el-Hayyat. Scale 1:5.

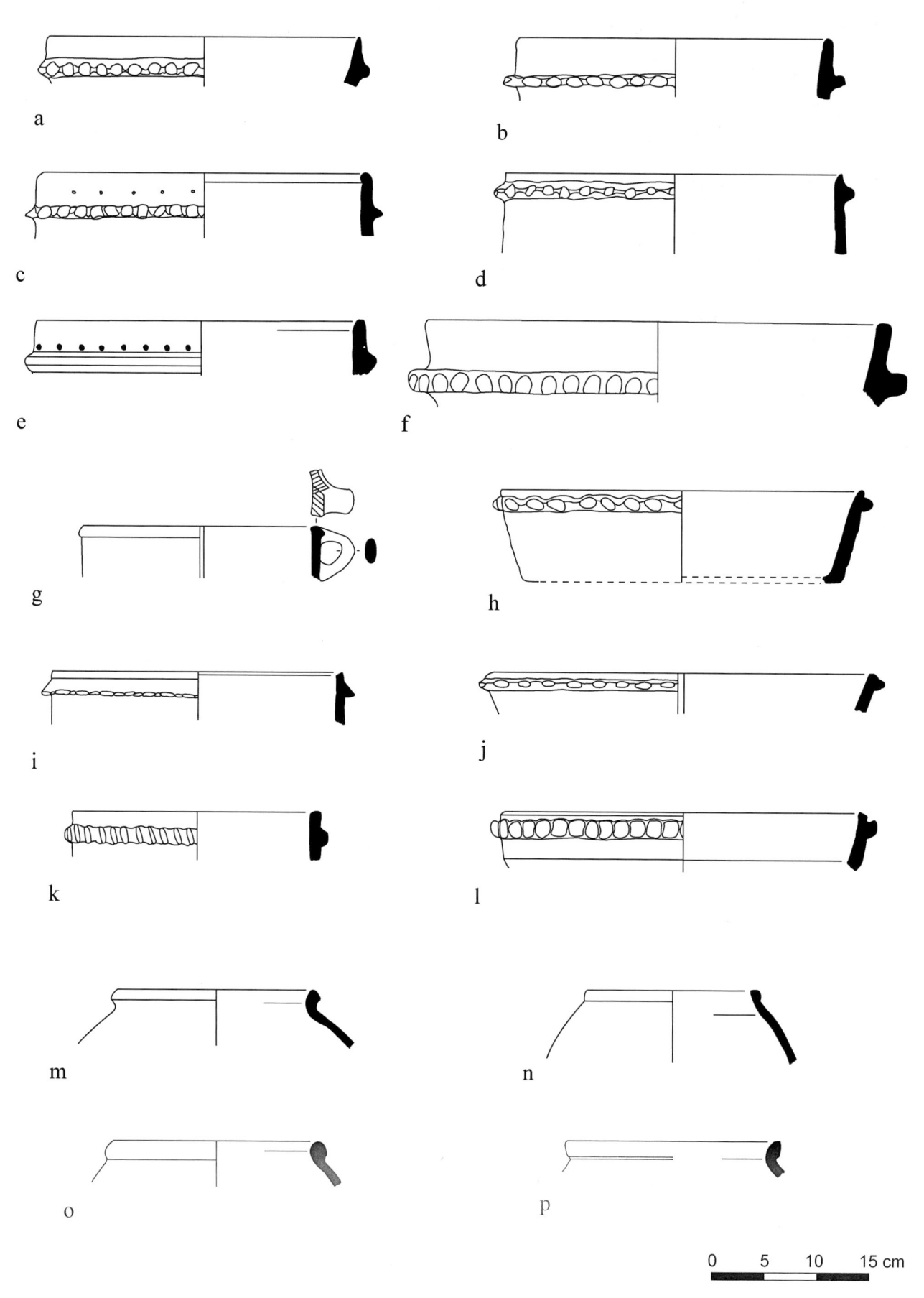

Figure 4.7 Middle Bronze IIA-B flat-bottomed cooking pots (a-l) and globular cooking pots (m-p) from Phase 3 at Tell el-Hayyat. Scale 1:5.

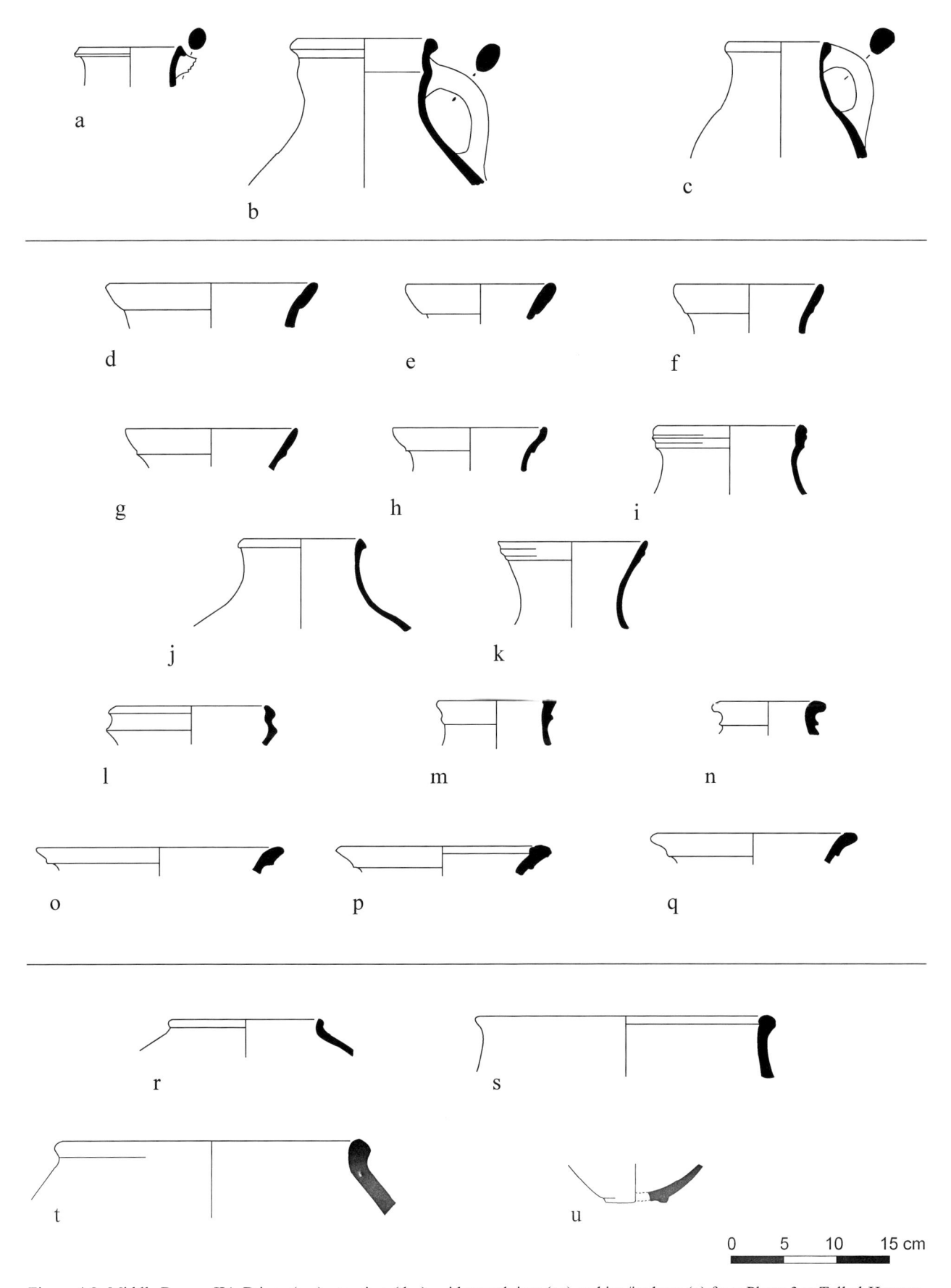

CERAMIC AND RADIOCARBON CHRONOLOGY FOR TELL EL-HAYYAT

Figure 4.8 Middle Bronze IIA-B jugs (a-c), storejars (d-q), widemouth jars (r-t) and jug/jar base (u) from Phase 3 at Tell el-Hayyat. Scale 1:5.

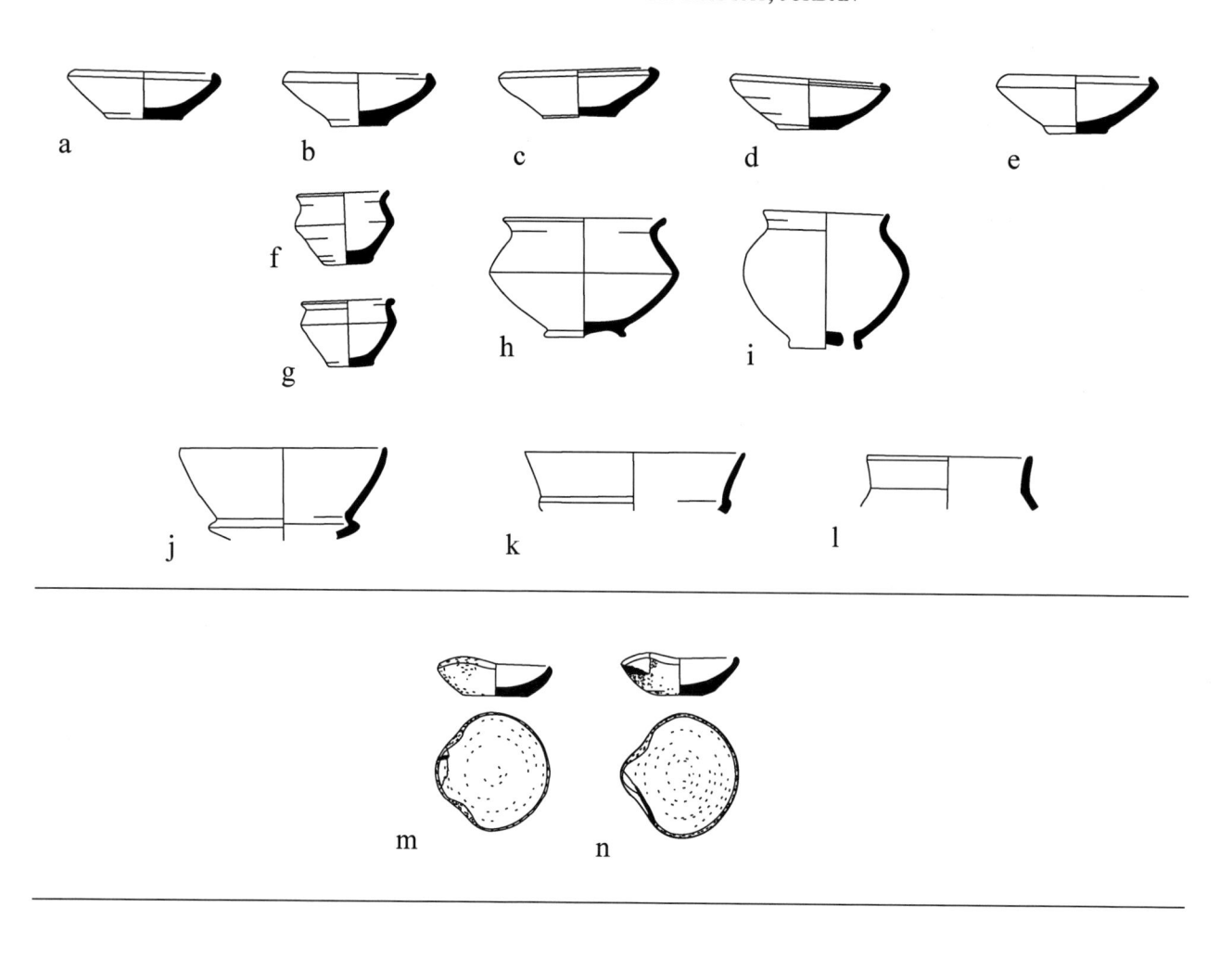

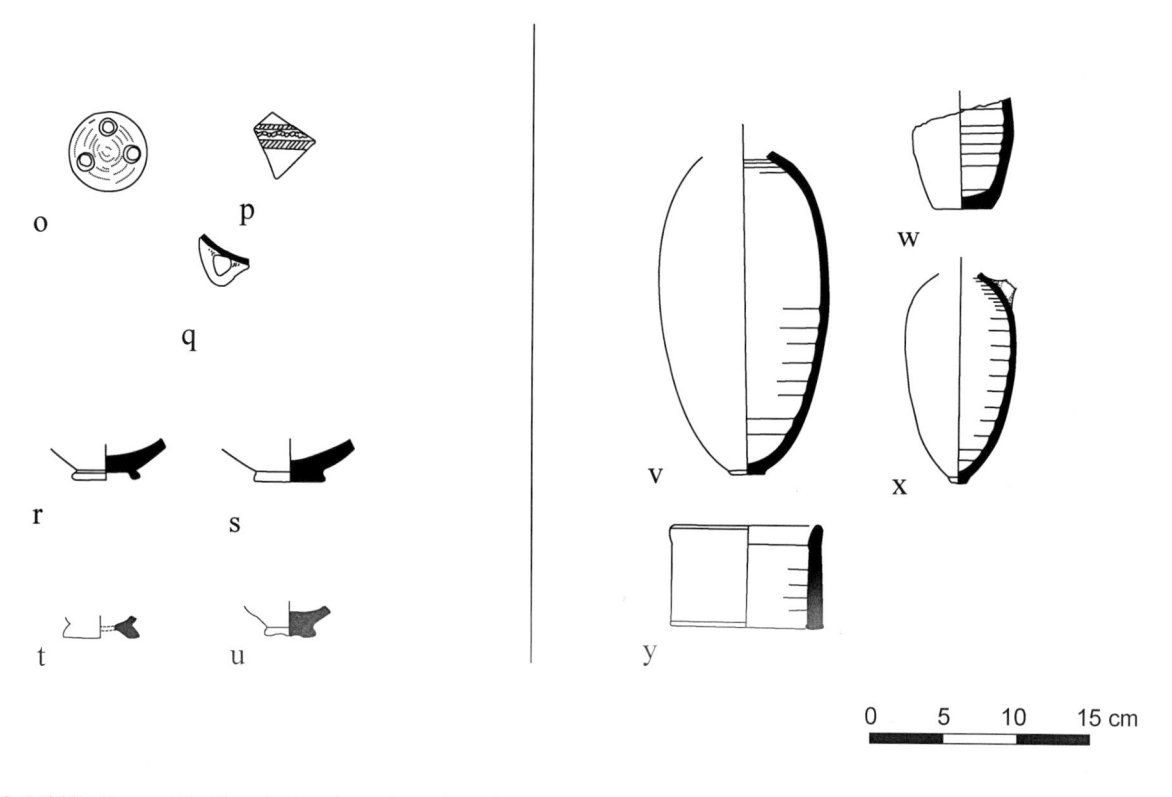

Figure 4.9 Middle Bronze IIB-C votive bowls (a-g), carinated and globular bowls (h-l), votive lamps (m, n), bowl bases (o, r-u), Chocolate on White ware (p, q), juglets (v-x) and pot stand (y) from Phase 2 at Tell el-Hayyat. Scale 1:5.

Figure 4.10 Cache of votive vessels (five shallow bowls, three carinated bowls and two lamps) from Tell el-Hayyat found buried in the Phase 2 temple forecourt, at the foot of the front temple wall.

globular cooking pots are characterized by a short outturned neck and a folded, thickened rim. Examples of this cooking pot, originally thought to date later than the flat-bottomed form (see Cole 1984: 65-66), are found in Middle Bronze IIA contexts at Megiddo (Ilan 2000: fig. 9.5: 13-17) and Nahariya (Ben-Dor 1950: 33). Thus, the changing mix of flat-bottomed and globular cooking pots between Phases 4 and 3 at Tell el-Hayyat is another hallmark of the subtle nature of ceramic changes from Middle Bronze IIA into IIB.

Phase 3 jugs (Figure 4.8: a-c) at Tell el-Hayyat usually have a handle attached between shoulder and rim. Rim forms generally are thickened externally (Figure 4.8: b-c) and occasionally everted (Figure 4.8: a). Internal concavity in the rim profile and red slip decoration are features of Middle Bronze IIA jugs, particularly at Megiddo (Ilan 2000). The absence of these features at Tell el-Hayyat indicates that Phase 3 represents a later manifestation of Middle Bronze IIA or IIB. Parallels to the Tell el-Hayyat examples are found at Megiddo (Ilan 2000: fig. 9. 7: 30), but the most similar examples come from Beth She'an (Maeir 1997a: pl. 19: 6, 20: 10, 21: 9).

Storejar rims from Phase 3 at Tell el-Hayyat show a wide variety of forms. The elongated, everted rims (Figure 4.8: d-h), some with a slight ridge at the bottom edge (Figure 4.8: g-h), now represent the most common jar rim form. At Aphek these everted rims appear at the beginning of Middle Bronze IIA (Beck 1975: fig. 5:11-12, fig. 7:19-21). Ridged rims (Figure 4.8: i-n), simple triangular rims (Figure 4.8: j), and molded rims with squared cross sections (Figure 4.8: o-q) also occur in quantity in Phase 3. These rims have parallels in the Pre-Palace phases at Aphek (Beck 2000), at Lachish (Singer-Avitz 2004), Megiddo (Ilan 2000) and Dan (Ilan 1996). The Middle Bronze IIA-B character of Phase 3 is underscored by the strong parallels of the storejars at Tell el-Hayyat to the Jericho (Kenyon and Holland 1982) and Beth She'an (Maeir 1997a) assemblages, where more elaborated rim forms also occur. The widemouth storejars (Figure 4.8: r-t) continue from Phases 5 and 4 and find parallels in Middle Bronze IIA contexts, such as Aphek (Beck 2000) and Megiddo (Ilan 2000).

Phase 2 Pottery

The Phase 2 pottery at Tell el-Hayyat belongs clearly to the Middle Bronze IIB-C ceramic horizon. The assemblage includes a cache of votive bowls (Figure 4.9: a-g) and lamps (Figure 4.9: m-n) buried near the entrance to the Phase 2 temple (see Figure 4.10). Among these votives, shallow miniature platter bowls have in-turned, slightly beveled rims and flat bases (Figure 4.9: a-e). Parallels for this type are found widely in Middle Bronze II, including early examples from Dan XII (Ilan 1996: fig. 4.77) and Lachish (Singer-Avitz 2004: fig. 16.1: 1-3), and later examples in Middle Bronze IIB-C contexts at Hazor III (Garfinkel 1997: fig. III. 12:10-11), Shechem (Cole 1984: pl. 19: j) and Tell Beth She'an (Maeir 1997a: pl. 6: 16). Another miniature Phase 2 hand-built carinated bowl exemplifies the high-necked profiles seen in Middle Bronze II B and C (Figure 4.11).

Figure 4.11 Miniature hand-built, high-necked carinated bowl from Phase 2 at Tell el-Hayyat.

Gently carinated and globular bowls are found in Phase 2 in votive (Figure 4.9: f-g) and full-sized (Figure 4.9: h-i) vessels. These bowl forms, which appear first at Tell el-Hayyat in slipped examples from Phase 4 (Figure 4. 4: n-o), have Middle Bronze IIA parallels from Stratum XII Dan (Ilan 1996: fig. 4. 78) and Aphek (Beck 2000), and from Middle Bronze IIB-C contexts at Shechem (Cole 1984: pl. 16), Tell Beth She'an (Maeir 1997a: pl. 5: 7, 10) and Jericho (Kenyon and Holland 1982: fig. 109). More sharply carinated "chalice" bowls with flaring rims (Figure 4.9: j-k) are found in Middle Bronze IIB-C at Jericho (Kenyon and Holland 1982: fig. 110: 1-5), Tell Beth She'an (Maeir 1997a: pl. 4: 11-13), the Hazor tombs (Maeir 1997b: fig. IV: 2-4), Shechem (Cole 1984: pl. 17: a-d) and Stratum X at Dan (Ilan 1996: fig. 4. 78).

Interestingly, one globular bowl from Tell el-Hayyat (Figure 4.9: i, o; Figure 4.12) features three holes drilled through its base, the function of which is not clear (see discussion in Gates 1988). Phase 2 ring bases and slightly concave disc bases (Figure 4.9: r-u) have parallels in the bowls of Middle Bronze IIB-C tomb groups 258, 644, and 645 at Megiddo (Guy 1938).

Phase 2 juglets at Tell el-Hayyat conform to one basic vessel form with three base variations. The illustrated examples (Figure 4.9: v-x; Figure 4.13) show the common internally ribbed dipper-juglet form, which is found variously with a button base, flat narrow base or flat wide base. The Phase 2 assemblage also features several wheel-thrown, string cut pot stands (Figure 4.9: y). Figure 4.14 shows a large Phase 2 juglet seated in one of these pot stands. These juglets find Middle Bronze IIB-C parallels, particularly at Hazor (Garfinkel 1997: fig. III: 13: 5) and Tell Beth She'an (Maeir 1997a: pl. 28. 14), while the base forms date early and late in the Middle Bronze Age, as seen at Dan (Ilan 1996: 224).

Lamps in Phase 2 (Figure 4.9: m-n) represent late Middle Bronze Age forms based on the accentuated angle between the vessel body and base seen in profile. The flatness of the base represents a morphological change from the earlier rounded bases, as exemplified in the Dan tomb assemblages (Ilan 1996: 221). The Tell el-Hayyat examples from Phase 2 are closely related to Stratum IX at Dan (Ilan 1996: fig. 4. 80) and Middle Bronze IIB-C Tell Beth She'an (Maeir 1997a: pl. 32: 6, 8). A small number of "Chocolate-on-White ware" sherds (Figure 4.9: p-q) includes a loop base from a tripod jar (Figure 4.9: q) as illustrated by Smith, McNicoll, and Hennessy (1981: fig. 26:7) from Tombs 23 and 24 at Pella. This aspect of the ceramic assemblage also signals a Middle Bronze IIB-C date for Phase 2 at Tell el-Hayyat.

Figure 4.12 Examples of Carinated Bowls from Phase 2 at Tell el-Hayyat; note three holes drilled through the base of the bowl on the right.

Figure 4.13 Three button-based juglets from Phases 3 and 2 at Tell el-Hayyat.

Figure 4.14 Juglet and pot stand from Phase 2 at Tell el-Hayyat.

Phase 1 Pottery

Phase 1 pottery comes from a small number of contexts associated with very fragmentary earthen floors and stone wall foundations just below the modern surface of Tell el-Hayyat. Sherds from the Middle Bronze IIB-C horizon provide the most common elements in the Phase 1 assemblage, including three good examples of Middle Bronze II platter bowls (Figure 4.15: c-e). These bowls, related to the EB rolled rim type (Dever 1973), occur from the outset of the Middle Bronze Age, including Tell el-Hayyat Phase 4 (Figure 4.4: a, c). Close parallels also come from Middle Bronze IIB levels at Shechem (Cole 1984: pl. 4), Tell Beth She'an (Maeir 1997a: pl. 3: 1-8) and Hazor (Garfinkel 1997: fig. III. 7: 14-15). A ribbed globular vessel found in Phase 1 (Figure 4.15: f) is a generic form related to necked globular bowls from Tell Beth She'an (Maeir 1997a: pl. 5: 7), Stratum IX at Dan (Ilan 1996: fig. 4.77) and Shechem (Cole 1984: pl. 14). The ribbing is a feature favored by the Tell el-Hayyat potters across all phases (see above). Phase 1 bases continue to incorporate the mix of ring bases and concave disc bases on bowls (Figure 4.15: g-h) and juglet button bases (Figure 4.15: i) seen in Phases 3 and 2 at Tell el-Hayyat.

The small Phase 1 assemblage also includes an example of a late Middle Bronze II straight-sided cooking vessel with subtle rope molding decoration (Figure 4.15: j). This vessel finds parallels in most Middle Bronze IIB-C

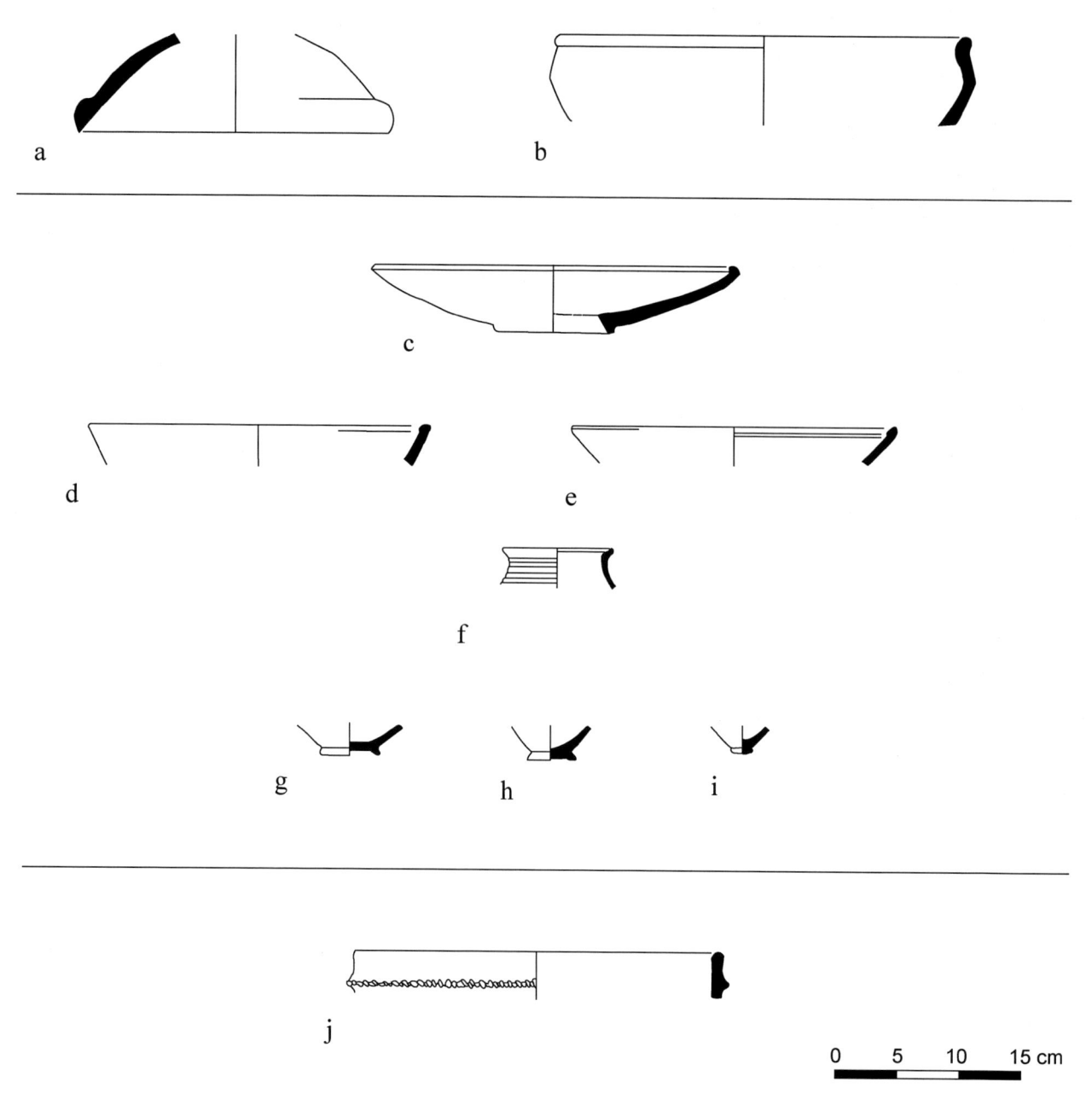

Figure 4.15 Middle Bronze IIC platter bowls (c-e), large carinated bowl (b), globular vessel (f), ring and concave bowl bases (g, h), juglet button base (i) and flat-bottomed cooking pot (j) from Phase 1 at Tell el-Hayyat. A single example of a mortarium (a) belongs to the Persian Period. Scale 1:5.

assemblages, including Shechem (Cole 1984: pl. 23: d) and Jericho (Kenyon and Holland 1982: fig. 147: 8). A few fragments of Tell el-Yehudiyeh Ware also were found in this level. Miscellaneous intrusive examples illustrate the fragmentary and potentially disturbed nature of Phase 1 deposits. A mortarium lid (Figure 4.15: a) belongs to the Persian period (Gitin 1990), while a large open carinated bowl (Figure 4.15: b) seems to belong to an early phase of the Iron Age (Amiran 1970: pl. 60: 1-3).

Decorative Techniques at Tell el-Hayyat (Phases 6-1)

The ceramic assemblages from Tell el-Hayyat include small quantities of Early Bronze IV and Middle Bronze II decorated ceramic wares, especially in Phases 6-4 (Figure 4.16). Early Bronze IV decoration typically involved trickle painting on cups and bowls (Figures 4.1: a-b; Figure 4.2: b), and rope molding on narrow-necked and

Figure 4.16 Examples of painted and applied decorative techniques commonly utilized on the pottery from Tell el-Hayyat.

holemouth jars (Figure 4.1: j, m). A variety of decorative techniques are combined on an idiosyncratic vessel in Phase 5 (Figure 4.2: g). Flat-bottomed cooking pots in Phases 4-2 are characterized by a variety of styles of rope molding (Figures 4.4: q; Figure 4.7: a-l). Storejars are marked with horizontal and wavy combing (Figure 4.5: r), as well as applied and impressed decoration. These two decorative techniques are quite common throughout the Middle Bronze Age (Amiran 1970: 102-3; Gerstenblith 1983). Red-slipped bowls and juglets, sometimes burnished, are found among the Middle Bronze IIA pottery (Figures 4.4: c, n-o; Figure 4.5: a). Painted decoration in Phases 4 and 3 includes examples of "trichrome" ware (Figure 4.4: p), similar in form and painted motif to a painted krater from Megiddo (Amiran 1970: pl. 31:2, pl. 33:14). A variety of straight, wavy, and cross-hatched red lines are found painted on store jars (Figure 4.5: m; Figure 4.16; discussion in Amiran 1970: 113). Linear painted decoration of this kind is confined to the Pre-Palace phase at Ras el-'Ain (Beck 1975: 45). In general, the ceramics of Tell el-Hayyat are characterized by a relatively limited repertoire of decorative motifs.

CHRONOLOGICAL IMPLICATIONS

The stratified pottery assemblages from Tell el-Hayyat provide a detailed, continuous typological sequence spanning the occupational history of this village through the Middle Bronze Age. The ceramics from Tell el-Hayyat include unusual transitional forms between late Early Bronze IV and early Middle Bronze IIA. Only a handful of sites in the southern Levant provide evidence of settlement during both Early Bronze IV and the Middle Bronze Age, including Lachish (Singer-Avitz 2004), Tell Beit Mirsim (Albright 1932), Megiddo (Loud 1948), Manahat (Edelstein et al. 1998), Nahal Rafa'im (Eisenberg (1993), Jericho (Prag 1974) and Hazor (Yadin 1972). However, these sites reveal ephemeral occupations during Early Bronze IV or reoccupation following a hiatus early in the Middle Bronze Age. The ceramic evidence across the southern Levant suggests generally that the abandonment of Early Bronze IV settlements occurred toward the end of the third millennium, and that the reoccupation of towns in Middle Bronze IIA occurred earliest on the Coastal Plain (Ilan 1995) at sites such as Aphek (Beck 2000) and Tell Ifshar (Marcus 2003; see also Cohen 2002 for a discussion). According to Maeir (1997a; 2002), the Middle Bronze IIA cultural horizon did not appear in the Jordan Valley until Middle Bronze IIA-B, an argument based in part on the lack of well-stratified Middle Bronze IIA settlement assemblages in the Jordan Valley. In contrast, the settlement record at Tell el-Hayyat includes a well-stratified late third to second millennium B.C. transition and lengthy Middle Bronze IIA occupation.

Early Bronze IV ceramics are particularly characteristic of Phases 6 and 5 at Tell el-Hayyat, although these ceramics are found mixed into later phases as well. The pottery assemblage of Phase 6 contains a combination of features that indicate a late Early Bronze IV date (i.e., EB IVC), as well as geographical variation. Some features of Hayyat's late Early Bronze IV pottery, such as holemouth jars, flaring, necked jars with rope decoration, and the absence of red paint seem out of place in the northern Jordan Valley (e.g., see Cohen 1999). However, the trickle-painted bowls and cups attest to a strong regional pottery tradition that continues from the nearby and chronologically earlier village of Tell Abu en-Ni'aj (Falconer et al. 1998, 2001; Jones 1999; Czarzasty 2001) into Tell el-Hayyat's Phases 6 and 5.

At Tell el-Hayyat, Phase 5 represents a unique transitional horizon that incorporates both Early Bronze IV and Middle Bronze II ceramic forms. The co-occurrence of trickle-painted bowls, late Early Bronze IV straight-sided cooking pots, heavy carinated bowls and closed externally rilled bowls/cups reflects an unusual assemblage that must be placed at the very beginning of Middle Bronze IIA, strikingly earlier than either Aphek (Beck 2000) or Tell Ifshar (Marcus 2003) on pure typological grounds. Indeed, Aphek and Ifshar, which purportedly contain the earliest Middle Bronze IIA assemblages in the southern Levant, find little in common with Tell el-Hayyat pottery forms until Phase 4. The transitional Early Bronze IV-Middle Bronze II assemblages from the Jordan Valley such as Tell el-Hayyat Phase 5 and the Hagosherim tombs (Covello-Paran 1996) may be contemporary with Middle Bronze IIA assemblages from the Coastal Plain, whose attributes appear later at these inland sites (see Maeir 2002). However, the transitional nature of the Phase 5 pottery reflects important, culturally indigenous processes. Typologically at least, Tell el-Hayyat Phase 5 seems to predate the Middle Bronze IIA assemblages from the Coastal Plain and the larger sites in the Jordan Valley, including Pella.

The similarity of Hayyat's Phase 4 pottery with the early Middle Bronze IIA assemblages on the Coastal Plain is best exemplified by the in-turned kraters, shallow platter bowls, carinated and globular bowls, the classic straight-sided cooking pot, and finally the handle-less, squat jars with elongated rims (Figures 4.4 and 4.5). Tell el-Hayyat's Phase 4 assemblage demonstrates a relatively complete group of vessels that fits neatly within other published early Middle Bronze IIA assemblages, particularly as seen in Aphek's Pre-Palace phase (see Beck 2000), as well as from Megiddo, Nahariya and Munhatta. The similarities with the last three sites are not surprising in light of their relative proximity to Tell el-Hayyat.

While Tell el-Hayyat's Phase 4 pottery constitutes a classic Middle Bronze IIA assemblage, Phase 3 ceramics attest to the development of later forms running from Middle Bronze IIA into IIB. Phase 3 is characterized by the virtual disappearance of painted vessels, the emergence of necked bowls, and the proliferation of great diversity in vessel morphology, particularly among deep bowls and cooking pots (see Maeir 1997b for discussion of the Middle Bronze IIA-B transition). Our Phase 3 assemblage finds much in common with Aphek's Palace phase (see Beck 2000).

Phase 2 at Tell el-Hayyat features Middle Bronze IIB and IIC ceramics that represent elaborations of vessel forms seen in earlier phases. The general Middle Bronze IIB-C ceramic chronology for the southern Levant suggests that rim and base forms become exaggerated as bowl carination sharpens and rim profiles grow more flared (see Cole 1984). For example, the walls of the straight-sided (*Cf*) cooking pot become progressively more inverted, assuming an almost globular form by Middle Bronze IIC (see Berelov 2006 for discussion). Most Phase 2 pottery from Tell el-Hayyat shows modest exaggeration in rim and base forms, and vessel morphology, in keeping with late Middle Bronze IIB and early Middle Bronze IIC ceramics elsewhere. The best evidence of habitation at Tell el-Hayyat into later Middle Bronze IIC comes from a small number of Chocolate-on-White Ware sherds from Phases 2 and 1, which are ascribed traditionally to the late 17th or early 16th centuries B.C. (Smith et al. 1981; cf. Johnson 1982 for earlier appearance of Cypriot pottery in Palestine).

The ceramic assemblage from Tell el-Hayyat consequently suggests original settlement of the village in late Early Bronze IV and its abandonment during the latter part of Middle Bronze IIC. This chronology may be specified further by considering Bronze Age radiocarbon determinations from the southern Levant (see Marcus 2003), including a suite of radiocarbon determinations from Tell el-Hayyat (presented below).

RADIOCARBON CHRONOLOGY FROM TELL EL-HAYYAT

A suite of 12 AMS radiocarbon dates were determined for plant macrofossil samples from Phases 5 and 4 (Table 4.2). These results help refine the chronology for the earlier occupations of Tell el-Hayyat. The AMS radiocarbon laboratories at the University of Arizona (AA), Oxford University (OxA) and the Vienna Environmental Research Accelerator (VERA) supplied four dates each. Samples for the Oxford and VERA dates were solicited by and submitted to the Middle Bronze Chronology Project (Marcus 2003). The Oxford and VERA dates are comprised of four sample pairs of a single plant taxon from the same excavation locus. As prescribed by Marcus, this sampling method permits comparison of inter-laboratory consistency. The results show that the Oxford and VERA dates are consistent and comparably precise.

When calibrated, the Arizona and VERA dates for Phase 5 provide two sigma ranges starting before 2000 cal B.C. The calibrated ranges for the Oxford dates, based on somewhat smaller standard deviations, start around 1900 cal B.C. The calibrated two sigma ranges end around 1700-1770 cal B.C. for all but AA-1236, whose range extends to roughly 1525 cal B.C. The early beginnings of these ranges, especially those for the results from Arizona

Table 4.2 Results of AMS ^{14}C on samples from Tell el-Hayyat calibrated in November 2005 with Calib 5.0 on the basis of Stuiver, M., and Reimer, P.J., 1993 (VERA and OxA dates were analyzed and compiled by Ezra Marcus for the MB chronology project, a sub-project of SCIEM2000, funded by the Jubily Fund of the City of Vienna, Austrian Academy of Sciences. SCIEM2000 is a special program of the Austrian Academy of Sciences, headed by Professor Manfred Bietak)

Lab.-Nr.	Sample Name	^{13}C [‰]	^{14}C-age [yr.B.P.]	Calibrated Age [cal. B.C.]: 2 sigma range
AA-1236	Tell el-Hayyat Ph 5 (lower), *Lens culinaris*		3460±100	2026BC (100%) 1526BC
AA-1239	Tell el-Hayyat, Ph 5 (upper), unidentified seeds		3600±60	2136BC (89%) 1865BC 1849BC (11%) 1773BC
AA-1238	Tell el-Hayyat, Ph 4 (lower), *Lens culinaris*		2930±80	1380BC (5%) 1335BC 1323BC (95%) 923BC
AA-1237	Tell el-Hayyat, Ph 4 (middle), *Olea* stones		3280±100	1874BC (1%) 1843BC 1816BC (1%) 1799BC 1779BC (97%) 1375BC 1339BC (1%) 1319BC
VERA-2037	Tell el-Hayyat, Ph 5 L.102, *Triticum aestivum* humic acids	-21.1 ± 1.3	3555±40	2020BC (5%) 1993BC 1981BC (95%) 1769BC
VERA-2038	Tell el-Hayyat, Ph 5 L.067, *Triticum aestivum*	-21.9 ± 2.1	3530±60	2025BC (98%) 1735BC 1714BC (2%) 1694BC
VERA-2039	Tell el-Hayyat, Ph 4 L.092, *Olea* stones humic acids	-23.4 ± 1.5	3495±35	1915BC (99%) 1739BC 1707BC (1%) 1699BC
VERA-2040	Tell el-Hayyat, Ph 4 *Olea* stones	-24.0 ± 1.5	3500±35	1922BC (100%) 1739BC
OxA-10986	Tell el-Hayyat, Ph 5 L.102, *Triticum aestivum*	-22.4	3470±36BP	1887BC (91%) 1728BC 1721BC (9%) 1691BC
OxA-10987	Tell el-Hayyat, Ph 5 L. 067, *Triticum aestivum*	-22.9	3497±37BP	1921BC (99%) 1738BC 1708BC (1%) 1698BC
OxA-10988	Tell el-Hayyat, Ph 4 L.092, *Olea* stone	-21.3	3502±37BP	1926BC (99%) 1739BC 1705BC (1%) 1700BC
OxA-10989	Tell el-Hayyat, Ph 4 L.074, *Olea* stone	-21.3	3523±39BP	1950BC (100%) 1745BC

and VERA, are in keeping our inference of an early start for Phase 5 settlement at Tell el-Hayyat (ca. 2000 B.C.) based on ceramic typology. The full two sigma ranges leave open the possibility that these samples may date as late as the 18th century B.C. However, comparison of the Phase 5 pottery with assemblages from other Middle Bronze Age sites suggests that Phase 5 dates well before the 18th century B.C.

The Phase 4 samples from Tell el-Hayyat provide calibrated two sigma ranges from VERA, Oxford and AA-1237 that begin between 1950 and 1875 B.C. The two sigma ranges from VERA and Oxford end about 1745-1700 B.C. One of the samples processed by the University of Arizona (AA-1238) provides anomalously late results, while the relatively large standard deviation of AA-1237 extends its calibrated two sigma range to around 1300 cal B.C. A beginning date for Phase 4 ca. 1900 B.C., in keeping with the calibrated ranges for five of these six samples, is consistent with our chronological inferences based on Bronze Age comparative ceramic typologies. While the end dates for the Arizona samples clearly seem anomalous, the two sigma ranges for the other four samples allow for a calibrated date as late as the 18th century B.C.

TELL EL-HAYYAT PHASES AND CHRONOLOGY

The comparative typological analysis of ceramics from Tell el-Hayyat, coupled with the radiocarbon results summarized above, help clarify the occupational history of Tell el-Hayyat (see Table 4.1). In keeping with Early Bronze IV evidence across the southern Levant, the stratified ceramics at the base of Tell el-Hayyat must date to the late third millennium B.C. The similarities with apparently late Early Bronze IV pottery from other sites, coupled with the beginning of the calibrated ranges for the Phase 5 radiocarbon dates, indicate clearly that Phase

6 predates 2000 cal B.C. The interface between Phases 5 and 4 may be estimated at ca. 1900 cal B.C. from the very early typological character of the Phase 5 ceramic assemblage, the classic Middle Bronze IIA ceramic repertoire of Phase 4, and the beginning of the calibrated ranges for the Phase 4 radiocarbon dates. The duration of Phase 4 fits well between ca. 1900 and 1800 cal B.C. based on the classic Middle Bronze IIA character of Tell el-Hayyat's Phase 4 ceramic assemblage, in conjunction with the two-sigma ranges for the Phase 4 calibrated radiocarbon dates (especially those from VERA and Oxford).

At the other end of the Tell el-Hayyat chronology, stratified Chocolate-on-White Ware suggests ages for the later portion of Phase 2 in the late 17th century B.C. and early Phase 1 at the beginning of the 16th century B.C. Accordingly, we may estimate a transition from Phase 2 to Phase 1 ca. 1600 B.C. The ephemeral remains of Phase 1 do not dictate occupation any later than ca. 1550 B.C. The earlier (i.e., Middle Bronze IIB) typological elements of the Phase 2 pottery would suggest a beginning date for that phase ca. 1700 B.C. This reasoning leaves the interval between 1800 B.C. (the estimated end of Phase 4) and 1700 B.C. (the estimated beginning of Phase 2) to accommodate Phase 3.

In overview, the occupational history of Tell el-Hayyat spans approximately five and one-half centuries, as represented in six stratified phases of village architecture and their associated material culture. We infer the chronology for Hayyat's habitation based on comparative analysis of excavated ceramics and a set of 12 AMS radiocarbon ages for botanical samples from Phases 5 and 4. These data reveal a sequence of village occupations, each lasting an average of about one century, between the late third millennium and the mid-second millennium B.C. Phase 6 provides limited evidence from late Early Bronze IV. Phase 5 dates to the very beginning of the Middle Bronze Age, offering a unique assemblage of transitional Early Bronze IV-Middle Bronze IIA ceramics. Phase 4 holds a classic Middle Bronze IIA pottery repertoire. Phase 3 incorporates a broadened typological range of Middle Bronze IIA and IIB ceramics. Phase 2 reveals elements of Middle Bronze IIB and IIC pottery. Phase 1 caps the history of Tell el-Hayyat with ceramics from Middle Bronze IIC. Thus, Tell el-Hayyat provides a record of village life from the latter portion of the Early Bronze IV urban collapse through the reappearance of towns in Middle Bronze IIA and their growth and proliferation in Middle Bronze IIB and IIC.

CHAPTER 5: ECONOMY AND SUBSISTENCE AT TELL EL-HAYYAT

Patricia L. Fall and Mary C. Metzger

AGRICULTURAL CROPS AND THE EXPANSION OF ORCHARDS

Despite the severity of local forest resource exploitation by Neolithic villagers, the Levantine hill country still featured large tracts of oak/pistachio woodland at the advent of Bronze Age cities in the third millennium B.C. (Gophna et al. 1986; Liphschitz et al. 1989). Roughly 5000 years after the Neolithic domestication of cereals and legumes, a second wave of agricultural innovation, featuring intensive orchard cultivation, became pronounced during the third and second millennia B.C. (Miller 1991). As a consequence, lowlands and river valleys, like the lands around Tell el-Hayyat (Figure 5.1), became checkered with annual subsistence crops, while perennial fruit-bearing trees and vines encroached on the rockier slopes of neighboring uplands (Stager 1985). Despite the likelihood of *localized* Neolithic deforestation, palynological analysis of lake cores from the Sea of Galilee and the Dead Sea show that *regional* impacts on forests and woodlands emerged clearly only in the wake of Bronze Age urbanism (see Chapter 1). Thus, one major impetus for the anthropogenic vegetation so characteristic of the Eastern Mediterranean stems from Bronze Age agricultural intensification – especially for the export of wine, olive oil, and dried fruit – to serve emerging urban markets, including Egypt and its trading partners (Stager 1985; Ben-Tor 1986). The domestication of orchard taxa, featuring olive (*Olea europea*), grape (*Vitis vinifera*), fig (*Ficus carica*), date (*Phoenix dactylifera*), pomegranate (*Punica granatum*) and sycamore fig (*Ficus sycomorus*) was accomplished by the fourth millennium B.C. (Helbaek 1959; Zohary and Spiegel-Roy 1975; Neef 1990). Cultivation originated in the Levant (olive, grape, fig, and pomegranate), Mesopotamia (date), and the Nile Valley (sycamore fig). However, the economic and environmental effects of this second wave of agricultural innovation did not become pronounced until at least a millennium after their domestication and roughly 5000 years after the domestication of cereals and legumes (see Miller 1991). The consequences of widespread orchard cultivation are clearly illustrated by botanical and archaeological evidence for intensive olive, grape, and fig cultivation in the southern Levant during the Bronze Age (McCreery 1980; Lines 1995).

The Domestication of Fruit Trees in the Levant

Arboriculture, the cultivation of trees for fruit and nuts, is a central component of agriculture in a wide variety of early civilizations around the world. The more celebrated

Figure 5.1 View of Tell el-Hayyat looking across the fields of the *ghor* in the foreground to the hills of Israel and Palestine in the background, facing west. Note the backdirt piles framing Tell el-Hayyat during the 1985 excavations. The Jordan River flows at the foot of the trees in the middle distance at the right (photo by Karen Scholz).

domestication of annual cereals and legumes in the Near East was followed by the domestication of an array of perennial orchard species that produced marketable secondary products (Zohary and Spiegel-Roy 1975). Olive, grape, date palm, fig, and pomegranate were the first, or among the very first, fruit trees cultivated in human history (Zohary and Hopf 1988; van Zeist 1991).

The wild progenitors of these species were exploited by hunter-gatherers for thousands of years prior to domestication (Miller 1991). Kislev et al. (1992) report carbonized fruit seeds from Ohalo II (ca. 17,000 B.C.), an Epipaleolithic site located on the southwestern shore of the Sea of Galilee. A combination of fruits apparently consumed at this site include wild grape (*Vitis vinifera sylvestris*), wild pistachio (*Pistacia atlantica*) and wild almond (*Amygdalus communis*.) The evidence from Ohalo II for wild grape is particularly noteworthy as the beginning of the evolution of grape as one of the major sources of secondary products traded in the Bronze Age. Other instances of well-documented wild almond use include Hayonim cave (ca. 10,000 B.C.), an Epipaleolithic site in northern Israel (Hopf and Bar-Yosef 1987).

Hallmark Neolithic assemblages from Jericho and 'Ain Ghazal (ca. 7000 B.C.) include carbonized remains of wild fruit trees, including fig, almond, pistachio, and carob (*Ceratonia siliqua*) (Hopf 1983; Rollefson and Simmons 1988). A larger inference to be drawn from this range of carbonized wood and wild fruit seeds is that forest communities in the southern Levant were still relatively intact during the Neolithic period. During the inception and growth of early Neolithic farming, deforestation remained localized, most notably around large Pre-Pottery Neolithic communities (Rollefson and Kohler-Rollefson 1992; Falconer and Fall 1995). Agricultural landscape change would become expanded and reconfigured dramatically with the rise of cities and the intensification of orchard agriculture in the Bronze Age.

Orchard Development and the Rise of Cities

Annual crop cultivation, largely for subsistence needs and orchard management, especially for production of marketable commodities, entail fundamentally different ecological considerations and social implications. Orchards require long-term commitment revolving around secure land tenure, residential stability, and a significant initial investment of labor and capital (Perevolotsky 1981; Stager 1985; LaBianca 1990). These considerations stem largely from the expectation than an orchard cultivator will not see a return on their initial investment for several years. Grape and olive require five years of cultivation before bearing fruit, and olive trees may grow for up to two decades prior to reaching their full fruit-bearing potential (Stager 1985). Given these needs for stability and peaceful conditions, as well as pronounced commercial potential, it is unsurprising that the date palm, olive branch and fig tree have become historic symbols of peace and prosperity in the Near East and elsewhere (Zohary 1982; Stager 1985).

The Early Bronze Age marks the roughly contemporaneous and clearly related beginnings of regional orchard cultivation, urbanized settlement in the southern Levant, and the development of state-level societies in Egypt and Mesopotamia (Stager 1985). These processes led to vastly increased economic specialization and trade throughout the Near East (Curtin 1984; Ben-Tor 1986). The southern Levant experienced influences from the export of orchard products to Egypt and Syria (Stager 1985; Ben-Tor 1986). Within the Levant, intra-regional interdependence grew as tree crops from the highlands were exchanged for surplus grain produced in the lowlands and river valleys (where cities were located) (Stager 1985). Market demands emanating from towns and cities grew as their residents became specialized (e.g., as artisans, merchants or bureaucrats), leading to increasingly market-oriented horticulture to produce a broadened array of products such as dried fruit, olive oil, wine and honey, further stimulating fruit orchards throughout the region (Ben-Tor 1986).

Pronounced evidence for orchard cultivation arises from a variety of locales and archaeological contexts in the Early Bronze Age. Ceramic innovations offered distinctive new vessels for storage and transport of rendered orchard products (Ben-Tor 1986). New manufacturing technologies adopted aluminum-silicate clay and wood resin to make pottery physically stronger and durable for storing acidic liquids such as olive oil and wine (earlier containers made from aluminum-calcium clay lacked these properties) (Ben-Tor 1986). These aspects of pottery design and manufacture changed in response to the rapid spread of Early Bronze Age grape and olive orchards, as signaled by the appearance of carbonized seeds recovered archaeologically across the Near East. Grape emerges abundantly from settlements in Israel and Palestine (e.g., Arad and Jericho), Jordan (e.g., Bab adh-Dhra' and Numeira), eastern Iran (e.g., Malyan and Shahr-i Sohkta) and the Tigris/Euphrates Valley (e.g., Tell Taya) (Miller 1991). Olive stones are a major component of the carbonized plant remains recovered from Bab adh-Dhra' and Numeira, Jordan, and Arad in Israel (Hopf 1978; McCreery 1980).

The abundance and variety of Early Bronze Age orchard crops is attested particularly well at Bab adh-Dhra', Jordan, near the eastern shore of the Dead Sea (McCreery 1980). Here carbonized grape and fig seeds increase steadily through the Early Bronze Age sequence, coinciding with the growth of a walled town at Bab edh-Dhra' and the development of town life across the southern Levant. Cultivated grape, olive and fig figure prominently, and are accompanied by evidence for wild fruit trees, including date palm, pistachio (*Pistacia*

Figure 5.2 Patchwork of remnant Mediterranean forests, olive groves, and agricultural fields near Ajlun, Jordan about 1000 masl on the Jordan Plateau overlooking the northern Jordan Valley (photo by Pat Fall).

atlantica), jujube (*Zizyphus spina-christi*), almond (*Amygdalus communis*) and peach (*Prunus persica*) (McCreery 1980).

Urban growth and the related spread of orchard cultivation also triggered widespread changes in the natural forest communities of the Near East (Miller 1985; Falconer and Fall 1995; Fall et al. 2002) (Figure 5.2). Sedentary inhabitants of villages, towns and cities consumed significant amounts of fuel wood, building materials, and specialized orchard products, leading to dramatic shifts in arboreal species composition (Miller 1985). These transitions are particularly apparent in the long-term pollen and plant macrofossil records from localities across southwestern Asia (e.g., Miller 1985; Baruch 1990; Bottema and Woldring 1990; Fall 1990; Roberts 1990; Rollefson et al. 1992; and see discussion in Chapter 1).

Levantine Arboriculture

Many fundamental differences between the cultivation of annual and perennial crops derive from characteristics of the plants themselves. Annual cereals and legumes are planted from seed, and harvested as new seeds several months later. Annual crop cultivation, therefore, represents an expedient strategy for low-investment seasonal agriculture by non-sedentary populations (Zohary and Hopf 1988; LaBianca 1990). Among perennials, wild fruit trees are cross-pollinated and also reproduce by seed (Zohary and Spiegel-Roy 1975; Liphschitz et al. 1991). Wild olives, grapes, figs, dates, pomegranates and sycamore figs carry the additional potential of vegetative propagation. These taxa may be reproduced as clones through cuttings (grape, fig, sycamore fig, and pomegranate), basal knobs (olive) or transplanting offshoots (dates) (Zohary and Spiegel-Roy 1975). These cultivated clones may survive for hundreds or even thousands of years (Zohary and Hopf 1988). Accordingly, the classic fruit trees of the Near East have changed little since their first domestication as the result of minimal cycles of sexual reproduction and genetic recombination.

Olive trees are well adapted to the warm, wet winters and hot, dry summers of Mediterranean climates, and make optimum use of well-drained hill slope soils (Polunin and Huxley 1965; Renfrew 1973) (Figure 5.3). Olive has proven not only productive, but versatile, being prized in antiquity for eating and cooking oil, ointments, fuel for lamps, and as a solvent for ingredients of perfumes and cosmetics (Goor 1966a; Zohary 1982). Rendered olive oil is well suited to transport and marketing, and long-term storage. The olive's enduring value made it a time-honored symbol of peace and wealth throughout the Mediterranean Basin (Goor 1966a; Zohary and Hopf 1988).

Little evidence for the use of olive wood for construction or fuel is apparent prior to the Chalcolithic (Liphschitz et al. 1991). Some Chalcolithic samples consist of *jift*, olive pits crushed during pressing, which elude ready identification as being wild or domesticated. The Jordan Valley provides the best evidence for olive cultivation during the Chalcolithic. Excavated wood samples from Abu Hamid and Tell esh-Shuna [North] are predominantly olive, including abundant fragments from ash deposits, indicating substantial burning of olive fuel

Figure 5.3 Domestic olive (*Olea europea*) trees near Umm Qeis, Jordan, like those planted in Classical period orchards (photo by Pat Fall).

wood (Dollfus and Ibrahim 1988; Neef 1990: table 2). Olive wood construction timbers are reported from Chalcolithic Teleilat Ghassul and Abu Hamid (Hennessy 1969; Dollfus and Ibrahim 1988). Olive utilization rose significantly with the growth of Bronze Age towns, as revealed in a sample of 47 archaeological sites in Israel. Olive wood fragments are identified in 20-30% of Chalcolithic charcoal samples and 40-60% of Early Bronze Age samples (Liphschitz et al. 1991: table 3). This evidence suggests increased harvesting of domesticated orchards for fuel wood and construction timbers by the Bronze Age, probably as a response to diminished wild sources (e.g., oak). Thus, the evidence for olive cultivation entails a variety of adaptations to urban mercantilism and increasingly anthropogenic landscapes.

Intensive arboriculture also entailed clearance of crop land for vineyards, which produced fruits that could be eaten fresh, dried into raisins, or pressed for their juice (Zohary 1982). Grapes were particularly valuable when rendered into wine, which (like olive oil) could be stored and transported in ceramic jars, making it eminently suitable for regional exchange (Goor 1966b; Stager 1985). The importance of ancient Levantine viticulture, particularly for winemaking, is attested by the use of the grapevine as a national symbol in the Old Testament (Zohary 1982: 54) (Figure 5.4). As with the olive, Chalcolithic settlements provide the earliest carbonized seeds and fruits, followed by more common appearance of grape remains in the Early Bronze Age, for example at Lachish (Helbaek 1958), Arad (Hopf 1978), Bab adh-Dhra` (McCreery 1980) and Jericho (Hopf 1983).

Figure 5.4 Domestic grape (*Vitis vinifera*) vine (photo by Pat Fall).

Domesticated fig and date, two other particularly successful fruit trees, also produced edible commodities, which could be stored and eaten year round (Figure 5.5). Sun drying allows the fig's sugar to crystallize on the surface as a natural preservative (Renfrew 1973: 136; Zohary 1982: 58) that enhanced their marketability. Fig and grape were sometimes planted side by side,

Figure 5.5 Domestic fig (*Ficus carica*) tree (photo by Pat Fall).

permitting the vine to climb on the fig (Goor 1965). Once harvested, figs were dried singly, on strings, or as pressed cakes. Excavated evidence for fig cultivation in the Levant begins in the Chalcolithic (Hopf 1983; Meadows 1996). Whereas fig, grape and olive flourish in Mediterranean environments, date palms prefer warmer and drier environments (Zohary and Hopf 1988). Dates were first cultivated during the fourth millennium B.C. in Mesopotamia (Zohary and Spiegel-Roy 1975) and do not appear commonly among plant remains excavated in the southern Levant. Following the domestication of orchard taxa by the Chalcolithic, fruit products became distributed widely in the Early Bronze Age. With the advent of town life and regional mercantilism in the third millennium B.C., olive, grape and fig products had become the three major food commodities traded throughout the dry farming regions of the Mediterranean basin (Zohary and Hopf 1988).

Crop Management at Tell el-Hayyat

The domestication of cereals and legumes and the increasing reliance on sheep and goat husbandry, which began with the Neolithic Revolution about 10,000 years ago, continued through the Holocene. By the fourth millennium B.C., subsistence strategies expanded to include new plant cultigens (orchard crops) and domesticated animals, including cattle, pigs and equids (horses and donkeys) (Figure 5.6). Agricultural intensification increased the available arable land with new technologies like the plow and irrigation, pushing settlements into more marginal areas, as well as concentrating populations in the richest agricultural regions, such as the Jordan Valley. Rivers, springs and *wadis* along the Rift Valley were utilized for expanded agricultural features, including check dams and garden plots (Joffe 1993: 32) (Figure 5.7). Today, farmers in the southern *ghor* around Wadi Fidan and Bab adh-Dhra' use irrigation water from nearby springs to augment the annual precipitation of 50-150 mm (McCreery 1980: 15). Alluvial terraces along the Jordan Valley were utilized through most of the year, with cultivation curtailed only during the extremely hot summer months. An annual precipitation of 300 mm or greater in the northern Jordan Valley is sufficient for dry farming, where today's wheat fields are still rain fed. Modern orchards and gardens in the vicinity of Tell el-Hayyat are irrigated from the King Abdullah Canal, which diverts water from the Yarmouk River, the northern-most tributary of the Jordan River (30 km north of these sites). In antiquity, irrigation water could have been diverted from springs at the foot of the hills bounding the Jordan Valley on the east. Most prominent among these is the spring at the foot of the ancient town of Pella.

Figure 5.6 Local farmer plowing the fields west of Tell el-Hayyat, 1982, facing west (photo by Bob Erskine).

Figure 5.7 The Zarqa River near its confluence with the Jordan River in the Jordan Valley, facing northeast (photo by Pat Fall).

Published floral analyses for Bronze Age archaeological sites in the Jordan Valley (e.g., Feinbrunn 1938; Helbaek 1958; Hopf 1969; Western 1971) show that three species retained paramount importance through the Early and Middle Bronze Ages: olive (*Olea* sp.), emmer wheat (*Triticum dicoccum*), and hulled barley (*Hordeum distichum*) (Helbaek 1958: 309, table 4). Jericho is unique in that it provides floral data from Neolithic through Early Bronze deposits. Hopf (1969: 357) reports that the diversity of cultigens in the Early Bronze Age numbered 15 species, dropping to nine in Early Bronze IV, before climbing back to 16 in Middle Bronze II. The excavations at Tell el-Hayyat produced 151 sediment samples for flotation processing, yielding 852 liters of sediment. Over 8000 carbonized seeds were recovered and identified from Tell el-Hayyat (Fall 1983; Lines 1995). The resulting collection of plant macrofossils includes the predictable staples of olives, hulled barley and emmer wheat, with lesser amounts of other cereals and legumes. Mixed dry farming is inferred from these cultigens, as well as by the presence of crop-following weeds, such as *Chenopodium* and *Amaranthus*.

The floral remains recovered from Tell el-Hayyat by water flotation include four main categories of plants: cultivated cereals, cultivated legumes, fruit-bearing trees and vines, and wild plants (Fall 1983; Lines 1995; Fall et al. 2002) (Figure 5.8). The cultivated plant assemblage at Tell el-Hayyat is dominated by domesticated cereals. Wheat is represented by three species, einkorn (*Triticum monococum*), emmer (*Triticum dicoccum*) and bread wheat (*Triticum aestivum*). Substantial quantities of hulled two-row barley (*Hordeum distichum*), and hulled (*Hordeum vulgare*) and naked six-row varieties (*Hordeum vulgare* var. *nudum*) also are present. Other cultivated cereals include oat (*Avena sativa*) and rye

Figure 5.8 Pat Fall recovering seeds from Tell el-Hayyat by water flotation (photo by Steve Falconer).

(*Secale cereale*). Wild cereals (e.g., *Phalaris* sp. and *Bromus* sp.) are relatively common at Hayyat. Cereal grains were the main staple food and could have been ground and baked as bread or cooked as porridge.

Cultivated legumes are less common than cultivated cereals in the carbonized seed assemblage from Tell el-Hayyat. The most common cultivated legumes are lentil (*Lens culinaris*), bitter vetch (*Vicia ervilla*), and garden pea (*Pisum sativum*). Other cultivated legumes include chick pea (*Cicer arietinum*), grass pea (*Lathyrus sativus*) and fava bean (*Vicia faba*). Wild legumes (e.g., *Medicago* sp.) are relatively common at Tell el-Hayyat. Legume cultivation supplemented the cereals, as it has since the advent of mixed agriculture. These pulses could be cooked and eaten whole, or ground into meal and combined with grains or other legumes in soups or cakes (Zohary 1982: 82-84).

The Bronze Age initiated the intensification of agriculture and the cultivation and exchange of fruits and fruit products. Tell el-Hayyat's fruit assemblages primarily feature olives (*Olea europaea*), figs (*Ficus carica*) and grapes (*Vitus vinifera*). Other orchard species that are occasionally found in Levantine flotation samples, date palm, pomegranate and pistachio seeds, are notably absent from Tell el-Hayyat. Olive was a particularly prominent fruit, which rapidly became a widely traded commodity, especially when rendered into oil (Stager 1985).

Summarized seed counts associated with major crop categories from Tell el-Hayyat are presented in Table 5.1 (detailed floral data are found in Appendices E-G). Orchard crops (i.e., grape, fig and olive) comprise 17% of the carbonized plant remains from Tell el-Hayyat. Cultivated cereals (e.g., wheat and barley) account for roughly one-third of the carbonized seeds; cultivated legumes make up less than five percent of the overall seed assemblage. Wild plants are exceptionally abundant, comprising almost one-half of the carbonized seeds recovered from Tell el-Hayyat. Seeds from wild plants include weedy species from the following genera: *Chenopodium, Rumex, Polygonum, Malva, Plantago, Amaranthus* and *Galium*. All of these plants can be found in agricultural fields and along paths and waterways. *Rumex/Polgonum, Galium* and *Malva* are the most common weed plants found in samples from Tell el-Hayyat. The carbonized seeds of *Prosopis*, a wild leguminous species, are common in the seed assemblage.

Floral data from Tell el-Hayyat are presented as seed counts and percentages (Table 5.1), and as density ratios, expressed as the total number of seeds per kiloliter of sediment (Table 5.2; and see discussion in Chapter 2). Density ratios are used for temporal comparisons of seed volumes between phases of occupation at Tell el-Hayyat. Species of wheat and barely dominate the cultivated plants recovered from Tell el-Hayyat, while cultivated legumes are relatively uncommon. Wild cereals, wild legumes, and weeds abound in the samples from Hayyat and further indicate the close proximity of cultivated land to the village. Large quantities of carbonized fruit seeds illustrate the importance of orchard cultivation for this ancient village. Grape vines, and olive and fig trees, most likely were grown at higher elevations a few kilometers away on either side of the Rift Valley, as they are today. Cereals and legumes require the planting of mature seeds, but may not entail intensive maintenance before producing a harvest of new seeds within several months.

Table 5.1 Seeds identified from Tell el-Hayyat; summarized by crop categories; data presented as numbers of seeds (and % of total seeds)

Taxa	Common Name	Seed Count (% total)
Orchard crops		
Vitis vinifera	grape	26
Olea europaea	olive	121
Ficus carica	fig	1194
Subtotal		**1341 (17%)**
Cultivated cereals		
Triticum	wheat	765
Hordeum	barley	1108
Avena	oat	233
Secale	rye	355
Subtotal		**2461 (30%)**
Cultivated legumes		
Lens culinaris	lentil	117
Pisum sativum	garden pea	63
Cicer arietinum	chick pea	19
Vicia faba	fava bean	12
Lathyrus sativus/ V. ervilla	grass pea/ bitter vetch	124
Subtotal		**318 (4%)**
Wild species*		
Poaceae family	wild cereals	447
Papillionaceae family	wild legumes	549
Prosopis	Prosopis	172
Weed species	Weeds	2793
Subtotal		**3961 (49%)**
Total		**8081**

*See Appendix G for full list of wild species identified.

Table 5.2 Floral taxa recovered from Tell el-Hayyat presented as seed densities (number of seeds per kiloliter of sediment); summarized by crop categories

Species	Common Name	Seed Density
Orchard crops		
Vitis vinifera	Grape	31
Olea europaea	Olive	142
Ficus carica	Fig	1401
Subtotal		**1574**
Cultivated cereals		
Triticum	Wheat	898
Hordeum	Barley	1300
Avena	Oat	273
Secale	Rye	417
Subtotal		**2888**
Cultivated legumes		
Lens culinaris	Lentil	137
Pisum sativum	garden pea	74
Cicer arietinum	chick pea	22
Vicia faba	fava bean	14
Lathyrus sativus/ V. ervilla	grass pea/ bitter vetch	146
Subtotal		**373**
Wild species*		
Poaceae family	wild cereals	525
Papillionaceae family	wild legumes	644
Prosopis	Prosopis	202
Weed species	Weeds	3278
Subtotal		**4649**
Total Seed Density (seeds/ kiloliter)		**9484**

*See Appendix G for full list of wild species identified.

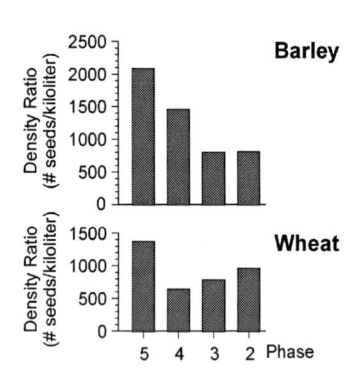

Figure 5.9 Density ratios of wheat and barley by phase at Tell el-Hayyat (drafting by Barbara Trapido-Lurie).

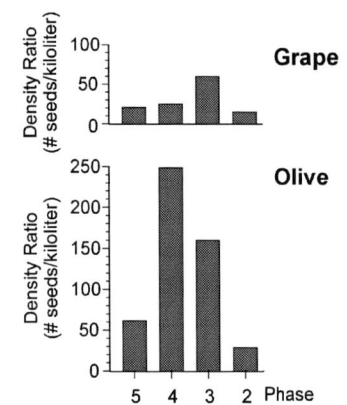

Figure 5.10 Density ratios of olive and grape seeds by phase at Tell el-Hayyat (drafting by Barbara Trapido-Lurie).

Thus, the cultivation of annual crops permits discontinuous seasonal cultivation by mobile populations (Zohary and Hopf 1988; LaBianca 1990). In contrast, the cultivation of fruit trees requires more continuous horticultural management and a shift from sexual (i.e., involving seeds) to vegetative reproduction (Liphschitz et al. 1991).

A brief summary of the evidence from Tell el-Hayyat shows that consumption of barley, the most common cultivated plant, declined through the occupation of the site (Figure 5.9). While wheat consumption fluctuated over time, the most noteworthy trend is an increase from Phase 4 through Phase 2, due largely to rising deposition of bread wheat, a potentially marketable commodity. Similarly, olive density ratios are highest in Phases 4 and 3, in concert with increases in market opportunities during the Middle Bronze Age (Figure 5.10). The floral data clearly reflect sedentary farming strategies at Tell el-Hayyat, with a growing emphasis on crops with greater market potential, which are detailed further in chapters 6, 7 and 8. The two major horticultural shifts, in which bread wheat became more dominant among cereals, and fruit cultivation grew to be dominated by olive, are most accentuated within the Middle Bronze Age.

FAUNAL REMAINS FROM TELL EL-HAYYAT

The animal husbandry regime of the Bronze Age Levant illustrates dependence upon domesticated sheep, goats, cattle and pigs. By this era, wild fauna supplemented human subsistence rather than underpinned it, as had been true in the early Neolithic. Bronze Age archaeological sites in the Levantine hill country, the Jordan Valley and southern Israel demonstrate a focus on sheep and goat management complemented by pig and cattle husbandry in varying levels of intensity. The animal economy at Arad revolved around ovicaprid husbandry with concern for meat and dairy yields, and apparently less focus on wool (Lernau 1975; 1978; Davis 1976). Pastoralists at Middle Bronze Tell Jemmeh pursued a management strategy focused on dairy production (Wapnish and Hesse 1984). The inhabitants of the coastal village at Nahal Alexander exploited sheep and goats, but also maintained a relatively large cohort of cattle and pigs (Dar 1977). Faunal remains at Middle Bronze Jericho illustrate a self-sufficient animal economy based on the four primary regional domesticates (Clutton-Brock 1979). The assemblage at the inland site of Tell Aphek suggests an emphasis on secondary products from sheep and goats (Hellwing and Gophna 1984). Ovicaprid-centered husbandry is evidenced at Bab edh-Dhra' (Finnegan 1977; 1981) and Zahrat adh-Dhra' (Edwards et al. 2001), both located on the Dead Sea plain in southern Jordan. In the moister central Jordan Valley at the site of Tell abu en-Ni'aj, pig raising had a significant role alongside sheep and goat herding (Falconer et al. 2004).

The faunal remains recovered during the three field seasons at Tell el-Hayyat numbered about 95,000 bones and bone fragments. Approximately 27,500 of the bones could be assigned into rough categories by size and type. The number of identifiable specimens (NISP) totaled 12,650. The faunal remains identified are listed in Table 5.3. All specimens were identified alongside remains from comparative collections. Wim Van Neer of the Royal Museum of Central Africa in Tervuren, Belgium, identified the Hayyat fish remains. Shells were identified by David Reese with reference to his own collections. All other reference specimens are curated at the Smithsonian Museum of Natural History in Washington, D.C. and the Field Museum in Chicago. All bones were retrieved from excavated soil that was dry-screened. Bones were washed, and received preliminary sorting in the Hayyat field laboratory (Figure 5.11). Bone measurements follow the conventions established by von den Driesch (1976). Bones identifiable in the NISP total were shipped to the United States for detailed analysis. The cataloged bones are stored at Arizona State University.

Table 5.3 Animal taxa from Tell el-Hayyat presented as number of identified specimens (NISP)

Species	Common Name	NISP
Domesticates		
Equus sp.	horse and/or ass	4
Bos taurus	Cow	1566
Ovis/Capra	Sheep/goat	8649
including		
Ovis aries	sheep	544
Capra hircus	goat	505
Sus scrofa domesticus	pig	2129
Canis sp.	domestic/ wild canid	10
Subtotal (domesticates)		**12,358**
Wild species		
Hemiechinus auritus	long-eared hedgehog	2
Gerbillus sp.	gerbil	2
Meriones sp.	jird	5
Meriones libycus	Libyan jird	1
Meriones crassus	Sundevall's jird	1
Mus musculus	house mouse	8
Spalax ehrenbergi	Palestine mole rat	8
Rattus rattus	black rat	1
Gazella sp.	gazelle	2
Vulpes vulpes	red fox	13
Meles meles	Eurasian badger	20
Mustela nivalis	common weasel	2
Felis silvestris	wild cat	1
Herpestes ichneumon	African mongoose	1
Fish		
Clarias gariepinus	North African catfish	1
Clarias sp.	labyrinth catfishes	1
Clariidae indet.	labyrinth catfishes	26
Barbus canis	Barb	8
Barbus esocinus	mangar	6
Barbus sp.	barbels	6
Cyprinidae indet.	minnows	7
Birds		
Aquila chrysaetos	golden eagle	1
B. buteo vulpinus	steppe buzzard	4
Coturnix coturnix	quail	12
Francolinus francolinus	black francolin	1
Alectoris chukar	chukar partridge	1
Ammoperdix heyi	sand partridge	2
Columba palumbus	wood pigeon	4
Columba livia	rock dove	8
Streptophilia decaocto	collared dove	2
Anus platyrhyncos	mallard	8
Rallus aquaticus	water rail	2
Gallinule chloropus	moorhen	1
Crex crex	corncrake	1
Larus ribidundus	black-headed gull	1
Anthus similes	long-billed pipit	1
Athena noctua	little owl	1
Oenanthe lugens	mourning wheatear	1
Tyrdoides sqamiceps	brown (Arabian) babbler	1
Galerida cristata	crested lark	1
Passer hispaniolensis	Spanish sparrow	1
Carduelis chloris	greenfinch	1
Molluscs		
Melanopsis sp.	freshwater snail	56
Unio sp.	freshwater snail	44
Glycymeris	dog cockle (marine)	3
Semicassis saburon	helmet shell	1
Murex brandaris	murex	1
Subtotal (wild)		292
Total		12,650

Figure 5.11 Mary Metzger at the Deir 'Alla dighouse with pots from Deir 'Alla on the top three shelves and bones from Tell el-Hayyat on the bottom two shelves, 1985 (photo by Jon Kline).

Domestic Animals

Over 97% of the bones recovered at Tell el-Hayyat represent domestic animals. Most of these remains were recovered from Phases 5-2. The largest component of the domestic assemblage belongs to ovicaprids. Pig bones and cattle bones follow in frequency, in that order. One of the four equid bones postdates the abandonment of the site.

Table 5.4 presents the distribution of domesticate bones, according to NISP, excluding equids, by phase. Phase 0 represents evidence that either postdates the abandonment of the site or was compromised by rodent burrowing.

The majority of domesticate bones correlate with Phases 3, 4 and 5. Sheep and goat bones are most numerous in Phase 4, and in all phases are more numerous than bones of pigs or cattle (Figure 5.12). Among the bones in the sheep/goat assemblage, just over 1,000 could be attributed specifically to either sheep or goat. The totals for Phase 4 are nearly equal. Goat bones are more frequent than sheep bones for Phase 5 and less frequent in Phases 3 and 2. Most of the cattle bones belong to Phase 5, in which cattle bones outnumber pig bones. In Phases 4 and 3 this pattern is reversed. The apparent trend may indicate that cattle were chiefly used for draft purposes and that fewer animals needed to be maintained, relative to the pig and ovicaprid populations.

Table 5.4 Bone counts (n = NISP) and relative frequencies (%) of domesticated animal taxa at Tell el-Hayyat, Phases 0-6

Phase	Sheep/Goat n (%)	Sheep n	Goat n	Pig n (%)	Cattle n (%)	Total n
0	72 (32.6)	0	0	121 (54.8)	28 (12.7)	221
1	23 (74.2)	0	0	5 (16.1)	3 (9.7)	31
2	527 (78.9)	50	32	70 (10.5)	71 (10.6)	668
3	2264 (69.6)	181	77	763 (23.5)	224 (6.9)	3251
4	3036 (70.7)	191	205	742 (17.3)	514 (12.0)	4292
5	2700 (71.8)	122	191	414 (11.0)	645 (17.2)	3759
6	26 (44.8)	1	1	11 (19.0)	21 (36.2)	58

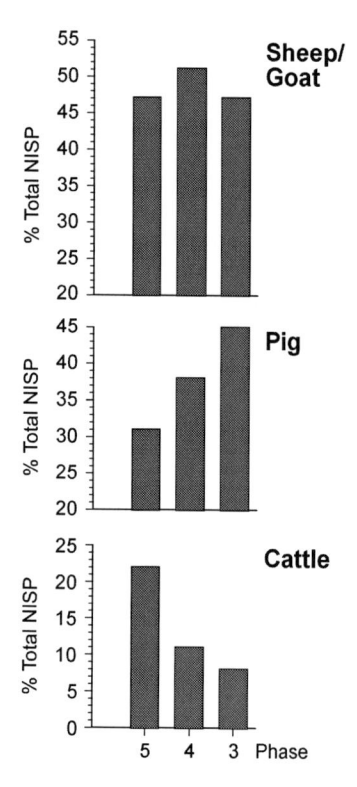

Figure 5.12 Relative frequencies of domestic animal bones by phase at Tell el-Hayyat (data based on NISP; drafting by Barbara Trapido-Lurie).

Table 5.5 Bone counts (n = NISP) and relative frequencies (%) of sheep/goat, pig and cattle at Tell el-Hayyat by excavation area

Excavation Area	Sheep/Goat n (%)	Pig n (%)	Cattle n (%)
A	396 (4.6)	208 (9.8)	154 (10.2)
B	145 (10.7)	96 (4.5)	52 (3.5)
C	172 (2.0)	127 (6.0)	92 (6.1)
D	140 (1.6)	59 (2.8)	28 (1.9)
E	190 (2.2)	214 (10.1)	42 (2.8)
F	148 (1.7)	67 (3.2)	31 (2.1)
G	113 (1.3)	75 (3.5)	27 (1.8)
H	323 (3.7)	180 (8.5)	68 (4.5)
I	156 (1.8)	105 (4.9)	36 (2.4)
J	384 (4.4)	176 (8.3)	88 (5.8)
K	139 (1.6)	53 (2.5)	19 (1.3)
L	439 (5.1)	151 (7.1)	128 (8.4)
M	583 (6.7)	45 (2.1)	78 (5.2)
N	675 (7.8)	30 (1.4)	97 (6.4)
P	1691 (19.6)	26 (1.2)	114 (7.6)
Q	1299 (15.0)	59 (2.8)	170 (11.3)
R	986 (11.4)	64 (3.0)	171 (11.4)
S	462 (5.3)	254 (11.9)	65 (4.3)
T	189 (2.2)	132 (6.2)	45 (3.0)
U	18 (0.2)	5 (0.1)	1 (0.1)

Table 5.5 illustrates the distribution of domesticate bones by excavation area. Sheep and goat bones are most numerous in areas identified with the temples, particularly Areas P, Q and R. The distribution of pig bones at Tell el-Hayyat is skewed in favor of areas at the perimeter of the site, particularly areas A, E, H, S and T. Pig bones were far less abundant in areas associated with the temple precinct. This pattern does not hold for the cattle bones. Cattle bones are most frequent around the village perimeter and temples, especially in areas A, Q, and R. Estimates of minimum numbers of individuals by phase are illustrated in Table 5.6. Ovicaprid remains predominate in all phases, while pig remains generally out number cattle bones.

The villagers at ancient Tell el-Hayyat depended upon their flocks and herds for meat, as well as for secondary products such as hair, wool, dairy products, and draft labor (Figures 5.13 and 5.14). Slaughter schedules can be gauged using tooth eruption and wear, and bone fusion. Tooth eruption sequences are based on Silver (1969). The tooth wear findings are based on models presented by Payne (1973) and Crabtree (n.d.) for sheep and goats, and Grant (1982) for pigs and cattle. Adaptations of the Grant models for pigs are taken from Hambleton (2001). Bone fusion guidelines are derived from data presented in Silver (1969).

Tooth wear data for sheep/goat (Table 5.7) suggest that in Phases 5 and 4, the villagers optimized meat production with a secondary emphasis on dairying. Payne (1973) suggests that meat production is maximized when most young males are killed as they reach optimum weight at about age two. In these two phases, somewhat less than half of the combined sheep/goat herd survived past the animals' second year. Sheep and goat milk destined for human use is maximized by killing lambs when they are several months old. Balasse's study (2003) suggests that milk let-down, which must be stimulated in cattle by the presence of a calf, is not imperative for milk production in sheep and goats. Therefore, the villagers were not risking a catastrophic loss of milk production by slaughtering surplus animals at less than one year of age.

Table 5.6 Domesticated animal taxa at Tell el-Hayyat presented as minimum number of individuals (MNI), Phases 2-5

Bone Element	Phase 2			Phase 3			Phase 4			Phase 5		
	o/c	pig	cattle	o/c	pig	cattle	o/c	pig	cattle	o/c	pig	cattle
Atlas	3	0	0	13	7	2	15	16	0	13	7	5
Axis	4	0	0	8	2	0	11	4	4	17	0	6
L. mandible	10	1	1	37	16	1	48	14	1	39	15	2
R. mandible	13	0	1	30	29	0	35	21	2	36	8	3
L. distal humerus	7	2	0	18	6	3	23	3	3	33	3	8
R. distal humerus	6	1	0	21	5	4	34	7	4	30	4	8
L. distal tibia	4	1	0	14	1	0	9	5	2	4	0	2
R. distal tibia	0	0	2	10	1	2	8	5	0	8	0	3
L. astragalus	4	0	2	17	3	5	28	7	3	16	0	4
R. astragalus	13	0	1	17	4	3	43	5	2	20	1	3
Total	64	5	7	185	74	20	254	87	21	216	38	44

Figure 5.13 The goat (*Capra hircus*) was a major source of meat and dairy products at Tell el-Hayyat, and became favored for ritual consumption associated with Hayyat's temples (photo by Mary Metzger).

Figure 5.14 Sheep (*Ovis aries*) management became accentuated at Tell el-Hayyat, reflecting increased production of wool, one of the major trade commodities of the secondary products revolution. View from the top of Tell Abu en-Ni'aj[N], 1985, facing southeast (photo by Karen Scholz).

Table 5.7 Sheep/Goat survivorship (% survival) at Tell el-Hayyat based on tooth wear, Phases 2-5

Stage	Age (mo.)	Phase 2 (n=95)	Phase 3 (n=554)	Phase 4 (n=657)	Phase 5 (n=598)
A	3	99	99.6	99.6	99.3
B	6	96.4	97.1	96.8	96.5
C	12	83.4	78.8	74.1	72.5
D	24	62.6	55.4	46.9	43.4
E	36	43.8	38.5	29.3	25.6
F	48	29.7	19	14.2	12.6
G	72	12.2	7.9	4.0	4.3
H	96	.8	1.2	.9	1.1
I	120	0	0	0	.1

The survivorship curve based on tooth wear moderated somewhat in Phase 3 and did so noticeably in Phase 2, when more than half of the combined herd survived to two years of age. Tooth wear data must be compared to survivorship patterns based on bone fusion. Bones fuse according to predictable schedules, although correlating ancient fusion rates with data assembled over the past century presents some inconsistencies (Reitz and Wing 1999). Table 5.8 displays the sheep/goat fusion data. The fused percentages are a rough estimate of herd survivorship at various ages (Table 5.8). The moderated survivorship curve in Phase 2 may reflect increased production of wool, obtained from post-mature animals.

Table 5.9 supplies data from which to estimate bone fusion at logical break points. These points include, for example, the slaughter of young animals, particularly males, at about one year to facilitate milk and meat production, and the slaughter of surplus two-year olds to reduce grazing pressure (Redding 2003).

The bone fusion grouping estimates offer close correlations with data for tooth wear for Phases 3 and 2.

However, the bone fusion groupings show lower survivorship rates for two year-olds in Phases 5 and 4. Bone fusion evidence, however, is dependent upon the survival of bones post-slaughter. Most importantly, bones which do not fuse early do not survive post-depositional processes as well as those which fuse later. This is particularly true for long bones. Therefore, the implication that sheep/goat survivorship was steep during the earlier phases of the site may reflect reduced preservation of bones that fuse after one year.

Pig slaughter schedules have fewer variations than those for sheep and goats, since meat is the primary product. Table 5.10 illustrates survivorship schedules based on tooth eruption and wear. These data are adapted for mandibles and individual teeth from Grant (1982) and Hambleton (2001), who provide mandible age models. The ancient villagers slaughtered sucklings at less than one year and slaughtered animals reaching optimum weight gain early in the second year. In general, the data suggest that most pigs did not live past age three (Figure 5.15).

Pig slaughter strategies also can be evaluated from bone fusion data (Table 5.11). As was provided for the sheep/goat cohort, the pig fusion tables first present data by individual bone maturation points and then by fusion groupings (Table 5.12). The bone fusion data point to a consistent kill-off of animals in the first two years. As with sheep/goat bones, however, the lower archaeological survival rate of late-fusing bones enhances the attrition picture.

Cattle survivorship is gauged from tooth eruption and wear (Table 5.13), and bone fusion (Table 5.14). The tooth data are adapted from Grant (1982). Most of the teeth show light to moderate wear. Teeth come into wear

Table 5.8 Sheep/Goat survivorship at Tell el-Hayyat based on bone fusion, Phases 2-5

Element	Fusion Range (mo.)	Phase 2 n=131 Not fused	Fused # (%)	Total	3 n=440 Not fused	Fused # (%)	Total	4 n=712 Not fused	Fused # (%)	Total	5 n=643 Not fused	Fused # (%)	Total
Pelvis	6-10	4	12 (75)	16	22	25 (53)	47	46	24 (34)	70	54	22 (28)	76
Scapula	6-8	3	4 (57)	7	6	38 (86)	44	20	21 (51)	41	19	20 (51)	39
D. humerus	10	8	13 (62)	21	13	34 (72)	47	21	46 (68)	67	18	50 (73)	68
P. radius	10	1	9 (90)	10	2	37 (95)	39	6	34 (85)	40	7	29 (80)	36
P. Phalange 1	13-16	3	12 (80)	15	19	35 (65)	54	70	47 (40)	117	73	45 (38)	118
P. Phalange 2	13-16	4	12 (75)	16	6	29 (57)	35	50	45 (47)	95	47	31 (40)	78
D. tibia	18-24	2	3 (60)	5	15	24 (62)	39	36	13 (20)	49	34	9 (21)	43
D. metacarpal	18-24	0	1 (100)	1	9	11 (55)	20	12	3 (20)	15	3	4 (57)	7
D. metatarsal	20-28	2	4 (66)	6	14	2 (12.5)	16	13	1 (7)	14	9	3 (25)	12
P. ulna	30	4	0 (0)	4	5	2 (29)	7	18	1 (5)	19	17	2 (11)	19
Calcaneus	30-36	4	3 (42)	7	17	9 (34)	26	54	10 (15.6)	64	48	7 (12)	55
P. femur	30-36	5	0 (0)	5	16	10 (38)	26	37	6 (14)	43	39	5 (11)	44
D. radius	36	6	3 (33)	9	9	3 (25)	12	18	2 (10)	20	25	2 (7)	27
P. humerus	36-42	0	0 (0)	0	4	1 (20)	5	7	1 (12.5)	8	4	0 (0)	4
D. femur	36-42	6	0 (0)	6	12	2 (14)	14	25	9 (26)	34	13	2 (13)	15
P. tibia	36-42	2	0 (0)	2	12	3 (20)	15	15	1 (6.25)	16	18	1 (5)	19

*Based on Silver 1969; "D" refers to distal and "P" proximal.

Table 5.9 Sheep/Goat survivorship at Tell el-Hayyat based on bone fusion groupings (% fused), Phases 2-5

Fusion Range Element	Fusion (mo.)*	Phase 2 %	3 %	4 %	5 %
Age 6-10 mo.					
Pelvis	6-10				
Scapula	6-8				
D. umerus	10				
P. radius	10	70.4	75.7	57.3	55
Age 13-16 mo.					
P. phalange 1	13-16				
P. phalange 2	13-16	77.4	72	43.4	38.8
Age 18-28 mo.					
D. tibia	18-24				
D. metacarpal	18-24				
D. metatarsal	20-28	66.7	49	21.8	25.8
Age 30-36 mo.					
P. ulna	30				
Calcaneus	30-36				
P. femur	30-36	18.8	35.6	13.5	20.3
Age 36-42 mo.					
D. radius	36				
P. humerus	36-42				
D. femur	36-42				
P. tibia	36-42	17.6	19.6	16.7	7.6

*Based on Silver 1969; "D" refers to distal and "P" proximal.

Table 5.10 Pig survivorship at Tell el-Hayyat based on tooth eruption and wear, Phases 2-5

Eruption Stage (mo.)	No.	V	Erupted, unworn	In Wear	In wear (%)
Phase 2 (n= 5)					
2-3	2	0	0	2	100
4-6	0	0	0	0	N/A
7-13	1	0	1	0	0
12-16	1	0	0	1	100
17-22	1	0	0	1	100
Phase 3 (n= 69)					
2-3	5	0	0	5	100
4-6	20	0	6	24	100
7-13	20	0	3	17	85
12-16	17	6	3	8	47
17-22	7	2	2	3	50
Phase 4 (n = 78)					
2-3	1	0	0	1	100
4-6	39	2	3	34	87
7-13	17	1	4	12	70
12-16	5	1	1	3	60
17-22	16	2	5	9	56
Phase 5 (n = 71)					
2-3	6	0	0	6	100
4-6	30	0	4	26	86.7
7-13	14	0	4	10	71
12-16	13	2	1	10	77
17-22	8	2	1	5	62

"V" indicates unerupted teeth in mandible or maxilla

Table 5.11 Pig survivorship at Tell el-Hayyat based on bone fusion, Phases 2-5

Element	Fusion Range (mo.)	Phase 2 (n = 13) Not fused	Fused # (%)	Total	Phase 3 (n = 109) Not fused	Fused # (%)	Total	Phase 4 (n = 117) Not fused	Fused # (%)	Total	Phase 5 (n = 41) Not fused	Fused # (%)	Total
Pelvis	12	1	0 (0)	1	18	10 (35.7)	28	13	8 (38)	21	3	0 (0)	3
Scapula	12	0	0 (0)	0	0	2 (100)	2	8	7 (46.7)	15	1	1 (50)	2
D. humerus	12	0	2 (100)	2	4	10 (71.4)	14	5	6 (54.5)	11	1	6 (85.7)	7
P. radius	12	1	0 (0)	1	2	6 (75)	8	3	6 (66.7)	9	0	2 (100)	2
P. phalange 2	12	0	0 (0)	0	2	6 (75)	8	2	10 (83.3)	12	3	3 (50)	6
P. phalange 1	24	3	0 (0)	3	4	5 (55.6)	9	5	2 (28.6)	7	3	0 (0)	3
D. tibia	24	1	0 (0)	1	1	2 (66.7)	3	8	0 (0)	8	2	3 (60)	5
D. metacarpal	24	1	0 (0)	1	11	1 (8.3)	12	9	0 (0)	9	1	2 (66.7)	3
D. metatarsal	26	1	1 (50)	2	4	2 (33.3)	6	4	1 (20)	5	1	0 (0)	1
Calcaneus	24-30	1	0 (0)	1	3	1 (25)	4	5	0 (0)	5	1	0 (0)	1
Ulna	36-42	0	0 (0)	0	6	1 (14.3)	7	7	3 (30)	10	4	0 (0)	4
P. humerus	42	0	0 (0)	0	1	0 (0)	1	0	0 (0)	0	0	0 (0)	0
D. radius	42	1	0 (0)	1	1	0 (0)	1	1	0 (0)	1	0	0 (0)	0
P. femur	42	0	0 (0)	0	1	0 (0)	1	0	0 (0)	0	1	0 (0)	1
D. femur	42	0	0 (0)	0	1	0 (0)	1	2	0 (0)	2	2	0 (0)	2
P. tibia	42	0	0 (0)	0	4	0 (0)	4	2	0 (0)	2	1	0 (0)	1

*Based on Silver 1969; "D" refers to distal and "P" proximal.

many weeks after first erupting. For example, a heavily worn third molar, a fourth premolar, and often a third premolar, are indicative of an animal well into its fourth year of age. Comparatively few teeth in the Hayyat cattle assemblage show this attrition (Figure 5.16).

Cattle survivorship based on fusion suggests kill-off of surplus immature animals in their third year (Table 5.15). A minority of mature animals (age four) were maintained for dairying and labor.

Table 5.12 Pig survivorship at Tell el-Hayyat based on bone fusion groupings (% fused), Phases 2-5

Phase Fusion Range Element	Fusion (mo.)*	2 (n=13) %	3 (n=109) %	4 (n=117) %	5 (n=41) %
Age 12-23mo.					
Pelvis	12				
Scapula	12				
D. humerus	12				
P. radius	12				
P. phalange 2	12	50	56.7	54.4	60
Age 24-35mo.					
P. phalange 1	24				
D. tibia	24				
D. metacarpal	24				
D. metatarsal	26				
Calcaneus	24-30	12.5	32.5	8.9	38.5
Age 36-42mo.					
Ulna	36-42				
P. humerus	42				
D. radius	42				
P. femur	42				
D. femur	42				
P. tibia	42	0	6.6	20	0

*Based on Silver 1969; "D" refers to distal and "P" proximal.

Table 5.13 Cattle survivorship at Tell el-Hayyat based on tooth eruption and wear, Phases 2-5

Teeth	Eruption Stage	No.	V	Erupted, unworn	Light wear	Mod. wear	Post-mature wear
Phase 2 n = 7							
dp4	Birth-3 wks	1	0	0	0	1	0
M1	5-6 mo.	0	0	0	0	0	0
M2	15-18	1	0	1	0	0	0
M1/M2	5-18	2	0	0	1	1	0
M3	24-30	1	0	0	0	1	0
P4	28-36	0	0	0	0	0	0
P3/P4	18-36	2	0	0	0	0	2
Phase 3 n = 30							
dp4	Birth-3 wks	0	0	0	0	0	0
M1	5-6 mo.	1	0	0	1	0	0
M2	15-18	3	0	0	1	2	0
M1/M2	5-18	13	0	0	4	9	0
M3	24-30	7	0	0	2	5	0
P4	28-36	1	0	0	0	1	0
P3/P4	18-36	5	0	0	0	0	5
Phase 4 n = 83							
dp4	Birth-3 wks	10		1	6	2	1
M1	5-6 mo.	1	0	0	1	0	0
M2	15-18	2	0	0	2	0	0
M1/M2	5-18	52	1	4	26	17	4
M3	24-30	7	0	0	6	1	0
P4	28-36	1	0	0	1	0	0
P3/P4	18-36	11	0	0	04	4	7
Phase 5 n = 76							
dp4	Birth-3 wks	10	0	3	6	1	0
M1	5-6 mo.	0	0	0	0	0	0
M2	15-18	2	0	0	1	1	0
M1/M2	5-18	41	0	3	11	25	2
M3	24-30	10	0	3	5	0	2
P4	28-36	6	0	0	6	0	0
P3/P4	18-36	7	0	0	5	0	2

"V" indicates unerupted teeth in mandible or maxilla

Table 5.14 Cattle survivorship at Tell el-Hayyat based on bone fusion, Phases 2-5

Element	Fusion Range (mo.)*	Phase 2 (n = 17) Not fused	Fused # (%)	Total	Phase 3 (n = 47) Not fused	Fused # (%)	Total	Phase 4 (n = 105) Not fused	Fused # (%)	Total	Phase 5 (n = 141) Not fused	Fused # (%)	Total
Pelvis	7-10	0	1 (100)	1	0	5 (100)	5	2	5 (71)	7	2	11 (85)	13
Scapula	7-10	0	0 (0)	0	1	0 (0)	1	1	3 (75)	4	1	4 (80)	5
D. humerus	12-18	0	0 (0)	0	0	2 (100)	2	0	4 (100)	4	1	8 (89)	9
P. radius	12-18	0	0 (0)	0	0	1 (100)	1	1	8 (89)	9	1	11 (92)	12
P. phalange 1	18	0	5 (100)	5	1	15 (94)	16	13	19 (59)	32	7	10 (59)	17
P. phalange 2	18	0	6 (100)	6	1	8 (89)	9	2	21 (91)	23	1	21 (95)	22
D. tibia	24-30	1	0 (0)	1	2	0 (0)	2	1	2 (67)	3	5	6 (55)	11
D. metacarpal	24-30	0	1 (100)	1	0	2 (100)	2	0	4 (100)	4	1	15 (94)	16
D. metatarsal	27-36	0	0 (0)	0	0	1 (100)	1	0	2 (100)	2	0	3 (100)	3
Calcaneus	36-42	0	0 (0)	0	0	1 (100)	1	3	0 (0)	3	2	0 (0)	2
P. femur	42	0	0 (0)	0	1	1 (50)	2	0	3 (100)	3	2	1 (33)	3
P. humerus	42-48	0	0 (0)	0	0	0 (0)	0	0	0 (0)	0	1	2 (67)	3
D. radius	42-48	1	0 (0)	1	0	1 (100)	1	4	1 (20)	5	5	5 (50)	10
Ulna	42-48	0	0 (0)	0	1	0 (0)	1	1	0 (0)	1	5	1 (17)	6
D. femur	42-48	0	0 (0)	0	1	1 (50)	2	0	3 (100)	3	4	4 (50)	8
P. tibia	42-48	2	0 (0)	2	1	0 (0)	1	2	0 (0)	2	3	1 (25)	4

*Based on Silver 1969; "D" refers to distal and "P" proximal.

Figure 5.15 Evidence for consumption of pig (*Sus scrofa*) illustrates a trend of increased household economic autonomy at Tell el-Hayyat (photo by Will Falconer).

Figure 5.16 The remains of cattle (*Bos taurus*) at Tell el-Hayyat indicate their use as traction animals and their declining importance as sources of beef often associated with urban elites. Cattle in the modern village of Mashara, facing north (photo by Jon Kline).

Table 5.15 Cattle survivorship at Tell el-Hayyat based on bone fusion groupings (% fused), Phases 2-5

Phase		2 (n=17)	3 (n=47)	4 (n=10)	5 (n=141)
Fusion Range Element	Fusion (mo.)	%	%	%	%
Age 7-18 mo.					
Pelvis	7-10				
Scapula	7-10				
D. humerus	12-18				
P. radius	12-18				
P. phalange 1	18				
P. phalange 2	18	100	91	76	78
Age 18-36 mo.					
D. tibia	24-30				
D. metacarpal	24-30				
D. metatarsal	27-36	50	60	89	30
Age 36-42 mo.					
Calcaneus	36-42				
P. femur	42				
P. humerus	42-48				
D. radius	42-48				
Ulna	42-48				
D. femur	42-48				
P. tibia	42-48	0	59	41	39

*Based on Silver 1969; "D" refers to distal and "P" proximal.

Wild Fauna

The wild animals at Tell el-Hayyat are suggestive of the ancient environmental conditions at the site and the extent of human involvement with non-domestic animals. Van Neer (n.d.) has identified all of the fish as freshwater species from the Jordan River. Likewise, nearly all of the shells are freshwater species from the Jordan River (Melanopsis and Unio). Only five Mediterranean marine shells (*Murex [=Bolinus] brandaris, Semicassis [=Phalium, =Cassis] saburon,* and three specimens of *Glycymeris* [dog cockle]) were brought to the site (Reese n.d.). Descriptions of the mammals and birds represented at the site follow.

Insectivores

Hemichinus auritus. The long-eared hedgehog is represented by seven jaw and skull bones that appear to have come from one individual. Common in the Near East, this type of hedgehog occupies an intermediate ecological niche between forest and desert-dwelling species. It is found on both semi-arid and cultivated land (Atallah 1977: 269-270).

Rodents

Meriones libycus and *Meriones crassus.* Two species of jird are represented. Both are commonly found near wadis and cultivated areas in the Near East. Atallah (1978) notes that these jirds eat the stems, leaves, and seeds of nearly every species of shrub within reach. Like the hedgehog, jirds shelter in burrows.

Spalax ehrenbergi. Palestine mole rats are abundant in areas of the Levant with rainfall above the 100 mm isohyet. They construct burrows, both below ground and in mounds above ground. Some of the mole rat bones recovered from Hayyat are probably owl pellet remnants. This attests to their nocturnal surface activity (Bate 1945 and Dor 1947, as cited in Atallah 1978: 20).

Gerbillus sp. Species identification of gerbil remains could not be made. However, a likely comparison lies with Wagner's gerbil, which inhabits many areas in the steppe region (Atallah 1978: 6-7).

Rattus rattus. The black rat is found worldwide. It is often associated with human habitation and contributes crop losses (Nowak 1991: 788-90). The bone representing this species at Hayyat is post-occupational.

Mus musculus. The house mouse is native to much of Eurasia and now is found partly as a commensal species worldwide (Nowak 1991: 858-60).

Ungulates

Gazella sp. This specimen could not be identified to species.

Carnivores

Canis sp. These specimens could represent either wild or domestic canids. Two of the bones are post-occupation.

Felis silvestris. The wild cat occupies a variety of habitats, including forested hills and open country. It eats mainly rodents and other small mammals (Nowak 1991: 1190).

Vulpes vulpes. The red fox is a widespread and successful predator. Its variable diet includes fruits, insects, small mammals, and the refuse from human settlements (Nowak 1991: 1048-50). Two of the specimens at Hayyat are post-occupation.

Meles meles. The Eurasian or Old World badger is found throughout most of the Levant. It prefers wooded areas into which it digs burrow systems. Its omnivorous diet includes reptiles and frogs (Nowak 1991: 1126-27).

Mustela nivalis. The least, or common weasel, is characterized by Nowak as the smallest carnivore. Resident in the Asia Minor region, the weasel subsists primarily on rodents (Nowak 1991: 1104-08).

Herpestes ichneumon. The range of the African mongoose is considerable, extending from most of sub-Saharan Africa northward through the Levant and into Asia Minor. It occupies a wide variety of habitats, from forested hilly areas to arid plains (Nowak 1991: 1164-66).

Birds

Aquila chrysaetos. The golden eagle is a resident species, but Andrews (1995: 68) suggests that it was once much more common than it is today.

B. buteo vulpinus. The steppe buzzard is a spring and autumn migrant through the Jordan Valley (Andrews 1995: 66; Hue and Etchecopar 1970: 159-60).

C. cortunix. The quail is normally a winter migrant to the Jordan Valley (Hue and Etchecopar 1970: 225). Andrews (1995: 75) suggests that they may breed in agricultural areas in northern Jordan.

F. francolinus. The black francolin is a resident and breeding species in the Jordan Valley which prefers dense vegetation (Bakig and Horani 1993: 71; Andrews 1995: 75)

Alectoris chukar. The chukar partridge breeds in Jordan, including the Jordan Valley (Bakig and Horani 1993: 68; Andrews 1995: 74). The bone representing this species postdates the site's occupation.

Ammoperdix heyi. The sand partridge is another common game bird that breeds in Jordan (Andrews 1995: p.75).

Columba palumbus. Hue and Etchecopar (1970: 385) note that the wood pigeon's Near Eastern home range is north of Jordan. It is a migrant to the Jordan Valley.

Columbia livia. The rock dove is a common breeding species in the hills of the Jordan Valley. It is scarce in the Eastern Desert (Andrews 1995: 98).

Streptophilia decaocto. The collared dove is resident in the Jordan Valley, and was more common here in the past (Andrews 1995: 99).

Anas platyrhynchos. The mallard is a winter migrant to the Jordan River valley. The literature debates whether it once lived permanently in the area and bred along the banks of the Jordan River (Andrews 1995: 59; Bakig and Horani 1993: 51).

Rallus aquaticus. The water rail is a passage breeder, but formerly could have been a resident species of the Jordan Valley (Andrews 1995: 76).

Gallinula chloropus. The moorhen is resident in the Jordan Valley (Hue and Etchecopar 1970: 247; Andrews 1995: 77).

C. crex. The corncrake is a spring migrant to the Jordan Valley (Hue and Etchecopar 1970: 244; Andrews 1995: 77).

Larus ribidundus. The black-headed gull can be seen in parts of Jordan year-round, but is a common resident in winter and on spring passage (Andrews 1995: 2; Bakig and Horani 1993: 99).

Anthus similes. The long-billed pipit is a Jordan Valley resident (Andrews 1995: 120; Hue and Etchecopar 1970: 761).

Athena noctua. The little owl is diurnal and a resident throughout Jordan (Andrews 1995: 104; Bakig and Horani 1993: 114). The bone representing this species postdates the site's occupation.

Oenanthe lugens. The mourning wheatear is a year-round resident of the Jordan Valley (Andrews 1995: 130; Hue and Etchecopar 1970: 604).

Tyrdoides sqamiceps. The brown (Arabian) babbler is a characteristic bird of the Jordan Valley (Andrews 1995: 144; Bakig and Horani 1993: 175).

Galerida cristata. The crested lark is a resident breeding bird in Jordan, particularly in the north (Andrews 1995: 116; Bakig and Horani 1993: 131).

Passer hispaniolensis. The Spanish sparrow, common in the Jordan Valley, is associated with human settlements (Andrews 1995: 153).

Carduelis chloris. The greenfinch is a common resident in the northern Jordan Valley, and can be seen in most areas of the Rift (Andrews 1995: 156; Hue and Etchecopar 1970: 818).

The residents of Tell el-Hayyat encountered a wide variety of wild fauna, although wild animals must have comprised only a very small component of their diet. The wild faunal remains are representative of the Irano-Turanian climatic zone, and none of the animals' distributions are suggestive of exclusively forested or desert habitats. A few species, such as the gazelle and golden eagle, have more restricted distributions today than they had in the past.

Conclusions

The evidence from wild faunal remains, coupled with the record of the domestic regime, suggests an environment closely similar to that of today, though deforestation and river-water diversion for modern agriculture have affected water supply. Villagers in the earliest full-occupation of the site (Phase 5) appear to have been more reliant on sheep/goat and cattle than on pigs. Possibly time was needed to establish a watering regime for pigs. Steady reliance on pigs followed. There is also some evidence that in the earliest phase goats were slightly more important in the sheep/goat cohort than sheep. Goats would have offered secondary products such as milk in quantities not provided by sheep, as well as hair for shelters. Thereafter, sheep represented an increasing proportion of the ovicaprid flock, perhaps reflecting the growing mercantile importance of their own secondary product: wool. In general, animal husbandry patterns at Tell el-Hayyat suggest well-maintained herd security and over time, successful production of marketable secondary products.

CHAPTER 6: TEMPLE ECONOMY AND RITUAL AT TELL EL-HAYYAT

INTRODUCTION

In ancient Near Eastern society, temples emerge as the best documented interface between institutional authority and individual communities. Temples served the interests of both in keeping the gods fed, clothed, informed and pleased with human activities (Jacobsen 1975). It was widely understood that only by propitiating the gods through performance of rituals and sacrifices could society at large be assured of peace and prosperity. The knowledge of when, where and how to perform rituals was a source of considerable power on many levels within society (Bell 1992: 120). Therefore, ritual systems may be viewed as a fundamental mechanism by which social relations were constantly renegotiated (Bell 1992: 130). Here we examine temples as the most immediate foci for community ritual behavior, but more importantly as they reflect social relations within the village of Tell el-Hayyat. Tell el-Hayyat is noteworthy as an early rural community with a significant ritual component embodied in a stratified series of four mudbrick Middle Bronze Age temples. Material evidence of ritual activities at Hayyat provides a rural perspective on temple-community relations in the larger context of early urbanization in the Southern Levant.

THE ORGANIZATION OF RITUAL

Ancient texts record many overt secular and sacred functions of Near Eastern religious institutions, but non-literate archaeological evidence reveals more subtle social implications of ritual behavior. Akkadian texts from Hazor (Landsberger and Tadmor 1964; Hallo and Tadmor 1977; Horowitz and Shaffer 1992), Gezer (Shaffer 1970), Shechem (Bohl 1926) and Hebron (Anbar and Na'aman 1986-1987) document the existence of Bronze Age bureaucracies in the southern Levant, but they tell us little of the relations between temples and their communities. The much richer documentary record of ancient Mesopotamia and Syria provides appropriate historical parallels for the southern Levant based on the proximity of the regions, their shared material culture (Dever 1987), and a common body of West Semitic dialects.

The fundamental relationship between temples and their communities is reflected most vividly in Akkadian texts from Mesopotamia (e.g., from the Old Babylonian Period roughly contemporaneous with the Levantine Middle Bronze Age), which refer to a temple as *bitum* or "house." The owner of such a house was a deity, and the house was where that deity could be found (Jacobsen 1976: 16). The sacred nature of the god's house differentiated it from human domiciles. Otherwise, it had much in common with other great households (Gelb 1979): the god owned property and employed a large staff. The staff provided food and drink for the god, bathed the cult image, and dressed it in finery (Jacobsen 1976: 16). Unlike secular households, however, the temple was the site of cult drama, sacrifice, and hymns of praise and lament (Jacobsen 1976: 14-15). From the community's perspective the temple was a divine residence, and thus the locus of sanctified power, but also a source of employment, a bank, and a charity (Renger 1979).

Syrian temples employed terminology, concepts, and rituals similar to those in Mesopotamian temples (Xella 1982), although elements of local Syrian belief and practice also were strong (Margueron 1982). Once again, the temple was referred to as the "house of the god" in which priests fed the deity, washed and clothed its image, and occasionally paraded the image before the population (Dalley 1984: 116). Although Mesopotamian temple institutions often were independent economic entities, archives from ancient Syrian cities portray temples as firmly embedded within state (Mari, Alalah and Ugarit) or community (Emar) economies. The data from Mari and Alalah are contemporary with the Levantine Middle Bronze Age, while those from Ugarit and Emar date to the Late Bronze Age (see Figure 6.1).

State-administered temples were built by royal artisans, staffed by state personnel, and provisioned by state stores. At Mari, for example, the palace archives and private records of the royal diviner and chief priest registered hundreds of withdrawals of animals for the king's table, ritual sacrifices, and acts of divination (Lafont 1984: 232; Charpin 1985: 457-458). Interestingly, all of these animals were obtained from internal palace sources suggesting the economic integration of temple ritual activity within the palace economy. Close association between royal and temple economies also is apparent in the rationing of priests by the royal administration at Alalah (Klengel 1979: 448-49) and Ugarit (Heltzer 1982: 135; Lipinski 1988). At Alalah, this dependence was reinforced by the physical incorporation of the temple into Alalah's palace in the Late Bronze Age. Although state temples tended to be urban phenomena linked to central seats of authority, the presence of a temple in the countryside is implied by a text from Ugarit in which the king ordered timbers for the repair of a village sanctuary (KTU 2.26).

Textual accounts of community-supported temples are limited to fewer and more laconic sources. In one instance, a king of Mari scheduled a trip that included stops at local shrines to pay homage to the resident gods. Before leaving the capital city, the king sent messages to the village leaders assuring them that in the course of his

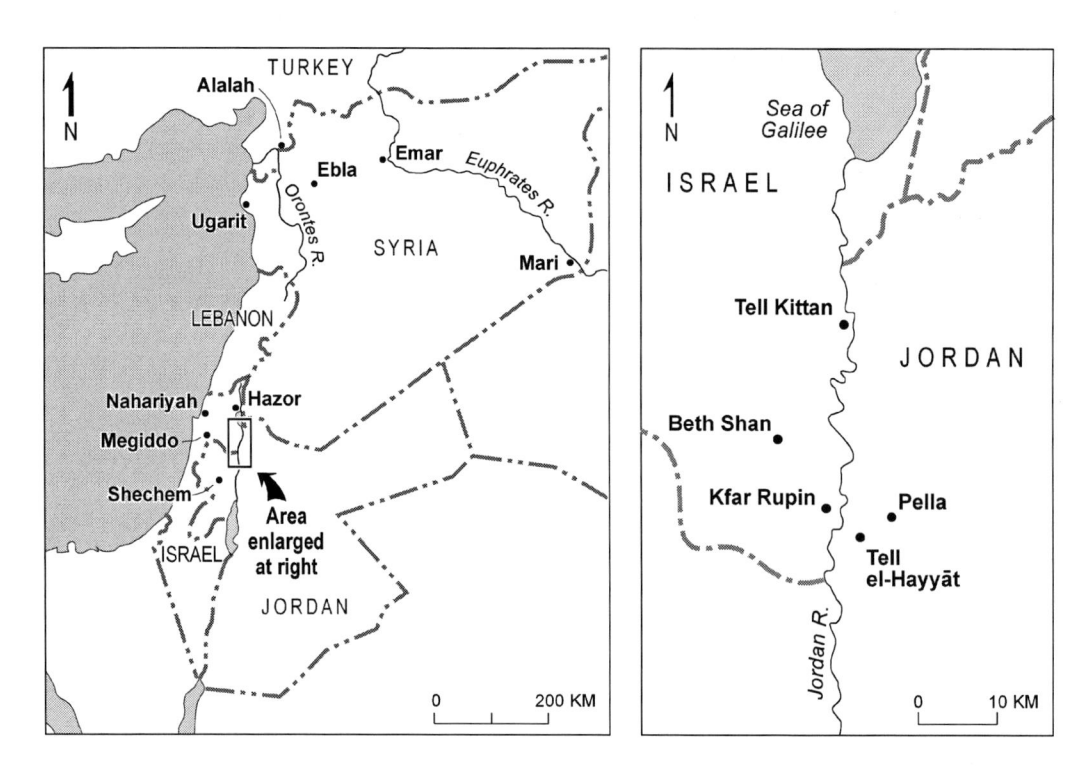

Figure 6.1 Regional map of Syria and the southern Levant showing locations of archaeological sites with temples mentioned in text (drafting by Barbara Trapido-Lurie).

visit he would not usurp their authority (Matthews 1978: 153). On another occasion, a local tribe petitioned the king at Mari for the return of its "gods" so that proper sacrifices could be made in the village (Matthews 1978: 154; ARM XIV 8). The ritual responsibilities of village leaders implied in these letters suggests that shrines and temples located in rural settlements were largely autonomous. The same situation is implied for a more metropolitan setting by the archive from Temple M1 at Emar (Margueron 1993). In this city, the citizenry supplied women to be priestesses and most materials for ritual observances. Palace authorities had little control over temple affairs, although palace officials played a part in some rituals (Fleming 1992: 103-104).

Ancient Near Eastern ritual was far from a uniform expression of the social relations between temples and communities. In some cases, particularly in capital cities, temples reflect extreme intimacy between institutions of secular and religious authority. Elsewhere, including some noteworthy urban cases, temples provide a material expression of communal economic and ritual organization. Perhaps the key to understanding the social significance of ritual lies in clarifying the nature of non-elite access to temples and priests, and participation in sanctified activities.

TEMPLES AND RITUAL BEHAVIOR

Ritual texts (Matthews 1978; Badre 1980) describe a variety of religious beliefs and their implementation through ritual activities. For example, accession rituals legitimized the installment of officials, from kings to priestesses (AT 1; Fleming 1992). Calendric rituals were celebrated with regularly scheduled feasts, sacrifices and processions (de Tarragon 1980: 120-26, 133; Dalley 1984: 133; Fleming 1992: 236-48). Ancestor worship featured ritual meals and the raising of memorial *stelae* (Graesser 1972: 39-41; Talon 1978; Levine and de Tarragon 1984). Although texts suggest that ritual procedures were shared across society, such documents carry inherent elite and institutional biases. The challenge of inferring ritual practice and its social implications for non-elite populations falls primarily to archaeological interpretation.

We pose two broad questions in examining archaeological evidence of rural ritual, as exemplified at Tell el-Hayyat: 1) how does ritual reflect social and economic relations in rural society, and 2) to what extent do village temples symbolize urban social and economic intervention in the countryside or the autonomy of rural communities? Perhaps most fundamentally, the social relations represented by ritual behavior at Tell el-Hayyat may be assessed according to the congruences or disjunctions between temple and domestic deposition of faunal, floral, ceramic and other remains. The time depth of temple and domestic evidence from Hayyat also reveals changes in ritual activities that may parallel or diverge from other trends in society.

Temple architecture provides the sanctified setting for ritual observances, while its form, size, decoration and construction materials also symbolize the wealth, power

TEMPLE ECONOMY AND RITUAL AT TELL EL-HAYYAT

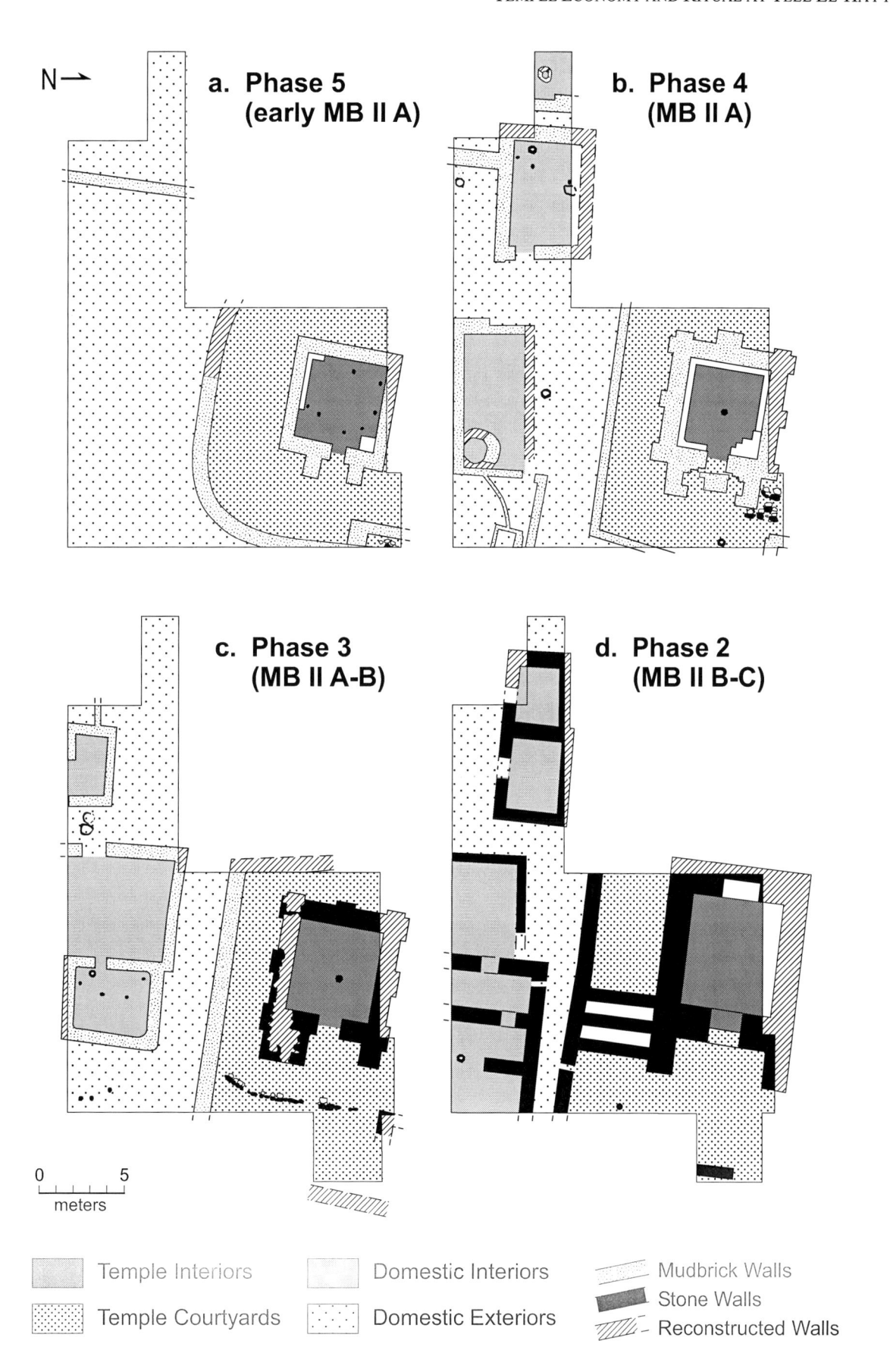

Figure 6.2 Plan view of Middle Bronze Age temple and domestic architecture at Tell el-Hayyat, Phases 5-2 (drafting by Barbara Trapido-Lurie).

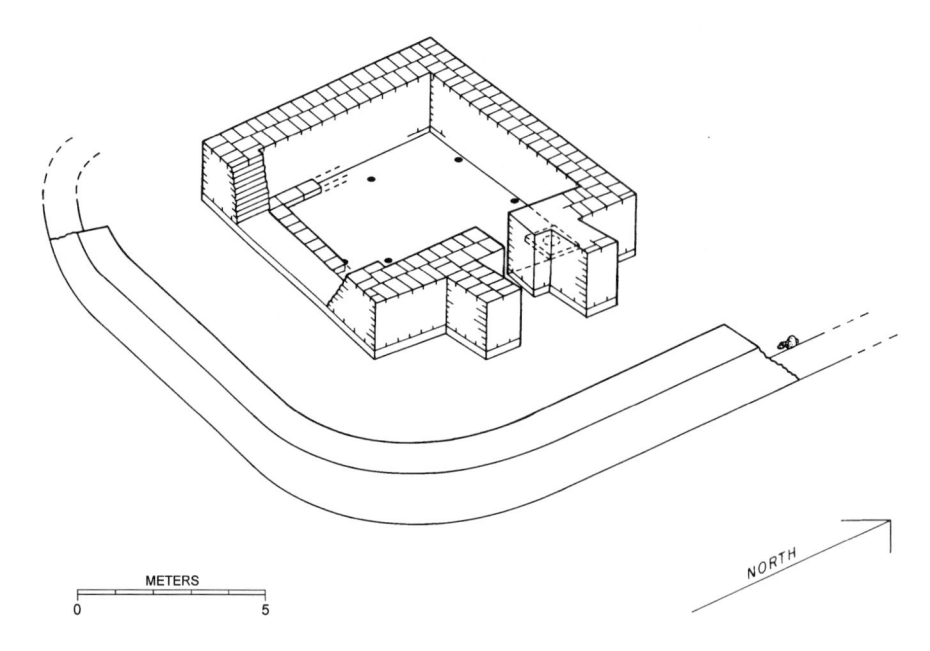

Figure 6.3 Isometric reconstruction of Phase 5 (early Middle Bronze IIA) temple at Tell el-Hayyat (drafting by Chuck Sternberg).

Figure 6.4 Tell el-Hayyat Phase 5 temple, facing west. Note temple interior with platform in northeast corner and low curb along south and west walls; Steve Falconer in foreground, Glen Peterman at back of temple (photo by Karen Scholz).

and knowledge of its builders (Hurowitz 1992). Depositional patterns of faunal and floral remains, and ceramic vessels for processing and storing food, illuminate ritual activities and their integration in village economies. Objects used in formal observances or given as temple donations are far less numerous, but their distribution also conveys a social dimension of ritual.

THE BRONZE AGE TEMPLES AT TELL EL-HAYYAT

Hayyat's first architecture consists of a small, centrally located shrine dating to Phase 5, which is the first in a stratified series of mudbrick temples that were enlarged and elaborated in Phases 4 through 2 (Figure 6.2). The changing size, plan and elements of these temples and

Phase 5 (early Middle Bronze IIA: ca. 2000-1900 B.C.)

The Phase 5 temple is the only building recovered from the initial phase of Middle Bronze Age occupation at Tell el-Hayyat (Figure 6.3). This temple was razed and replaced in precisely the same location and orientation by new temples in each of the three successive phases. The foundations of the Phase 5 temple, measuring 6.1 x 6.7 m in exterior dimensions, is constructed very simply of compacted earth (*terre pise*) resting directly on the Pleistocene age lacustrine sediments beneath Tell el-Hayyat (i.e., there are no Phase 6 deposits under this temple). Remnants of brick on top of this foundation hint at mudbrick walls, in keeping with subsequent Hayyat temples. Two anterior "buttresses" or *antae* flank the entrance to the temple on its eastern face. The base of a small mudbrick platform or "altar" occupies the northeastern corner of the temple, and a low curb runs along portions of its southern and western walls (Figure 6.4). Seven shallow, pebble-lined depressions (perhaps pot-stands) are arranged around the temple interior. The very ephemeral remains of two cornering compacted earth wall foundations lie northeast of the temple. These wall foundations are overlain by compacted earth foundations for an enclosure wall that encircled the temple. In association with this enclosure wall, a single meter-high smoothed limestone standing stone, accompanied by additional flat-lying stones, was exposed in the northeastern portion of the forecourt (Figure 6.5).

Figure 6.5 Standing stone and adjacent flat-lying stones in northeast portion of Phase 5 temple forecourt at Tell el-Hayyat, facing east (photo by Karen Scholz).

Specialized paraphernalia found in association with the Phase 5 temple illustrate a variety of ritual behaviors. A broken ceramic pedestal found on a temple interior surface probably served as an incense burner (Figure 6.6).

Figure 6.6 Ceramic incense burner from surface in Phase 5 temple interior at Tell el-Hayyat (photo by Karen Scholz).

Figure 6.7 Copper alloy plates resembling miniature "oxhide" ingots from Phase 5 temple interior surface (l) and jar in Phase 4 temple altar (r) at Tell el-Hayyat (photo by Karen Scholz).

A small copper alloy plate resembling a miniature "oxhide" ingot also found on an interior surface may have served as a ritual offering (Figure 6.7). Most strikingly, excavation of the low mudbrick curb inside the temple revealed an anthropomorphic copper-alloy figurine, possibly a depiction of the Canaanite goddess Astarte posed with her arms out to her sides (Figures 6.8 and 6.9).

The Phase 5 shrine corresponds to Hayyat's later temples in overall form, orientation, and physical separation from domestic structures. However, it differs from later temples on the site and other contemporary temples elsewhere in its size and construction techniques. For example, it is smaller by far than any of the temples *in antis* known from contemporary Syria. The only other Levantine Middle Bronze IIA temple *in antis* lies at Nahariyah (Dothan 1956: 16-17), but these two temples are by no means identical. The *antae* at Nahariyah extend directly from the corners of the temple façade, while the *antae* at Hayyat are inset to frame the entrance more closely. Although comparable in size to the Hayyat temples of Phases 5 and 4, the Nahariyeh temple foundations are made of up to three courses of stone. Stone foundations are consistent with more elaborate Syrian temple conventions (Matthiae 1975), while the compacted earth foundations at Hayyat represent an unusual construction technique (Wright 1985: 361).

The seemingly isolated appearance of this temple might be interpreted to reflect the implantation of an urban institution in the countryside. However, the floral, faunal and ceramic deposition outside the Phase 5 temple enclosure more strongly resemble the domestic assemblages of Phases 4-2 than any of the temple interior or courtyard assemblages (see discussions below and in Chapter 7). Indeed a domestic wall lies to the west of the Phase 5 temple. Therefore, we infer that there must have been dwellings in the unexcavated areas outside the Phase 5 temple enclosure (see discussion in Chapter 3). Further, the small size of the structure at Tell el-Hayyat and its simple construction are in keeping with an independent community with some knowledge of proper temple form, but without the means to engage in more impressive structures and expensive building materials.

Phase 4
(Middle Bronze IIA: ca. 1900-1800 B.C.)

At the end of its use life, the Phase 5 temple and its enclosure wall apparently were leveled off, leaving only the lower wall foundations, prior to the construction of the Phase 4 temple on the same location. This second temple represents a slight enlargement, to 6.9 x 7.2 m, and a definite elaboration of its predecessor, incorporating well-formed mudbrick for its foundation, superstructure and enclosure wall (Figure 6.10). The Phase 4 temple enclosure wall now has angular corners unlike the curved contours of the Phase 5 complex (Figure 6.11). Using the brick to good effect, the Phase 4 temple walls have decorative pilasters on three exterior wall faces. The *antae* framing the door also are stepped back in an elaborate inset-offset niched pattern (Figure 6.12). A low mudbrick curb runs around the temple's interior walls, while a stepped mudbrick altar occupies the northeast corner just inside the door (Figure 6.13). A small painted jar was set into the altar (Figure 6.14), inside of which we found another miniature oxhide ingot (Figure 6.7) and a finely-crafted set of carnelian necklace beads (Figure 6.15). Traces of a circular depression at the center of the interior floor hint at the former presence of a central pedestal (perhaps the basalt pedestal found in the Phase 2 temple forecourt; see below). Individual

Figure 6.8 Copper alloy anthropomorphic figurine, possibly depicting the Canaanite goddess Astarte, found embedded in the mudbrick curb inside the Phase 5 temple at Tell el-Hayyat (photo by Karen Scholz).

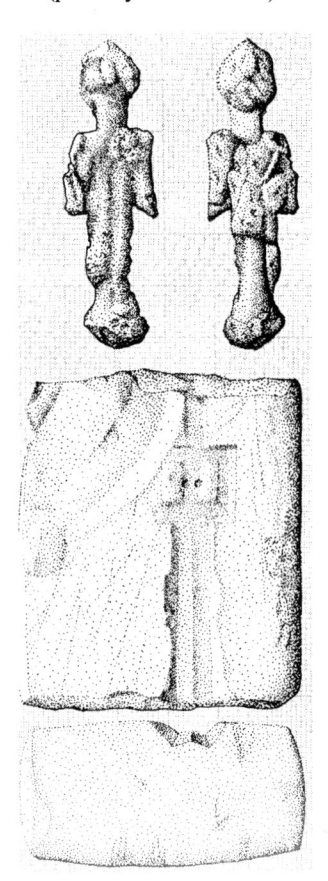

Figure 6.9 Front and back views of copper alloy anthropomorphic figurine found embedded in the mudbrick curb inside the Phase 5 temple at Tell el-Hayyat. Front and end views of carved limestone mold for casting anthropomorphic figurines; mold found in forecourt of the Phase 3 temple (drawings by Jonathan Mabry).

Figure 6.10 Tell el-Hayyat Phase 4 temple, facing west. Note temple interior with central depression for pedestal, low mudbrick curb, mudbrick altar in northeast corner; Paula Marcoux in foreground, Steve Falconer behind back temple wall (photo by Karen Scholz).

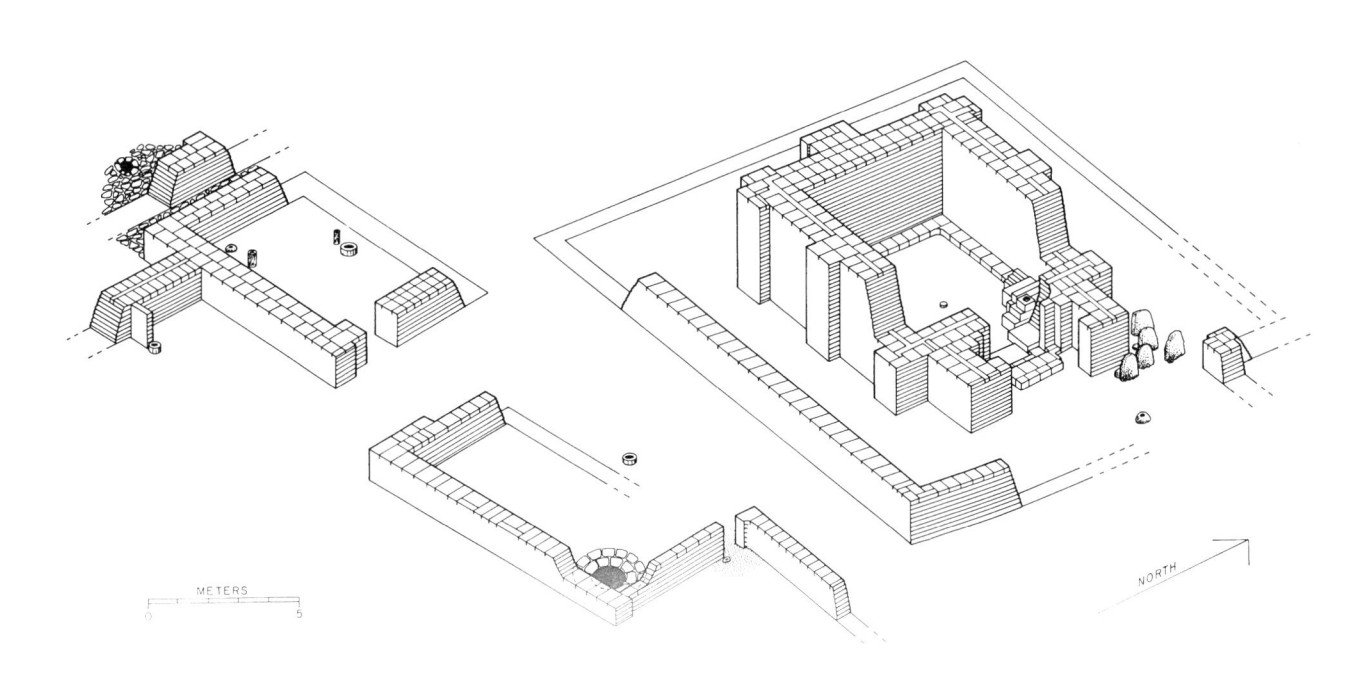

Figure 6.11 Isometric reconstruction of Phase 4 (Middle Bronze IIA) temple and domestic structures at Tell el-Hayyat (drafting by Chuck Sternberg).

Figure 6.12 Inset-offset niching of southern temple *anta* framing the entry to the Phase 4 temple at Tell el-Hayyat, facing southwest. Brickwork shows lower, original construction and subsequent remodeling, both Phase 4 (photo by Karen Scholz).

Figure 6.13 Stepped mudbrick platform or "altar" in northeast corner of Phase 4 temple at Tell el-Hayyat (photo by Karen Scholz).

Figure 6.14 Painted jar set into altar in northeast corner of Phase 4 temple at Tell el-Hayyat (photo by Karen Scholz).

Figure 6.15 Carnelian beads found in Phase 4 temple altar at Tell el-Hayyat (photo by Karen Scholz).

well-formed, pale-colored bricks were laid to define interior and exterior wall faces, leaving a hollow wall core that was filled with a more *ad hoc* combination of broken bricks and brick debris. The scale and construction techniques applied to the temple are matched in the domestic buildings on the site, although the form and contents of the temple buildings are quite distinct.

The decorative use of mudbrick, for example, is not paralleled elsewhere in the southern Levant, either in domestic or public architecture.

In the courtyard, a single large limestone basin lies outside the temple entrance, and once again a pair of cornering walls appears in the northeast corner of the

Figure 6.16 Standing stones and associated flat-lying stones around north buttress of the Tell el-Hayyat Phase 4 temple shown after excavation to its founding level, facing northwest. Level of chinking stones around bases of the standing stones indicate the stones were added after the initial construction of the northern *anta* and before the subsequent enlargement of the *anta* (photo by Karen Scholz).

Figure 6.17 Mudbrick steps just outside the temple entrance added late in Phase 4 at Tell el-Hayyat, facing northwest; Pat Fall at corner of altar (photo by Karen Scholz).

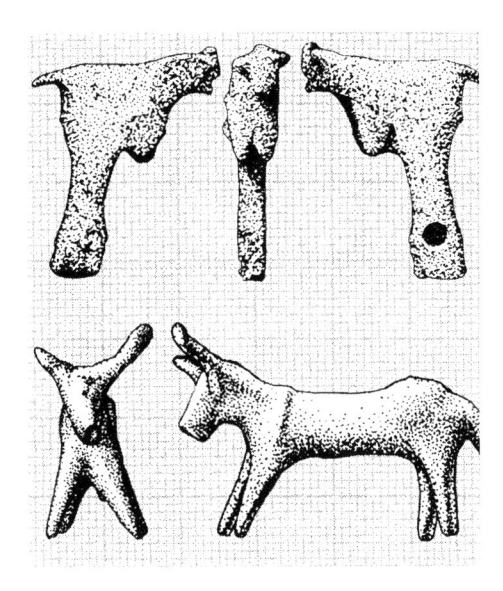

Figure 6.18 Zoomorphic figurines from surface of Phase 4 temple interior at Tell el-Hayyat; upper figurine has perforated base, presumably for hafting (drawings by Jonathan Mabry and Ronald Beckwith).

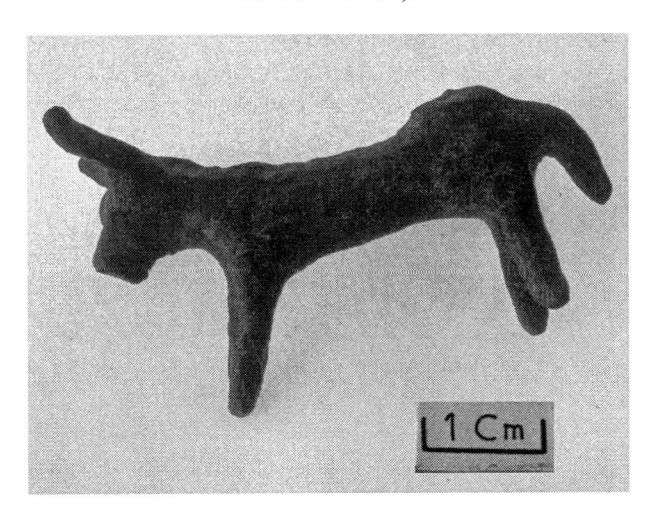

Figure 6.19 Copper alloy zoomorphic figurine, possibly bovine, from surface in Phase 4 temple interior at Tell el-Hayyat (photo by Karen Scholz).

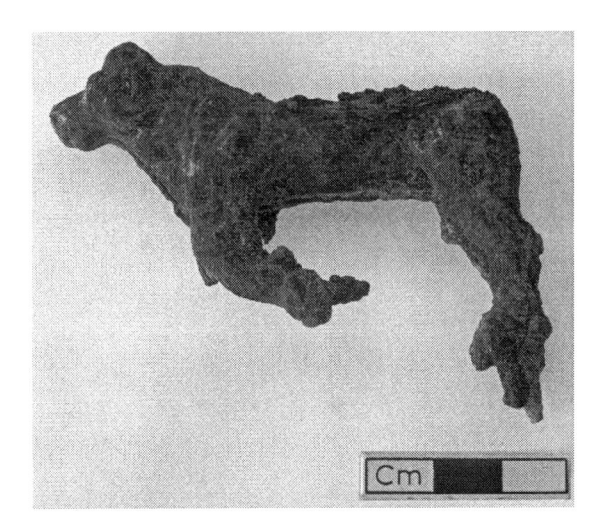

Figure 6.20 Copper alloy zoomorphic figurine from surface deposits (Phase 0) in Area N at Tell el-Hayyat.

Figure 6.21 Large ceramic krater with two appended anthropomorphic figures recovered from an interior surface in the Phase 4 temple at Tell el-Hayyat (photo by Karen Scholz).

forecourt. Most strikingly, six one-meter-tall river stones are clustered with adjacent flat-lying stones around the temple's north *anta* (Figure 6.16). Standing stones such as these may serve many functions depending on context and intent. This set of identical stones probably does not represent deities or patrons, as they would have been individualized in some way (Dalley 1984: 117-18; Durand 1985: 81, note 9). It is more likely that the stones were raised for memorial and votive purposes by families honoring the dead (Graesser 1972; Lewis 1989: 53-70). During the latter portion of Phase 4, two slightly misaligned mudbrick steps were added, apparently to hold back the accumulation of mudbrick debris and large amounts of animal bones in the temple forecourt (Figure 6.17; see discussion below). In addition to the apparent offerings left in the altar jar, further ritual evidence recovered from temple interior surfaces includes copper alloy zoomorphic figurines (one possibly bovine; Figures 6.18 and 6.19). (A well-preserved copper alloy figurine from Phase 0 illustrates another example of the animal figurine repertoire at Tell el-Hayyat [Figure 6.20]). Phase 4 temple interior surfaces also revealed fragments of a krater with appended anthropomorphic figures (Figure 6.21). Temple courtyard surfaces from Phases 4 and 3 produced fragments from a number of kernos vessels (Figures 6.22 and 6.23), reinforcing the importance of ritual behavior immediately outside the Hayyat temples. These courtyards also revealed well-preserved copper alloy points, which appear to have been left intentionally on exterior surfaces just prior to the leveling of the Phase 4 temple (Figures 6.24 and 6.25). Further metallurgical evidence includes a pair of tongs, and a variety of tanged and pointed implements from the Phase 4 temple interior and courtyards (Figure 6.26). In addition to the wide array of copper alloy figurines and tools from Phase 4, carved limestone molds for casting tools and figurines from Phases 4 and 3 (Figures 6.9 and 6.27) and a ceramic ladle from Phase 4 (Figure 6.28) attest to the importance of local metallurgy in the Middle Bronze Age village of Tell el-Hayyat.

Figure 6.22 Kernos fragments from courtyard surfaces associated with the Phase 4 and Phase 3 temples at Tell el-Hayyat (photo by Karen Scholz).

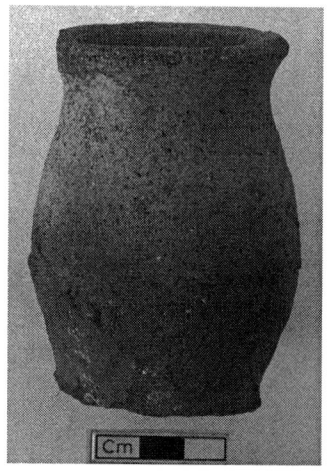

Figure 6.23 Kernos fragment from Phase 4 temple courtyard at Tell el-Hayyat (photo by Karen Scholz).

Figure 6.24 Well-preserved copper alloy spear points from the courtyard of the Phase 4 temple at Tell el-Hayyat (photo by Karen Scholz).

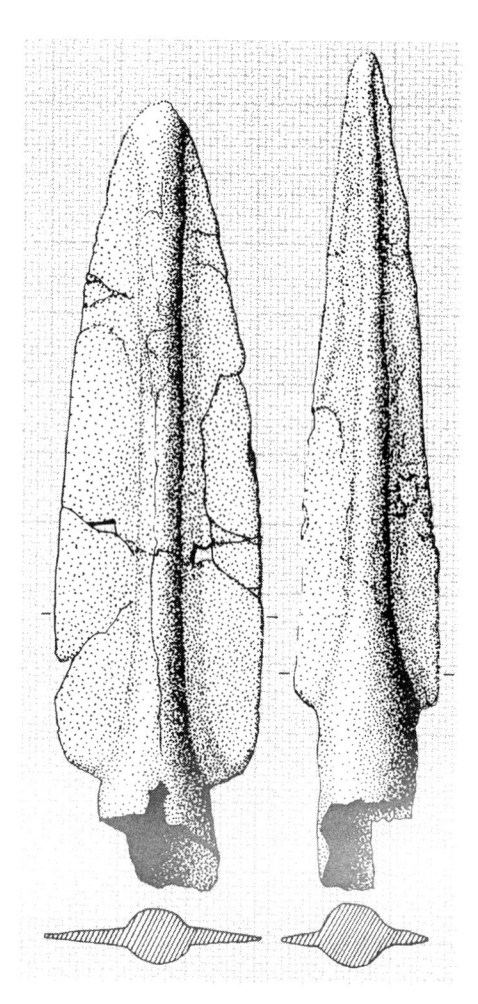

Figure 6.25 Copper alloy spear points from the courtyard of the Phase 4 temple at Tell el-Hayyat (drawing by Jonathan Mabry).

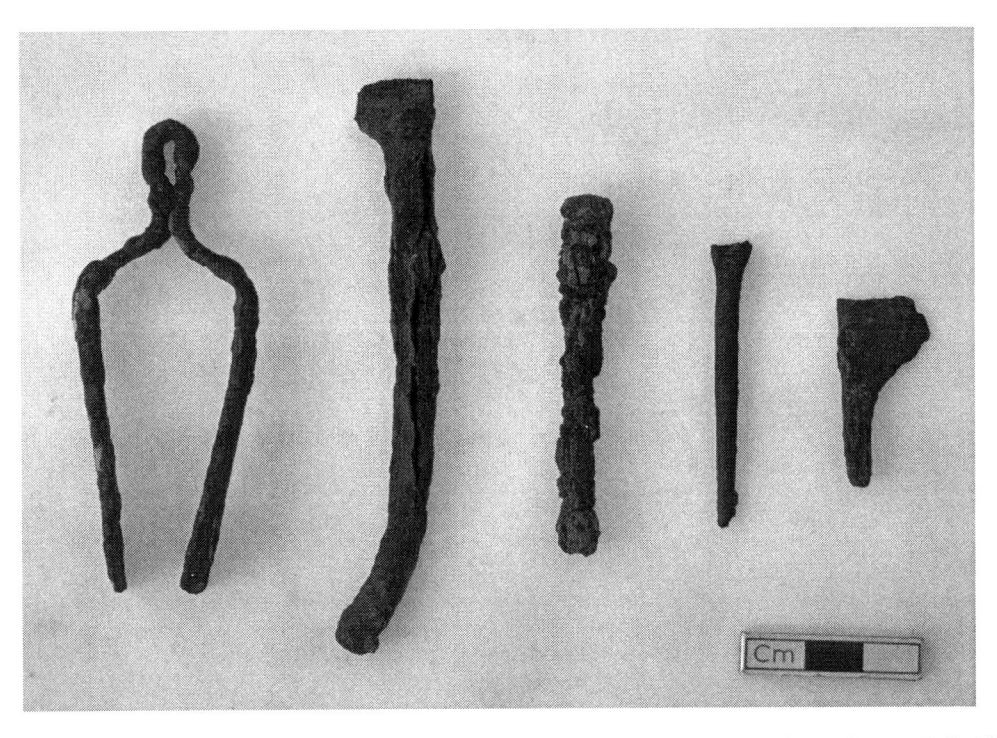

Figure 6.26 Copper alloy tongs, tangs and points from Phase 4 temple courtyard and interior surfaces at Tell el-Hayyat (photo by Karen Scholz).

Figure 6.27 Carved limestone molds for casting metal anthropomorphic figurines (mold from Phase 3 Temple Forecourt) and tanged tools (mold from Phase 4 East Alley) at Tell el-Hayyat (photo by Karen Scholz).

Figure 6.28 Fragments of a ceramic ladle with solidified copper in its cracks, suggesting its use for pouring molten copper to cast tools or figurines; found in Phase 4 surface in the East Alley at Tell el-Hayyat (photo by Karen Scholz).

Figure 6.29 Tell el-Hayyat Phase 3 temple, facing west. Note asymmetrical *antae* and temple interior with central depression for pedestal. Some foundation stones for south wall were removed by Phase 2 foundation trench; Jonathan Mabry at left, John Meloy at right (photo by Karen Scholz).

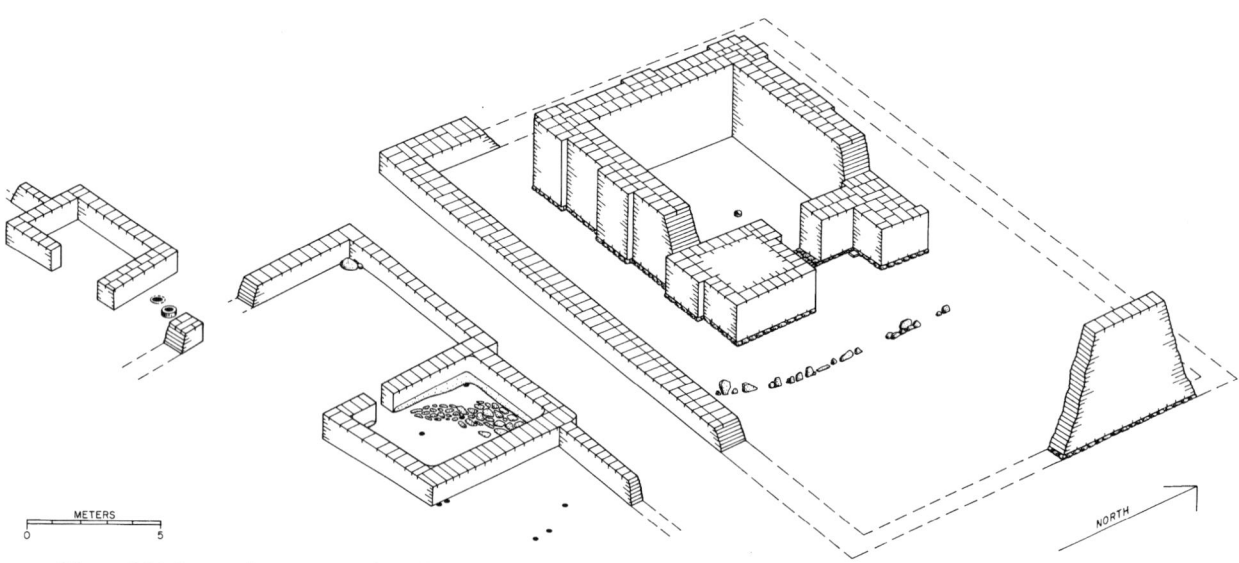

Figure 6.30 Isometric reconstruction of Phase 3 (Middle Bronze IIA-B) temple and domestic structures at Tell el-Hayyat (drafting by Chuck Sternberg).

Phase 3
(Middle Bronze IIA/B: ca. 1800-1700 B.C.)

Repeating the pattern between Phases 5 and 4, the Phase 4 temple was leveled at a height of five brick courses. A single course of foundation stones was laid directly on the remains of the Phase 4 walls and the mudbrick walls of the Phase 3 temple were then built on this stone foundation (Figure 6.29). Stone foundations represent an architectural innovation at Tell el-Hayyat, while the tradition of a mudbrick superstructure with inset-offset decoration continues (Figure 6.30). The Phase 3 temple measures 6.9 x 7.4 m, occupying virtually the same footprint as its predecessor. However, the size of its forecourt was increased substantially, perhaps to accommodate a new alignment of standing and flat-lying stones in a shallow arc outside the doorway (Figures 6.31 - 6.33). The full height of the Phase 3 temple enclosure wall (almost 4 m) was measured from a portion of its eastern perimeter, which was exposed in the temple

Figure 6.31 Tell el-Hayyat Phase 3 temple with accompanying standing stones arrayed in a shallow arc outside the temple entrance, facing east; Jonathan Mabry in foreground, John Meloy by standing stones (photo by Karen Scholz).

Figure 6.32 Group of standing stones and their accompanying flat-lying stones in forecourt of Phase 3 temple at Tell el-Hayyat, facing east. Note that the stones are founded at different levels, suggesting they were installed at different times (photo by Karen Scholz).

Figure 6.33 Group of standing stones, including stacked stones, and accompanying flat-lying stones in the forecourt of the Phase 3 temple at Tell el-Hayyat, facing east (photo by Karen Scholz).

Figure 6.34 Portion of collapsed Phase 3 temple enclosure wall at Tell el-Hayyat with its excavator,
Area U supervisor Susan Morton, facing northwest. Note diagonal coursing of fallen bricks in north balk (photo by Karen Scholz).

Figure 6.35 Area P at Tell el-Hayyat, showing collapsed mudbrick wall from Phase 3 temple (directly in front of Area Supervisor Glen Peterman) lying under preserved portions of Phase 2 temple interior plaster floor (behind Peterman and under hand picks at right), facing southwest (photo by Karen Scholz).

forecourt where it had collapsed in tact (Figures 6.30 and 6.34). Similarly, portions of the western wall of the Phase 3 temple were found collapsed under subsequently constructed plaster floors in the interior of the Phase 2 temple (Figure 6.35).

At the eastern end of the Phase 3 standing stone alignment, a wall corner barely emerges into the northeast corner of the forecourt. The temple's southern *anta* was enlarged substantially, perhaps as the foundation for a tower, lending the building a greater sense of mass (Mathhiae 1975: 59). The northern *anta*, however, is much smaller and fits precisely the plan of its predecessor. If it had been enlarged like its southern counterpart, the anta would have covered over the previous set of standing stones from Phase 4. It appears that the builders of the Phase 3 temple knew of, and respected, the placement of these earlier standing stones. The elements of continuity here are very strong and would seem to indicate a stable population and conservative religious tradition, although the increase in the number of standing stones between Phases 5 and 3 over approximately 200 years might signal an increase in the number of families, clans or lineages present in the village. Metallurgical activity associated with the Hayyat temples continued to figure prominently in Phase 3, as signaled by carved limestone molds for casting tools and anthropomorphic figurines (Figures 6.9 and 6.27), like the possible Astarte found in the Phase 5 temple. In contrast to the general concentration of metal artifacts in temple contexts, household ritual behavior is signaled by other materials, exemplified by a ceramic anthropomorphic figurine (perhaps another Astarte) found on a surface in the Phase 3 Eastern Courtyard (Figure 6.36). Specialized ceramic artifacts found in association with the Phase 3 temple include fragments of miniature cart wheels (Figure 6.37).

TEMPLE ECONOMY AND RITUAL AT TELL EL-HAYYAT

Figure 6.36 Fragment of ceramic anthropomorphic figurine, possibly a depiction of Astarte, from a surface in the Phase 3 East Courtyard at Tell el-Hayyat (photo by Karen Scholz).

Other contemporary temples have been recovered in the Jordan Valley at Kfar Rupin and Tell Kittan (Figure 6.38). The initial temple at Tell Kittan dates to Middle Bronze IIB (Eisenberg 1977). It differs from the Hayyat Phase 3 temple in its use of interior and exterior pillars. Like the Hayyat temple, the temple at Kittan is built of mudbrick on a river stone foundation, with an arc of standing stones placed before the entrance. The temple at Kfar Rupin was not excavated, but merely surveyed after the draining of a fishpond (Gophna 1979). Its meter-thick walls, square room and walled enclosure are sufficient to identify its function as a temple.

Phase 2
(Middle Bronze IIB/C: ca. 1700-1600 B.C.)

The Phase 3 temple was razed to its foundations to make way for the last of Hayyat's temples in Phase 2. Larger than its predecessors at 8.3 x 10.2 m, this structure

Figure 6.37 Miniature ceramic cart wheel fragments from the Phase 3 temple forecourt at Tell el-Hayyat (photo by Karen Scholz).

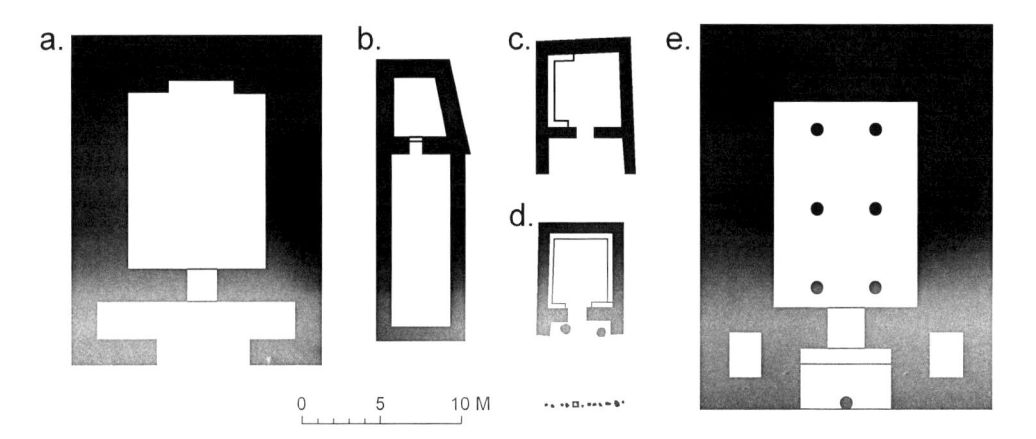

Figure 6.38 Middle Bronze Age temples *in antis* from towns and villages in the southern Levant. a. Megiddo, Temple 2048 (Dunayevsky and Kempinski 1973: fig. 2), b. Kfar Rupin (Gophna 1979: fig. 2), c. Nahariyeh (Mazar 1992: 162), d. Tell Kitan, Stratum V (Eisenberg 1977: 80), e. Shechem, Temple 1a (Wright 1965: fig. 41) (drafting by Barbara Trapido-Lurie).

Figure 6.39 Tell el-Hayyat Phase 2 temple, facing west. Pat Fall in foreground, Susan Morton at back left. Note portions of two white plaster temple interior floors shown in section at back right. Two superimposed exterior plaster surfaces are preserved in the north balk face behind Pat Fall. Some foundation stones in south wall were removed by Byzantine and later pits and burials (photo by Karen Scholz).

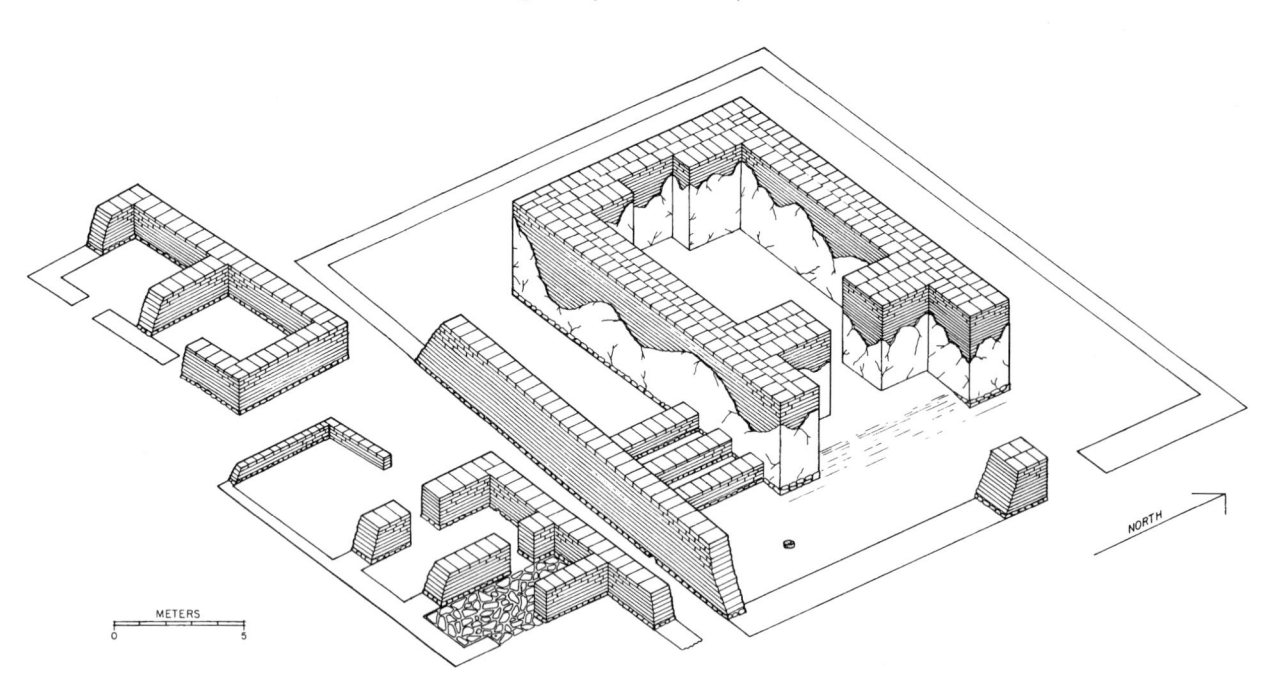

Figure 6.40 Isometric reconstruction of Phase 2 (Middle Bronze IIB-C) temple and domestic structures at Tell el-Hayyat (drafting by Chuck Sternberg).

perpetuated the illusion of mass with a multi-course stone foundation (Figure 6.39) set on a sub-foundation of river stone and rubble, thicker walls, and the elevation of the temple floor a half-meter above ground level (Figure 6.40). Two stratified plaster surfaces mark earlier and later floors inside the temple (Figure 6.41). Small traces on the east façade show that the exterior walls were plastered and painted red. The construction of the Phase 2 temple entailed a roughly 1.5 m deep foundation trench that removed much of the underlying stone foundations for the Phase 3 temple (see missing wall stones in Figures 6.2 and 6.29). Three stone foundation walls attach the temple to the enclosure wall, probably as supports for a tower at the temple's southeastern corner, and perhaps as

Figure 6.41 Section view of stratified white plaster floors in the interior of the Phase 2 temple at Tell el-Hayyat, facing south (photo by Karen Scholz).

Figure 6.42 Basalt pedestal shown *in situ* in forecourt of Phase 2 temple at Tell el-Hayyat, facing south. Note foundation stones under the pedestal, and portion of hard-packed surface cut by a burial (photo by Karen Scholz).

a continuation of the tower design suggested for the Phase 3 temple. In the Phase 2 temple forecourt, a short cylindrical basalt pedestal was found seated in the courtyard to the southwest of the temple entrance (Figure 6.42). The temple entrance may have been marked by two broad basalt steps (Figure 6.43) that were subsequently removed and found in pits that cut into the Phase 2 sediments after the Bronze Age. A cache of votive bowls and lamps was buried under two stratified exterior plaster surfaces in the temple forecourt (Figure 6.44). Although the temple at Hayyat is much smaller than its urban contemporaries, its massive appearance, elevation above ground level, and external tower are consistent with development of "Tower Temples" in the towns of Shechem and Megiddo (Figure 6.38). The village temple at Tell Kittan shows the same enlargement of size and walls in Middle Bronze IIC (Eisenberg 1977: 80). The trend toward increased size and mass in temple buildings seems common in the southern Levant. This tendency is most apparent in Hayyat's Phase 2 domestic architecture, which incorporates substantial stone foundations, more rooms and plastered floors.

THE TEMPLES IN OVERVIEW

Given the rather surprising presence of temples in a 0.5 ha hamlet, this site could be interpreted as a rural shrine or pilgrimage destination. This possibility would seem reinforced by the virtual absence of domestic architecture in the excavated exposures of Phase 5. Other instances of Bronze Age shrines, however, have no associated domestic architecture whatsoever, and are situated very near large towns that they presumably served (e.g., Ben-

Figure 6.43 Basalt pedestal from the Tell el-Hayyat Phase 2 temple forecourt, and two basalt steps probably related to the Phase 2 temple entrance shown after excavation (photo by Karen Scholz).

Dor 1950; Dothan 1956; Boling 1969). Hayyat's village houses and its location seven km from the nearest Bronze Age town at Pella also do not follow the pattern of a rural shrine. Instead, Hayyat's plan, size and setting are very much in keeping with those of contemporaneous domestic villages, as exemplified at Tell Kittan and Kfar Rupin. Further, if Tell el-Hayyat began as a rural shrine, which later developed into a residential community, we might expect the evidence from Phase 5 to be ritually oriented, in a manner similar to the temple assemblages of Phases 4-2. Likewise, we should expect pronounced distinctions between the general assemblages of Phases 5 and 4. Instead, the remains outside the Phase 5 temple enclosure wall consist of domestic refuse, generally similar to the refuse found in and around the houses of Phases 4-2. These analyses also show distinctions between Phases 5 and 4 comparable to those between Phases 4 and 3, two strata clearly embodying village settlement (see discussions in subsequent chapters). In sum, Tell el-Hayyat emerges as a village of sedentary farming households from which we can infer common rural responses to town life in the Jordan Valley. We view these responses as symptoms of Bronze Age urban-rural interaction in the southern Levant more generally.

The development of the Tell el-Hayyat temples over perhaps four centuries reveals a number of striking characteristics. Through the process of enlargement over the Middle Bronze Age, the four temples show remarkable consistency in placement and orientation. Each iteration of the temple is built directly over the remains of its predecessor, always with the main entrance facing east-southeast. At least two of the temples (Phases 4 and 3) had a central pedestal, perhaps the cylindrical basalt upright found *in situ* in the Phase 2 courtyard, potentially representing the reuse of a central ritual feature over multiple centuries. This continuity leaves little doubt that these temples represent a sequence of intentional rebuildings in which the people of Tell el-Hayyat were quite conscious of the location and plan of each previous temple.

TEMPLES AND COMMUNITY

Architectural forms, features and contents tell us both about temple function and integration in the community. Several aspects of the Hayyat temples make them comparable to urban and rural temple buildings elsewhere in Syria and the southern Levant (Magness-Gardiner and Falconer 1994). In this cultural sphere, temples usually have a single room with an opening in the center of one wall and a niche or altar at the back, in line with the door (Mazar 1992) (Figures 6.38 and 6.45). In each case, the entrance is framed by two exterior *antae*, as seen at Hayyat, and the open space in front of the entrance generally is larger than the interior space. Stone *stelae* are often grouped in pairs or larger numbers in the forecourt (Graesser 1972), and the forecourt frequently is set off from secular areas of the site by an enclosure wall, as at Megiddo (Dunayevsky and Kempinski 1973: Fig. 2) and Mari (Margueron 1984: 48).

Figure 6.44 Gaetano Palumbo (l, holding miniature carinated bowl) and Steve Falconer (r) excavate a cache of Middle Bronze IIB-C votive bowls and lamps buried under two stratified plaster surfaces in the Phase 2 temple forecourt at Tell el-Hayyat, facing north. East temple wall is behind Palumbo (photo by Karen Scholz).

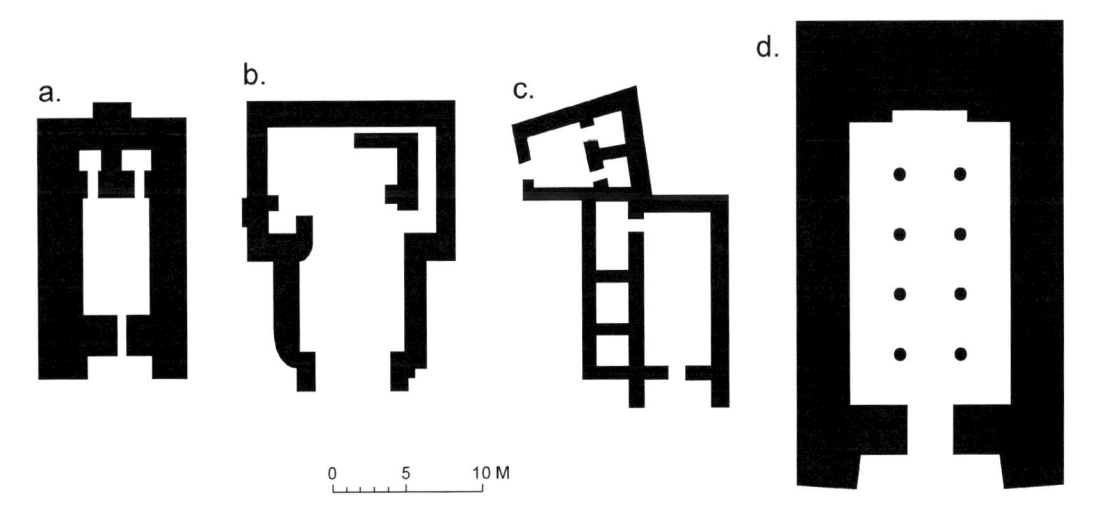

Figure 6.45 Temples *in antis* from towns and cities in Syria. a. Mari, Temple of Dagan (Margueron 1984: 48), b. Ugarit, Temple of Ba'al (Yon 1984: fig. 2), c. Emar, Temple of the Diviner (Margueron 1984a: fig. 7), d. Ebla, Temple P2 (Matthiae 1989: fig. 5) (drafting by Barbara Trapido-Lurie).

The broad functional areas of the temple are apparent in the distribution of space, the use of *antae* as an architectural framing device, and the arrangement of *stelae* facing the door. The latter two features serve to focus attention on the entrance of the building. The amount of space allocated to temple interiors is in all cases much smaller than necessary to accommodate even a small percentage of the resident population. Although ritual texts do not prohibit the general public from entering the temple, the small size of interior rooms implies they were the domain of specialists and specialized activities. The large temple forecourts and the architectural focus on temple entrances suggests that priests directed rituals and communal observances in temple courtyards (Wright 1985: 226).

PATTERNS OF RITUAL BEHAVIOR AND THE ROLES OF TEMPLES

We infer patterns of ritual behavior at Tell el-Hayyat based on faunal, floral and ceramic remains from a range of depositional contexts in and around the temples. As discussed in Chapter 2, we focus on the analysis of data from contexts most likely to contain primary refuse (i.e., use surfaces, occupational build-up immediately above surfaces, and shallow ash lenses and pits embedded in surfaces). We generate comparisons of ritual and domestic behavior at Tell el-Hayyat by segregating assemblages recovered within temple compounds (found in Areas L, M, N, P, Q, R and U; see Figure 2.3) from those associated with household structures (Areas C, D, E, F, G, H, I, J, K, S and T) and the site's southern periphery (Areas A and B). In some cases, ritual activities may be specified further by sub-dividing temple evidence into interior and courtyard assemblages (see Figure 2.22).

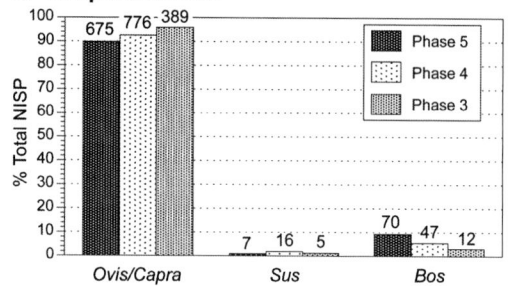

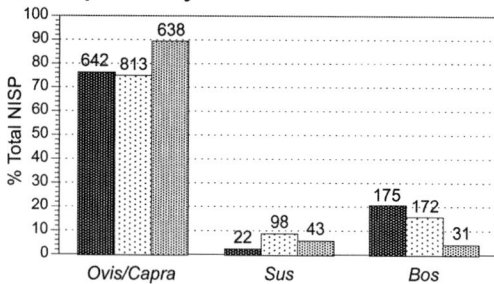

Animal Deposition and Temple Ritual

Several fundamental distinctions emerge when comparing temple and domestic bone assemblages from Phases 5-3, which offer the most robust data (Figure 6.46 and Table 6.1). Sheep and goat remains, the dominant constituents of temple assemblages, are particularly abundant in temple interiors. In contrast, domestic bone deposition features comparable frequencies of ovicaprid and pig bones. The predominance of ovicaprid remains in the temple interior and forecourt is consistent with ritual texts that stipulate the use of sheep and goat for sacrifice and ritual meals (de Tarragon 1980: 32-40; Dalley 1984: 119; Fleming 1992: 152-153).

Table 6.1 Chi-square statistics for comparisons of domesticated animal taxa in temple interiors, temple courtyards and domestic areas at Tell el-Hayyat, Phases 3-5

Phase	χ^2	df	p	NISP
3	500.325	4	< .001	1821
4	559.893	4	< .001	2804
5	548.621	4	< .001	2423

Table 6.2 Sheep:goat ratios based on NISP identifiable as *Ovis* or *Capra* in temple vs. domestic contexts at Tell el-Hayyat, Phases 3-5

a. Ratios

Phase	Temple Interiors	Temple Courtyards	Domestic Areas	χ^2	df	p
3	2.25:1	2.72:1	3.64:1	1.234	2	.539
4	0.59:1	0.97:1	1.46:1	9.581	2	.008
5	0.37:1	0.54:1	1.00:1	7.633	2	.022

b. Bone Counts

Phase	Temple Interiors		Temple Courtyards		Domestic Areas		NISP
	Ovis	Capra	Ovis	Capra	Ovis	Capra	
3	45	20	49	18	40	11	183
4	55	93	38	39	38	26	289
5	22	60	21	39	27	27	196

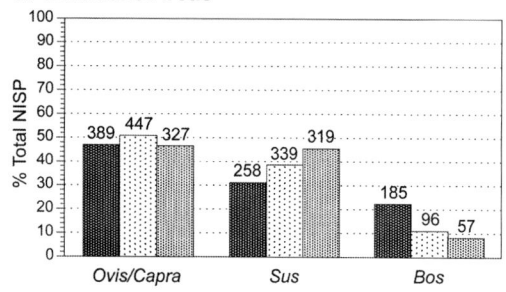

Figure 6.46 Relative bone frequencies for major domesticated animal taxa in temple interiors, courtyards and domestic areas at Tell el-Hayyat, Phases 5-3, expressed as percentages of total number of identified specimens (NISP; here NISP excludes other domesticates and wild taxa) (drafting by Barbara Trapido-Lurie). Tests of null hypothesis: a. Temple interiors: $\chi^2 = 21.989$, df = 4, p < .001; Temple courtyards: $\chi^2 = 120.463$, df = 4, p < .001; Domestic areas: $\chi^2 = 86.686$, df = 4, p < .001.

Noteworthy chronological trends include accentuated temple deposition of ovicaprid bones, particularly in temple interiors, a steady rise in household pig consumption, and decreasing deposition of cattle bones in all temple and domestic settings. The increasingly high frequencies of sheep/goat in temple interiors reflect specialized ritual activities and more restrictive rules regarding appropriate sacrifice. Among the ovicaprid data there is a consistent increase in the ratio of sheep to goats in temple and domestic contexts (Table 6.2). These ratios are consistently lower in temple settings, particularly temple interiors, suggesting relatively greater consumption of goats in ritual contexts than in households.

Relative frequencies of head, foot, and limb and trunk bones reveal body part profiles for temple compounds and domestic areas that are more similar to each other

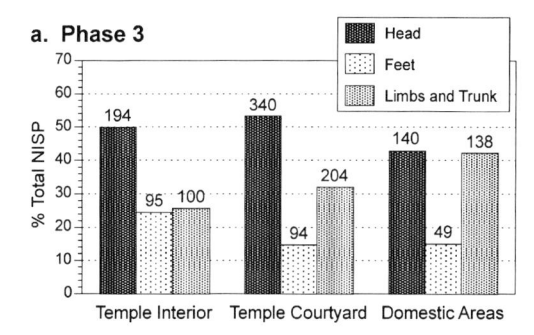

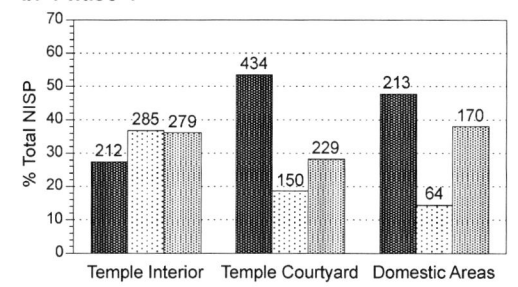

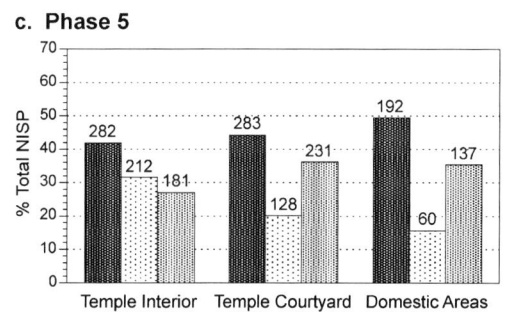

Figure 6.47 Frequencies of ovicaprid bone elements in temple interiors, temple courtyards and domestic areas at Tell el-Hayyat, Phases 5-3, expressed as percentages of NISP (drafting by Barbara Trapido-Lurie). Tests of null hypothesis: Phase 5: χ^2 = 45.545, df = 4, p < .001; Phase 4: χ^2 = 157.432, df = 4, p < .001; Phase 3: χ^2 = 34.295, df = 4, p < .001.

than to temple interiors (Figure 6.47). While the mix of body parts in domestic and courtyard settings tends to be consistent, temple interiors vary more obviously from phase to phase. Temple courtyards and domestic areas generally feature higher frequencies of limb and trunk bones, which may be considered "consumption offal" (e.g., Hellwing and Gophna 1984), and may reflect meat consumption. However, a more apparent spatial distinction lies in the elevated frequencies of foot bones in temple interiors. The high proportion of foot bones in temple contexts may reflect ritual prescriptions for certain body parts, as indicated by texts from Emar (Fleming 1992: 152) and Ugarit (de Tarragon 1980: 33). Head fragments are comparably abundant in all settings and do not appear to be ritually prescribed here. The most obvious and generally most informative pattern in these data lies in the congruence of domestic and temple courtyard assemblages, as an indication of the intimate ties between household economies at Tell el-Hayyat and communal ritual behavior in and around its temples.

While the frequencies of pig bones (*Sus*) are remarkably small in temple settings, particularly interiors, they increase dramatically in domestic areas to approach ovicaprid frequencies by the end of the Middle Bronze Age. A growing emphasis on pig husbandry is symptomatic of increased economic autonomy, particularly at the household level (see discussion in Chapter 7). Therefore, the near absence of pig bones in temple settings is especially noteworthy. Whereas most depositional patterns of ovicaprid and cattle bones in temple settings mirror those in households, pig deposition embodies a clear dichotomy between ritual and subsistence consumption. One might attribute this to a desire among Hayyat's households to retain firm control over this aspect of animal husbandry. However, the ovicaprid data suggest local control over sheep and goat consumption that does not preclude the use of ovicaprids in ritual observances. Therefore, the dearth of pig bones in temple settings, particularly by virtue of its stark contrast to sheep and goat, probably signals an effect of ritual proscription.

Plant Deposition and Temple Ritual

The unexpected discovery of a temple compound at Tell el-Hayyat suggests that rural Bronze Age villages in the Jordan Valley were characterized by complex social behavior. Plant deposition in the temples and their surrounding temple compounds illustrates some of these behaviors. Cereals, legumes, fruit-bearing trees and vines, and wild plants constitute the four categories of plant taxa recovered from Tell el-Hayyat (see Chapter 5). One of the main floral trends at Tell el-Hayyat is a pronounced transition between Phases 4 and 3 in both the temple and domestic assemblages, in much the same way as is noted above for sheep:goat ratios (Figure 6.48). After negligible change between phases 5 and 4, the relative frequency of cereals rises in domestic areas, while in temple compounds cereals decline and fruits jump sharply. The temple remains feature the conspicuous presence of fig and grape seeds in the forecourt, which may reflect the ritual offering of fresh fruit at the temple. Olive stones are found in very small quantities within the temple compound. This is not surprising since fresh olives are not suitable for human consumption (raw olives are very bitter and pickling was not introduced until Hellenistic times) and olive production was represented in the temple as olive oil. Similarly, wine as a temple offering would not have resulted in the deposition of carbonized seeds in the temple areas. On the other hand, wild legumes and weeds are very common in temple settings. This may reflect the ritual offering of fresh flowers and wild fruit. The high fruit frequency in temple compounds primarily reflects the abundance of fig pips, particularly in the forecourts of the Phase 5 and 3 temples (Table 6.3). The floral assemblage suggests generally distinct patterns of

a. Temple Compounds

b. Domestic Areas

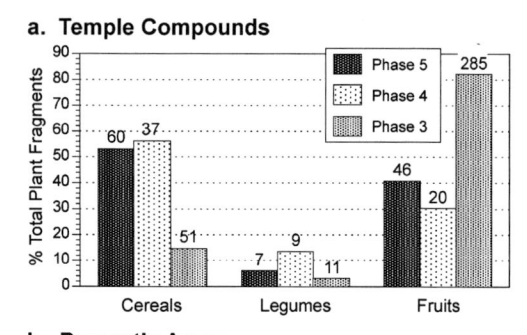

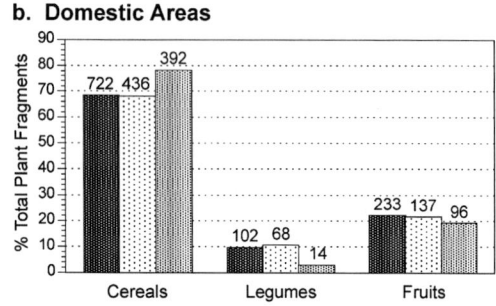

Figure 6.48 Relative frequencies of cultivated plant macrofossils in temple compounds and domestic areas at Tell el-Hayyat, Phases 5-3, expressed as percentages of total identified fragments (drafting by Barbara Trapido-Lurie). Tests of null hypothesis: Temple compounds: $\chi^2 = 114.664$, df = 4, p < .001; Domestic areas: $\chi^2 = 31.376$, df = 4, p < .001.

Table 6.3 Chi-square statistics for comparisons of taxonomic frequencies for seeds in temple vs. domestic contexts at Tell el-Hayyat, Phases 3-5

Phase	χ^2	df	p	Seeds (n)	Samples (n)
3	339.623	2	< .001	1170	33
4	3.932	2	.140	707	37
5	19.755	2	< .001	849	43

Table 6.4 Relative frequencies of domesticated fruit taxa in temple vs. domestic contexts at Tell el-Hayyat, Phases 3-5

a. Temple Compounds

Ph	Ficus %	Olea %	Vitis %	Prosopis %	Seeds (n)	Samples (n)
3	98.6	0.0	1.1	0.4	285	13
4	100.0	0.0	0.0	0.0	20	16
5	89.1	0.0	2.2	8.7	46	12

b. Domestic Areas

Ph	Ficus %	Olea %	Vitis %	Prosopis %	Seeds (n)	Samples (n)
3	76.0	7.3	7.3	9.4	96	20
4	67.2	13.9	1.5	17.5	137	21
5	84.1	5.2	0.9	9.9	233	31

Pottery Deposition and Temple Ritual

Ritual texts and archaeological remains show that sacrifice and consumption of animal and plant foods was a major focus of activity in the temple compound. Textual references to sacrifice and ritual meals specify the quality and quantity of the foods, rather than special preparation techniques or the use of ritual vessels necessary for preparation or presentation of the meal. Although we expected to find more specialized, elaborate, and costly serving pieces in the temple, as befitted the status of the god within, this proved not to be the case. Temple ceramic assemblages are remarkably consistent with those of domestic areas in the range and quality of types represented.

The ceramic assemblages from Tell el-Hayyat include three major functional categories distinguished by clay/temper composition, vessel morphology and ethnographic analogy: cooking vessels, storage vessels and serving vessels. Cooking pots appear in a flat-bottomed, straight-sided form (e.g., Figure 4.2: k; Figure 4.4: q; Figure 4.7: a-l) and in ovoid varieties with everted or rolled rims (e.g., Figure 4.2: l, m; Figure 4.7: m-p). These pots incorporate a porous clay matrix and large, angular chrystalline inclusions; both features enhance ceramic resistance to thermal shock (Rye 1976; Bronitsky and Hamer 1986). Storage vessels appear most commonly as tall jars with very contricted necks (e.g., Figure 4.2: n-t; Figure 4.5: c-r; Figure 4.8: a-q) and less frequently as smaller, more squat jars with wider mouths (e.g., Figure 4.2: u-y; Figure 4.5: t-y; Figure 4.8: r-t).

Serving vessels include a variety of open bowls (e.g., Figure 4.2: a; Figure 4.4: a-h; Figure 4.6: a-f, m) and closed cups and bowls (e.g., Figure 4.2: c-f, h-j; Figure 4.4: l-p; Figure 4.6: g-l, n-q). A modest number of special function vessels, including small jugs, votive bowls, crucibles and oil lamps, constitute only 1-3% of the Hayyat assemblages. Because very few whole or reconstructable vessels were recovered, this study concentrates on rim sherds, which are particularly diagnostic of vessel morphology in the southern Levant. When calculating relative frequencies of vessel classes

ritual and domestic plant deposition. While domestic fruit assemblages include substantial remains from all four fruit taxa, the temple assemblages in all three phases are dominated overwhelmingly by fig pips and, to a lesser extent, grape pips (Table 6.4). Even considering the large number of seeds produced by each fig, the clear contrast between domestic and temple assemblages, and the near absence of other fruit taxa in temple settings, are quite striking. Thus, the emphasis on figs may reflect ritual behavior guided by specific religious rules. Ritual texts mention a variety of breads, including fruit bread (Fleming 1992: 140), and fruits themselves (de Tarragon 1980: 44-45; Fleming 1992: 147) as acceptable for ritual meals and donations to the gods. In concert with the bone assemblages, these floral data also reflect the influence of specific ritual prescriptions as manifested in pronounced emphases on fig and ovicaprid consumption in temple settings.

Table 6.5 Chi-square statistics for comparisons between functional categories of ceramic vessels in temple interiors, temple courtyards and domestic areas at Tell el-Hayyat, Phases 3-5

Phase	χ^2	df	p	Rims (n)
3	34.101	4	< .001	1349
4	30.220	4	< .001	1685
5	17.716	4	< .001	833

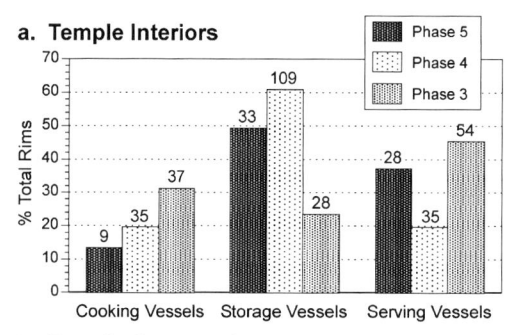

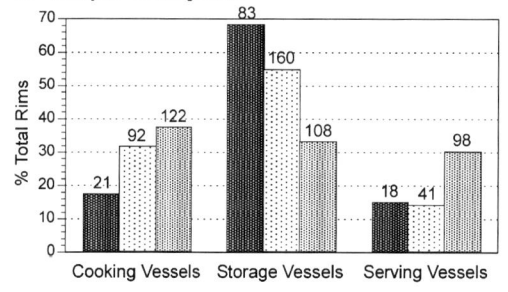

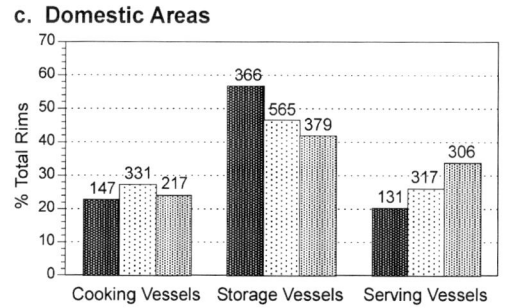

Figure 6.49 Frequencies of rim types by functional categories in temple interiors, temple courtyards and domestic areas at Tell el-Hayyat, Phases 5-3, expressed as percentages of total identified rims. (drafting by Barbara Trapido-Lurie). Tests of null hypothesis: a. Temple interiors: $\chi^2 = 44.914$, df = 4, p < .001; Temple courtyards: $\chi^2 = 61.279$, df = 4, p < .001; Domestic areas: $\chi^2 = 48.243$, df = 4, p < .001.

this approach also minimizes the problem of counting multiple fragments, particularly body sherds, from the same vessel. As noted in Chapter 2, in all cases rim frequencies are corrected for joins.

The ceramic assemblages from temple interiors, temple courtyards and domestic areas show significant functional distinctions in each of the three phases analyzed here (Table 6.5). This is not surprising, since textual accounts suggest that different activities and scales of activity occurred in these three settings. Despite these distinctions, domestic and temple pottery deposition reveal many aspects of generally similar functional change over time, although they are often more subtle and less consistent than those seen in Hayyat's faunal data. The relative frequency of cooking pots increases steadily in temple interiors and courtyards, with no clear trend in domestic areas. The proportion of storage vessels shows a net decrease in all three settings, although it rises in the Phase 4 temple interior before dropping in Phase 3 (Figure 6.49). The frequency of serving vessels increases in all settings, although again the temple interior values are discontinuous, with a drop in Phase 4 before rising in Phase 3. Temple interiors provide the smallest rim assemblages in all three phases, so these last two characteristics may be artifacts of sampling. This evidence suggests a mix of changes that are parallel in some cases and discontinuous in others. However, in contrast to Hayyat's floral data, there are no clear examples of divergent trends in temple and domestic pottery deposition. This observation is borne out in greater detail by a closer look at pottery deposition involving cooking and storage vessels.

Cooking Vessels

The modest changes among cooking vessel frequencies in domestic contexts may reflect greater repetition in the household activities in which ceramic vessels were used, broken and discarded. Preparation of food, for example, occurred several times a day, offering a number of opportunities for ceramic breakage and discard. Ritual texts and calendars indicate that ritual activities were conducted at regularly scheduled intervals, but not on a daily basis. It would seem that the sporadic nature of ritual activity might contribute to the more diverse patterning within temple compounds. For instance, the rise in cooking pot frequency suggests an increase in the frequency or amount of foodstuffs being prepared for sacrifices and ritual meals, possibly resulting from modified ritual prescription. Alternatively, the increasing wealth of the community may have allowed larger contributions for ritual occasions.

Further insights on Hayyat's temple economy are apparent when we consider distinctions in cooking vessel morphology that suggest multiple modes of manufacture. In most parts of the world, cooking pots have smooth contours, and lack sharp angles that contribute to uneven heating and thermal shock (Rye 1981: 27; Woods 1986). Hayyat's flat-bottomed cooking pots violate this convention, but their straight sides and bottom create an appropriate vessel form for simple coil or slab construction (Rye 1981: 67-72; Rice 1987: 125-128). In addition, their rectilinear shape, with its inherently weak joint between vessel base and wall, renders them exceedingly poor vessels for transport. These structural characteristics make Hayyat's flat-bottomed cooking pots particularly likely candidates for highly localized manufacture and use. This likelihood is strengthened by neutron activation analysis, which shows chemical composition of flat-bottomed cooking pots to be very consistent *within* Bronze Age sites, but clearly distinguishable *between* sites in the Jordan Valley (Falconer 1987a; 1994b).

Ovoid pots, on the other hand, conform more closely with expected cooking vessel morphology, and their form holds greater potential for specialist manufacture. They provide more consistent evidence of wheel-thrown construction (or at least rim finishing) in the form of "rilling" left on vessel interior and exterior walls by Bronze Age potters (Rye 1981: 75; Rice 1987: 129). In addition, their nearly spherical shape is more resistant to breakage during transport, which opens the possibility of more centralized manufacture.

Therefore, a ratio of flat-bottomed to ovoid cooking pots provides a rough measure of the relative importance of very simple, possibly household construction versus potentially more specialized village or regional manufacture. Data from Tell el-Hayyat show a significant increase in these ratios through time, regardless of the architectural setting from which they are drawn (Table 6.6). The spatial uniformity of this trend is reinforced by chi-square statistics showing that cooking pot ratios did not vary significantly across settings during any of the three phases analyzed here. These data reveal increasingly localized manufacture of cooking pots at Tell el-Hayyat, and the congruity of cooking pot use in both temple and domestic contexts.

Table 6.6 Ratios of flat-bottomed to ovoid cooking pots in temple interiors, temple courtyards and domestic areas at Tell el-Hayyat, Phases 3-5

a. Ratios

Phase	Temple Interiors	Temple Courtyards	Domestic Areas	χ^2	df	p
3	6.40:1	16.43:1	6.75:1	4.575	2	.102
4	1.92:1	2.41:1	3.36:1	3.259	2	.196
5	0.50:1	0.91:1	2.59:1	9.948	2	.077

b. Rim Counts

Phase	Temple Interiors Flat	Temple Interiors Ovoid	Temple Courtyards Flat	Temple Courtyards Ovoid	Domestic Areas Flat	Domestic Areas Ovoid	Rims (n)
3	32	5	115	7	189	28	376
4	23	12	65	27	255	76	458
5	3	6	10	11	106	41	177

Storage Vessels

As with cooking vessels, morphological variations among storage jars carry economic implications. Tall, narrow-necked jars may be sealed easily, and provide effective containers for long-term storage and transportation of goods, particularly liquids (Ericson and Stickel 1973; Parr 1973; Henrickson and McDonald 1983; Smith 1985). Shorter, wide-mouth forms permit easier access, are less appropriate for transportation of goods, and are more commonly used for short-term storage of both dry and liquid commodities (Henrickson and McDonald 1983; Smith 1985). Therefore, ratios of constricted- to open-necked store jar rims suggest the relative significance of long- versus short-term storage of commodities, and the potential for store jars to serve as vehicles of exchange with other communities. These ratios decrease through time at Tell el-Hayyat, regardless of the architectural setting considered (Table 6.7). These shifting storage vessel patterns cannot be attributed simply to changing stylistic preferences. Elsewhere in the Southern Levant storage jar rims often become more elaborate, but both jar forms remain very common throughout the Middle Bronze Age (Cole 1984: 47-48, 73-78).

TABLE 6.7 Ratios of long-term to short-term storage vessels in temple interiors, temple courtyards and domestic areas at Tell el-Hayyat, Phases 3-5

a. Ratios

Phase	Temple Interiors	Temple Courtyards	Domestic Areas	χ^2	df	p
3	6.00:1	2.72:1	3.16:1	1.924	2	.382
4	12.63:1	11.31:1	5.49:1	9.352	2	.009
5	33.0:0	26.67:1	6.32:1	9.243	2	.010

b. Rim Counts

Phase	Temple Interiors Long-term	Temple Interiors Short-term	Temple Courtyards Long-term	Temple Courtyards Short-term	Domestic Areas Long-term	Domestic Areas Short-term	Rims (n)
3	24	4	79	29	288	91	515
4	101	8	147	13	478	87	834
5	33	0	80	3	316	50	482

As with the cooking pot ratios discussed above, this trend is most pronounced in temple settings. The Phase 5 and 4 temple and domestic store jar ratios are significantly different, indicating segregated storage and exchange activities in various settings within Hayyat. The tremendous predominance of constricted-neck store jars in temple settings implies the importance of temples in coordinating communal storage and local exchange. However, by Phase 3 these ratios have converged, and this storage and exchange distinction has vanished. Chi-square statistics suggest little difference between the use of pottery for storage and exchange in the temple compound and individual households.

Although temple and domestic ceramic assemblages show undeniable functional distinctions, cooking pot and storage jar ratios change in concert, and these ratios converge through time. This line of analysis could potentially document functionally divergent ritual and household use of ceramics (we see an element of this in the floral data), yet the pottery data are striking for the lack of any signature of increasing temple versus domestic spatial distinctions through the Middle Bronze Age.

Objects of Symbolic and Intrinsic Value

Faunal, floral and ceramic remains exhibit distinct spatial patterns because of their frequent use, utilitarian nature, and relatively low intrinsic value. Other forms of material culture also were manufactured, used and deposited at Tell el-Hayyat, but in smaller numbers. The quantity and spatial distribution of objects in metal, stone, ceramic and bone are tabulated in Table 6.8. While the overall sample is too modest to support diachronic analysis, its general spatial distribution reveals noteworthy similarities and contrasts between domestic and temple assemblages.

These objects also are grouped according to their functions as symbols or tools. Objects designated as symbolic, since they have no obvious utilitarian function, include human and animal figurines, miniature "oxhide" ingots, miniature vessels, miniature cart wheels, and other manufactured items whose odd shape (*kernoi* and "incense burners") or context lead one to infer a ritual function. For example, most of the beads on the site were found in groups embedded within temple altars, and because of their consistent context they are classified here as symbolic. The miniature vessels, cart wheels and ingots appear to be replicas of full size objects used as offerings or in temple ritual. As a case in point, carts were used to carry divine images in rituals at Emar (Fleming 1992: 237).

At Tell el-Hayyat, deposition of symbolic objects made of metal or stone was restricted to temple compounds, while ceramic objects of symbolic value were found in equal numbers in both temple and domestic contexts. Two inferences may be derived from this pattern: first, material value is an important consideration in ritual paraphernalia and donations, and second, the distribution of symbolic ceramic objects suggests that rituals took place in households, as well as in temples. The prevalence of domestic ritual is well documented at Emar (Fleming 1992: 236-248).

Metallurgical debris and equipment for producing both tools and figurines were found in the temple compounds of Phases 5 and 4. In this case, both the instrinsic value of metal and the technological ability to work it seem to have been important factors determining spatial deposition. Although metal tools and weapons function well as cutting and thrusting implements, chipped stone tools provided a more accessible and less costly utilitarian alternative. Therefore, the deposition of metal objects, particularly with such clear spatial preferences, provides a highly visible expression of material wealth or social privilege. The deposition of metals suggests that wealth in its symbolic form often was manifested in temple deposition, while the distribution of faunal and botanical evidence suggests that wealth in its practical (edible, wearable, reproduceable) form was concentrated in the flocks and fields owned and managed by Tell el-Hayyat's villagers.

TABLE 6.8 Distribution of manufactured objects in temple and domestic sectors at Tell el-Hayyat categorized by material (unidentifiable fragments and production debris excluded)

	Temple	Domestic	Total
A. Metal (Copper Alloy or Silver Alloy)			
Figurine	2	0	2
Miniature "Oxhide" Ingot	2	0	2
Pin	0	2	2
Point	4	0	4
Blade	1	0	1
Tang	1	1	2
Eyelet	1	0	1
Tweezers	1	0	1
Shaft	1	0	1
Sheet	2	0	2
Wire	1	0	1
Subtotal	**16**	**3**	**19**
B. Stone			
Bead	17	1	18
Miniature Cart-Wheel	1	0	1
Spindle Whorl	0	15	15
Loom-weight	1	0	1
Mould	1	1	2
Mortar	0	1	1
Bowl	1	0	1
Disc	1	0	1
Sphere	1	0	1
Subtotal	**23**	**18**	**41**
C. Ceramic			
Figurine	3	4	7
"Incense Burner"	1	0	1
Miniature Vessel	13	14	27
Kernos	7	5	12
Miniature Cart-Wheel	2	1	3
Crucible	2	1	3
Spindle-Whorl	2	1	3
Disc	26	119	145
Scraper	2	37	39
Jar Stopper	0	3	3
Subtotal	**58**	**185**	**243**
D. Bone			
Astragalus	0	4	4
Awl	0	9	9
Point	6	10	16
Pin	0	2	2
Tube	1	5	6
Needle	0	1	1
Shuttle	0	1	1
Smoothing Tool	0	1	1
Subtotal	7	33	40

RITUAL AND COMMUNITY AT TELL EL-HAYYAT

In the foregoing analyses we delineate how depositional patterns indicate the embeddedness of ritual activities in the village economy of Tell el-Hayyat. Comprehending the economic basis of temple activities is crucial for understanding the social implication of ritual in society, and for making archaeological inferences from evidence that is obviously linked with ritual by virtue of its setting, constituent elements or spatial patterning. Therefore, we suggest that the material remains of ritual behavior may be inspired by three major driving forces: (1) ritual rules, prescriptions and proscriptions; (2) demands of larger regional institutions; and (3) dependence on community support and economy, in which temples may be an expression of communal behavior.

It is highly unlikely that any one of these forces acted alone in determining the nature of ritual behavior and its archaeological signatures. However, we can ascertain the relative mix of different factors and their social implications archaeologically. We suggest that ritual behavior primarily reflecting ceremonial rules will be manifested by preferential distribution of specific taxa or material culture, in this case metal objects, ovicaprids, cultivated fruits (figs and grapes), and the fruits and flowers of wild plants. The increasing specificity of animal taxa in Hayyat's temple interiors suggests a correspondingly greater specificity of, or adherence to, those rules. Perhaps it is not surprising that during a period of increasing specialization and complexity in other spheres of activity, ritual activities should become increasingly specialized as well. However, rather than illustrating the dominance of a social class or political elite, the widespread acceptance of these rules would seem to reflect the contiguity of language and culture in urban and rural settlements of Syria and the Levant during the Middle Bronze Age.

Little evidence exists of any stringent economic ties between Tell el-Hayyat and institutionalized authority. However, an increasing preference for sheep over goat and the importation of metals for temple observances suggest the influences of a regional market economy. The embedded, communal nature of Hayyat's ritual economy is indicated by temporal trends in temple assemblages that generally mirror those found in domestic deposition. This congruity is revealed by parallel trends in temple and household architecture, consumption of cattle and ovicaprids, and cooking and storage vessel manufacture and use.

The construction of Hayyat's temples and the regular observance of formal rituals may also have been designed to enhance the economic success of the community, as resident villagers would have expected such observances to insure the fertility of the people, the land and the flocks. As the wealth of the community increased, so did the size of its temple and perhaps even the frequency of ritual occasions. Yet, some economic rationality may still be visible in the greater preference for goat, rather than sheep, for sacrifice. Both were ritually acceptable, but sheep were more valuable for their secondary products and, therefore, a more "expensive" gift. Thus, knowledge, choice and enlightened self-interest characterized the behavior of the community as a whole. Participation in ritual activities and economic support for the temple not only bound the community together in worship of common gods and their own ancestors, it was also another means for the farming villagers of Tell el-Hayyat to survive as a rural community amid the growth of urbanized society during the Middle Bronze Age.

CHAPTER 7: HOUSEHOLD ECONOMY AT TELL EL-HAYYAT

INTRODUCTION

The development of early social complexity in southwestern Asia generates considerable archaeological discussion on a variety of fronts, most notably the emergence of localized polities and urbanized socio-economic systems. Both topics are particularly amenable to macroscopic analysis of centralized decision-making institutions and the metropoli that housed them. The essence of growing complexity lay not so much in cities or state institutions themselves, however, but in their interactions with the vast majority of society that lived in the countryside, and supported burgeoning specialized economies and professional bureaucracies.

Textual analysis and ethnographic analogy provide a variety of insights on the structure of village life in urbanized societies, but are subject to inherent limitations and biases. Ancient texts were commissioned at the behest of central authorities, and reflect the immediate concerns and larger world view of city dwellers. Ethnographic data from southwestern Asia that may illuminate the more distant past are drawn from societies that postdate the advent of Islam and modern technology, and their potential social and economic influences. Therefore, these avenues must be augmented with analyses of the potentially eloquent material remains of ancient rural communities themselves.

Wilk and Rathje suggested that "many archaeological dilemmas . . . have their roots in the organizational structure of household groups," and that the resolution of these dilemmas depends on inferring "the relation of the household to the core of the socioeconomic structure of society" (1982:636). In the same spirit, a comprehensive understanding of early urbanism must relate the responses of small communities and their constituent households to the benefits and liabilities of early urbanism (e.g., see Schwartz and Falconer 1994a). Spatial and temporal patterns of faunal, floral and ceramic deposition at Tell el-Hayyat reflect rural responses to early urbanism. These patterns suggest communal and household economic strategies, and thereby illustrate the changing nature of town-village interactions that lay at the root of developing complex society in this region.

HISTORICAL AND ETHNOGRAPHIC INSIGHTS ON RURALISM

The early towns and cities of southwestern Asia depended to varying extents on agricultural surpluses provided by the countryside (Figure 7.1). According to most anthropological models of ruralism (e.g., Redfield 1953; Wolf 1966), these surpluses would have supported ruling elites, professional bureaucrats, and a variety of other religious and secular specialists who were only minimally involved in food production. Urban centers often maintained this social differentiation, and the economic inequality it engendered, by practicing a "carrot and stick" management strategy toward rural hinterlands. Early cities commonly offered their surrounding villages a rather limited set of benefits (e.g., military protection, access to regional markets) in return for a more imposing set of demands (e.g., taxation, corvee labor, and military conscription) (Adams 1984; Gilman 1981; Diakonoff 1975). Successful urbanism depended on the ability of central authorities to tap rural assets to the greatest extent possible without discouraging agrarian life in the countryside altogether. Failure to do so was a prescription for collapse (Adams 1978; Yoffee 1979).

Historical texts relating directly to social and economic organization in the southern Levant are extremely sparse prior to the Iron Age. A variety of Bronze Age archives from Syrian cities, however, describe systems of land tenure and village ownership that probably encompass the range of contemporaneous practices in the southern Levant. Although Syrian cities and polities developed on larger scales than their Levantine counterparts, these regions enjoyed extensive economic interchange and shared a common technology, material culture and written language. Syrian texts reveal that agricultural lands and entire villages could be incorporated in crown or temple estates, administered directly by elite families, or held as private property. Archives from the cities of Ugarit and Alalah, dating to the 2nd millennium B.C., show that the crown worked some fields using state dependents (Liverani 1982) and distributed other state lands to local elites who provided military or administrative services (Magness-Gardiner 1994). The state permitted these elites to collect a portion of surplus foodstuffs before passing the balance on to the crown.

Private land, which could be bought and sold as a commodity, was held by individuals and by larger social groups. Individual land ownership often involved urban-based entrepreneurial landlords who engaged sharecropping peasants to work the fields (Diakonoff 1975; Adams 1982). While some rural households may have owned or leased their own fields, collective ownership is attested more commonly. Archives from the city of Nuzi in Northeastern Iraq, as well as those from Ugarit, describe transactions involving private family farmlands and corporate agrarian villages (Heltzer 1976; Zaccagnini 1979, 1984; Morrison 1987). In the case of Ugarit, the surrounding countryside was populated by approximately 200 villages, most of which had collective tax, military, and labor obligations to the crown (Heltzer

Figure 7.1 Rural mudbrick farmstead and agricultural fields in the *ghor*, looking northwest to the *zor*, or active floodplain of the Jordan River, 1985 (photo by Bob Erskine).

Figure 7.2 Mudbrick "bee hive" houses at the Deir 'Alla Agricultural Station, 1983 (photo by Steve Falconer).

1976:18-47). The evidence from Tell el-Hayyat fits well with forms of communal village structure suggested by ancient texts and ethnographic analogy.

Communal landholding persisted among rural communities in southwestern Asia until the late 19th and early 20th centuries A.D. (Figure 7.2) as a means of coordinating the sometimes conflicting requirements of grain cultivation and sheep/goat grazing (Lewis 1987:63, 221-222). In one formerly common corporate system, known as *mesha'a* in Arabic, garden and orchard plots immediately surrounding a village (*hawakir* land) were cultivated intensively, and owned as private property by individual families (Grannott 1952: 198-199; Lutfiyya 1966: 29). Most fields beyond the *hawakir* holdings were planted in annual crops and worked jointly as *mesha'a* land by members of a family or several families, or by the inhabitants of an entire village (Grannott 1952: 174; Poyck 1962: 27; Lutfiyya 1966: 104; Antoun 1972: 20; Sweet 1974: 48; Atran 1986; Graham-Brown 1990). Parcels of *mesha'a* land were redistributed at regular intervals (Grannott 1952: 215; Poyck 1962: 27; Atran 1986). Grazing lands included *mesha'a* parcels that were harvested or lay fallow, as well as less arable lands, such as hill slope woodlands and remnant forests. This system of communal land tenure allowed villages to meet tax and labor obligations collectively and share long-term agricultural risks in uncertain natural and political environments.

Rural populations in ancient southwestern Asia exercised a variety of economic strategies in the face of urban pressures. The most radical option of curtailing sedentary farming in favor of mobile pastoralism played a major role in more than one instance of political disintegration (Adams 1978; Dever 1989). Short of this extreme response, however, urban-rural relations balanced the diverse, often conflicting interests of city and countryside (see Schwartz and Falconer 1994a).

Village ownership by institutional estates, royal families, or absentee landlords engendered intimate urban-rural economic relations in which villagers had little option but to provide the bulk of their harvest to urban landholders (Magness-Gardiner 1994). The acquisition and improvement of private property by villagers were effectively discouraged. Liverani (1982) notes that the royal estates of Ugarit kept their resident labor force at a bare subsistence level. In contrast, household or communal landholding permitted more autonomous village organization and less intense interaction with cities. Greater autonomy required villages to perform some activities otherwise concentrated in cities, but permitted these communities to accumulate material wealth and develop their own economic base. Just as successful urban authority refrained from excessive predation on villages, successful rural autonomy must have avoided excessive dependence on cities.

BRONZE AGE RURALISM AT TELL EL-HAYYAT

The leading Bronze Age towns in the vicinity of Tell el-Hayyat would have been Pella (about 7 km to the northeast) and Beth She'an (about 15 km to the northwest across the Jordan River). The occupation of Pella, fortified with a mudbrick wall built in Middle Bronze IIA, is represented by five major archeological strata spanning the Middle Bronze Age (McNicoll et al. 1993). Beth She'an, which has revealed no fortifications, contains two strata dating to Middle Bronze IIB-C (Mazar 1993). In contrast to coastal sites, several of which exceed 10 ha (Falconer 1994a), the tells at Pella and Beth She'an measure only approximately 7 and 4 ha, respectively, and reflect the modest scale of town life in the Jordan Valley.

Chapters 3 and 6 discuss how the village at Tell el-Hayyat developed architecturally and socially through the Middle Bronze Age. Its structures, both domestic and ritual, improved in building materials and grew in size as this community apparently succeeded in adapting to the opportunities and challenges of increasingly urbanized society over the course of four or more centuries, before being abandoned at the end of the Middle Bronze Age. The excavated evidence from Areas A and B reflects industrial and midden deposits of the sort that would have surrounded the Bronze Age village. Using Areas A and B as a guide for the extent of the domestic architecture we can estimate the habitable space at Tell el-Hayyat to have been approximately 3850 m^2 (roughly circular with a 35 m radius). Part of this habitable space was filled by Hayyat's temple compounds, which grew from roughly 250 m^2 in Phase 5 to perhaps 400 m^2 in Phase 2. The excavated samples of the *tell* revealed roughly two houses in Phases 4 and 3, and perhaps 1.5 houses in Phase 2. Based on these estimates, we may extrapolate a village of perhaps 35 households in Phase 4, 40 households in Phase 3 and 30 households in Phase 2. The reduced estimate of Phase 2 households stems from our excavation of only about half of the large multi-room West Building. Given the lack of excavated Phase 5 domestic architecture, the village at that time must have had fewer households than during subsequent phases.

In overview, the small Phase 5 hamlet at Tell el-Hayyat would have had very modest population and abundant open domestic space. A denser village of perhaps 150 people in Phase 4 and as many as 200 people in Phase 3 inhabited single-room structures with attached courtyards, which were separated from the temple compound and each other by narrow earthen alleyways (Figures 7.3 and 7.4). While the temple compound grew incrementally through Phases 5-3, its most striking expansion occurred in Phase 2 as the temple became more massive, may have added an attached tower, and pushed its enclosure walls into former domestic space. Phase 2 houses likewise increased in investment (with stone foundations) and size (as suggested by the multi-room house and attached courtyard in the Phase 2 East Building). Although Tell el-Hayyat would have been relatively modest in size and population through the Middle Bronze Age, these changes in domestic and public architecture reflect a larger phenomenon of dynamic rural behavior that must have fueled Hayyat's changing interactions with other settlements, both large and small.

The critical measure of any urbanized society lies in the relations between central and peripheral communities. Within the context of the Jordan Valley, Tell el-Hayyat provides a venue for inferring the economic influences of local towns and coastal cities from a rural vantage point. Given its small size amid the florescence of Bronze Age urbanism, conventional logic would predict that Tell el-Hayyat became increasingly interactive with urban places and increasingly dedicated to agrarian production to feed town and city populations. While the inhabitants of Hayyat did adopt some market-oriented strategies, the interpretations presented below also suggest that they compensated with a variety of behaviors that must have enhanced village autonomy. Although these farmers participated in the local and regional economies either voluntarily or by compulsion, they also hedged their bets significantly. Tell el-Hayyat provides a detailed glimpse of a rural community balancing the benefits of interaction with nearby towns against those of economic independence. This case study also suggests a relatively

Figure 7.3 Excavation of Phase 2 architecture at Tell el-Hayyat, 1983, facing southwest. Stone foundation for temple enclosure wall at right; room in Sector EB1 at left; room in Sector WB2 in background (photo by Jon Kline).

Figure 7.4 Excavation of Phase 2 architecture at Tell el-Hayyat, 1983, facing south. Stone foundation for southeast temple corner in foreground with two abutting tower foundation walls. Room in Sector EB1 in background (photo by Jon Kline).

limited influence of urban economies on many Middle Bronze Age villages in the southern Levant.

Animal Management and Consumption

As with most agrarian communities in southwestern Asia, the majority of the identifiable animal bones at Tell el-Hayyat come from domesticated taxa, including sheep (*Ovis aries*), goats (*Capra hircus*), pigs (*Sus scrofa*) and cattle (*Bos taurus*) (Metzger 1984; see Chapter 5). The overwhelming majority of domesticated animal bones recovered from Tell el-Hayyat are from sheep and goats. The relative frequency of ovicaprid bones from all architectural settings increases slightly between Phases 5 and 3 (Figure 7.5a). Over this same time span the ratio of sheep to goat also increases, most notably between Phase 4, in which goat bones are slightly more numerous, and Phase 3, in which sheep bones assume an almost 3 to 1 majority (Table 7.1). Bone counts from all settings show that the ratios of sheep to goat differ significantly between phases. Rising sheep: goat ratios suggest an increasing potential for market-oriented or centrally-managed animal husbandry (Zeder 1991: 38). While goats are more suitable for long distance pastoralism away from agricultural fields, sheep may be managed locally in conjunction with crop cultivation. Further, sheep have more meat and generate more "secondary products" (especially wool), which are renewable and well-suited for transport and exchange (Sherratt 1981; Davis 1984). The dramatic shift from approximately even deposition of sheep and goat in Phase 3 is one of several such trends noted in the faunal, floral,

Table 7.1 Sheep: goat ratios at Tell el-Hayyat, Phases 3-5 based on NISP*

	Phase 3	Phase 4	Phase 5
All Settings	2.73:1	0.83:1	0.56:1
NISP	183	289	196
Temple Compounds	2.47:1	0.70:1	0.43:1
NISP	132	225	142
Domestic Areas	3.64:1	1.46:1	1.00:1
NISP	51	64	54

* All settings: χ^2= 57.998, df = 2, p<.001
Temple compounds: χ^2= 49.859, df = 2, p<.001
Domestic areas: χ^2= 9.343, df = 2, p<.009.

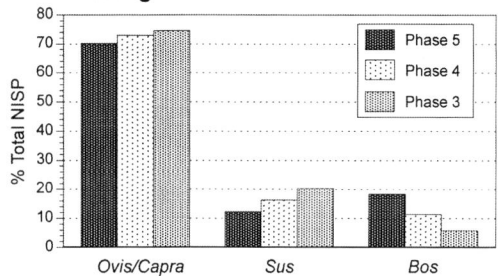

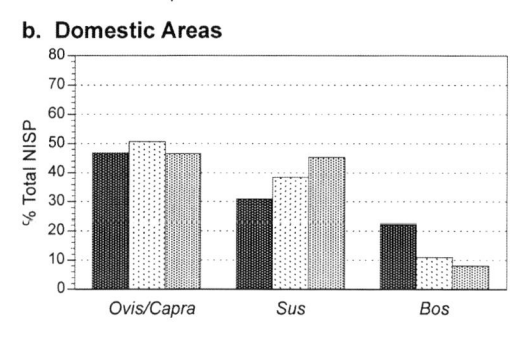

Figure 7.5 Relative bone frequencies for major domesticated animal taxa at Tell el-Hayyat, Phases 5-3, expressed as percentages of total number of identified specimens (NISP), excluding other domesticates (equids) and wild taxa. A. All architectural settings, χ^2 = 183.21, df = 4, p < 0.001; NISP: Phase 5 = 2427, Phase 4 = 2802, Phase 3 = 1822. B. Domestic areas, χ^2 = 86.69, df = 4, p < 0.001; NISP: Phase 5 = 832, Phase 4 = 882, Phase 3 = 703 (drafting by Barbara Trapido-Lurie).

and ceramic data, suggesting adjustments in economic strategy at Tell el-Hayyat between Middle Bronze IIA and IIB.

Spatial patterns of animal bone deposition also reveal several aspects of social and economic organization at Hayyat (see Figure 6.2). Bone assemblages from temple compounds are dominated by ovicaprid remains (82-92% NISP in Phases 5-3), probably reflecting communal ritual behavior focused on sheep and goats. A similar emphasis on ovicaprids indicates formal offerings and sacrifices associated with Early Bronze IV and Middle Bronze II burials in the southern Levant (Horwitz 1987). In contrast, Hayyat's domestic assemblages contain substantial, but less overwhelming, frequencies of ovicaprid bones (47-51% NISP). The sheep: goat ratios from temple compounds mirror those for the site generally (Table 7.1). The ratios from domestic sectors also follow the same general trend but, interestingly, sheep remains are more prominent in all three phases. These results show that ovicaprid use was marked by a greater preference for sheep in households than in temple contexts.

The other major animal taxa at Tell el-Hayyat reveal more pronounced changes through time in which the relative abundance of pigs increases, while that of cattle decreases (see Figure 7.5a). These trends are reiterated in domestic assemblages that feature substantial amounts of pig bones (Figure 7.5b). A drop in cattle frequency follows from a shift toward sheep husbandry. Although cattle may be important traction animals, as grazers they complete for forage more often with sheep, which both graze and browse, than with goats, which prefer browsing (Redding 1984). One might suspect that decreased deposition of cattle bones represents a change in management strategy, perhaps due to increased demand for mature draft animals.

Bos survivorship curves, however, show minimal differences between phases and no trend of change through time (Figure 7.6a). The same characteristics are true of *Sus* survivorship curves (Figure 7.6b). These curves show maximum mortality rates for both taxa prior to ages when the rate of food intake starts to exceed that of increased meat weight (Horwitz 1989; Cribb 1984, 1987; Payne 1973). Therefore, these data demonstrate that both cattle and pig were managed primarily for meat. While the management of each taxon changed little from phase to phase, the occupants of Tell el-Hayyat increasingly augmented their sheep and goat husbandry with herds of swine, rather than cattle.

In contrast to the enhanced potential for market-oriented ovicaprid husbandry noted above, increased pig and diminished cattle bone deposition through the Middle Bronze Age generally reflect a growing emphasis on a household-based subsistence economy. Pigs provide few secondary products, have high water requirements, and are poorly suited for herding to market (Wapnish and Hesse 1988; Horwitz and Tchernov 1989). At the same time, among southwestern Asian domesticates their meat carries the highest fat and caloric value, they produce the largest number of offspring per birth, and they reach harvestable age faster than any bovid (Zeder 1991: 30). Swine can subsist as domestic scavengers and may be managed effectively by individual families (Grigson 1982). Because pig husbandry engendered little participation in market exchange, it provided an effective hedge against regulation and taxation by central institutions. Therefore, pig husbandry was actively discouraged by some urban authorities (Diener and Robkin 1978), and flourished when institutional controls were relaxed (Redding 1991; Zeder 1990). Accordingly, it is symptomatic of economic autonomy at both village and household levels.

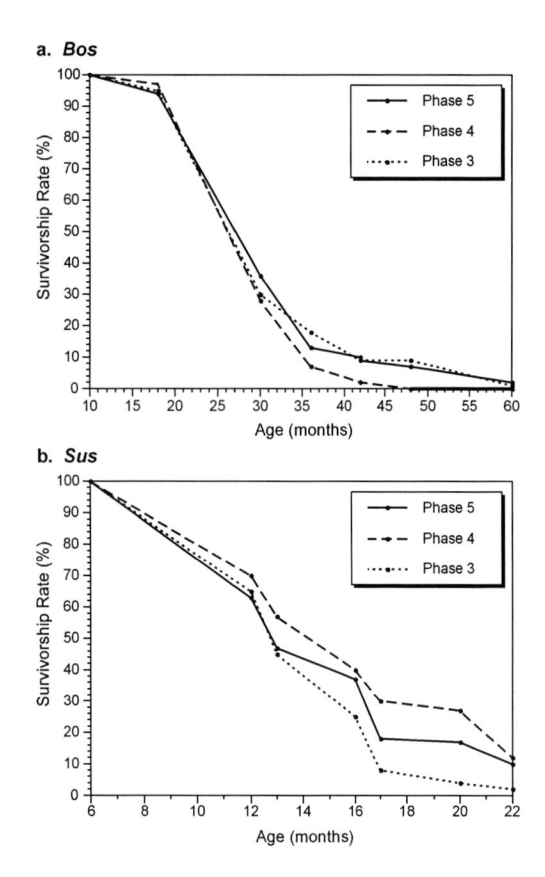

Figure 7.6 Faunal survivorship curves at Tell el-Hayyat, Phases 5-3; data from all architectural settings expressed in percentages of NISP that could be aged by bone fusion or tooth eruption. A. *Bos taurus* (cattle), NISP: Phase 5 = 137, Phase 4 = 109, Phase 3 = 44. B. *Sus scrofa* (pig); NISP: Phase 5 = 60, Phase 4 = 67, Phase 3 = 51 (drafting by Barbara Trapido-Lurie).

The frequency of pig bones in domestic settings at Tell el-Hayyat (31-45% NISP) is extremely high in comparison to that in contemporaneous settlements in southwestern Asia. Most Levantine Middle Bronze Age sites report *Sus* frequencies on the order of 10% NISP (e.g., Clutton-Brock 1979; Hellwing and Gophna 1984; Wapnish and Hesse 1988; Horwitz 1989). The Egyptian Old Kingdom village of Kom el-Hisn provides a notable exception to this tendency. The age profile of the cattle assemblage from Kom el-Hisn is consistent with natural rates of cattle mortality, suggesting that local villagers consumed cattle that died of natural causes (Redding 1992). Meanwhile, most of their animal protein was provided by pigs. This dietary pattern is reflected by frequencies of cattle bones (2% NISP) and pig bones (56% NISP) more comparable to those of Tell el-Hayyat.

The abundance of pig bones at Hayyat is particularly intriguing given the village's distance from permanent water sources. To meet their water needs, these swine may have been herded periodically in the *zor*, the active floodplain of the Jordan River, as a specialized aspect of pig husbandry. Regardless of where they foraged, pigs were intended for domestic consumption, as indicated by the patterning of bones in and around household architecture. In contrast to temple compounds and domestic exteriors, pig bones constitute the majority of the faunal assemblages from domestic interiors. A spatial comparison of *Sus* bone element deposition in Phases 4 and 3 reveals significantly greater representation of head fragments in domestic exteriors, whereas domestic interiors produce more abundant limb, trunk, and foot bones (Table 7.2). The higher frequencies of trunk and limb elements, often categorized as "consumption offal" (e.g., Hellwing and Gophna 1984), suggest that interior assemblages are more indicative of household dietary refuse. Greater exterior frequencies of head fragments, elements of the "slaughter offal," reflect the deposition of butchering refuse in alleyways. Paradoxically, pig foot bones, also considered slaughter offal, are more abundant in domestic interiors. This may reflect cases in which feet remained attached intentionally or unintentionally to butchered limbs. More intriguingly, this pattern parallels historical cases in which pig feet were preferred ingredients in soups or stews among lower status households because of their high fat content (Crader 1990).

Table 7.2 Frequencies of pig bone elements in domestic areas at Tell el-Hayyat, Phases 4 and 3 presented as percentages of NISP*

Setting	Head (%)	Feet (%)	Llimbs/trunk (%)	NISP
Phase 4				
Interior	46.2	17.9	35.9	106
Exterior	61.5	10.5	28	200
Phase 3				
Interior	39.2	37.3	23.5	51
Exterior	67.5	13.9	18.7	252

* Phase 4: $\chi^2 = 7.186$, df = 2, p=.028
Phase 3: $\chi^2 = 18.909$, df = 2, p<.001

Table 7.3. Frequencies of ovicaprid bone elements in domestic areas at Tell el-Hayyat, Phases 4 and 3 presented as percentages of NISP.*

Setting	Head (%)	Feet (%)	Limbs/trunk (%)	NISP
Phase 4				
Interior	35.6	9.6	54.8	73
Exterior	47.1	16.7	36.2	323
Phase 3				
Interior	51.3	7.7	41	39
Exterior	41	17	42.1	271

* Phase 4: $\chi^2 = 8.879$, df = 2, p=.012
Phase 3: $\chi^2 = 2.727$, df = 2, p=.256

A similar comparison of ovicaprid bones (Table 7.3) shows a predictable dichotomy between interior dietary refuse and exterior butchering refuse in Phase 4. The Phase 3 assemblages, however, reveal very similar interior and exterior distributions. Two aspects of this patterning are noteworthy for their contrasts with the pig bone evidence. First, in both phases ovicaprid feet, with their substantially lower fat content, are more abundant in exterior assemblages with other elements of slaughter offal. This implies that ungulate feet were routinely severed from butchered limbs, and that the interior co-occurrence of pig limbs and feet reflects an intentional dietary preference among Hayyat's households. Second, while the segregation of pig body parts becomes more marked between Phases 4 and 3, interior/exterior distinctions in the ovicaprid data become insignificant by Phase 3. This result may simply reflect small interior sample size, or it may suggest that with increased pig consumption, ovicaprid bone elements provide a less distinct signature of household diet.

The salient characteristics of these zooarchaeological data indicate mixed strategies of animal husbandry at Tell el-Hayyat. The general importance of sheet/goat husbandry and escalating sheep:goat ratios suggest potentially increased involvement in regional exchange of animal goods, particularly secondary products associated with sheep. This village was far from a dedicated producer of goods for urban markets, however. Hayyat's households show a marked preference for sheep *consumption*, as well as marketing. Further, these households consumed greater amounts of pork and lesser amounts of beef, reflecting an increased emphasis on household-managed animal husbandry through the Middle Bronze Age. Some aspects of growing market potential, combined with persistent household autonomy, also are embodied in Hayyat's botanical evidence.

Consumption and Exchange of Cultivated Plants

The floral remains recovered from Tell el-Hayyat include three main categories of cultivated taxa: cereals, legumes, and fruit-bearing trees and vines (Fall 1983; Lines 1995; see Chapter 5). Again in keeping with most post-Neolithic sites in southwestern Asia (see Miller 1991; Zohary and Hopf 1988), these assemblages are dominated by domesticated cereals, especially hulled two-row barley (*Hordeum distichum*), bread wheat (*Triticum aestivum/T. compactum*), einkorn (*T. monococcum*) and emmer (*T. dicoccum*) wheat. Legume cultivation supplemented the cereals, as it has since the advent of mixed agriculture. Hayyat's most common legumes include peas (*Pisum sativum*), lentils (*Lens culinaris*) and bitter vetch (*V. ervilia*). In addition to these long-standing staple crops, the Bronze Age introduced intensive cultivation and inter-regional exchange of fruits and fruit products. Tell el-Hayyat's fruit assemblages primarily feature olives (*Olea europaea*), figs (*Ficus carica*) and grapes (*Vitus vinifera*).

The most striking floral change occurs between Phases 4 and 3, in which the frequency of fruit macrofossils rises and that of cultivated cereals drops (Figure 7.7). More specific implications of this shift are clarified when the major taxonomic categories are recombined into annual cultigens (i.e., cereals and legumes) and perennial fruits. Cultivated annuals generally prefer deep loam or clay soils (Renfrew 1973; Borowski 1987: 89-96), and would have constituted the major crops in the Jordan Valley bottomlands around Tell el-Hayyat. These crops were grown in bulk for local subsistence and required large-scale storage in grain pits or granaries (Borowski 1987:71-72).

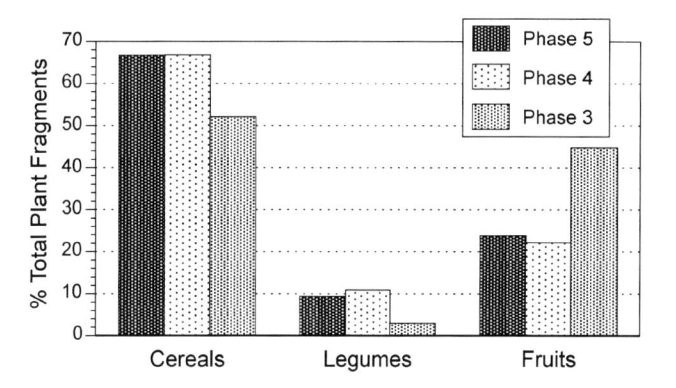

Figure 7.7 Relative frequencies of cultivated plant macrofossils from all architectural settings at Tell el-Hayyat, Phases 5-3, expressed as percentages of total identified seeds. $\chi^2 = 150.08$, df = 4, p < 0.001; number: Phase 5 = 1170, Phase 4 = 707, Phase 3 = 849 (drafting by Barbara Trapido-Lurie).

Grape vines, and olive and fig trees, on the other hand, prefer thinner sandy or rocky soils more commonly found in the Levantine hills, where they continue to flourish today (Renfrew 1973:131-134; Zohary 1982:56-58; Borowski 1987:114). Even if the surrounding bottomlands were dedicated to annual crops, Hayyat's farmers probably produced orchard commodities, since suitable hill slopes lay only 3 km to the east. Grapevines and fig trees appear in the Old Testament as symbols of stability and prosperity because they, along with olive trees, require up to a decade of maintenance before producing abundantly (Boardman 1976:189; Hopkins 1985:227; Borowski 1987:103, 114). Further, olive trees generally fruit only once every two years (Forbes and Foxhall 1978). Once in production, however, these fruit taxa yielded commodities (olive oil, wine, and dried figs) that could be marketed effectively in ceramic vessels using simple overland transport (Stager 1985). Unlike bulk grain crops, these products carried great value, even when traded in relatively modest quantities. For example, the natural preservation of dried figs made them a highly desired commodity when other fresh crops were out of season (Zohary 1982:58). In addition to their versatility, olives were prized for their high oil content. They were the most important among very few sources of vegetable oil (Renfrew 1973: 134; Forbes and Foxhall 1978). Thus, a ratio of annual to perennial plant macrofossils reflects the relative consumption of locally-grown subsistence crops versus those with greater potential significance for regional trade.

When data are combined from all architectural settings, ratios of annual to perennial macrofossils show a major disjunction between Phases 4 and 3 (Table 7.4), very much in keeping with a similar shift in sheep:goat ratios (see Table 7.1). In this case, the ratio drops substantially, indicating a relative increase in fruit fragments. The annual:perennial ratios for temple compounds are highly variable, but also show this decline. The domestic macrofossils, on the other hand, show higher rates of cereal grain deposition, and statistically insignificant changes in the mix of annual and perennial crops through time.

Table 7.4 Ratios of annual to perennial plant macrofossils at Tell el-Hayyat, Phases 3-5 based on number of identified seeds*

Phase	Annual: perennial	Seeds (n)	Samples (n)
All Settings			
3	1.23:1	849	33
4	3.50:1	707	37
5	3.19:1	1170	43
Temple Compounds			
3	0.22:1	347	13
4	2.30:1	66	16
5	1.46:1	113	12
Domestic areas			
3	4.23:1	502	20
4	3.68:1	641	21
5	3.54:1	1057	31

* All settings: $\chi^2 = 131.090$, df = 2, p<.001
Temple compounds: $x^2 = 110.993$, df = 2, p<.001
Domestic areas: $\chi^2 = 1.758$, df = 2, p<.415.

Table 7.5 Ratios of annual to perennial plant macrofossils at Tell el-Hayyat, Phases 4 and 3 based on number of identified seeds*

Setting	Annual: perennial	Seeds (n)	Samples (n)
Phase 4			
Interior	10.84:1	296	11
Exterior	3.38:1	241	8
Phase 3			
Interior	5.79:1	326	10
Exterior	2.42:1	164	10

* Phase 4: $\chi^2 = 21.654$, df = 1, p<.001
Phase 3: $\chi^2 = 14.651$, df = 1, p<.001

These ratios distinguish communal display behavior involving highly valued, marketable fruit products in temple compounds from household plant consumption, which emphasized grain and legume subsistence crops. This inference is strengthened by distinction between domestic interiors and exteriors comparable to those for distributions of ovicaprid and pig bone elements. Interior assemblages in Phases 4 and 3 produce much higher ratios that reiterate the domestic orientation of annual crop consumption, particularly involving cereal grains (Table 7.5).

As with the evidence for domestic animal management at Tell el-Hayyat, these data generate a mixed message of increased exchange tempered by subsistence-oriented household consumption. Increased fruit deposition from Phase 4 to Phase 3 implies greater participation in regional economies. While this is apparent at the community level in Hayyat's temple deposits, it is not true of household remains. Domestic plant deposition, in which annual:perennial ratios remain effectively static, indicates that intensified fruit cultivation was not triggered simply by the needs of a growing population at Hayyat, since increased fruit production did not trickle down to the level of individual household consumption. This theme of mixed economic strategies continues in a consideration of ceramic vessels that once contained Hayyat's plant products. In the face of growing potential for exchange of commodities, most changes in pottery production and function reflect trends toward greater household autonomy.

POTTERY MANUFACTURE AND FUNCTION

The Tell el-Hayyat ceramic assemblages may be divided into three major functional categories based on clay/temper composition, vessel morphology, and ethnographic analogy: cooking pots (flat-bottomed and ovoid varieties), storejars (for long-term or short-term storage) and serving vessels (see discussion in Chapter 6). Rim frequencies from all architectural settings in Phases 5 through 3 show fairly static patterns of cooking pot deposition, a decrease in storage vessels and an increase in serving vessels (Figure 7.8a). These trends are reiterated in data pertaining to domestic areas from which the majority of the ceramics was excavated (Figure 7.8b). Data from the temple compounds also show a decrease in storage jar rim frequency, but cooking pot rims become more frequent through time, while serving vessels drop, then rise sharply in frequency (Figure 7.8c). The economic implications of these changes may be clarified by considering trends within, as well as between, functional categories.

The generally-increased relative abundance of serving vessels, particularly in Phase 3, may stem from a variety of factors. These relatively simple, but finely crafted, bowl forms are particularly amenable to standardized, wheel-thrown construction and centralized production in larger communities. One neutron activation analysis of Middle and Late Bronze Age pottery from the Jordan Valley suggests that most fineware ceramics were distributed from central workshops in towns like Pella and Beth She'an (Knapp et al. 1988; Knapp 1989). With this in mind, it is tempting to infer that Tell el-Hayyat received more centrally manufactured ceramics through time. However, another neutron activation analysis of Middle Bronze Age ceramics in the Jordan Valley suggests an element of fineware bowl manufacture at Hayyat itself (Falconer 1987a, 1994b). Therefore, a more conservative interpretation simply proposes that the increased consumption and deposition of serving vessels at Tell el-Hayyat probably derived from both urban and rural production sites. Although somewhat equivocal, these results suggest increased exchange of manufactured goods between Hayyat and neighboring communities. In

HOUSEHOLD ECONOMY AT TELL EL-HAYYAT

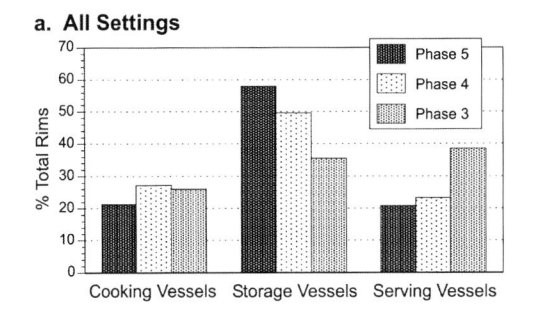

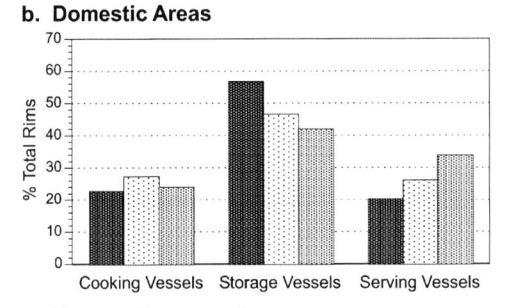

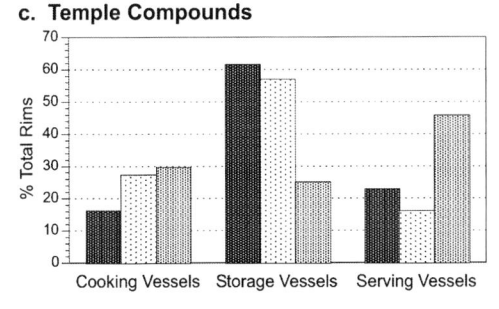

Figure 7.8 Relative rim frequencies for major functional categories of pottery at Tell el-Hayyat, Phases 5-3, expressed as percentages of total identified rims, corrected for multiple sherds from the same vessel. A. All architectural settings, $\chi^2 = 156.17$, df = 4, p < 0.001; number: Phase 5 = 833, Phase 4 = 1685, Phase 3 = 1449. B. Domestic areas, $\chi^2 = 48.24$, df = 4, p < 0.001; number: Phase 5 = 644, Phase 4 = 1213, Phase 3 = 902. C. Temple compounds, $\chi^2 = 166.16$, df = 4, p < 0.001; number: Phase 5 = 189, Phase 4 = 472, Phase 3 = 547 (drafting by Barbara Trapido-Lurie).

contrast, deposition patterns for cooking and storage vessels reveal more demonstrative trends toward increased village autonomy through the Middle Bronze Age.

Cooking Vessels

Distinctions in cooking vessel morphology denote multiple models of manufacture, as discussed in Chapter 6. Data from Tell el-Hayyat show a significant diachronic increase in ratios of flat-bottomed to ovoid cooking pots, with a marked rise from Phase 4 to Phase 3 (Table 7.6). Interestingly, this result is not simply a reflection of changing stylistic preferences during the Middle Bronze Age. At most Levantine sites, flat-bottomed cooking pots become less abundant in Middle Bronze IIB and IIC (Amiran 1970:101-102; Cole 1984:61-63). Instead, these data reveal an increasing element of local, unspecialized manufacture of cooking pots through the Middle Bronze Age, even as the towns and cities of the southern Levant presented growing potential for more centralized manufacture and exchange.

Table 7.6 Ratios of flat-bottomed to ovoid cooking vessels at Tell el-Hayyat, Phases 3-5 based on rim counts corrected for joins*

Phase	All settings	No.	Temple compounds	No.	Domestic areas	No.
3	8.40:1	376	12.25:1	159	6.75:1	217
4	2.98:1	458	2.26:1	127	3.36:1	331
5	2.05:1	177	0.76:1	30	2.59:1	147

* All settings: $\chi^2 = 43.664$, df = 2, p<.001
Temple compounds: $\chi^2 = 46.674$, df = 2, p<.001
Domestic areas: $\chi^2 = 13.607$, df = 2, p=.001.

Storage Vessels

As with cooking vessels, morphological variations among storage jars have functional implications. Both tall and squat storejars were wheel-thrown, and required similar technology and craftsmanship. Further, both forms were produced at numerous sites in the Jordan Valley, including Tell el-Hayyat, judging from the results of neutron activation analysis (Falconer 1987a, 1994b) and the presence of rims from both tall and squat storage jars among the ceramic wasters recovered from Hayyat. Ratios of long-term to short-term storejars decrease through time at Tell el Hayyat, regardless of the architectural setting considered (Table 7.7). The pervasive shift in relative rates of rim deposition reveals that Hayyat's repertoire of jars became increasingly dedicated to short-term storage, and held less potential for exchange (e.g., of wine and olive oil) with neighboring villages and towns.

Table 7.7 Ratios of long-term to short-term storage vessels at Tell el-Hayyat, Phases 3-5 based on rim counts corrected for joins*

Phase	All settings	No.	Temple compounds	No.	Domestic areas	No.
3	3.15:1	515	3.12:1	136	3.16:1	379
4	6.72:1	834	11.81:1	269	5.49:1	565
5	8.09:1	482	37.67:1	116	6.32:1	366

* All settings: $\chi^2 = 40.394$, df = 2, p<.001
Temple compounds: $\chi^2 = 16.655$, df = 2, p<.001
Domestic areas: $\chi^2 = 35.801$, df = 2, p<.001.

HOUSEHOLD MATERIAL CULTURE

Tell el-Hayyat's house interiors and especially alleyways provide a variety of evidence pertaining to household activities. Careful excavation of domestic and temple remains (Figure 7.9) produced assemblages indicative of both household and communal activities (Figure 7.10).

Figure 7.9 Ron Gardiner and Bonnie Magness-Gardiner excavate mudbrick walls in the southwest corner of the Phase 4 temple at Tell el-Hayyat, facing southwest (photo by Karen Scholz). A pick and shovel rest against the Phase 4 temple southern enclosure wall to the left; the brick coursing of the Phase 3 western enclosure wall is clearly visible in the balk face to the right.

Domestic evidence includes the pottery discussed in Chapter 4, as well as other ceramics, such as perforated disks (often interpreted as spindle whorls) and half of a clay bulla. More whimsical artifacts feature an apparent toy, in the form of a hand-molded clay bowl with several marble-sized clay balls, plus a unique clay jar stopper (Figures 7.11 and 7.12). Both items were recovered from a pit with pottery manufacturing debris, including two wasters, in the East Building of Phase 4. Non-ceramic vessels include ground and polished stone bowls (e.g., Figures 7.13 and 7.14). The ground stone industry produced a variety of grinding and pounding implements, plus an array of perforated stone disks (Figures 7.15-7.17). Abundant ceramic spindle whorls, and worked animal bone awls, shuttles and scrapers (Figures 7.18 and 7.19) suggest possible household industries, such as weaving. Squared off sheep/goat astragali attest to possible household gaming. More enigmatic remains include hollowed-out sheep/goat long bones (Figure 7.20), some of which are shaved to triangular or square cross-sections, with various combinations of drilled holes (Figure 7.21). Forms of personal adornment are exemplified by marine shell jewelry (Figures 7.22). Tell el-Hayyat's Phase 2 includes two surprising examples of glyptic evidence. A complete scarab emerged from fill deposits in the East Building, Room 1 (Figure 7.23) and a fragment of an apparent seal impression was recovered from a surface in the West Building, Room 1 (Figure 7.24). These remains provide a strikingly rich record of household behavior amid the development of Middle Bronze Age village life at Tell el-Hayyat.

Figure 7.10 Smashed jars, a juglet and grinding stone lie in Phase 2 occupational debris (Locus T022) just above an earthen surface in the East Building (Sector EB) at Tell el-Hayyat, facing east (photo by Karen Scholz).

Figure 7.11 Clay pinch pot with clay marbles from a shallow Phase 4 pit (Locus K064) in the East Building (Sector EB) at Tell el-Hayyat.

Figure 7.12 Clay jar stopper from a shallow Phase 4 pit (Locus K064) in the East Building (Sector EB) at Tell el-Hayyat.

Figure 7.13 Basalt bowl from a Phase 4 surface (Locus J059) in the East Alley (Sector EA) at Tell el-Hayyat.

Figure 7.14 Polished porphery bowl fragment, probably Middle Bronze Age, but found in mixed Phase 0 deposits in Area H at Tell el-Hayyat.

Figure 7.15 Examples of the ground stone industry from domestic contexts at Tell el-Hayyat, including a large stone mortar, basalt grinding stones, and drilled and perforated cobbles.

Figure 7.16 Examples of domestic ground stone from Tell el-Hayyat, including basalt grinders, a perforated stone weight and worked limestone

Figure 7.17 Perforated ceramic (center top) and stone disks from domestic contexts at Tell el-Hayyat.

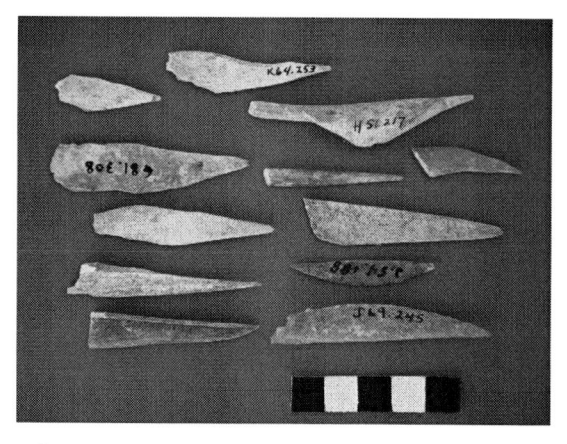

Figure 7.18 Worked animal bone tools from households at Tell el-Hayyat, including scrapers, awls and shuttles.

Figure 7.19 Finely sharpened animal bone awl or needle fragments from domestic contexts at Tell el-Hayyat.

Figure 7.20 Hollowed sheep/goat long bones found amid Phase 3 and Phase 4 household remains at Tell el-Hayyat.

Figure 7.21 Hollowed and perforated sheep/goat tibiae from Phase 3 and Phase 4 domestic contexts at Tell el-Hayyat.

Figure 7.22 Marine shell amulet from fill in the Central Alley, Phase 4 at Tell el-Hayyat.

Figure 7.23 Scarab from fill in the East Building, Room 1, Phase 2 at Tell el-Hayyat.

Figure 7.24 Seal impression on a clay fragment from a surface in the West Building, Room 1, Phase 2 at Tell el-Hayyat. Arrow indicates 1 cm.

CONCLUSIONS

Patterns of faunal, floral and ceramic deposition, as well as household paraphernalia, reveal several salient aspects of household and village economy at Tell el-Hayyat. In turn, these data provide a glimpse of urban-rural relations and the economic structure of Middle Bronze Age society in the southern Levant. The inhabitants of Tell el-Hayyat responded to the influence of Jordan Valley towns with a mixture of strategies that primarily enhanced their economic autonomy, but also expanded some avenues for regional interaction.

Although its temples might suggest that Tell el-Hayyat was part of an institutional estate (e.g., similar to those attested near Ugarit and Alalakh), only limited aspects of Hayyat's economy reveal the intimate ties to external markets that we might expect for such a community. For example, sheep became the more important oviacprid, presumably for their marketable secondary products. Increased relative frequencies of fruit taxa and serving vessels reflect greater exchange of high-value agricultural and manufactured products in keeping with larger economic trends in the southern Levant. Enhanced fruit consumption is not expressed at the household level, in which plant deposition remains oriented toward annual cereals and legumes. Orchard cultivation may have become directed toward external markets or managed at a supra-household level.

These trends, however, are overshadowed by a predominance of data suggesting accentuated economic autonomy at Tell el-Hayyat. For instance, while the potential for ovicaprid secondary products grew, sheep remained important sources of meat for domestic consumption. The market potential of sheep husbandry was tempered further by increased pig herding with a pronounced household orientation. While the increased deposition of serving vessels can only hint at greater interaction with neighboring villages and towns, most ceramic data signal a more demonstrable shift toward household pottery production. The manufacture of cooking vessels became increasingly localized, storage jars became less suitable for exchange of commodities, and the storage functions of Hayyat's temples and households converged.

These changes are most pronounced between Phases 4 and 3, which span the transition from the initial redevelopment of towns in Middle Bronze IIA to the peak of Canaanite urbanism in Middle Bronze IIB. Because the Jordan Valley shows little alteration in settlement patterns during the Middle Bronze Age (Falconer and Savage 1995), some of these shifts may have been responses to the opportunities and impositions created by more distant Levantine towns and cites.

In overview, the economic behaviors reflected at Tell el-Hayyat were more strongly predicated on self-interest than on the demands of estate managers or absentee landowners. Most of the interpretations above are consistent with the development of an increasingly independent economic base at Tell el-Hayyat. In keeping with our expectations for autonomous settlements, growing community investments are reflected in the increased size and elaboration of Hayyat's temple and domestic architecture. Likewise, this village performed activities otherwise concentrated in cities, including the manufacture of copper alloy tools, weapons, and figurines, and of a variety of ceramic vessels (Falconer 1987a; 1994b; Falconer and Magness-Gardiner 1989).

In light of these characteristics, it is tempting to portray Tell el-Hayyat as an archaeological example of a collectively owned village, analogous to those known historically from ancient Syria and ethnographically from a variety of locales throughout southwestern Asia. We may conclude more assuredly that Tell el-Hayyat illustrates the resilient nature of many rural communities at the foundation of Middle Bronze Age society in the southern Levant, in which production and consumption were inspired more by long-term community survival than short-term economic maximization (see Adams 1978). This resilience is embodied in household and village economics that exploited some opportunities presented by town and city markets, but simultaneously insured community autonomy in the face of the inevitable liability of urbanism.

CHAPTER 8: BRONZE AGE AGRARIAN ECOLOGY ALONG THE JORDAN RIFT

INTRODUCTION

Tell el-Hayyat provides a vantage point for inferring rural ecology, not only on a local scale, but in terms of larger patterns that characterized the regional agrarian development of Bronze Age communities along the Jordan Rift. A variety of settlements along the Rift illustrate the effects of the mid-Holocene "secondary products revolution" (Sherratt 1981), during which a wave of agricultural intensification caused widespread impacts on rural agriculture, urban-rural relations, and their physical and social landscapes. In Sherratt's estimation, the most significant effects of this revolution stemmed from the harnessing of domesticated animal power and a regime of animal husbandry dedicated increasingly to the marketing of derivative products. Here we consider, from the vantage point of Tell el-Hayyat, the larger context of Bronze Age economic shifts, especially in crop cultivation, as they affected Bronze Age rural communities and molded the natural and cultural landscapes of the southern Levant.

The village of Tell el-Hayyat developed during the growth of Middle Bronze Age mercantilism, which featured greater production of marketable goods, especially wool and dairy products (Sherratt 1981). This shift was augmented by the use of traction animals (i.e., cattle and equids) to expand and intensify cultivation, and for the transportation of agricultural products to burgeoning urban markets. We expand the concept of the secondary products revolution to include the ecological and social effects of the domestication of orchard crops and the marketing of *their* derivative commodities, especially since paleoenvironmental evidence from the Jordan Rift and excavated evidence from Tell el-Hayyat underscore the importance of arboriculture as the most important avenue for human impacts on Bronze Age landscapes. As Sherratt notes, the plow permitted agricultural exploitation of a wider range of soils and landscapes. This broadened agricultural regime entailed the clearance of large tracts of natural vegetation to establish orchards. Technological innovation also featured the inception of animal-drawn carts, which facilitated transport and trade of secondary products over wide regions. These included not only animal products, but the renderings of orchard crops: dried fruits (e.g., figs, dates), wine and olive oil. With the advent of plow agriculture and urbanized economies, Sherratt points out that the transmission of land carried greater economic implications, as long-term investment in perennial orchards triggered increasingly complex systems of ownership, inheritance and land tenure.

These general economic considerations might suggest that an overview of Bronze Age agrarian ecology would simply describe a gradual trajectory of linked urbanism, commercial agriculture and deforestation (Naveh and Dan 1973: 47; Naveh 1990). The seemingly impoverished modern landscapes of the Middle East would seem to be logical products of such processes. Upon closer analysis, however, these landscapes appear as intricate palimpsests that reflect the interactions of ever-changing agricultural and pastoral economies and a suite of impacts that vary over time and space (Falconer and Fall 1995). In southwestern Asia, a long history of sheep/goat pastoralism may have entailed significant defoliation. Indeed, the periodic collapse of Near Eastern cities often engenders hypotheses of greater non-sedentary pastoralism. This perspective is well exemplified in the literature surrounding the particularly dramatic region-wide abandonment of Levantine urbanism during Early Bronze IV (e.g., Dever 1995). A more nuanced interpretation shows, however, that the distinctly humanized environment of the Near East resulted from a series of cultural strategies with clear, sometimes dramatic, starts and stops. Even in the midst of these cultural and environmental fluxes, the Mediterranean basin, including the southern Levant, boasts agricultural systems and societies that have proven sustainable over particularly long time spans (Butzer 1996).

The inception of urbanized society, incorporating regional mercantile exchange, compounded the impacts of early agriculture, especially through renewed forest clearance and newly-expanded orchard cultivation. A diachronic study of cereal and fruit cultivation at four archaeological sites in the Jordan Rift illustrates the effects of the secondary products revolution over the fourth through second millennia B.C. and the larger ecological setting for Middle Bronze Age society, as exemplified at Tell el-Hayyat. In particular, the development of orchard cultivation carried profound economic and environmental implications, and left clearly discernible evidence of the anthropogenic landscape that surrounded the village of Tell el-Hayyat.

BRONZE AGE AGRICULTURE ALONG THE JORDAN RIFT

By the third millennium B.C. the secondary products revolution had utterly transformed the ways in which farmers utilized their fields and resources. The Bronze Age marked a watershed in agricultural intensification in the southern Levant and the widespread exchange of agricultural products throughout the Eastern

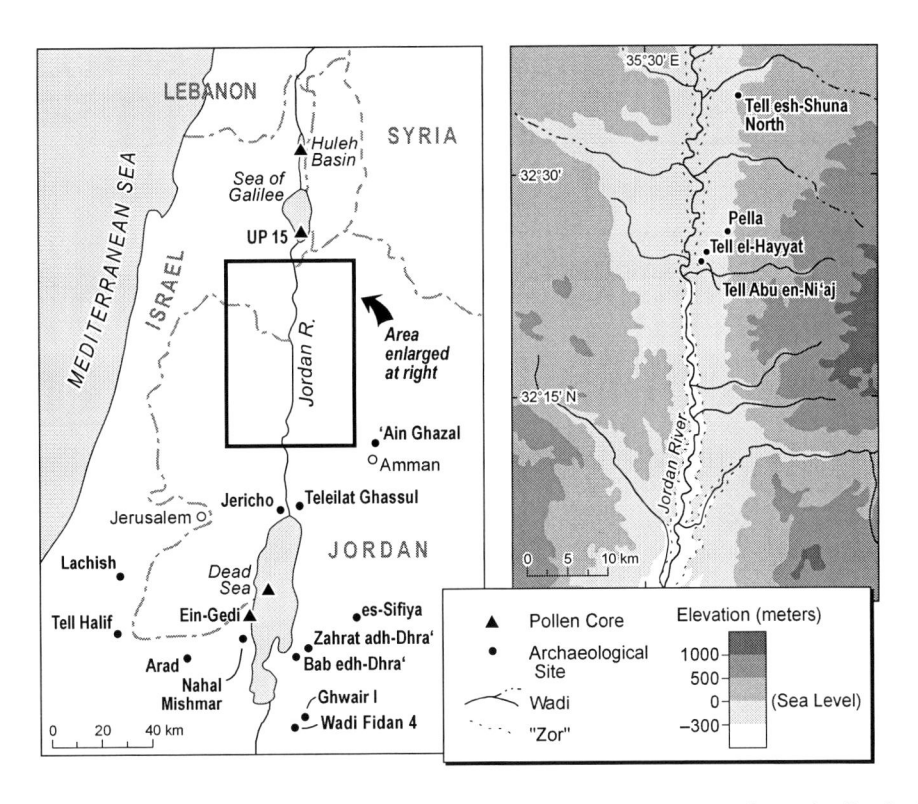

Figure 8.1 Archaeological sites and paleoenvironmental localities in the southern Levant, including Bab edh-Dhra' and Wadi Fidan 4 near the Dead Sea. Inset specifies locations of Tell el-Hayyat and Tell Abu en-Ni'aj in the northern Jordan Valley (drafting by Barbara Trapido-Lurie).

Mediterranean (Stager 1985; Ben-Tor 1986). Paleobotanical data from Tell el-Hayyat, when linked with evidence from three other Bronze Age settlements along the Jordan Rift, detail the most basic changes in crop production entailed by the secondary products revolution.

Research conducted at these sites features systematic recovery and quantified assessment of plant remains from the beginning of the Early Bronze Age to the end of the Middle Bronze Age, holding implications for our understanding of the advent, abandonment, and rebirth of towns and regional economies (see Table 1.1). The course of Bronze Age agricultural development is exemplified in the floral evidence from two settlements in the Dead Sea basin and two villages in the northern Jordan Valley (Figure 8.1). Around the southern Dead Sea, Wadi Fidan 4 and Bab dh-Dhra' reveal agrarian trends through the Early Bronze Age, while Tell Abu en-Ni'aj (Figure 8.2) and Tell el-Hayyat document the effects of the Early Bronze IV urban collapse and the redevelopment of towns in the Middle Bronze Age, respectively (see also Fall et al. 1998; 2002).

At the beginning of the Early Bronze Age (Early Bronze IA), Wadi Fidan 4 was a modest village of nearly one hectare perched on a rocky plateau above the Wadi Fidan (Adams and Genz 1995), south of the Dead Sea. As discussed earlier for Tell el-Hayyat, Middle Eastern village ethnographies (e.g., Kramer 1980; 1982) suggest

Figure 8.2 Pat Fall and Steve Falconer at Tell Abu en-Ni'aj, view facing southwest and the edge of the *ghor*, 1985 (photo by Karen Scholtz).

population densities between 200 and 250 people/ha, implying that Wadi Fidan 4 probably had a population of about 200. However, population estimates based on contemporaneous sites in comparably arid settings (e.g., the Negev; see Levy 1983) suggest that Wadi Fidan 4 may have housed no more than 100 (Meadows 1996: 13). The ruins of Bab edh-Dhra' spread along a plateau 220-230 mbsl (meters below sea level) overlooking the Wadi Kerak to the north and the broad Wadi Araba to the west. Following non-sedentary use of the site in Early Bronze IA, a sedentary village of perhaps 2-3 ha was inhabited during Early Bronze IB and II (Schaub and Rast 1984: 35-43; Rast and Schaub 1980: fig. 19). An expanded settlement of about 4 ha was fortified with substantial stone walls in Early Bronze III (Rast and Schaub 1980: fig. 19; Schaub and Rast 1984: 43-50, fig. 4). Most Early Bronze IV evidence is found east of the Early Bronze I-III settlement, suggesting a relocation of the village during its last occupation (Schaub and Rast 1984: 36, 55-58; Rast and Schaub 1980: 32, fig. 2). Use of ethnographic parallels would suggest populations ranging between 400 and 1,000 through the history of Bab edh-Dhra'. Tell Abu en-Ni'aj, lying about 1.5km southwest of Tell el-Hayyat, incorporates the remains of an Early Bronze IV village covering 2.5ha located 250 mbsl at the edge of the *ghor*, overlooking the *zor* (Falconer and Magness-Gardiner 1989). Architecture in seven major strata reflects successive rebuilding of the village over the course of Early Bronze IV. Ethnographic analogy suggests that the occupants of Tell Abu en-Ni'aj would have numbered 500-600 (while its successor village at Hayyat housed no more than 200; discussion in Chapter 7). Thus, these settlements represent modestly-sized villages (perhaps a small town at Bab edh-Dhra'), like the majority of those that populated the Bronze Age landscape of the Jordan Rift.

The excavation of these settlements involved intensive sediment sampling for plant macrofossils that reflect crop production and consumption, and the local environment. At all four sites flotation samples were collected non-randomly from domestic contexts that clearly contained carbonized remains, and were processed using simple water flotation (McCreery 1980: 34, 37; Lines 1995; Meadows 1996: 13, 16; see discussion in Chapter 2 for Tell el-Hayyat). We have converted seed counts for selected taxa into relative percentages to permit inference of trends through time. We present relative frequencies for barley, wheat, grape, and olive for each of the assemblages from these four sites, running from Early Bronze IA at Wadi Fidan 4 to Middle Bronze IIB-C at Tell el-Hayyat (Figures 8.3 and 8.4). Due to the potential for figs to produce very large numbers of pips, relative frequencies for fig are presented separately (Figure 8.5). The resulting values provide a long-term portrait of trends in crop production that illustrate the effects of the secondary products revolution over the Early and Middle Bronze ages (see Miller 1988; Pearsall 1989).

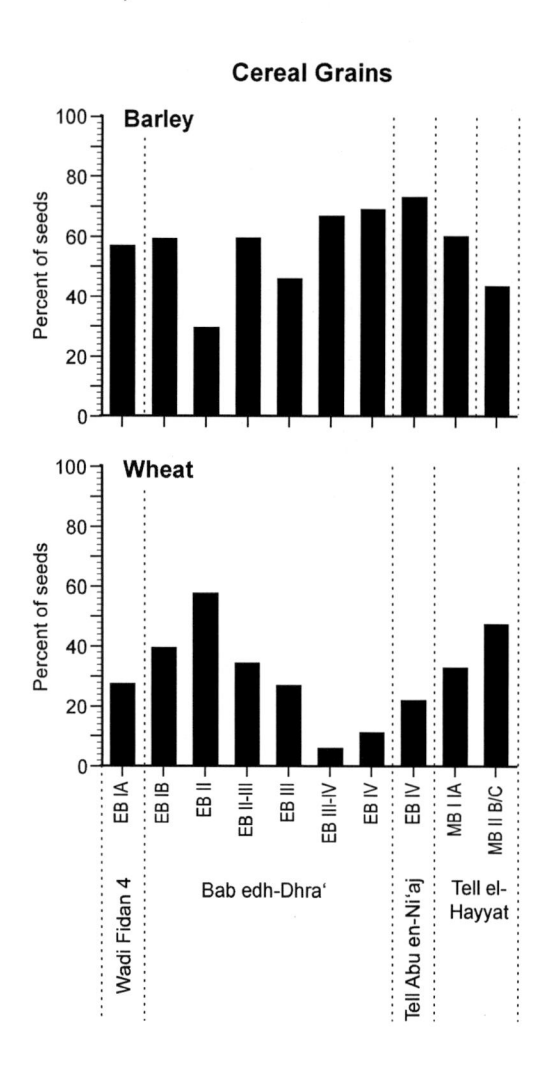

Figure 8.3 Relative frequencies of barley and wheat macrofossils recovered from Bronze Age archaeological sites along the Jordan Rift (drafting by Barbara Trapido-Lurie). Data from McCreery (1980), Lines (1995), Meadows (1996), Fall et al. (1998).

Plant macrofossils from these sites reflect four main categories of agrarian taxa: cultivated cereals, cultivated legumes, fruit-bearing trees and vines, and wild species indicative of pastures and agricultural fields. This discussion concentrates on the most abundant cereal and fruit taxa, which provided the foundation for ancient Levantine agriculture: wheat, barley, olive, grape, and fig. Wheat types include einkorn (*Triticum monococcum*), emmer (*T. dicoccum*), and bread wheat (*T. aestivum/T. compactum*), while barley is found in hulled two-row form (*Hordeum distichum*), and hulled (*H. vulgare*) and naked six-row varieties (*H. vulgare* var. *nudum*) (McCreery 1980: 73-84; Fall 1983; Lines 1995: 26-27; Meadows 1996: 24-30; see Chapter 5).

Barley frequencies undulate through the Early Bronze Age, dipping at Bab edh-Dhra during its maximum size and fortification in Early Bronze III (Figure 8.3). During Early Bronze IV, barley values peak at both Bab edh-Dhra' and Tell Abu en-Ni'aj, then drop through the

BRONZE AGE AGRARIAN ECOLOGY ALONG THE JORDAN RIFT

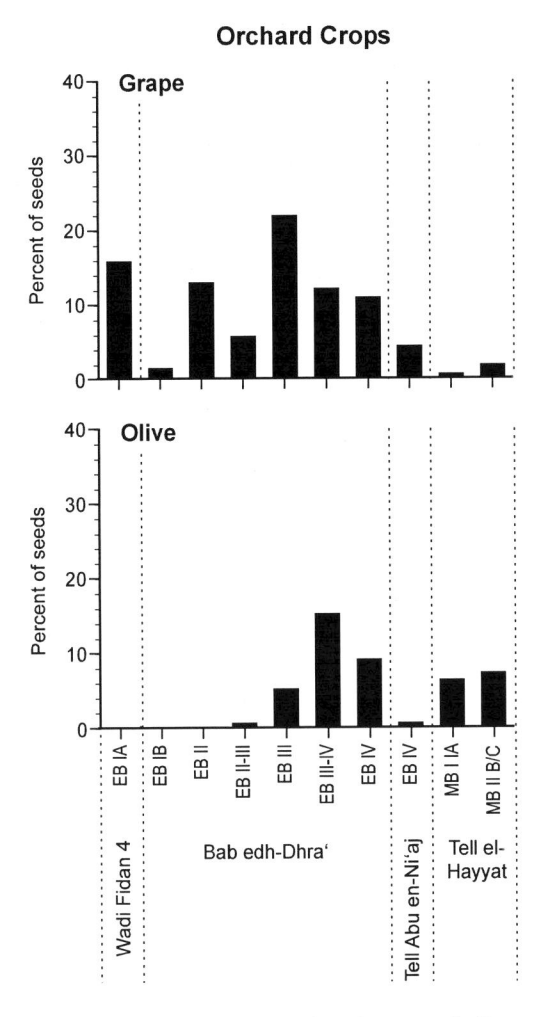

Figure 8.4 Relative frequencies of grape and olive macrofossils recovered from Bronze Age archaeological sites along the Jordan Rift (drafting by Barbara Trapido-Lurie). Data from McCreery (1980), Lines (1995), Meadows (1996), Fall et al. (1998).

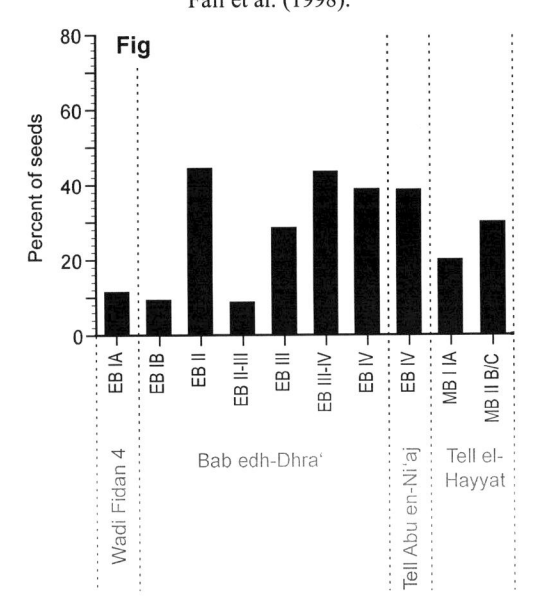

Figure 8.5 Relative frequencies of fig macrofossils recovered from Bronze Age archaeological sites along the Jordan Rift (drafting by Barbara Trapido-Lurie). Data from McCreery (1980), Lines (1995), Meadows (1996), Fall et al. (1998).

Middle Bronze Age at Tell el-Hayyat. At all four sites barley appears most commonly in the hulled six-row variety. Since this form is used primarily for feeding livestock, these data are particularly valuable indicators of long-term shifts in the importance of pastoralism. This line of interpretation tends to affirm the hypothesis of increased pastoralism during the urban collapse of Early Bronze IV, and conversely less emphasis on herding during the appearance of towns in Early Bronze II and III, and their rejuvenation in the Middle Bronze Age, as seen at Tell el-Hayyat.

Table 8.1 Macrobotanical samples and barley:wheat ratios from Bronze Age sites along the Jordan Rift. Data from McCreery (1980); Lines (1995); Meadows (1996); Fall, et al. (1998)

Site	Period	Samples (n)	Barley: Wheat Ratio
Tell el-Hayyat	Middle Bronze IIB/C	38[1]	0.9:1
Tell el-Hayyat	Middle Bronze IIA	50[2]	1.8:1
Tell Abu en-Ni'aj	Early Bronze IV	60[3]	3.3:1
Bab edh-Dhra'	Early Bronze IV	12	6.2:1
Bab edh-Dhra'	Early Bronze III-IV	7	11.2:1
Bab edh-Dhra'	Early Bronze III	17	1.7:1
Bab edh-Dhra'	Early Bronze II-III	10	1.7:1
Bab edh-Dhra'	Early Bronze II	5[4]	0.5:1
Bab edh-Dhra'	Early Bronze I	16[5]	1.5:1
Wadi Fidan 4	Late Chalcolithic	21	2.1:1

[1] Combines data from Phases 3 and 2.
[2] Combines data from Phases 5 and 4.
[3] Combines data from Phases 7-1.
[4] Includes two samples from Early Bronze I-II.
[5] Excludes one sample from Early Bronze IA.

In contrast, evidence for wheat provides a more subtle indication of both environmental influences and market forces. Wheat remains at Wadi Fidan 4 and Bab edh-Dhra', most commonly in the form of emmer (McCreery 1980: 82-83; Meadows 1996: 24-25), increase through Early Bronze II, before dwindling through Early Bronze IV. Wheat cultivation at Bab dh-Dhra' may have involved irrigation from local springs. The trend of declining wheat frequencies during the latter half of the Early Bronze Age at Bab edh-Dhra' may be explained by coordinating multiple lines of floral evidence. Barley to wheat ratios indicate a greater emphasis on wheat among cereal grains up to Early Bronze II, followed by a return to previous levels in the next two periods (Table 8.1). The greater tolerance of barley for drought conditions and saline soils traditionally makes it a preferred crop in the face of environmental deterioration. At Bab edh-Dhra', the trend of increased barley cultivation coupled with high boron concentrations in cereal grains suggest that intensified Early Bronze Age irrigation may have led to significant soil salinization (McCreery 1980: 187-188, 199). Barley:wheat ratios register their greatest rise in late Early Bronze III and Early Bronze IV, perhaps

127

implicating local salinization due to the growth of Early Bronze Age town life or the effects of a long-term regional drought hypothesized for the late third millennium B.C. from historical and sedimentological evidence from Egypt (e.g., Bell 1971) and Syria (Weiss, et al. 1993; Courty and Weiss 1997; see discussion in Chapter 1). Thus, agricultural trends at Hayyat may reflect a relative improvement from the environmental conditions of Early Bronze IV, as well as the influence of urban markets in the Middle Bronze Age.

As discussed previously, the most abundant evidence of arboriculture and the production of trade commodities is seen in fruit taxa: olive (*Olea europaea*), grape (*Vitus vinifera*) and fig (*Ficus carica*). The remains of fruit taxa are modest among the Early Bronze I samples, except for moderately abundant grape remains at Wadi Fidan 4 (Figures 8.4 and 8.5). However, orchard crops increase substantially in Early Bronze II, probably in response to the development of towns and mercantile economies. Once olive remains appear in significant numbers, all three major fruit taxa rise through Early Bronze III and III-IV, as Bab edh-Dhra' grows to its maximum size. Increased fruit cultivation would have been triggered locally by the expansion and fortification of Bab edh-Dhra', and regionally by the development of towns during Early Bronze II and III.

The remains of olive, grape and fig continue abundantly during the abandonment of towns in Early Bronze IV. This unexpected result suggests that although cereal cultivation shifted to barley as settlement at Bab edh-Dhra' moved outside the former town walls, local farmers continued the cultivation of well-established orchards and vineyards. Despite the substantial water and maintenance requirements of grape vines (White 1970: 229), excavated evidence from sites in particularly arid settings characteristically features a combination of abundant grape and barley remains (Fall et al. 2002). As cases in point, Early Bronze IA Wadi Fidan 4 and the Early Bronze IV villages of Bab edh-Dhra' and Tell Abu en-Ni'aj produced small amounts of wheat and little or no olive (crops with market potential), but generated substantial evidence of grape and barley (a crop often linked with drought or salinity). Excavations at Middle Bronze Age sites along the Wadi al-'Ajib, in the dry eastern desert of Jordan, adhered to this crop profile by producing grape seeds amid a predominance of barley grains, with only trace amounts of wheat and no olives (Eames 2001). This pattern suggests a tendency for agrarian populations to maintain grapevines, despite their water and maintenance requirements, even in the driest periods and environmental settings.

As we move from the collapse of towns at the end of the Early Bronze Age to their redevelopment in the Middle Bronze Age, evidence from the northern Jordan Valley shows a fundamental transition in arboriculture from grape cultivation at Tell Abu en-Ni'aj to pronounced olive production at Tell el-Hayyat (Fall et al. 1998). Significant grape remains at Ni'aj parallel those reported at Bab edh-Dhra', and suggest continued availability of water along the Jordan Rift. Greater olive cultivation at Tell el-Hayyat signals a reorientation of arboriculture, probably based on expanded orchard clearance and land holdings involving the farmers of Tell el-Hayyat, since olive trees, unlike grape vines, have broad root systems requiring spacing of ten meters between trees (Turrill 1952). This shift is especially pronounced within the Middle Bronze Age, between Hayyat Phases 4 and 3 (see discussion in Chapter 7), suggesting it was inspired by the mercantile opportunities afforded by the apex of Middle Bronze Age urbanism, and perhaps a restructuring of regional land tenure (with possible implications for the institution or expansion of *hawakir*-type land holdings; see discussion in Chapter 7).

These four ancient villages reveal a variety of trends in crop management, and the marketing and consumption of agricultural products over the rise, collapse and rejuvenation of Bronze Age town life along the Jordan Rift. Cultivation of cereals may be particularly indicative of animal management, and further implicate the effects of long-term irrigated agriculture, resulting most notably in soil salinization around Bab edh-Dhra'. The evidence for orchard management reflects a mix of climatic and cultural factors, especially the waxing and waning of Levantine towns. The households that populated these villages clearly altered their cultivation strategies in response to the mercantile opportunities and authoritarian impositions of urban institutions, especially as they involved regional trade. Agriculture tailored to the production of secondary products, especially orchard commodities, emerged foremost among village agrarian responses to the changing natural and social environments of urbanized society. The increased cultivation of orchards particularly entailed intensified environmental manipulation on a regional scale, creating, even by the Bronze Age, largely anthropogenic landscapes in the countryside surrounding villages like Tell el-Hayyat (Figure 8.6).

CONCLUSIONS

The formation of the agricultural landscapes of the southern Levant resulted from a complex overlay of ecological influences, conditioned by a variety of environmental and cultural factors operating on local and regional scales. While climatic trends must have figured prominently, the farmers of Tell el-Hayyat responded most clearly to accommodate the changing political and economic world around them. Foremost among the

Figure 8.6 Tell el-Hayyat during excavation, 1983; Christ-thorn (*Ziziphus spina-christii*) tree in fields in the foreground; hills rise to the east from the Jordan Rift Valley in the background, 1983 (photo by Jon Kline).

factors that influenced Hayyat's inhabitants were the mercantile incentives and impositions of urbanization, often revolving around the production and exchange of secondary products. This detailed consideration of Bronze Age crop management along the Jordan Rift describes complex patterns of expanded vineyard, orchard and wheat cultivation during peaks in town life, and greater barley consumption during its collapse, and perhaps during intervals of soil salinization. Detailed study of the agrarian economy of Tell el-Hayyat specifies the variety of responses implemented by rural farmers to the opportunities and inroads of growing Middle Bronze Age urban centers and political authority. Increased production of olives, wheat, sheep, and their marketable products suggests that Hayyat's farmers clearly availed themselves of commercial opportunities in local towns such as Pella. The increasingly mercantile elements of Hayyat's agricultural regime were tempered, however, by equally pronounced strategies to enhance local economic autonomy. These results challenge us to amend our preconceptions of Bronze Age ruralism. In particular, they signal the need for interpretations of early rural communities, not simply as antitheses of towns and cities, but as they reveal a foundation of ruralism essential to all complex agrarian societies, with its own trends of agricultural adjustment and readjustment in the face of urban rise and collapse.

REFERENCES CITED

Adams, R. McC. 1978. Strategies of maximization, stability, and resilience in Mesopotamian society, settlement, and agriculture. *Proceedings of the American Philosophical Society* 122: 329-333.

Adams, R. McC. 1981. *Heartland of Cities: Surveys of Ancient Settlement and Land Use on the Central Floodplain of the Euphrates*. Chicago: University of Chicago Press.

Adams, R. McC. 1982. Property rights and functional tenure in Mesopotamian rural communities, in M. A. Dandamayev, I. Gershevitch, H. Klengel, G. Komoroczy, M. T. Larsen, and J. N. Postgate (eds.), *Societies and Languages of the Ancient Near East: Studies in Honour of I. M. Diakonoff*, pp. 1-14. London: Aris and Phillips.

Adams, R. McC. 1984. Mesopotamian social evolution: old outlooks, new goals, in T. K. Earle (ed.), *On the Evolution of Complex Societies. Essays in Honor of Harry Hoijer, 1982*, pp. 79-129. Malibu, CA: Undena Press.

Adams, R. M. & Genz, H. 1995. Excavations at Wadi Fidan 4: a Chalcolithic village complex in the copper ore district of Feinan, southern Jordan. *Palestine Exploration Quarterly* 127: 8-20.

Albright, W. F. 1932. The excavations of Tell Beit Mirsim in Palestine I: the pottery of the first three campaigns. *Annual of the American Schools of Oriental Research* 12. New Haven: Yale University Press.

Albright, W. F. 1949. *The Archaeology of Palestine*. London: Penguin Books.

Albright, W. F. 1962. The chronology of MB I (Early Bronze-Middle Bronze). *Bulletin of the American Schools of Oriental Research* 168: 36-42.

Albright, W. F. 1966. Remarks on the chronology of Early Bronze IV – Middle Bronze IIA in Phoenicia and Syria-Palestine. *Bulletin of the American Schools of Oriental Research* 184: 26-35.

Alon, D. 1973. Tell Halif. *Hadashot Arkhiologiyot* 47: 19-20.

Amiran, R. 1970. *Ancient Pottery of the Holy Land: From Its Beginnings in the Neolithic Period to the Iron Age*. Ramat Gan, Israel: Massada.

Anbar, M. & Na'aman, N. 1986-1987. An account tablet of sheep from ancient Hebron. *Tel Aviv* 13-14: 3-12.

Anderson, J.D. 1995. The impact of Rome on the periphery: the case of Palastina--Roman Period (63 B.C.E.-324 B.C.E.), in T. E. Levy (ed.), *The Archaeology of Society in the Holy Land*, pp. 446-468. New York: Facts on File.

Andrews, I. J. 1995. *The Birds of the Hashemite Kingdom of Jordan*. Midlothian, Scotland: Ian J. Andrews.

Antoun, R. T. 1972. *Arab Village*. Bloomington, IN: Indiana University Press.

Atallah, S. I. 1977. Mammals of the eastern Mediterranean region; their ecology, systematics and zoogeographical relationships. *Sugetierkundlichen Mitteilungern* 25: 241-320.

Atallah, S. I. 1978. Mammals of the eastern Mediterranean region; their ecology, systematics and zoogeographical relationships. *Sugetierkundlichen Mitteilungern* 26: 1-50.

Atran, S. 1986. *Hamula* organization and *masha'a* tenure in Palestine. *Man* 21: 271-295.

Badre, L. 1980. *Les Figurines Anthropomorphes en Terre-Cuite a L'age du Bronze en Syrie*. Paris: Geuthner.

Bakig, A. R. & Horani, H. K. 1993. *Birds of Jordan*. Amman: A.R. Bakig.

Balasse, M. 2003. Keeping the young alive to stimulate milk production? Differences between cattle and small stock. *Anthropozoologica* 37: 3-10.

Baruch, U. 1986. The late Holocene vegetational history of Lake Kinneret (Sea of Galilee), Israel. *Paleorient* 12: 37-48.

Baruch, U. 1990. Palynological evidence of human impact on the vegetation as recorded in Late Holocene lake sediments in Israel, in S. Bottema, G. Entjes-Nieborg and W. van Zeist (eds.), *Man's Role in the Shaping of the Eastern Mediterranean Landscape*, pp. 283-293. Rotterdam: A. A. Balkema.

Baruch, U. & Bottema, S. 1991. Palynological evidence for climate changes in the Levant 17,000-9,000 BP, in O. Bar-Yosef and F. Valla (eds.), *The Natufian Culture in the Levant*, pp. 11-20. Ann Arbor: International Monographs in Prehistory.

Bar-Yosef, O. 1986. The walls of Jericho: an alternative interpretation. *Current Anthropology* 27: 157-162.

Bar-Yosef, O. 1995. The earliest food producers—Pre-Pottery Neolithic (8000-5500), in T. E. Levy (ed.), *The Archaeology of Society in the Holy Land*, pp. 190-204. New York: Facts on File.

Bassett, T. J. 1988. The political ecology of peasant-herder conflicts in the northern Ivory Coast. *Annals of the Association of American Geographers* 78: 453-472.

Bate, D. 1945. Note on small mammals from the Lebanon Mountains, Syria. *Annals and Magazine of Natural History* 12(11): 141-158.

Beck, P. 1975. The Pottery of the Middle Bronze Age IIA at Tel Aphek. *Tel Aviv* 2: 45-85.

Beck, P. 2000. The Middle Bronze Age IIA pottery repertoire: a comparative study, in M. Kochavi, P. Beck and E. Yadin (eds.), *Aphek-Antipatris I; Excavation of Areas A and B, the 1972-1976 Seasons*, pp. 239-254. Tel Aviv: Emery and Claire Yass Publications in Archaeology of the Institute of Archaeology, Tel Aviv University.

Behre, K.-E. 1981. The interpretation of anthropogenic indicators in pollen diagrams. *Pollen et Spores* 23: 225-245.

Behre, K.-E. 1990. Some reflections on anthropogenic indicators and the record of prehistoric occupation phases in pollen diagrams from the Near East, in S. Bottema, G. Entjes, and W. van Zeist (eds.), *Man's Role in the Shaping of the Eastern Mediterranean Landscape*, pp. 219-230. Rotterdam: A. A. Balkema.

Bell, B. 1971. The Dark Ages in ancient history, I. The Dark Age in Egypt. *American Journal of Archaeology* 75: 1-26.

Bell, C. 1992. *Ritual Theory, Ritual Practice*. New York: Oxford University Press.

Ben-Dor, I. 1950. A Middle Bronze Age Temple at Nahariya. *Quarterly of the Department of Antiquities of Palestine*: 1-41.

Ben-Tor, A. 1986. The trade relations of Palestine in the Early Bronze Age. *Journal of the Economic and Social History of the Orient* 29:1-27.

Berelov, I. 2001. Zahrat adh-Dhra' 1: stranded on the Dead Sea Plain in the Middle Bronze Age, in A.Walmsley (ed.), *Australians uncovering Jordan; fifty years of Middle Eastern Archaeology*, pp. 165-172. Sydney: Research Institute for Humanities and Social Sciences, University of Sydney and the Department of Antiquities, Jordan.

Berelov, I. 2006. *Occupation and Abandonment of Middle Bronze Age Zahrat adh-Dhra' 1, Jordan. The Behavioral Implications of Quantitative Ceramic Analyses*. Oxford: British Archaeological Reports, International Series 1493.

Berelov, I. & Falconer, S. E. 2001. Zahrat adh-Dhra' 1, in A. Negev and S. Gibson (eds.), *Archaeological Encyclopedia of the Holy Land*, p. 551. New York: Continuum Publishing Group.

Berry, B. J. L. 1961. City size distributions and economic development. *Economic Development and Culture Change* 9: 573-588.

Boardman, J. 1976. The olive in the Mediterranean: its culture and use. *Philosophical Transactions of the Royal Society of London, Series* B 275: 187-196.

Bohl, F. M. Th. 1926. Sichem Keilschrifttafeln. *Zeitschrift für Deutsche Palestinien Verein* 49: 321-27.

Boling, R. G. 1969. Bronze Age buildings at the Shechem High Place: ASOR excavations At Tananir. *Biblical Archaeologist* 32: 81-103.

Borowski, O. 1987. *Agriculture in Iron Age Israel*. Winona Lake, IN: Eisenbrauns.

Bottema, S. 1982 [1985]. Palynological investigations in Greece with special reference to pollen as an indicator of human activity. *Palaeohistoria* 24: 257-289.

Bottema, S. & Woldring, H. 1990. Anthropogenic indicators in the pollen record of the eastern Mediterranean, in S. Bottema, G. Entjes, and W. van Zeist (eds.), *Man's Role in the Shaping of the Eastern Mediterranean Landscape*, pp. 231-264. Rotterdam: A. A. Balkema.

Bronitsky, G. & Hamer, R. 1986. Experiments in ceramic technology: the effects of various tempering materials on impact and thermal-shock resistance. *American Antiquity* 51: 89-101.

Broshi, M. 1979. The population of western Palestine in the Roman-Byzantine Period. *Bulletin of the American Schools of Oriental Research* 236:1-10.

Broshi, M. & Gophna, R. 1986. Middle Bronze Age II Palestine: its settlements and population. *Bulletin of the American Schools of Oriental Research* 261: 73-90.

Butzer, K. 1996. Ecology in the long view: settlement histories, agrosystemic strategies, and ecological performance. *Journal of Field Archaeology* 23(2): 141-50.

Charpin, D. 1985. Les archives du Devin Asqudum dans le residence du "Chantier A". *MARI* 4: 453-462.

Cleveland, R. L. 1960. The excavation of the Conway High Place (Petra) and the soundings at Khirbet Ader. *Annual of the American Schools of Oriental Research* 34/35: 79-97. New Haven: American Schools of Oriental Research.

Clutton-Brock, J. 1971. The primary food animals of the Jericho tell from the proto-Neolithic to the Byzantine Period. *Levant* 3: 41-55.

Clutton-Brock, J. 1979. The mammalian remains from the Jericho tell. *Proceedings of the Prehistoric Society* 45: 135-157.

Cohen, R. 1999. *Ancient Settlement of the Central Negev, Volume I: The Chalcolithic Period, the Early Bronze Age and the Middle Bronze I*. Israel Antiquities Authority Reports, No. 6. Jerusalem: The Israel Antiquities Authority.

Cohen, R. & Dever, W. G. 1981. Preliminary report of the third and final season of the Central Negev Highlands Project. *Bulletin of the American Schools of Oriental Research* 243: 57-77.

Cohen, S. 2002. Middle Bronze Age IIA ceramic typology and settlement in the southern Levant, in M. Bietak (ed.), *The Middle Bronze Age in the Levant; Proceedings of an International Conference on MB IIA Ceramic Material, Vienna, 24th-26th of January 2001*, pp. 113-131. Wien: Verlag der Osterreichischen Akademie der Wissenschaften.

Cole, D. P. 1984. *Shechem I: The Middle Bronze IIB Pottery*. Winona Lake, IN: American Schools of Oriental Research.

Courty M. & Weiss, H. J. 1997. The scenario of environmental degradation in the Tell Leilan region, NE Syria, during the late 3rd millennium abrupt climate change, in H. Dalfes, G. Kukla, and H. Weiss (eds.), *Third Millennium B.C. Climate Change and Old World Collapse*, pp. 107-147. Berlin: Springer Verlag.

Covello-Paran, K. 1996. Middle Bronze Age burial caves at Hagosherim, Upper Galilee. *Atiqot* 30: 71-84.

Crabtree, P. J. n.d. *Animal use and cultural change*. Unpublished ms.

Crabtree, P. J. 1990. Zooarchaeology and complex societies: some uses of faunal analysis for the study of trade, social status, and ethnicity, in M. B. Schiffer (ed.), *Archaeological Method and Theory, Volume 2*, pp. 155-205. Tucson: University of Arizona Press.

Crader, D. 1990. Slave diet at Monticello. *American Antiquity* 55: 690-717

Cribb, R. 1984. Computer simulation of herding systems as an interpretive and heuristic device in the study of kill-off strategies, in J. Clutton-Brock and C. Grigson (eds.), *Animals and Archaeology 3. Early Herders and Their Flocks*, pp. 161-70. Oxford: British Archaeological Reports, International Series 202.

Cribb, R. 1987. The logic of the herd: computer simulation of archaeological herd structure. *Journal of Anthropological Archaeology* 6: 367-415.

Cullen, H. M. & deMenocal, P. B. 2000. The possible role of climate in the collapse of the Akkadian Empire: evidence from the deep sea. *Geology* 28: 379-382

Cullen, H., Hajdas, I. & Bonani, G. 1997. A pervasive millennial-scale cycle in North Atlantic Holocene and glacial climates. *Science* 278: 1257-66.

Curtin, P. D. 1984. *Cross-Cultural Trade in World History.* Cambridge: Cambridge University Press.

Czarzasty, J. L. 2001. *The Ceramic Assemblage from Tell Abu en-Ni'aj.* Unpublished Master's Thesis. Department of Anthropology, Arizona State University, Tempe, AZ.

Dalley, S. 1984. *Mari and Karana.* New York: Longman.

Dar, S. 1977. *The Sites of Tell Nurit, Nahal Alexander and the Rockcut Tombs of Ma'abarot.* Ma'abarot, Israel.

Davies, C. P. & Fall, P. L. 2001. Modern pollen precipitation from an elevational transect in central Jordan and its relationship to vegetation. *Journal of Biogeography* 28: 1195-1210.

Davis, S. 1976. Mammal bones from the Early Bronze Age city of Arad, Northern Negev, Israel: some implications concerning human exploitation. *Journal of Archaeological Science* 3: 153-164.

Davis, S. 1984. The advent of milk and wool production in western Iran, in J. Clutton-Brock and C. Grigson (eds.), *Animals and Archaeology 3. Early Herders and Their Flocks*, pp. 265-278. Oxford: British Archaeological Reports, International Series 202.

Deal, M. 1985. Household pottery disposal in the Maya Highlands: an ethnoarchaeological interpretation. *Journal of Anthropological Archaeology* 4: 243-291.

deMenocal, P. J. 2001. Cultural responses to climate change during the late Holocene. *Science* 292: 667-673.

deMenocal, P., Ortiz, J., Guilderson, T. & Sarnthein, M. 2000. Coherent high- and low-latitude climate variability during the Holocene warm period. *Science* 288: 2198-2202.

Denevan, W. M. 1996. A bluff model of riverine settlement in prehistoric Amazonia. *Annals of the Association of American Geographers* 86(4): 654-681.

de Tarragon, J. M. 1980. *Le Cult a Ugarit d'apres les Textes de la Pratique en Cuneiformes Alphabetiques.* Cahiers de la Revue Biblique 19. Paris: Gabalda.

Dever, W. G. 1971. The peoples of Palestine in the Middle Bronze I Period. *Harvard Theological Review* 64: 197-226.

Dever, W. G. 1973. The EBIV-MBI Horizon in Transjordan and southern Palestine. *Bulletin of the American Schools of Oriental Research* 210: 37-63.

Dever, W. G. 1974. The Middle Bronze occupation and pottery of 'Araq en-Na'asaneh (Cave II), in P. W. Lapp and N. L. Lapp (eds.), *Discoveries in the Wadi ed-Daliyeh*, pp. 33-48. Cambridge, MA: American Schools of Oriental Research.

Dever, W. G. 1980. New vistas on the EB IV (MBI) Horizon in Syria-Palestine. *Bulletin of the American Schools of Oriental Research* 232: 35-64.

Dever, W. G. 1987. Palestine in the Middle Bronze Age: the zenith of the urban Canaanite era. *Biblical Archaeologist* 50(3): 149-177.

Dever, W. G. 1989. The collapse of the urban Early Bronze Age in Palestine, in P. De Microschedji (ed.), *L'urbanisation de la Palestine a l'age du Bronze Ancien*, pp. 215-246. Oxford: British Archaeological Reports, International Series 527.

Dever, W. G. 1995. Social structure in the Early Bronze IV Period in Palestine, in T. E. Levy (ed.), *The Archaeology of Society in the Holy Land*, pp. 282-296. New York: Facts on File.

Diakonoff, I. M. 1975. The rural community in the ancient Near East. *Journal of the Economic and Social History of the Orient* 18(2): 121-133.

Diener, P. & Robkin, E. 1978. Ecology and evolution and the search for cultural origins: the question of Islamic pig prohibition. *Current Anthropology* 19: 493-540.

Dollfus, G. & Ibrahim, M. 1988. *Abu Hamid – Village du 4e Millenaire de la Vallee du Jordain.* Amman: Centre National de la Recherche Scientifique.

Dor, M. 1947. Observations sur les micro-mammiferes trouves dans les pelotes de la Chouette Effraye (*Tyto alba*) en Palestine. *Mammalia* 11: 49-54.

Dothan, M. 1956. The excavations at Nahariyeh, preliminary report (seasons 1954/55). *Israel Exploration Journal* 6: 14-25.

Dunayevsky, I. & Kempinski, A. 1973. The Megiddo temples. *Zeitschrift fur Deutsche Palestinien Verein* 89: 161-87.

Durand, J.-M. 1985. Le Culte des Betyles en Syrie, in J.-M. Durand and J. R. Kupper (eds.), M*iscellanea Babylonica*, pp. 79-84. Paris: Editions Recherche sur les Civilisations.

Eames, S. 2001. Middle Bronze Age settlement in the Wadi al-'Ajib, in A.Walmsley (ed.), *Australians Uncovering Jordan; Fifty Years of Middle Eastern Archaeology*, pp. 173-180. Sydney: Research Institute for Humanities and Social Sciences, University of Sydney and the Department of Antiquities, Jordan.

Edelstein, G., Milevski, I. & Aurant, S. 1998. *The Rephaim Valley Project: villages, terraces, and stone mounds. excavations at Manahat, Jerusalem, 1987 – 1989.* Israel Antiquities Authority Reports, No. 3. Jerusalem: Israel Antiquities Authority.

Edwards, P. C., Falconer, S. E., Fall, P., Ariotti, A. & Swoveland, T. K. 2004. Archaeology and environment of the Dead Sea Plain: preliminary results of the third season of investigations by the joint La Trobe University/Arizona State University project. *Annual of the Department of Antiquities, Jordan* 48: 181-201.

Edwards, P. C., Falconer, S. E., Fall, P., Berelov, I., Czarzasty, J., Day, C., Meadows, J., Meegan, C., Sayej, G., Swoveland, T. K. & Westaway, M. 2002. Archaeology and environment of the Dead Sea Plain: preliminary results of the second season of investigations by the joint La Trobe/Arizona State Universities project. *Annual of the Department of Antiquities, Jordan* 46: 51-92.

Edwards, P. C., Falconer, S., Fall, P., Berelov, I., Meadows, J., Meegan, C., Metzger, M. & Sayej, G. 2001. Archaeology and environment of the Dead Sea Plain: preliminary results of the first season of investigations by the joint La Trobe University/Arizona State University project. *Annual of the Department of Antiquities, Jordan* 45: 135-57.

Eickelmann, D. F. 1989. *The Middle East: An Anthropological Approach*. Englewood Cliffs, NJ: Prentice Hall.

Eisenberg, E. 1976. The Middle Bronze Age temples at Tel Kitan. *Qadmoniot* 9(4): 106-8.

Eisenberg, E. 1977. The temples at Tell Kittan. *Biblical Archaeologist* 40(2): 77-81.

Eisenberg, E. 1993. Rephaim, Nahal. in E. Stern (ed.), *The New Encyclopedia of Archaeological Excavations in the Holy Land*, pp. 1277-1280. Jerusalem: Israel Exploration Society.

Ericson, J. E. & Stickel, E. G. 1973. A proposed classification system for ceramics. *World Archaeology* 4: 357-367.

Evenari, N., Shanan, L. & Tadmor, N. 1961. Ancient agriculture in the Negev. *Science* 133: 979-96.

Evenari, N., Shanan, L. & Tadmor, N. 1971. *The Negev, the Challenge of the Desert*. London: Oxford University Press.

Falconer, S. E. 1987a. Village pottery production and exchange: a Jordan Valley perspective, in A. Hadidi (ed.), *Studies in the History and Archaeology of Jordan, Volume 3*, pp. 251-259. London: Routledge and Kegan Paul.

Falconer, S. E. 1987b. *Heartland of Villages: Reconsidering Early Urbanism in the Southern Levant*. PhD dissertation, University of Arizona, Tucson. Ann Arbor: University of Microfilms.

Falconer, S. E. 1994a. The development and decline of Bronze Age civilization in the southern Levant: a reassessment of urbanism and ruralism, in C. Mathers. and S. Stoddart (eds.), *Development and Decline in the Mediterranean Bronze Age*, pp. 305-333. Sheffield: Sheffield Academic Press.

Falconer, S. E. 1994b. Early village life in the Jordan Valley: a study of rural social and economic complexity, in G. M. Schwartz and S. E. Falconer (eds.), *Archaeological Views from the Countryside: Village Communities in Early Complex Societies*, pp. 121-142. Washington, D.C.: Smithsonian Institution Press.

Falconer, S. E. 1995. Rural responses to early urbanism: Bronze Age household and village economy at Tell el-Hayyat, Jordan. *Journal of Field Archaeology* 22: 399-419.

Falconer, S. E. & Fall, P. L. 1995. Human impacts on the environment during the rise and collapse of civilization in the eastern Mediterranean, in J. I. Mead and D. Steadman (eds.), *Late Quaternary Environments and Deep History: A tribute to Paul S. Martin*, pp. 84-101. Hot Springs: SD: The Mammoth Site.

Falconer, S. E., Fall, P. L. & Jones, J. E. 1998. Winter 1996/97 excavations in the northern Jordan Valley: The Jordan Valley Village Project. *American Journal of Archaeology* 102(3): 588-589.

Falconer, S. E., Fall, P. L. & Jones, J. E. 2001. The Jordan Valley Village Project: excavations at Tell Abu en-Ni'aj, 2000. *American Journal of Archaeology* 105(3): 438-439.

Falconer, S. E., Fall, P. L., Metzger, M. C. & Lines L. 2004. Bronze Age rural economic transitions in the Jordan Valley. *Annual of the American Schools of Oriental Research* 58:1-17.

Falconer, S. E. & Magness-Gardiner, B. 1984. Preliminary report of the first season of the Tell el-Hayyat Project. *Bulletin of the American Schools of Oriental Research* 255: 49-74.

Falconer, S. E. & Magness-Gardiner, B. 1989. Bronze Age village life in the Jordan Valley: archaeological investigations at Tell el-Hayyat and Tell Abu en-Ni'aj. *National Geographic Research* 5: 335-347.

Falconer, S. E. & Savage, S. H. 1995. Heartlands and hinterlands: alternative trajectories of early urbanization in Mesopotamia and the southern Levant. *American Antiquity* 60(1): 37-58.

Fall, P. L. 1983. La Flore à Tell el-Hayyat. *Syria* 60(3-4): 309-310

Fall, P. L. 1990. Deforestation in southern Jordan: evidence from fossil hyrax middens, in S. Bottema, G. Entjes-Nieborg and W. van Zeist (eds.), *Man's Role in the Shaping of the Eastern Mediterranean Landscape*, pp. 271-281. Rotterdam: Balkema.

Fall, P. L., Falconer, S. E. & Lines, L. 2002. Agricultural intensification and the secondary products revolution in the southern Levant. *Human Ecology* 30(4): 445-82.

Fall, P. L., Lines, L. & Falconer, S. E. 1998. Seeds of civilization: Bronze Age rural economy and ecology in the southern Levant. *Annals of the Association of American Geographers* 88: 107-125.

Feinbrunn, N. 1938. New data on some cultivated plants and weeds of the Early Bronze Age in Palestine. *Palestine Journal of Botany* 1: 238-240.

Felix, Y. 1982. Jewish Agriculture in the Land of Israel in the period of the Mishna and the Talmund, in Z. Baras, S. Safrai, Y. Tsafrir, and M. Stern (eds.), *Eretz Israel from the Destruction of the Second Temple to the Muslim Conquest*, pp. 420-441. Jerusalem: Izhak Ben-Zvi Institute.

Ferembach, D. Furshpan, A. & Perrot, J. 1975. Une sequlture collective du Bronze Moyen IIA/B a Kh. Minha (Munhata), Israel. *Bulletin of the American Schools of Oriental Research, Supplemental Series* 21: 87-112.

Finkelstein, I. 1995. The great transformation: the "conquest" of the highlands frontiers and the rise of territorial states, in T. E. Levy (ed.), *The Archaeology of Society in the Holy Land,* pp. 349-365. New York: Facts on File.

Finnegan, M. 1978. Faunal remains from Bab edh-Dhra, 1975, in D. N. Freedman (ed.), *Preliminary excavation reports: Bab edh-Dhra, Sardis, Meiron, Tell el-Hesi, Carthage (Punic)*, pp. 51-54. Cambridge, MA: American Schools of Oriental Research.

Finnegan, M. 1981. Faunal remains from Bab edh-Dhra and Numeira, in W.E. Rast and R. T. Schaub (eds.), *The Southwestern Dead Sea Plain Expedition: An Interim Report*, pp. 177-180. Cambridge, MA: American Schools of Oriental Research.

Flanagan. J. W., McCreery, D. W. & Yassine, K. N. 1994. Tell Nimrin: preliminary report on the 1993 season. *Annual of the Department of Antiquities, Jordan* 38: 205-44.

Fleming, D. 1992. *The Installation of Ba'al's High Priestess at Emar*. Atlanta: Scholars Press.

Forbes, H. & Foxhall, L. 1978. The queen of all trees: preliminary notes on the archaeology of the olive. *Expedition* 21(1): 37-47.

Fritz, V. 1987. Conquest or settlement? The early Iron Age in Palestine. *Biblical Archaeologist* 50(2): 84-100.

Garfinkel Y. 1997. The Middle and Late Bronze Age phases in Area L, in A. Ben-Tor and R. Bonfil (eds.), *Hazor V: An Account of the Fifth Season of Excavations, 1968*, pp. 194-217. Jerusalem: Israel Exploration Society and Hebrew University of Jerusalem.

Gates, M. 1988. Dialogues between ancient Near Eastern texts and the archaeological record: test cases from Bronze Age Syria. *Bulletin of the American Schools of Oriental Research* 270: 63-91

Gebel, H. G., M. S. Muheisen & Nissen, H. J. 1988. Preliminary report on the first season of excavations at Basta, in A. N. Garrard and H. G. Gebel (eds), *The Prehistory of Jordan: The State of Research in 1986*, pp. 101-134. Oxford: British Archaeological Reports, International Series 396.

Gelb, I. J. 1979. Household and family in early Mesopotamia. *Orientalia Louvaniensia Analecta* 5: 1-97.

Gerstenblith, P. 1983. *The Levant at the Beginning of the Middle Bronze Age*. ASOR Dissertation Series, no. 5. Winona Lake, IN: Eisenbrauns.

Gilman, A. 1981. The development of social stratification in Bronze Age Europe. *Current Anthropology* 22: 1-23.

Gitin, S. 1975. Middle Bronze I domestic pottery at Jebel Qa'aqir: a ceramic inventory of Cave G23. *Eretz Israel* 12: 46-62.

Gitin, S. 1990. *Gezer III: A Ceramic Typology of the Late Iron II, Persian and Hellenistic Periods at Tell Gezer*. Jerusalem: Annual of the Nelson Glueck School of Biblical Archaeology.

Glueck, N. 1934. Explorations in Eastern Palestine, I. *Annual of the American Schools of Oriental Research 14*. New Haven: American Schools of Oriental Research.

Glueck, N. 1935. Explorations in Eastern Palestine, II. *Annual of the American Schools of Oriental Research 15*. New Haven: American Schools of Oriental Research.

Glueck, N. 1939. Explorations in Eastern Palestine III. *Annual of the American Schools of Oriental Research 18-19*. New Haven: American Schools of Oriental Research.

Glueck, N. 1951. Explorations in Eastern Palestine, IV. *Annual of the American Schools of Oriental Research 25-28*. New Haven: American Schools of Oriental Research.

Goor, A. 1965. The history of the fig in the Holy Land from ancient times to the present day. *Economic Botany* 19(2): 124-135.

Goor, A. 1966a. The place of the olive in the Holy Land and its history through the ages. *Economic Botany* 20(3): 223-243.

Goor, A. 1966b. The history of the grape-vine in the Holy Land. *Economic Botany* 20(1): 46-64.

Gopher, A. 1995. Early pottery bearing-groups in Israel—The Pottery Neolithic Period, in T. E. Levy (ed.), *The Archaeology of Society in the Holy Land*, pp. 205-225. New York: Facts on File.

Gophna, R. 1979. A Middle Bronze II village in the Jordan Valley. *Tel Aviv* 6: 28-33.

Gophna, R., Liphschitz, N. & Lev-Yadun, S. 1986. Man's impact on the natural vegetation in the central Coastal Plain of Israel during the Chalcolithic and the Bronze Ages (circa 4000-1600 B.C.). *Tel Aviv* 13: 69-82.

Gophna, R. & Portugali, J. 1988. Settlement and demographic processes in Israel's Coastal Plain from the Chalcolithic to the Middle Bronze Age. *Bulletin of the American Schools of Oriental Research* 269: 11-28.

Graesser, C. 1972. Standing stones in ancient Palestine. *Biblical Archaeologist* 35: 34-63.

Graham-Brown, S. 1990. Agriculture and labour transformation in Palestine, in K. Glavanis and P. Glavanis (eds.), *The Rural Middle East: Peasant Lives and Modes of Production*, pp. 53-69. London: Zed Books, Birzeit University.

Grannot, A. 1952. *The Land System in Palestine: History and Structure*. London: Eyre and Spottiswoode.

Grant, A. 1982. The use of tooth wear as a guide to the age of domestic ungulates, in B. Wilson, C. Grigson and S. Payne (eds.), *Ageing and Sexing Animal Bones from Archaeological Sites*, pp. 91-108. Oxford: British Archaeological Reports, British Series 109.

Grayson, D. K. 1984. *Quantitative Zooarchaeology. Topics in the Analysis of Archaeological Faunas.* New York: Academic Press.

Grigson, C. 1982. Porridge and pannage: pig husbandry in Neolithic England, in M. Bell and S. Limbrey (eds.), *Archaeological Aspects of Woodland Ecology*, pp. 297-314. Oxford: British Archaeological Reports, International Series 146.

Guy, P. L. O. 1938. *Megiddo Tombs.* Chicago: University of Chicago Press.

Hallo, W. & Tadmor, H. 1977. A lawsuit from Hazor. *Israel Exploration Journal* 27: 1-11.

Hambleton, E. 2001. A method for converting Grant Mandible Wear Stages to Payne Style Wear Stages in sheep, cow, and pig, in A. Millard (ed.), *Archaeological Sciences '97. Proceedings of the Conference Held at the University of Durham, 2nd-4th September 1997,* pp. 103-108. Oxford: British Archaeological Reports, International Series 939.

Harding, G. L. & Isserlin, B. 1953. An Early Bronze Age cave at el-Husn. *Palestine Exploration Fund, Annual* 6: 1-13.

Heim, C., Nowaczyk, N. R., Negendank, J. F. W., Leroy, S. A. G. & Ben-Avraham, Z. 1997. Near East desertification: evidence from the Dead Sea. *Naturawissenschaften* 84: 398-401.

Helbaek, H. 1958. Plant economy in ancient Lachish, in O. Tufnell (ed.), *Lachish (Tell ed-Duweir) IV. The Bronze Age. Appendix A*, pp. 309-317. London: Oxford University Press.

Helbaek, H. 1959. Domestication of food plants in the Old World. *Science* 130:365-372.

Hellwing, S., & Gophna, R. 1984. The animal remains from the Early and Middle Bronze Ages at Tel Aphek and Tel Dalit: a comparative study. *Tel Aviv* 11: 48-59.

Helms, S. W. 1986. Excavations at Tell Umm Hammad 1984. *Levant* 18: 25-49.

Heltzer, M. 1976. *The Rural Community in Ancient Ugarit.* Wiesbaden: Ludwig Reichert Verlag.

Heltzer, M. 1982. *The Internal Organization of the Kingdom of Ugarit.* Wiesbaden: Reichert Verlag.

Hennessy, J. B. 1969. Preliminary report on the first season of excavation at Teleilat Ghassul. *Levant* 1: 1-24.

Henrickson, E. F. & McDonald, M. M. A. 1983. Ceramic form and function: an ethnographic search and an archaeological application. *American Anthropologist* 85: 630-643.

Holladay, J.S., jr. 1995. The kingdoms of Israel and Judah: political and economic centralization in the Iron IIA-B (ca. 1000-750 B.C.E.), in T. E. Levy (ed.), *The Archaeology of Society in the Holy Land*, pp. 446-468. New York: Facts on File.

Hopf, M. 1969. Plant remains and early farming in Jericho, in P. J. Ucko and G. W. Dimbleby (eds.), *The Domestication and Exploitation of Plants and Animals*, pp. 355-59. New York: Aldine-Atherton.

Hopf, M. 1978. Plant remains, Strata V-I, in R. Amiran (ed.), *Early Arad*, pp. 64-82. Jerusalem: Israel Exploration Society.

Hopf, M. 1983. Jericho plant remains, in K. M. Kenyon and T. A. Holland (eds.), *Excavations at Jericho, Volume V*, pp. 576-621. London: British School of Archaeology at Jerusalem.

Hopf, M. & Bar-Yosef, O. 1987. Plant remains from Hayonim Cave, Western Galilee. *Paleorient* 13: 117-120.

Hopkins, D. C. 1985. *The Highlands of Canaan. Agricultural Life in the Early Iron Age.* Sheffield: Almond Press.

Horwitz, L. 1987. Animal offerings from two Middle Bronze Age tombs. *Israel Exploration Journal* 37: 251-255.

Horwitz, L. 1989. Diachronic changes in rural husbandry practices in Bronze Age settlements from the Refaim Valley, Israel. *Palestine Exploration Quarterly* 121: 44-54.

Horowitz, A. 1971. Climatic and vegetational developments in northeastern Israel during Upper Pleistocene-Holocene time. *Pollen et Spores* 13(2): 255-278.

Horowitz, A. 1979. *The Quaternary of Israel.* New York: Academic Press.

Horowitz, W. & Shaffer, A. 1992. An administrative tablet from Hazor. *Israel Exploration Journal* 42: 21-33.

Horwitz, L. & Tchernov, E. 1989. Animal exploration in the Early Bronze Age of the southern Levant, in P. de Mieroschedji (ed.), *L'urbanisation de la Palestine à l'age du Bronze ancient,* pp. 279-296. Oxford: British Archaeological Reports, International Series 527.

Hue, F. & Etchecopar, R. D. 1970. *Les Oiseaux du Proche and du Moyen Orient.* Paris: Editions N. Boubee & Cie.

Hurowitz, A. 1992. *I Have Built You an Exalted House.* Sheffield: Sheffield Academic Press.

Ibrahim, M., Sauer, J. A. & Yassine, K. 1976. The East Jordan Valley Survey, 1975. *Bulletin of the American Schools of Oriental Research* 222: 41-66.

Ibrahim, M., Sauer, J. A. & Yassine, K. 1988. The East Jordan Valley Survey, 1976 (second part), in K. Yassine (ed.), *Archaeology of Jordan: Essays and Reports,* pp. 187-207. Amman: University of Jordan.

Ilan, D. 1995. The dawn of internationalism: the Middle Bronze Age, in T. E. Levy (ed.), *The Archaeology of Society in the Holy Land,* pp. 297-320. New York: Facts on File.

Ilan, D. 1996. The Middle Bronze Age tombs, in A. Biran (ed.), *Dan I.* Jerusalem: Nelson Glueck School of Biblical Archaeology, Hebrew Union College – Jewish Institute of Religion.

Ilan, D. 2000. The Middle Bronze Age pottery, in I. Finkelstein, D. Ussishkin and B. Halpern (eds.), *Megiddo III, the 1992-1996 Seasons*, pp. 186-222. Tel Aviv: Emery and Claire Yass Publications in Archaeology, Institute of Archaeology, Tel Aviv University.

Jacobsen, T. 1975. Religious drama in ancient Mesopotamia, in H. Goedicke and J. J. M. Roberts (eds.), *Unity and Diversity*, pp. 65-97. Baltimore: Johns Hopkins University Press.

Jacobsen, T. 1976. *Treasures of Darkness*. New Haven: Yale University Press.

Joffe, A. H. 1991. *Settlement and Society in Early Bronze I and II Canaan*. Unpublished Ph.D. Dissertation, University of Arizona. Ann Arbor: University Microfilms.

Joffe, A. 1993. *Settlement and Society in the Early Bronze Bronze Age I and II, Southern Levant*. Sheffield: Sheffield Academic.

Johnson, G. A. 1977. Aspects of regional analysis in archaeology. *Annual Review of Anthropology* 6: 479-508.

Johnson, G. A. 1980. Rank-size convexity and system integration: a view from archaeology. *Economic Geography* 56(3): 234-247.

Johnson, P. 1982. The Middle Cypriot pottery found in Palestine. *Opuscula Atheniensia* 14: 49-72.

Jones, G. E. M. 1991. Numerical analysis in archaeobotany, in W. Van Zeist, K. Wasylikowa, K.-E. Behre (eds.), *Progress in Old World Palaeoethnobotany; A Retrospective View on the Occasion of 20 Years of the International Work Group for Palaeoethnobotany*, pp. 63-80. Rotterdam: A. A. Balkema.

Jones, J. E. 1999. *Local Ceramic Production in a Collapsed Early Urban Society in the Southern Levant*. Unpublished Ph.D. Dissertation, Department of Anthropology, Arizona State University, Tempe, AZ.

Kadane, J. B. 1988. Possible statistical contributions to paleoethnobotany, in A. Hastorf and V. S. Popper (eds.), *Current Paleoethnobotany: Analytical Methods and Cultural Interpretations of Archaeological Plant Remains*, pp. 206-214. Chicago: University of Chicago Press.

Kenyon, K. M. 1965. *Excavations at Jericho, Volume II: The Tombs Excavated in 1955-58*. London: British School of Archaeology in Jerusalem.

Kenyon, K. M. 1966. *Amorites and Canaanites*. London: Oxford University.

Kenyon, K. M. 1973. Palestine in the Middle Bronze Age. In *Cambridge Ancient History*, third edition, Volume 2, part 1: 77-116. Cambridge: Cambridge University Press.

Kenyon, K. M. 1981. *Excavations at Jericho, Volume III*. London: British School of Archaeology in Jerusalem.

Kenyon, K. M. & Holland, T. A. 1982. *Excavations at Jericho, Volume IV*. London: British School of Archaeology in Jerusalem.

Kenyon, K. M. & Holland, T. A. 1983. *Excavations at Jericho, Volume V*. London: British School of Archaeology in Jerusalem.

Kislev, M.E., Nadel, D. & Carmi, I. 1992. Epipalaeolithic (19,000) cereal and fruit diet at Ohalo II, Sea of Galilee, Israel. *Review of Palaeobotany and Palynology* 73: 161-166.

Klengel, H. 1979. Die Palastwirschaft in Alalah, in E. Lipinski (ed.), *State and Temple Economy in the Ancient Near East*, pp. 435-57. Leuven: Department Orientalistiek.

Knapp, A. B. 1989. Complexity and collapse in the north Jordan Valley: archaeometry and society in the Middle-Late Bronze Ages. *Israel Exploration Journal* 39(3-4): 129-148.

Knapp, A. B., Duerden, P., Wright, R. V. S. & Grave, P. 1988. Ceramic production and social change: archaeometric analysis of Bronze Age pottery from Jordan. *Journal of Mediterranean Archaeology* 1(2): 57-113.

Kramer, C. 1980. Estimating prehistoric populations: an ethnoarchaeological approach. In M.-T. Barrelet (ed.) *L'Archeologie de l'Iraq:* 315-334. Paris: Centre National de la Recherche Scientifique.

Kramer, C. 1982. *Village Ethnoarchaeology. Rural Iran in Archaeological Perspective*. New York: Academic Press.

LaBianca, O. S. 1990. *Hesban 1: Sedentarization and Nomadization*. Berrien Springs, MI: Andrews Univeristy Press.

Lafont, B. 1984. *Archives Administratives de Mari, I*. Archives Royale de Mari, Volume 23. Paris: ERC.

Landmann, G, Reimer, A., Lemcke, G. & Kempe, S. 1996. Dating late glacial abrupt climate changes in the 14,570 yr long continuous varve record of Lake Van, Turkey. *Palaeogeography, Palaeoclimatology, Palaeoecology* 122(1-4): 107-118.

Landsberger, B. & Tadmor, H. 1964. Fragments of clay liver models from Hazor. *Israel Exploration Journal* 14: 201-218.

Lapp, P. W. 1970. Palestine in the Early Bronze Age, in J. A. Sanders (ed.), *Near Eastern Archaeology in the Twentieth Century*, pp. 101-139. Garden City, NY: Doubleday.

Lernau, H. 1975. Animal remains, in Y. Aharoni (ed.), *Investigations at Lachish, Volume 5: The sanctuary and the residency*, pp. 86-103. Tel Aviv: Gateway.

Lernau, H. 1978. Faunal remains, strata III-I, in Ruth Amiran (ed.), *Early Arad: the Chalcolithic Settlement and Early Bronze Age City, 1*, pp. 83-113. Jerusalem: Israel Exploration Society.

Levine, B. A. & de Tarragon, J.-M. 1984. Dead kings and Rephaim: the patrons of the Ugaritic Dynasty. *Journal of the American Oriental Society* 104: 649-59.

Levy, T.E. 1983. The emergence of specialized pastoralism in the southern Levant. *World Archaeology* 15: 15-36.

Levy, T.E. 1995. Cult, metallurgy and rank societies—Chalcolithic Period (ca. 4500-3500 B.C.E.), in T. E. Levy (ed.), *The Archaeology of Society in the Holy Land*, pp. 446-468. New York: Facts on File.

Levy, T.E. & Bar-Yosef, O. 1995. Preface, in T. E. Levy (ed.), *The Archaeology of Society in the Holy Land*, pp. x-xvi. New York: Facts on File.

Lewis, N. N. 1987. *Nomads and Settlers in Syria and Jordan, 1800-1890*. Cambridge: Cambridge University Press.

Lewis, T. 1989. *Cults of the Dead in Ancient Israel and Ugarit*. Atlanta: Scholars Press.

Lines, L. 1995. *Bronze Age Orchard Cultivation and Urbanization in the Jordan River Valley*. Unpublished Ph.D. Dissertation. Department of Geography, Arizona State University, Tempe, AZ.

Lipinski, E. 1988. The socio-economic condition of the clergy in the kingdom of Ugarit, in M. Heltzer and E. Lipinski (eds.), *Society and Economy in the Eastern Mediterranean (c. 1500-1000 B.C.)*, pp. 125-150. Leuven: Peeters.

Lipschitz, N., Gophna, R., Hartman, M. & Biger, G. 1991. The beginning of olive (*Olea europaea*) cultivation in the Old World: a reassessment. *Journal of Archaeological Science* 18:441-453.

Liphschitz, N. Gophna, R. & Lev-Yadun, S. 1989. Man's impact on the vegetational landscape of Israel in the Early Bronze Age II-III, in P. Miroschedji (ed.), *L'urbanisation de la Palestine à l'âge du Bronze Ancien*, pp. 263-268. Oxford: British Archaeological Reports, International Series 527.

Liverani, M. 1982. Ville et campagne dans le Royaume d'Ugarit. Essai d'Analyse Economique, in I. M. Diakonoff (ed.), *Societies and Languages of the Ancient Near East: studies in honour of I. M. Diakonoff*, pp. 249-58. Warminster: Aris and Phillips.

Loud, G. 1948. *Megiddo II: Seasons of 1935-39*. Oriental Institute Publication 62. Chicago: University of Chicago Press.

Lutfiyya, A. M. 1966. *Baytin. A Jordanian Village*. Paris: Mouton and Company.

Maeir, A. 1997a. *The Material Culture of the Central and Northern Jordan Valley in the Middle Bronze Age II: Pottery and Settlement Pattern*. Unpublished Doctoral Dissertation. Jerusalem: Hebrew University.

Maeir, A. 1997b. Tomb 1181: a multiple-interment burial cave of the transitional Middle Bronze Age IIA-B, in A. Ben-Tor and R. Bonfil (eds.), *Hazor V: An Account of the Fifth Season of Excavations, 1968*, pp. 295-340. Jerusalem: Israel Exploration Society, Hebrew University of Jerusalem.

Maeir, A. 2000. Hamadiya-North: a rural MB II settlement in the Bet She'an Valley. *Atiqot* 39: 31-42.

Maeir, A. 2002. Perspectives on the early MB II Period in the Jordan Valley, in M. Bietak (ed.), *The Middle Bronze Age in the Levant; Proceedings of an International Conference on MB IIA Ceramic Material, Vienna, 24th-26th of January 2001*, pp. 261-267. Vienna: Verlag der Osterreichischen Akademie der Wissenschaften.

Magness-Gardiner, B. 1994. Urban-rural relations in Bronze Age Syria: evidence from Alalakh Level VII palace archives, in G. M. Schwartz and S. E. Falconer (eds.), *Archaeological Views from the Countryside: Village Communities in Early Complex Societies*, pp. 39-47. Washington, D.C.: Smithsonian Institution Press.

Magness-Gardiner, B. & Falconer, S. E. 1994. Community, polity and ritual in a Middle Bronze Age Levantine village. *Journal of Mediterranean Archaeology* 7(2): 3-40.

Mann, M. 1986. *The Sources of Social Power*. Cambridge: Cambridge University Press.

Marchetti, N. 2003. A century of excavations on the spring hill at Tell es-Sultan, Ancient Jericho: a reconstruction of its stratigraphy, in M. Bietak (ed.), *The Synchronization of Civilizations in the Eastern Mediterranean in the Second Millennium B.C. II*, pp. 295-321. Vienna: Verlag der Osterreichischen Akademie der Wissenschaften.

Marcus, E. S. 2003. Dating the early Middle Bronze Age in the southern Levant: a preliminary comparison of radiocarbon and archaeo-historical synchronizations, in M. Bietak (ed.), *The Synchronization of Civilizations in the Eastern Mediterranean in the Second Millennium B.C. II*, pp. 95-110. Vienna: Verlag der Osterreichischen Akademie der Wissenschaften.

Margueron, J.-Cl. 1982. Mari: originalite ou dependence. *Studi Eblaiti* 5: 121-44.

Margueron, J.-Cl. 1984. Le temple de Dagan. *Histoire et Archeologie* 80: 48.

Margueron, J.-Cl. 1993. Meskene (Imar/Emar) (Archaeologisch). *RLA* 8: 84-93.

Matthews, V. 1978. Government involvement in the religion of the Mari kingdom. *Revue d'Assyriologie* 72: 151-156.

Matthiae, P. 1975. Unite et developpement du temple dans la Syrie du Bronze Moyen, in *Le Temple et le Culte: Compte Rendu de la Vingtieme Rencontre Assyriologique Internationale Organisee a Leiden du 3 au 7 Juillet 1972 sous les Auspices due Nederlands Institut voor het Habije Oosten*, pp. 43-72. Nederlands Historisch-Archeologisch Institut te Istambul. Leiden: Brill.

Matthiae, P. 1989. Masterpieces of early and old Syrian Art. *Proceedings of the British Academy* 75: 25-56.

Mazar, A. 1992. Temples of the Middle and Late Bronze Ages and the Iron Age, in A. Kempinski and R. Reich (eds.), *The Architecture of Ancient Israel*, pp. 161-187. Jerusalem: Israel Exploration Society.

Mazar, A. 1993. Beth-Shean. Tel Beth-Shean and the Northern Cemetery, in E. Stern (ed.), *The New Encyclopedia of Archaeological Excavations in the Holy Land*, pp. 214-235. Jerusalem: Israel Exploration Society.

Mazar, B. 1968. The Middle Bronze Age in Palestine. *Israel Exploration Journal* 18: 65-97.

McCreery, D. W. 1980. *The Nature and Cultural Implications of Early Bronze Age Agriculture in the Southern Ghor of Jordan: An ArchaeologicalReconstruction*. Ph.D. Dissertation, University of Pittsburgh. Ann Arbor: University Microfilms.

McNicoll, A. W., Hennessy, J. B., Edwards, P. C., Potts, T. F. & Walmsley, A. (eds.) 1993. *Pella in Jordan 2. Second Interim Report of the Joint University of*

Sydney and the College of Wooster Excavations at Pella, 1982-1985. Sydney: University of Sydney.

McNicoll, A. W. & Smith, R. H. 1980. The 1979 Season at Pella of the Decapolis. *Bulletin of the American Schools of Oriental Research* 240: 63-84.

Meadow, R. H. & Zeder, M. A. (eds.) 1978. *Approaches to Faunal Analysis in the Middle East.* Peabody Museum Bulletin 2. Cambridge, MA: Harvard University.

Meadows, J. 1996. *The Final Straw: An Archaeobotanical Investigation of the Economy of a Fourth Millennium BC Site in the Wadi Fidan, Southern Jordan.* Unpublished M.Sc. Thesis, Department of Archaeology and Prehistory, University of Sheffield.

Mellaart, J. 1962. Preliminary report on the archaeological survey in the Yarmuk and Jordan Valley for the Point Four Irrigation Scheme. *Annual of the Department of Antiquities, Jordan* 6-7: 126-157.

Metzger, M. C. 1984. Faunal remains at Tell el-Hayyat: preliminary results. *Bulletin of the American Schools of Oriental Research* 255: 68-69.

Miller, N. F. 1985. Paleoethnobotanical evidence for deforestation in ancient Iran: a case study of urban Malyan. *Journal of Ethnobiology* 5: 1-19.

Miller, N. F. 1988. Ratios in paleoethnobotanical analysis, in C. A. Hastorf and V. S. Popper (eds.), *Current Paleoethnobotany: Analytical Methods and Cultural Interpretations of Archaeological Plant Remains,* pp. 72-85. Chicago: University of Chicago Press.

Miller, N. F. 1991. The Near East, in W. van Zeist, K. Wasylik-owa and K.-E. Behre (eds.), *Progress in Old World Palaeoethnobotony. A Retrospective View on the Occasion of 20 Years of the International Work Group for Palaeoethnobotany,* pp. 133-160. Rotterdam: A. A. Balkema.

Morrison, M. A. 1987. The Southwest Archives at Nuzi, in D. I. Owen and M. A. Morrison (eds.), *Studies on the Civilization and Culture of Nuzi and the Hurrians, Volume 1,* pp. 167-201. Winona Lake, IN: Eisenbrauns.

Murray, P. 1980. Discard location: the ethnographic data. *American Antiquity* 45(3): 490-502.

Naveh, Z. 1990. Ancient man's impact on the Mediterranean landscape in Israel: ecological and evolutionary perspectives, in S. Bottema, G. Entjes-Nieborg and W. van Zeist (eds.), *Man's Role in the Shaping of the Eastern Mediterranean Landscape,* pp. 43-50. Rotterdam: A. A. Balkema.

Naveh, Z. & Dan, J. 1973. The human degradation of Mediterranean landscapes in Israel, in F. di Castri and H. A. Mooney (eds.), *Mediterranean Type Ecosystems: Origin and Structure, Ecological Studies: Analysis and Synthesis, Volume 7,* pp. 373-389. Berlin: Springer Verlag.

Neef, R. 1990. Introduction, development and environmental implications of olive culture: the evidence from Jordan, in S. Bottema, G. Entjes-Nieborg and W. van Zeist (eds.), *Man's Role in the Shaping of the Eastern Mediterranean Landscape,* pp. 295-306. Rotterdam: A. A. Balkema.

Nowak, R. M. 1991. *Walker's Mammals of the World, Volume II* (5th ed.). Baltimore: Johns Hopkins University Press.

Olavarri, E. 1965. Sondages a l'Aro'er sur l'Arnon. *Revue Biblique* 72: 77-94.

Olavarri, E. 1969. Fouilles a l'Aro'er sur l'Arnon, les niveaux du Bronze Intermediare. *Revue Biblique* 76: 230-59

Oren, E. D. 1973. The Early Bronze IV Period in northern Palestine in its cultural and chronological setting. *Bulletin of the American Schools of Oriental Research* 210: 20-37.

Ory, J. 1936/37. Excavations at Ras el-Ain II. *Quarterly of the Department of Antiquities of Palestine* 6: 99-120.

Palumbo, G. 1987. 'Egalitarian' or 'stratified' society? Some notes on mortuary practices and social structure at Jericho in EB IV. *Bulletin of the American Schools of Oriental Research* 276: 43-59.

Palumbo, G. 1991. *The Early Bronze Age IV in the Southern Levant: Settlement Patterns, Economy and Material Culture of a "Dark Age."* Contributi Materiali di Archeologia Orientale III. Roma: Universita Degli Studi di Roma la Sapienza.

Parr, P. J. 1960. Excavations at Khirbet Iskander. *Annual of the Department of Antiquities, Jordan* 4-5: 128-33.

Parr, P. J. 1972. Settlement patterns and urban planning in the ancient Levant: the nature of the evidence, in P. J. Ucko, R. Tringham and G. W. Dimbley (eds.), *Man, Settlement and Urbanism,* pp. 805-810. Cambridge, MA.: Schenkman.

Parr, P. J. 1973. The origin of the Canaanite jar, in D.E. Strong (ed.), *Archaeological Theory and Practice,* pp. 173-181. London: Seminar Press.

Patrich, J. 1995. Church, State and the Transformation of Palestine—The Byzantine Period (324-640 C.E.), in T. E. Levy (ed.), *The Archaeology of Society in the Holy Land,* pp. 446-468. New York: Facts on File.

Payne, S. 1973. Kill-off patterns in sheep and goats: the mandibles from Asvan Kale. *Anatolian Studies* 23: 281-303.

Paynter, R. W. 1983. Expanding the scope of settlement analysis, in J. Moore and A. Keene (eds.), *Archaeological Hammers and Theories,* pp. 233-275. New York: Academic Press.

Pearsall, D. M. 1989. *Paleoethnobotany: A Handbook of Procedures.* San Diego: Academic Press, Inc.

Perevolotsky, A. 1981. Orchard agriculture in the high mountain region of southern Sinai. *Human Ecology* 9: 331-357.

Polunin, O. & Huxley, A. 1965. *Flowers of the Mediterranean.* London: Hogarth.

Poyck, A. 1962. Farm Studies in Iraq. *Medelingen van de Landboushogeschool et Wageningen* 62(1). Wageningen: H. Veenman and Zonen N.V.

Prag, K. 1974. The Intermediate Early Bronze-Middle Bronze Age; an interpretation of the evidence from

Transjordan, Syria, and Lebanon. *Levant* 6: 69-116.

Prag, K. 1988. Kilns of the Intermediate Early Bronze-Middle Bronze Age at Tell Iktanu. preliminary report, 1987 season. *Annual of the Department of Antiquities, Jordan* 32: 59-73.

Raikes, R. 1967. *Water, Weather and Prehistory*. London: Baker.

Rapoport, A. 1990. Systems of activities and systems of settings, in S. Kent (ed.), *Domestic Architecture and the Use of Space*, pp. 9-20. Cambridge: Cambridge University Press.

Rast, W. E. & Schaub, R. T. 1974. Survey of the southeastern plain of the Dead Sea, 1973. *Annual of the Department of Antiquities, Jordan* 19: 5-54.

Rast, W. E. & Schaub, R. T. 1978. A preliminary report of excavations at Bab edh-Dhra', 1975, in D. N. Freedman (ed.), Preliminary Excavation Reports: Bab edh-Dhra', Sardis, Meiron, Tell el-Hesi, Carthage (Punic). *Annual of the American Schools of Oriental Research* 43: 1-32.

Rast, W. E. & Schaub, R. T. 1980 Preliminary report of the excavation of the Dead Sea Plain, Jordan. *Bulletin of the American Schools of Oriental Research* 240: 21-61.

Rast, W. E. & Schaub, R. T. 2003. *Bab edh-Dhra': Excavations at the Town Site (1975-1981)*. Winona Lake, IN: Eisenbrauns.

Redding, R. 1984. Theoretical determinants of a herder's decisions: modeling variation in the sheep/goat ratio, in J. Clutton-Brock and C. Grigson (eds.), *Animals and Archaeology* 3. *Early Herders and Their Flocks*, pp. 161-170. Oxford: British Archaeological Reports, International Series 202.

Redding, R. 1991. The role of the pig in the subsistence system of ancient Egypt: a parable on the potential of faunal data, in P. J. Crabtree and K. Ryan, (eds.), *Animal Use and Culture Change. MASCA Research Papers in Science and Archaeology* 8, Supplement, pp. 20-30. Philadelphia: University Museum.

Redding, R. 1992. Egyptian Old Kingdom patterns of animal use and the value of faunal data in modeling socioeconomic systems. *Paleorient* 18(2): 99-107.

Redding, R. n.d. Personal communication, 2003.

Redfield, R. 1953. *The Primitive World and its Transformations*. Ithaca: Cornell University Press.

Reese, D. n.d. Personal communication, 1984.

Reitz, E. J. & Wing, E. S. 1999. *Zooarchaeology*. Cambridge: Cambridge University Press.

Renfrew, J. M. 1973. *Paleoethnobotany: The Prehistoric Food Plants of the New East and Europe*. New York: Columbia University Press.

Renger, J. 1979. Interaction of temple, palace and 'private enterprise' in the Old Babylonian economy, in E. Lipinski (ed.), *State and Temple Economy*, pp. 249-256. Leuven: Peeters.

Rice, P. M. 1987. *Pottery Analysis. A Sourcebook*. Chicago: University of Chicago.

Richard, S. 1980. Toward a consensus of opinion on the end of the Early Bronze Age in Palestine-Transjordan. *Bulletin of the American Schools of Oriental Research* 237: 5-34.

Richard, S. 1983. Report on the 1982 season of excavations at Khirbet Iskander. *Annual of the Department of Antiquities, Jordan* 27: 45-53.

Richard, S. & Boraas, R. S. 1984. Preliminary report of the 1981-82 seasons of the expedition to Khirbet Iskander and its vicinity. *Bulletin of the American Schools of Oriental Research* 254: 63-87.

Roberts, N. 1990. Human-induced landscape change in south and southwest Turkey during the later Holocene, in S. Bottema, G. Entjes-Nieborg and W. van Zeist (eds.), *Man's Role in the Shaping of the Eastern Mediterranean Landscape*, pp. 53-67. Rotterdam: A. A. Balkema.

Rollefson, G. & Köhler-Rollefson, I. 1989. The collapse of early Neolithic settlements in the southern Levant, in I. Herskovitz (ed.), *People and Culture in Change: Proceedings of the Second Symposium on Upper Paleolithic, Mesolithic, and Neolithic Populations of Europe and the Mediterranean Basin*, pp. 59-72. Oxford: British Archaeological Reports, International Series 508.

Rollefson, G. & Köhler-Rollefson, I. 1992. Early Neolithic exploitation patterns in the Levant: cultural impact on the environment. *Population and Environment* 13: 243-254.

Rollefson, G. O. & Simmons, A. H. 1988. The Neolithic settlement at 'Ain Ghazal, in A. N. Gebel and H. G. Garrard (eds.), *Prehistory of Jordan*, pp. 393-421. Oxford: British Archaeological Reports, International Series 587.

Rollefson, G., Simmons, A. & Kaffafi, Z. 1992. Neolithic cultures at 'Ain Ghazal, Jordan. *Journal of Field Archaeology* 19: 443-470.

Rosen-Ayalon, M. 1995. Between Cairo and Damascus: rural life and urban economics in the Holy Land during the Ayyubid, Mamluk and Ottoman Periods, in T. E. Levy (ed.), *The Archaeology of Society in the Holy Land*, pp. 446-468. New York: Facts on File.

Rye, O. S. 1976. Keeping your temper under control. *Archaeology and Physical Anthropology in Oceania* 11(2): 106-137.

Rye, O. S. 1981. *Pottery Technology: Principles and Reconstruction*. Washington, D.C.: Taraxacum.

Schiffer, M. B. 1987. *Formation Processes of the Archaeological Record*. Albuquerque: University of New Mexico Press.

Schaub, R. T. & Rast, W. E. 1984. Preliminary report of the 1981 expedition to the Dead Sea Plain, Jordan. *Bulletin of the American Schools of Oriental Research* 254: 35-60.

Schwartz, G. M. & Falconer, S. E. (eds.) 1994a. Rural approaches to social complexity, in G. M. Schwartz and S. E. Falconer (eds.), *Archaeological Views From the Countryside: Village Communities in Early Complex Societies*, pp. 1-9. Washington, D.C.: Smithsonian Institution Press.

Schwartz, G. M. & Falconer, S. E. (eds.) 1994b. *Archaeological Views From the Countryside: Village*

Communities in Early Complex Societies. Washington, D.C.: Smithsonian Institution Press.

Shaffer, A. 1970. Appendix B: Fragment of an inscribed envelope, in W. Dever, H. D. Lance, and G. E. Wright (eds.), *Gezer I,* pp. 111-13. Jerusalem: Hebrew Union College.

Sherratt, A. G. 1981. Plough and pastoralism: aspects of the secondary products revolution, in I. Hodder, G. Isaac, and N. Hammond (eds.), *Pattern of the Past: Studies in Memory of David Clarke,* pp. 261-305. Cambridge: Cambridge University Press.

Shipton, G. 1938. *Notes on the Megiddo Pottery of Strata VI-XX.* Chicago: University of Chicago Press.

Shmida, A. 1980. Kermes oak in the land of Israel. *Israel Land and Nature* 6(1): 9-16.

Silver, I. A. 1969. The ageing of domestic animals, in D. R. Brothwell and E. S. Higgs (eds.), *Science in Archaeology,* pp. 283-302. London: Thames and Hudson.

Singer-Avitz, L. 2004. The Middle Bronze Age pottery from areas D and P, in D. Ussishkin (ed.), *The Renewed Archaeological Excavations at Lachish (1973-1994), Volume 3,* pp. 900-970. Tel Aviv: Emery and Claire Yass Publications in Archaeology, Tel Aviv University.

Smith, M. F., jr. 1985. Toward an economic interpretation of ceramics: relating vessel size and shape to use, in B. A. Nelson (ed.), *Decoding Prehistoric Ceramics,* pp. 254-309. Carbondale, IL: Southern Illinois University Press.

Smith, R. H. 1973. *Pella of the Decapolis, Volume 1.* Wooster, OH: Wooster College.

Smith, R. H. 1993. Pella, in E. Stern (ed.), *The New Encyclopedia of Archaeological Excavations in the Holy Land,* pp. 1174-1180. Jerusalem: Israel Exploration Society.

Smith, R. H. McNicoll, A. W. & Hennessy, J. B. 1981. The 1980 Season at Pella of the Decapolis. *Bulletin of the American Schools of Oriental Research* 245: 1-30.

Smith, R. H. & Potts, T. F. 1992. The Middle and Late Bronze Ages. in A. W. McNicoll, P. C. Edwards, J. Hanbury-Tenison, J. B. Hennessy, T. F. Potts, R. H. Smith, A. Walmsley and P. Watson (eds.), *Pella in Jordan 2,* pp. 35-81. Sydney: University of Sydney.

Stager, L.E. 1985. The first fruits of civilization, in J. N. Tubb (ed.), *Palestine in the Bronze and Iron Ages. Papers in Honor of Olga Tufnell,* pp. 172-188. Institute of Archaeology Occasional Papers 11. London: Institute of Archaeology.

Stuiver, M. & Reimer, P. J. 1993. Extended C-14 database and revised Calib 3.0 C-14 age calibration program. *Radiocarbon* 35(1): 215-230.

Sweet, L. E. 1974. *Tell Toqaan, a Syrian Village.* Museum of Anthropology, University of Michigan Anthropological Papers 14. Ann Arbor: University of Michigan.

Talon, Ph. 1978. Les offrandes funeraires a Mari. *Annuaire de l'institut de Philologie et d'histoire Orientales et Slaves* 22: 53-75.

Thuesen, I. 1988. *Hama Fouilles et Recherches 1931-1938 I: The Pre- and Protohistoric Periods.* Copenhagen: Nationalmuseets Skrifter, Storre Beretinger XI.

Turrill, W. B. 1952. Wild and cultivated olives. *Kew Bulletin* 7: 437.

van der Kooij, G. & Ibrahim, M. 1989. *Picking up the Threads: A Continuing Review of Excavations at Deir Alla, Jordan.* Leiden: University of Leiden.

van Neer, W. n.d.Personal communication, 2004.

van Zeist, W. 1985. Past and present environments of the Jordan Valley, in A. Hadidi (ed.), *Studies in the History and Archaeology of Jordan II,* pp. 199-204. Amman: Department of Antiquities, Jordan.

van Zeist, W. 1991. Economic aspects, in W. Van Zeist, K. Wasylikowa, K.-E. Behre (eds.), *Progress in Old World Palaeoethnobotany: A Retrospective View on the Occasion of 20 years of the International Work Group for Palaeoethnobotany,* pp. 109-131. Rotterdam: A. A. Balkema.

van Zeist, W. & Bottema, S. 1991. *Late Quaternary Vegetation of the Near East.* Wiesbaden: Ludwig Reichert Verlag.

Vapnarsky, C. A. 1968. On rank-size distributions of cities: an ecological approach. *Economic Development and Culture Change* 17: 584-595.

Von den Driesch, A. 1976. *A Guide to the Measurement of Animal Bones from Archaeological Sites.* Peabody Museum Bulletin 1. Cambridge: Peabody Museum of Archaeology and Ethnology, Harvard University.

Wapnish, P. & Hesse, B. 1984. *Organization of animal production at Tell Jemmeh in the Middle Bronze Age.* Paper presented at the annual meeting of the American Schools of Oriental Research, Chicago, IL

Wapnish, P. & Hesse, B. 1988. Urbanization and the organization of animal production at Tell Jemmeh in the Middle Bronze Age Levant. *Journal of Near Eastern Studies* 47(2): 81-94.

Weinstein, J. M. 1991. Egypt and the Middle Bronze IIC/Late Bronze IA transition in Palestine. *Levant* 23: 105-115.

Weiss, H., Courty, M.-A., Wetterstrom, W., Guichard, F., Senior, L., Meadow, R. & Curnow, A. 1993. The genesis and collapse of third millennium north Mesopotamian civilization. *Science* 261: 995-1004.

Western, A. C. 1971. Ecological interpretation of ancient charcoals from Jericho. *Levant* 3: 31-40.

White, K. D. 1970. *Roman Farming.* Ithaca, NY: Cornell University Press.

Whitmore, T. M. & Turner, B. L. 1992. Landscapes of cultivation in Mesoamerica on the eve of the conquest. *Annals of the Association of American Geographers* 82: 402-425.

Wilk, R. R. & Rathje, W. L. 1982. Household Archaeology. *American Behavioral Scientist* 25: 617-639.

Wilkinson, T. J. 2003. *Archaeological Landscapes of the Near East.* Tucson: University of Arizona Press.

Wolf, E. R. 1966. *Peasants.* Englewood Cliffs: Prentice-Hall.

Woods, A. J. 1986. Form, fabric, and function: some observations on the cooking pot in antiquity, in W. D. Kingery (ed.), *Technology and Style. Ceramics and Civilization, Volume 2,* pp. 157-172. Columbus, OH: American Ceramic Society.

Wright, G. E. 1965. *Shechem: The Biography of a Biblical City.* New York: McGraw-Hill.

Wright, G. E. 1971. The archaeology of Palestine from the Neolithic through the Middle Bronze Age. *Journal of the American Oriental Society* 91: 276-93.

Wright, G. R. H. 1985. *Ancient Building in South Syria and Palestine.* Leiden: E. J. Brill.

Wright, H. E., jr. 1993. Environmental determinism in Near Eastern prehistory. *Current Anthropology* 34: 458-469.

Xella, P. 1982. L'influence Babylonienne a Ougarit, d'apres les textes alphabetiques, rituels et divinatoires, in J. Renger (ed.), *Mesopotamien und Seine Nachbarn,* pp. 321-338. Berlin: Reimer Verlag.

Yadin, Y. 1972. *Hazor. The Schweich Lectures of the British Academy.* London: Oxford University Press.

Yasuda, Y., Kitagawa, H. & Nakagawa, T. 2000. The earliest record of major anthropogenic deforestation in the Ghab Valley, northwest Syria: a palynological study. *Quaternary International* 73/74: 127-36.

Yoffee, N. 1979. The decline and rise of Mesopotamian civilizations: an ethnoarchaeological perspective on the evolution of complex society. *American Antiquity* 44: 5-35.

Yon, M. 1984. Sanctuaires d'Ougarit, in G. Roux (ed.), *Temples et Sanctuaires,* pp. 37-50. Lyons: Maison de l'Orient.

Zaccagnini, C. 1979. *The Rural Landscape of the Land of Arraphe. Quaderni di Geografia Storica, Volume 1.* Rome: Instituto di Studi del Vicino Oriente, Universita di Roma.

Zaccagnini, C. 1984. Land tenure and transfer of land at Nuzi, in T. Khalidi (ed.), *Land Tenure and Social Transformation in the Middle East,* pp. 79-94. Beirut: American University of Beirut.

Zeder, M. 1990. Animal exploitation at Tell Halif. *Bulletin of the American Schools of Oriental Research, Supplement* 26: 24-30.

Zeder, M. 1991. *Feeding Cities.* Washington, D.C.: Smithsonian Institution Press.

Zimmerer, K. S. 1991. Wetland production and smallholder persistence: agricultural change in a highland Peruvian region. *Annals of the Association of American Geographers* 81: 443-463.

Zimmerer, K. 1993. Agricultural biodiversity and peasant rights to subsistence in the Central Andes during Inca rule. *Journal of Historical Geography* 19: 15-32.

Zipf, G. K. 1949. *Human Behavior and the Principle of Least Effort.* Cambridge, MA: Addison-Wesley.

Zohary, M. 1973. *Geobotanical Foundations of the Middle East, Volume 1.* Stuttgart: Gustav Fischer Verlag.

Zohary, M. 1982. *Plants of the Bible.* Cambridge: Cambridge University Press.

Zohary, D. & Hopf, M. 1988. *Domestication of Plants in the Old World.* Oxford: Clarendon Press.

Zohary, D. & Spiegel-Roy, P. 1975. Beginning of fruit growing in the Old World. *Science* 187: 319–327.

APPENDIX A: CODES FOR TELL EL-HAYYAT DATABASES (APPENDICES B-S)

CODES FOR APPENDIX B Tell el-Hayyat excavated loci (filename: "TH LOCUS"):
"Sector"= Architectural Sector:
TB = Temple backcourt
TF = Temple forecourt
TFE = Temple forecourt exterior
TI = Temple interior
TS = Temple sidecourt
TT = Tower
WA = West alley
WB = West building
WE = West exterior
WR = West room
EA = East alley
EB = East Building
EC = East courtyard
CA = Central alley
CE = Central enclosure
CC = Central courtyard
CR = Central room
Temple Interiors – Sector TI only
Temple Courtyards – Sectors TF, TS, TB, and TT
Domestic Interiors – Sectors WR, CR, CE, EB, and WB
Domestic Exteriors – Sectors WA, CA, EA, CC, EC, WE and TFE

"Code"= Locus Code:
A = Ash lens (usually embedded in a surface)
B = Burial (i.e., modern)
DO = Occupational debris (i.e., buildup on surface)
DM = Mudbrick debris
DF = Fill debris
H = Posthole
I = Installation (unidentified industrial or architectural feature)
K = Kiln
M = Modern *tell* surface
P = Pit (usually shallow, embedded in surface)
R = Rodent burrow
S = Surface (earthen)
SP = Plaster surface
T = Tabun (earthen oven)
TF = Tabun fill
V = Virgin soil (i.e., archaeologically sterile deposit)
X = Test trench

CODES FOR APPENDIX C Tell el-Hayyat registered objects (filename: "TH REGISTERED OBJECTS"):
"Registration #"= Department of Antiquities, Jordan Registration number
"Max dim."= maximum dimension (in cm)
"Length," "Width," "Depth," "Diameter"= in cm
"Weight"= in grams

CODES FOR APPENDIX D Tell el-Hayyat registered object descriptions (filename: "TH REGISTERED OBJECTS DESCRIPTION"):
"Registration #"= Department of Antiquities, Jordan Registration number

CODES FOR APPENDIX E Tell el-Hayyat seed counts (filename: "TH FLORA SUMMARY"):
"Phase or Unit" = Excavated context:
Niaj = Tell Abu en-Ni'aj
Phase 5 = Tell el-Hayyat Phase 5
Phase 4 = Tell el-Hayyat Phase 4
Phase 3 = Tell el-Hayyat Phase 3
Phase 2 = Tell el-Hayyat Phase 2
Hayyat Total = total from Tell el-Hayyat
Temple = Tell el-Hayyat, temple interiors and courtyards, sectors TI, TF, TS
Outside Temple = Tell el-Hayyat, domestic interiors and domestic exteriors
TF = Tell el-Hayyat, temple forecourts
Temple 5 = Tell el-Hayyat, Phase 5 temple interior and courtyard
Outside 5 = Tell el-Hayyat, Phase 5 domestic interiors and domestic exteriors
Temple 4 = Tell el-Hayyat, Phase 4 temple interior and courtyard
Outside 4 = Tell el-Hayyat, Phase 4 domestic interiors and domestic exteriors
Temple 3 = Tell el-Hayyat, Phase 3 temple interior and courtyard
Outside 3 = Tell el-Hayyat, Phase 3 domestic interiors and domestic exteriors
Temple 2 = Tell el-Hayyat, Phase 2 temple interior and courtyard
Outside 2 = Tell el-Hayyat, Phase 2 domestic interiors and domestic exteriors
Surface = all use surface contexts, all loci coded as A, Do, P or S
Non-surface = all non-surface contexts, all other loci
All interiors = domestic interiors and Area A, Phases 5-2
All exteriors = domestic exteriors and Area A, Phases 5-2
Exterior 5 = temple exteriors and domestic exteriors, Phase 5
Interior 5 = temple interiors and domestic interiors, Phase 5
Exterior 4 = temple exteriors and domestic exteriors, Phase 4
Interior 4 = temple interiors and domestic interiors, Phase 4
Exterior 3 = temple exteriors and domestic exteriors, Phase 3
Interior 3 = temple interiors and domestic interiors, Phase 3
Exterior 2 = temple exteriors and domestic exteriors, Phase 2
Interior 2 = temple interiors and domestic interiors, Phase 2
Area A = all contexts in Area A
Tabun T,TF = tabun contexts, loci coded T or TF

"Volume" = volume of sediment in flotation sample (in liters)

Values for plant taxa shown as no. of identified seeds
"Pros" = *Prosopis*
"Wild C" = wild cereals
"OC" = other cereals
"Cult L" = cultivated legumes
"Wild L" = wild legumes
"UNID" = unidentified

CODES FOR APPENDIX F Tell el-Hayyat seed densities (filename: "TH FLORA DENSITY"):
See codes for Appendix E
All values shown in no. of seeds/kiloliter

CODES FOR APPENDIX G Tell el-Hayyat flotation samples and seed identifications (filename: "TH FLORA ALL PHASES")
"Code" = locus code
"Qty_saved" = quantity of sherds from locus; exponential notation rounded to nearest 100 (e.g., 1E+02=1x10^2)
"Volume" = flotation sample volume (in liters)
"C/H# undiff#" = Cereal/*Hordeum*, undifferentiated
"C/H# hulled var#" = Cereal/*Hordeum*, hulled
"C/H# naked var#" = Cereal/*Hordeum*, naked
"C/Rachis frag#" = Cereal/rachis fragment
"C/T# undiff#" = Cereal/*Triticum*, undifferentiated
"C/T# emmer" = Cereal/*Triticum*, emmer
"C/T# einkorn" = Cereal/*Triticum*, einkorn

"**C/T# bread**" = Cereal/*Triticum,* bread wheat
"**C/Spikelet frag#**" = Cereal/spikelet fragment
"**OC/Avena**" = Other cereal/*Avena*
"**WC/Phalaris**" = Wild cereal/*Phalaris*
"**CL/V# faba**" = Cultivated Legume/*Vicia faba*
"**F/Ficus**" = Fruit/*Ficus*
"**W/cf# Adonis**" = Weed/cf. *Adonis*

CODES FOR APPENDIX H   Tell el-Hayyat sheep/goat identifications (filename: "TH FAUNA SHEEP/GOAT")
"**SP**" = skeletal part

"**ELEM**" = bone element
4c = 4th carpal
Ic = intermediate carpal
In = innominate
cc 2/3 = os carpal 2+3
Sk = skull

"**LOC**" = locus
"**PH**" = phase and locus type
"**RF**" = relative frequency
"**REM**" = remarks (c = cut; b = burned)
"**TWEAR**" = tooth wear
"**FUST**" = fusion stage
"**SPE**" = species (o = *Ovis*; c = *Capra*)

CODES FOR APPENDIX I   Tell el-Hayyat pig bone identifications (filename: "TH FAUNA PIG")
See codes for Appendix H
"**WEAR**" = tooth wear
"**MWS**" = mandible wear stage

CODES FOR APPENDIX J   Tell el-Hayyat cattle bone identifications (filename: "TH FAUNA CATTLE")
see codes for Appendix I
"**Field6**" = disregard

CODES FOR APPENDIX K   Tell el-Hayyat wild animal identifications (filename: "TH FAUNA WILD")
See codes for Appendix J
"**Field6**" = disregard

CODES FOR APPENDIX L   Tell el-Hayyat analyzed Phase 5 ceramics (filename: "TH CERAMICS PHASE 5")
"**Sherd**" = sherd number
"**Code**" = locus code
"**Sherd type**" = sherd type:
BD = body sherd
RM = rim sherd
BS = base sherd

"**Appendage**" = appendage:
HD = handle
SP = spout

"**Joins**" = sherd joins with one or more other sherds
Y = yes

"**Same vessel**" = sherd is from same vessel as one or more other sherds
Y = yes

"Joins #s" = joins numbers; sherd numbers for joining sherds
"Condition" = sherd condition
1 = good
2 = fair
3 = worn

"Manufacture, Inclusions, Inclu size, Inclu freq, Color ext, Color int, Color core" = disregard
"EB IV ware" = Early Bronze IV ceramic
"Greenware" = greenish fabric possibly indicative of local manufacture

"Form code" = form code, following Cole 1984

BC	small closed bowl
BCA	small closed bowl
BCB	small closed bowl
BDA	deep open bowl
BDB	deep open bowl
BDC	deep closed bowl
BDE	deep open bowl
BDF	deep open bowl
BF	small flared-rim bowl
BFA	small flared-rim bowl
BFB	small flared-rim bowl
BFC	small flared-rim bowl
BG	small closed bowl
BGA	small closed bowl
BGB	small closed bowl
BGC	small closed bowl
BM	miniature bowl
BMA	miniature bowl
BMB	miniature bowl
BN	small necked bowl
BNA	small necked bowl
BNB	small necked bowl
BND	small necked bowl
BP	platter bowl
CF	open cooking pot
CFA	open cooking pot
CFB	open cooking pot
CFC	open cooking pot
CH	closed cooking pot
CRU	crucible
CU	closed cooking pot
JC	cylindrical juglet
JD	dipper juglet
JDC	dipper juglet
JG	jug
JGA	jug
JGB	jug
JGC	jug
JJ	medium jar
JL	large jar
JP	piriform jar
JS	small jar
KER	kernos
L	lamp
TR	baking tray

"Rim code, Base code, Hand code" = see Cole codes in 1984
"Max dimens" = maximum dimension (in cm)
"Body thick" = body thickness (in cm)
"Rim dia" = rim diameter (in cm)

"**Base dia**" = base diameter (in cm)
"**Base ht**" = base height (in cm)

"**Slip**" = surface slip color
1 = red
2 = white
3 = black/brown

"**Burnish**" = surface burnishing
1 = complete
2 = radial
3 = horizontal
4 = vertical
5 = sporadic/irregular

"**Paint**" = color of surface paint
1000 = red only
1100 = red and white
1110 = red, white and blue
1111 = red, white, blue and black

"**Bands**" = type of painted band(s)
First digit:
1 = horizontal
2 = wavy
3 = horizontal and wavy
4 = vertical
5 = vertical and horizontal
Second digit:
1 = single
2 = multiple
3 = multiple horizontal and single wavy
4 = other

"**Trickle**" = surface trickle painting
Y = present
N = absent

"**Comb teeth**" = combed surface decoration
First digit:
1 = multiple tooth
2 = single tooth
3 = multiple and single tooth
Second digit:
0 = horizontal and vertical band(s)
1 = horizontal band(s)
2 = wavy band(s)
3 = horizontal and wavy band(s)
4 = pattern combing
5 = pattern and band combing
6 = brief horizontal strokes
7 = horizontal strokes and bands
8 = overall horizontal combing
9 = other

"**Strokes**" = incised strokes
1 = incised single strokes
2 = herring bone strokes

"**Applique1**" = applied decoration
1 = raised continuous molding
2 = impressed continuous molding

3 = incised continuous molding

"Area dec" = area(s) of vessel decorated
10000 = rim
11000 = rim and neck
11100 = rim, neck and shoulder
11110 = rim, neck, shoulder and handle
11111 = rim, neck, shoulder, handle and body

CODES FOR APPENDIX M   Tell el-Hayyat comments on analyzed Phase 5 ceramics (filename: "TH CERAMICS PHASE 5 COMMENTS")
See codes for Appendix L

CODES FOR APPENDIX N   Tell el-Hayyat analyzed Phase 4 ceramics (filename: "TH CERAMICS PHASE 4")
See codes for Appendix L

CODES FOR APPENDIX O   Tell el-Hayyat comments on analyzed Phase 4 ceramics (filename: "TH CERAMICS PHASE 4 COMMENTS")
See codes for Appendix L

CODES FOR APPENDIX P   Tell el-Hayyat analyzed Phase 3 ceramics (filename: "TH CERAMICS PHASE 3")
See codes for Appendix L

CODES FOR APPENDIX Q   Tell el-Hayyat comments on analyzed Phase 3 ceramics (filename: "TH CERAMICS PHASE 3 COMMENTS")
See codes for Appendix L

CODES FOR APPENDIX R   Tell el-Hayyat analyzed Phase 2 ceramics (filename: "TH CERAMICS PHASE 2")
See codes for Appendix L

CODES FOR APPENDIX S   Tell el-Hayyat comments on analyzed Phase 2 ceramics (filename: "TH CERAMICS PHASE 2 COMMENTS")
See codes for Appendix L

APPENDIX B:
TELL EL-HAYYAT EXCAVATED LOCI
(filename: "TH LOCUS")

Tell El Hayyat Loci

Locus	Phase	Sector	Subphase	Description	Code	Contents	Number of Bags	Qty sherds excavated
A001	0				M		1	55
A002	0				DF		2	450
A003	0				DF		2	375
A004	0				DF		1	150
A005	0				S		1	29
A006	0				P		1	4
A007	0				P		0	0
A008	0				B		10	362
A009	0				X		2	33
A010	0				DF		2	290
A011	0				B		3	87
A012	0				B		5	127
A013	0				B		5	165
A014	0				DF		2	90
A015	0				S		1	200
A016	2				A		1	20
A017	0				P		3	47
A018	2				S		3	163
A019	0				P		1	12
A020	2				S		1	40
A021	2				S		2	225
A022	2				A		1	20
A023	2				S		1	40
A024	2				S		2	345
A025	0				WM		0	0
A026	2				A		1	50
A027	2				DF		1	150
A028	2				DF		1	200
A029	2				DF	slag	2	400
A030	2				A		1	40

Locus	Phase	Sector	Subphase	Description	Code	Contents	Number of Bags	Qty sherds excavated
A031	2				WM		1	8
A032	2				DO		3	269
A033	2				DF		1	50
A034	3				A		3	426
A035	3				A		4	450
A036	3				DF		6	1131
A037	3				S		2	35
A038	3				DF		2	200
A039	3				P		1	10
A040	3				P		1	1
A041	4				S		1	10
A042	4				S		0	0
A043	4				K		6	190
A044	4				DF		2	235
A045.1	4				DO	Split locus, bags A.045.185, 221, 1	10	384
A045.2	0				DO	Split locus, bags A.045. 241-242, 2	2	95
A046	4				DO		2	65
A047	4				P		4	136
A048	4				DO		1	15
A049	4				DF		5	508
A050	5				A		7	226
A051	5				DF		12	481
A052	0				M		1	23
A053	0				DF		1	60
A054	0				DF		1	70
A055	0				S		1	35
A056	0				DF		2	95
A057	0				S		3	65
A058	0				DF		1	35
A059	0				TF		0	0

Tell El Hayyat Loci

Tell El Hayyat Loci

Locus	Phase	Sector	Subphase	Description	Code	Contents	Number of Bags	Qty sherds excavated
A060	0				DF		2	73
A061	0				B		0	0
A062	0				S		1	20
A063	0				DF		2	80
A064	0				WM		0	0
A065	0				P		0	0
A066	0				S		1	15
A067	0				DO		1	15
A068	0				X		1	15
A069	0				DO		2	22
A070	0				B		1	20
A071	0				DO		5	202
A072	0				WM		1	30
A073	0				DF		2	110
A074	0				DO	slag	1	10
A075	0				DF		2	150
A076	2				A		5	110
A077	3				A	slag	1	100
A078	3				A		3	175
A079	3				DF	slag	1	125
A080	3				S		1	3
A081	3				DF		5	425
A082	0				B		4	65
A083	3				S		1	60
A084	3				DF	2 wasters	2	65
A085	4				DF	slag	1	15
A086	3				DF	slag	4	173
A087	0				B		1	15
A088	4				DO		4	45
A089	4				DF		9	276

Locus	Phase	Sector	Subphase	Description	Code	Contents	Number of Bags	Qty sherds excavated
A090	4				K		4	47
A091	4				DF	slag	10	492
A092	4				K		2	55
A093	4				T		2	11
A094	5				DF		5	160
A095	4				T		0	0
A096	5				WM		1	17
A097	5				A		1	45
A098	5				DF		1	60
A099	5				A		3	100
A100	5				DF		1	30
A101	4				S		0	0
A102	5				DF		1	50
A103	4				WM		2	72
A104	4				P		1	8
A105	5				DF		2	45
A106	5				DF		1	35
A107	0				V		0	0
B001	0				M		1	80
B002	0				DF		2	700
B003	0				DF		2	135
B004	0				DF		2	220
B005	0				DF		1	80
B006	0				A		1	2
B007	0				DF		1	75
B008	0				A		0	0
B009	0				A		0	0
B010	0				DM		4	238
B011	0				B		8	642
B012	0				DM		1	20

Tell El Hayyat Loci

Locus	Phase	Sector	Subphase	Description	Code	Contents	Number of Bags	Qty sherds excavated
B013	0				DM		2	375
B014	0				S		1	30
B015	0				DF		1	75
B016	0				DF		2	100
B017	0				A		0	0
B018	3				DF		2	32
B019	3				X		1	350
B020	0				B		4	77
B021	2				S		1	0
B022	2				A		0	0
B023.1	2				S	Split locus, bags B.023.094-96	1	150
B023.2	0				S	Split locus, bags B.023.091-93	1	75
B024	2				DF	slag	1	40
B025	3				DF		3	320
B026	0				B		4	261
B027	0				R		0	0
B028	3				DO	slag	2	260
B029	3				P		1	4
B030	3				DF		1	125
B031	0				R		1	30
B032	3				DM		1	100
B033	4				DF		1	30
B034	4				A		1	30
B035	4				DO		2	150
B036	4				A		1	6
B037	4				DO		1	175
B038	4				A		1	0
B039	4				DF		3	100
B040	5				S		2	100
B041	5				A		2	75

Tell El Hayyat Loci

Locus	Phase	Sector	Subphase	Description	Code	Contents	Number of Bags	Qty sherds excavated
B042	5				DO		1	30
B043	0				U	Unused locus numbers: B.043-B.04	0	0
B050	3				DF		2	51
B051	3				D0		1	110
B052	3				DF		1	45
B053	3				DM		2	160
B054	4				DO		2	175
B055	0				B		0	0
B056	4				DF		1	30
B057	5				S		1	70
B058	5				A		1	150
B059	0				B		0	0
C001	0				M		2	37
C002	0				DF		2	160
C003	0				DF		3	270
C004	0				P		3	53
C005	1				WS		1	25
C006	0				P		3	113
C007	0				B		3	34
C008	0				DF		5	500
C009	1				S		2	80
C010	1				S		2	32
C011	0				P		1	6
C012	1				WS		0	0
C013	0				P		2	70
C014	0				X		0	0
C015	0				P		2	150
C016	0				P		1	15
C017	1				S		1	15
C018	0				R		2	30

Tell El Hayyat Loci

Locus	Phase	Sector	Subphase	Description	Code	Contents	Number of Bags	Qty sherds excavated
C019	1				S		1	25
C020	0				X		4	240
C021	2	CA		NORTH-SOUTH DR	WS		2	2
C022	3	CA	LATE		T		4	98
C023	3	CA	LATE		T		3	50
C024	3	CA	LATE		DF		2	50
C025	3	CA	LATE		DM		1	8
C026	3	CA	LATE		S		2	25
C027	0				R		2	27
C028	3	CA	LATE		DF		2	15
C029	0				R		1	35
C030	3	CA	LATE		S		1	9
C031	2	CA			WS		2	37
C032	0				X		1	25
C033	3				WM		1	0
C034	3				WM		1	15
C035	2	CA			WS		0	0
C036	2	CA			WM		1	30
C037	2	CA			WM		1	12
C038	3			N-S WALL	WM		1	45
C039	3	WB	EARLY		S		1	20
C040	3	CA	LATE		DF		1	50
C041	0				R		1	35
C042	2	CA	LATE		S		1	50
C043	2	CA	LATE		S		1	10
C044	2	CA	LATE		S		1	10
C045	2	CA		PART OF C021	WS		1	25
C046	2	CA		PART OF C021	WS		2	3
C047	0				X		1	30
C048	3	CA	LATE		S		1	50

Tell El Hayyat Loci

Locus	Phase	Sector	Subphase	Description	Code	Contents	Number of Bags	Qty sherds excavated
C049	0				X		2	65
C050	3	CA	LATE		DF		1	150
C051	3	CA	LATE		S		2	115
C052	2	CA	EARLY		S		1	5
C053	3	CA	LATE		DO		2	95
C054	3	WB	LATE		DF		2	335
C055	3	CA			WM		2	35
C056	3	CA	LATE		S		1	20
C057	3	CA	LATE		WM		1	150
C058	3	CA	LATE		DM		2	225
C059	3	CA	EARLY		DF		1	125
C060	0				R		2	65
C061	3	CA	LATE		DF		4	333
C062	3	CA	EARLY		DF		1	200
C063	4	CA	LATE		DF		1	350
C064	4	CA	LATE		DF		2	300
C065	4	CC	LATE		DF		1	200
C066	4	CA	LATE		DF		2	500
C067	4	CA	EARLY		S		1	350
C068	4	CA	EARLY		DO		1	50
C069	4	CC	EARLY		DO		1	50
C070	4	CA	EARLY	C070=I081	S		1	275
C071	4	CA	EARLY		DO	CHECK CERAMICS, THIS MAY	1	250
C072	5				DO		1	50
C073	5				DO		1	240
C074.1	5				P	Duplicate locus number, bag P.073.	1	11
C074.2	5				P	Duplicate locus number, bags P.07	2	345
C075	5				A	1 waster	1	185
C076	5				S		1	52
C077	5				A		2	125

Tell El Hayyat Loci

Locus	Phase	Sector	Subphase	Description	Code	Contents	Number of Bags	Qty sherds excavated
C078	5				DF		1	200
C079	5				DF		1	450
C080	5				DF		2	350
C081	5				S	slag	1	200
C082	5				A		1	100
D001	0				M		1	20
D002	0				DF		2	70
D003	0				X		1	100
D004	0				A		0	0
D005	0				S		1	25
D006	0				B		3	190
D007	0				B		2	120
D008	0				B		2	20
D009	0				B		1	25
D010	0				DM		1	175
D011	0				DM		2	50
D012	0				DF		1	35
D013	0				S		2	55
D014	0				DF		1	50
D015	0				B		3	125
D016	0				DF		2	92
D017	2	WA	EARLY		S		1	25
D018	2	WA	EARLY		DF		1	15
D019	2	WA	EARLY		DF		2	145
D020	0				DM		1	0
D021	0				B		1	9
D022	3	WA	LATE		S		1	15
D023	3	WA	LATE		A		0	0
D024	3	WA	LATE		S		1	250
D025	3	WA	LATE		S		1	200

Tell El Hayyat Loci

Tell El Hayyat Loci

Locus	Phase	Sector	Subphase	Description	Code	Contents	Number of Bags	Qty sherds excavated
D026	3				A		0	0
D027	3	WA	LATE		S		1	60
D028	3	WB	LATE		DF		6	372
D029	3				WM		1	25
D030	4	CC	LATE	Wall running north-s	DM		2	50
D031	3				WM		0	0
D032	3	WE	EARLY		A		2	135
D033	3	WE	EARLY		S		1	75
D034	3				WS		0	0
D035	3	WB	EARLY		S		1	75
D036	4	CC	LATE		S		2	250
D037	4	CC	LATE		DM		2	20
D038	4	CC	LATE		S		1	20
D039	4	CC	LATE		P		3	215
D040	4		LATE		WM	STRATIGRAPHICALLY PHASE	2	190
D041	4	WA	EARLY	Wall runs north-south	WM		3	125
D042	4	CC	LATE		TF		1	2
D043	4	CC	LATE		P		1	30
D044	4	CC	EARLY		S		2	220
D045	4	CC	LATE		P		3	650
D046	4	CC	EARLY		P		2	320
D047	4		EARLY	Wall in C/D balk run	WM		0	0
D048	5				A		1	70
D049	5				WM		1	25
D050	5				S		1	75
D051	5				A		1	7
D052	5				DM		1	5
D053	5				DF		3	158
D054	0				V		0	0
D055	4	WA	EARLY		DF		3	43

Locus	Phase	Sector	Subphase	Description	Code	Contents	Number of Bags	Qty sherds excavated
D056	5				S		5	151
D057	4	WA	EARLY		S		1	30
D058	4	WA	EARLY		DF		1	40
D059	5				S		1	50
D060	5				A		1	25
D061	5				S		1	50
D062	5				S		1	25
D063	5				DF		1	25
D064	5				DF		1	30
D065	5				A		1	40
D066	5				A		2	75
D067	5				A		1	8
D068	5				A		1	60
D069	0				U	Unused locus number	0	0
D070	5				A		2	64
D071	5				WM		1	50
D072	5				DF		2	170
E001	0				M		1	35
E002	0				DF		4	455
E003	0				DF		2	115
E004	0				B		5	164
E005	0				S		2	17
E006	0				P		2	62
E007	0				P		1	30
E008	0				S		1	15
E009	0				DF		1	25
E010	0				DF		3	115
E011	0				B		6	276
E012	0				WM		1	25
E013	0				S		1	20

Tell El Hayyat Loci

Locus	Phase	Sector	Subphase	Description	Code	Contents	Number of Bags	Qty sherds excavated
E014	0				DF		1	30
E015	0				WM		0	0
E016	0				U	Unused locus number	0	0
E017	0				P		2	55
E018	0				P		2	27
E019	0				B		1	25
E020	0				B		0	0
E021	0				B		0	0
E022	0				B		4	160
E023	0				WM		3	350
E024	0				X		1	30
E025	0				WM		1	20
E026	0				DF		2	85
E027	2	WB1	EARLY		S		1	20
E028	0				R		0	0
E029	0				WM		0	0
E030	0				WM		0	0
E031	0				A		0	0
E032	2	WB1	EARLY		T		2	32
E033	2	WB1	EARLY		TF		1	55
E034	0				P		1	40
E035	0				P		1	20
E036	0				R		1	25
E037	2	WB1	EARLY		S		0	0
E038	0				R		0	0
E039	0				X		2	60
E040	0				A		1	20
E041	2	WB1	EARLY		A		1	25
E042	2	WB1	EARLY		S		4	275
E043.1	2	WB1	EARLY		S	Split locus, bags E.043.173-175	1	30

Tell El Hayyat Loci

Locus	Phase	Sector	Subphase	Description	Code	Contents	Number of Bags	Qty sherds excavated
E043.2	0				S	Split locus, bags E.043.179-181	1	15
E044	2	WB		NORTH-SOUTH W	WS		1	35
E045	2	WB		EAST-WEST WALL	WS		0	0
E046	0				B		0	0
E047	0				WM		1	15
E048	0				DF		0	0
E049	0				DF		0	0
E050	0				M		1	15
E051	0				DF		1	50
E052	0				DF		1	25
E053	0				DF		4	62
E054	0				B		3	62
E055	0				P		1	30
E056	0				DF		1	50
E057	0				P		6	117
E058	0				X		1	30
E059.1	2	WB2	LATE		S	Split locus, bags E.059.232-234	1	25
E059.2	0				S	Split locus, bag E.059.235	1	10
E060	0				R	1 waster	2	65
E061	2	WB2	LATE		S		1	50
E062	0				X		2	90
E063	2	WB2	LATE		DF		2	60
E064.1	2	WB1	LATE		S	Split locus, bags E.064.256, 270, 2	2	9
E064.2	0				S	Split locus, bags E.064.290-291	1	58
E065	0				P		3	45
E066	0				R		1	12
E067	0				R		4	114
E068	2	WB1	LATE		A		1	60
E069	0				R		2	100
E070.1	2	WB2	LATE		DF	Split locus, bags E.070.283-286	2	80

Tell El Hayyat Loci

Locus	Phase	Sector	Subphase	Description	Code	Contents	Number of Bags	Qty sherds excavated
E070.2	0				DF	Split locus, bags E..070.281-282	1	50
E071	2	WB2	EARLY		S		0	0
E072	0				R		1	28
E073	2	WB1	EARLY		S		1	45
E074	3	WA	EARLY		S		2	180
E075	2	WB2	EARLY		S		2	102
E076	3	WA	LATE		DF		3	365
E077	0				R		4	172
E078	2	WB		EAST-WEST WALL	WS		0	0
E079	0				R		1	30
E080	4		EARLY	Mudbrick wall on so	WM		0	0
E081	3	WA	LATE		DM		2	145
E082	3	WA	EARLY		P	Reassign bags from E.086, bags E.	10	1982
E083	0				B		0	0
E084	3	WA	EARLY		S		1	15
E085	3	WA	EARLY		S		1	200
E086	4	CR			X	Exclude bags E.086.379-386, 391,	15	2188
E087	4	CR	LATE	Wall added after E an	WM		1	12
E088	4	CR	LATE		S		4	760
E089	4	CR	EARLY		S		3	75
E090	4	CR	EARLY		S		1	12
E091	0				R		1	20
E092	4	CR	LATE		TF		2	32
E093	4	CR	EARLY		S		1	25
E094	4	CR	LATE		H		2	21
E095	4	CR	LATE		H		1	12
E096	4		EARLY		WS		1	12
E097	4	CR	EARLY		S		1	12
E098	4	CR	EARLY		X		5	370
E099	4	CR	EARLY		S		1	10

Locus	Phase	Sector	Subphase	Description	Code	Contents	Number of Bags	Qty sherds excavated
E100	5				S		3	390
E101	5				WM		0	0
E102	5				A		2	71
E103	5				S		1	57
E104	5				DF		1	50
E105	5				S		0	0
E106	5				S		1	100
E107	5				S		1	200
F001	0				M		1	25
F002	0				DF		2	450
F003	0				DF		2	20
F004	0				DF		2	240
F005	0				A		0	0
F006	2	WB		NORTH-SOUTH W	WS		1	35
F007	0				DM		1	30
F008	2	WB		EAST-WEST WALL	WS		0	0
F009	0				B		3	215
F010.1	2	WE	EARLY		DM	Split locus, bags F.010.32-35	1	110
F010.2	0				DM	Split locus, F.010.36-38	1	400
F011	2	WB1	EARLY		DO		0	0
F012	2	WB1	EARLY		S		2	80
F013	3	WA	LATE		S		2	75
F014	0				B		0	0
F015	3	WA	LATE		S		2	135
F016	0				R		0	0
F017	3	WA	EARLY		S		2	72
F018	3	WA	EARLY		DO		3	435
F019	3	WA	LATE		S		1	20
F020	3	WA	LATE		S		1	15
F021	3	WA	EARLY		A		1	35

Tell El Hayyat Loci

Locus	Phase	Sector	Subphase	Description	Code	Contents	Number of Bags	Qty sherds excavated
F022	3	WA	EARLY		DO		3	195
F023	3	WA	EARLY		A		0	0
F024	3	WA	EARLY		D0		1	30
F025	3	WA	EARLY		A		0	0
F026	4	WR	EARLY		WM		0	0
F027.1	4	WR	LATE		DO	Split locus, bags F.027.102, 103, 10	2	40
F027.2	0	WR			R	Split locus, bags F.027.99-101	1	40
F028	0				R		1	8
F029	0	WR	EARLY		WM		1	40
F030	4	WR	LATE		DM		6	210
F031	4	WA	LATE		DM		2	22
F032	4	WR	LATE		WM		1	7
F033	4	WA	LATE		S		0	0
F034	4	WA	LATE		S		1	2
F035	4	WR	EARLY		DO		4	245
F036	4	WA	LATE		DF		2	50
F037	4	WA	LATE		S		0	0
F038	4	WR	EARLY		DO		2	40
F039	4	WA	EARLY		DF		3	40
F040	4	WR	EARLY		S		3	130
F041	4	WR	EARLY		S		3	140
F042	4	WR	EARLY		T		1	7
F043	4	WR	EARLY	Stratified fill from cla	P		1	15
F044	5				DO		3	95
F045	5				A		0	0
F046	5				DO		1	40
F047	5				DO		5	77
F048	5				DO		2	100
F049	5				DO		3	69
F050	5				A		3	97

Tell El Hayyat Loci

Locus	Phase	Sector	Subphase	Description	Code	Contents	Number of Bags	Qty sherds excavated
F051	0				V		0	0
F052	4	WR	LATE		WM		0	0
F053	4	WA	EARLY		S		0	0
F054	4	WR	EARLY	Stratified fill from cla	P		3	130
F055	4	WR	EARLY	Stratified fill from cla	P		1	30
F056	4	WR	EARLY	Stratified fill from cla	P		0	0
F057	4	WA	EARLY		S		0	0
G001	0				M		1	15
G002	0				DF		3	70
G003	0				B		4	65
G004	0				DF		1	10
G005	0				DF		1	30
G006	0				B		2	20
G007	0				DF		1	15
G008	0				DF		1	20
G009	0				B		0	0
G010	1				S		1	25
G011	0				B		2	90
G012	0				DF		5	125
G013	0				B		1	3
G014	0				B		1	30
G015	0				B		5	255
G016	0				B		5	250
G017	0				B		1	55
G018	2	CA	LATE		DM		0	0
G019	0				S		2	88
G020	0				B		0	0
G021	2	CA	LATE		DF		1	15
G022	2	CA	LATE		DM		1	45
G023	0				B		5	397

Tell El Hayyat Loci

Locus	Phase	Sector	Subphase	Description	Code	Contents	Number of Bags	Qty sherds excavated
G024	2	CA	LATE		DF		2	65
G025	2	CA	LATE		A		3	87
G026	2	CA	LATE		DF		1	25
G027	2	CA	LATE		P		1	15
G028	2	CA	LATE		DF		1	60
G029	2	CA	LATE		DF		3	140
G030	1				WS		1	10
G031	1				S		1	50
G032	2	CA	LATE		DF		1	80
G033	0				B		1	70
G034.1	2	WB2	LATE		DM	Split locus, bags G.034.93-95; 100-	4	95
G034.2	0				DM	Split locus, G.034.96-98	1	50
G035	2	CA	EARLY		S		1	35
G036	2	WB2	LATE		DF		4	200
G037	2	CA	LATE		DF		1	15
G038	2	WB2	LATE		DM		1	25
G039	2	WB2		LEVELLING COUR	WM		2	17
G040	2	CA	LATE		DF		2	55
G041	2	WB2	EARLY		A		0	0
G042	2	CA	EARLY		DO		2	60
G043	0				T		0	0
G044	2	CA	EARLY		DO		1	40
G045	2	CA	EARLY		A		1	50
G046	2	CA	EARLY		DO		1	20
G047	2	WB2			WS		0	0
G048	2	WB2		NORHT-SOUTH W	WS		1	40
G049	0				X		1	7
G050	0				R		1	7
G051	2	WB2	EARLY		S		1	130
G052	2	WB2			WS		0	0

Tell El Hayyat Loci

Locus	Phase	Sector	Subphase	Description	Code	Contents	Number of Bags	Qty sherds excavated
G053	2	WB2	EARLY	LEVELLING COUR	DF		1	20
G054	2	CA	EARLY		DO		1	50
G055	2	CA	EARLY	PART OF DRAIN C	I		0	0
G056	0				U	Unused locus number	0	0
G057	2	CA	EARLY		DO		2	40
G058	0				DM		1	60
G059	2	CA	EARLY	PART OF DRAIN C	I		0	0
G060	2	CA	EARLY	DRAIN COMPLEX	I		2	120
G061	2	WB2	EARLY	LEVELLING COUR	DF		1	35
G062	3	CA	LATE		DF		1	100
G063	3	CA	LATE		DF		1	150
G064	3	CE		CENTRAL ENCLOS	WM		3	355
G065	3	CA	LATE		X		2	95
G066	2	CA	EARLY	CURB WALL, EQU	WS		1	6
G067	3	CA	EARLY		S		7	1380
G068	3	CA	EARLY		DF		4	107
G069	4	CR		Wall in south balk ru	WM		0	0
G070	0				R		1	70
G071	3	CA	EARLY		DF		2	470
G072	4	CR	LATE		X		1	30
G073	4	CR	LATE		X		2	175
G074	4	CA	LATE		DM		5	735
G075	0	CR	LATE		R		1	220
G076	4	CA		A hole (possible post below 100.60 m	H		0	0
G077.1	4	CA	LATE		DM	Split locus, Ph 4 Late = bags 266-2	2	530
G077.2	3	CA	EARLY		DM	Split locus, Ph 3 early = bags 260-2	2	450
G078.1	4	CA	LATE		DM	Split locus, CA late = bags 272-277	2	500
G078.2	4	CR	LATE		DM	Split locus, CR late = bags 278-299	1	75
G079.1	4	CA	LATE		X	Split locus, CA late = bags 289-299	4	765
G079.2	4	CR	EARLY		DO	Split locus, CR early = bags 281-28	3	220

Tell El Hayyat Loci

Locus	Phase	Sector	Subphase	Description	Code	Contents	Number of Bags	Qty sherds excavated
G080	4	CA	EARLY		DF		1	325
G081	4	CA	EARLY	Lowest clean Ph 4 su	A		1	200
G082	5			Perhaps not entirely c	A		1	135
G083	5				A		2	95
H001	0				M		1	20
H002	0				DF		5	160
H003	0				DF		1	50
H004	0				B		2	16
H005	0				B		2	27
H006	0				B		1	20
H007	0				B		4	40
H008	0				B		1	3
H009	0				DF		5	212
H010	0				DF		3	160
H011	0				DF		2	253
H012	0				P		2	68
H013	0				P		2	70
H014	0				DF		1	200
H015	0				B		5	205
H016	0				B		1	25
H017	0				B		2	85
H018	1				WS		0	0
H019	1				S		1	20
H020	1				S		1	9
H021	1				DO		3	50
H022	1				S		1	45
H023	1				S		1	7
H024	1				S		2	25
H025	2	EA	LATE	ENCLOSURE WAL	DM		2	130
H026	0				B		2	37

Tell El Hayyat Loci

Locus	Phase	Sector	Subphase	Description	Code	Contents	Number of Bags	Qty sherds excavated
H027	2	TE		TEMPLE ENCLOSU	WS		0	0
H028	2	EA	LATE		DO		2	155
H029	2	EA	LATE		DO		4	350
H030	2	EA	LATE		DO		1	50
H031	2	EA	EARLY		S		4	195
H032	2	EA	LATE		S		1	40
H033	2	EA	LATE		S		1	75
H034	2	EA	LATE		S		1	100
H035	2	EA	EARLY	EARLIEST SURFA	S		1	40
H036	2	EA	EARLY		A		1	20
H037	2	EA	EARLY		A		0	0
H038	3	CE		SINGLE LARGE RO	WS		1	4
H039	0				B		2	60
H040	0				X		1	100
H041	3	EA	LATE	EAST-WEST WALL	WM		1	80
H042	2	EA	EARLY		DO		1	75
H043	3	CE	LATE		DO		2	220
H044	2	EA	EARLY		S		2	325
H045	3	EA	LATE	LATEST PH 3 LOC	DO		2	275
H046	3	EA	LATE		DO		2	175
H047	3				WM		1	26
H048	3	EA	LATE		DO		3	720
H049	3	CE	MIDDLE		S		4	431
H050	3	CE	MIDDLE		S		2	175
H051	3	EA	EARLY		DF	slag	7	1875
H052	3	EA	EARLY		P		1	8
H053	3	EA	EARLY		S		2	290
H054	3	EA	EARLY		DO	slag	1	230
H055	4	EA	LATE		DO		1	675
H056	4	EA	LATE		S		4	565

Tell El Hayyat Loci

Locus	Phase	Sector	Subphase	Description	Code	Contents	Number of Bags	Qty sherds excavated
H057	4	EA	LATE		S		8	658
H058	4	EA	EARLY		DO		11	860
H059	4	EA	EARLY		DO		2	125
H060	4	EA	EARLY		S		1	30
H061	4	EA	EARLY		A		2	75
H062	4	EA	EARLY		DF		1	70
H063	4	EA	EARLY		DO		5	195
H064	5				S		4	255
H065	5				S		3	225
H066	5				DO		14	607
H067	5				A		1	7
H068	5				DO		8	778
H069	5				TF		2	32
H070	5				S		11	965
H071	5				S		2	110
H072	5				S		6	575
H073	6				S		6	615
H074	5				DO		3	51
H075	5				S		1	150
H076	6				S		3	88
H077	6				S		2	9
H078	6				S		1	3
H079	6				S		1	1
I001	0				M		1	1
I002	0				DF		6	203
I003	0				B		1	12
I004	0				B		2	45
I005	0				B		2	52
I006	0				B		1	30
I007	0				B		2	50

Tell El Hayyat Loci

Locus	Phase	Sector	Subphase	Description	Code	Contents	Number of Bags	Qty sherds excavated
I008	0				B		1	20
I009	0				B		3	125
I010	0				B		7	190
I011	1				WS		4	115
I012	0				B		1	2
I013	0				B		2	30
I014	1				S		4	110
I015	0				B		0	0
I016	0				B		3	105
I017	0				DF		4	210
I018	0				B		3	65
I019	0				B		1	1
I020	0				B		4	200
I021	0				U	Unused locus number	0	0
I022	0				B		0	0
I023	0				DF		1	25
I024	0				B		1	15
I025	0				DF		1	40
I026	2	CE	LATE		S		1	90
I027	0				U	Unused locus number	0	0
I028	0				B		0	0
I029	2	CE	LATE		A		1	25
I030	2	CE	LATE		S		1	150
I031	2	CE	LATE		S		1	30
I032	0				B		1	8
I033	0				B		1	60
I034.1	0				X	Split locus, bags I.034.94, 104-106,	2	285
I034.2	3	CE	LATE		DF	Split locus, bags I.034.107, 107b, 1	5	97
I035	2	CE	LATE		DC		2	160
I036	0				B		2	84

Tell El Hayyat Loci

Locus	Phase	Sector	Subphase	Description	Code	Contents	Number of Bags	Qty sherds excavated
I037	2	CE	EARLY		DM		1	100
I038	3	CE	LATE		DO		1	150
I039	0				DF		1	200
I040	3	CE	LATE		S		4	220
I041	3	CE	LATE		DF		3	112
I042	0				B		0	0
I043	2	CE	LATE		TF		0	0
I044	2	CE	LATE		DM		0	0
I045	2	CE	LATE		A		0	0
I046	2	CE	LATE		DM		0	0
I047.1	3	CE	LATE		S	Split locus, bags I.047.178-181 slag	1	405
I047.2	0				DF	Split locus, bags I.047.161-163, 17	2	350
I048	3	CE	LATE		X		1	140
I049	3	CE	LATE		DO		2	160
I050	3	CE	LATE		DO		4	470
I051	2	CE	EARLY		DF		0	0
I052	2	CE	EARLY		DF		0	0
I053	3	CE	LATE		S		1	30
I054	3	CE	MIDDLE	SURFACE THAT P	S		1	80
I055	3	CE	MIDDLE		P		2	130
I056	3	CE	MIDDLE		S		2	405
I057	3	CE	MIDDLE		P		2	100
I058	3	CE	EARLY		S		1	140
I059	3	CE	EARLY		DO		1	480
I060	3	CE	EARLY		P		2	37
I061	3	CE	EARLY		P		1	8
I062	3	CE	EARLY		DO		1	400
I063	3	CE	EARLY		DO		1	60
I064	3	CE	EARLY		P		2	120
I065	4	CE	LATE		DF		1	100

Tell El Hayyat Loci

Locus	Phase	Sector	Subphase	Description	Code	Contents	Number of Bags	Qty sherds excavated
I066	4	CA	LATE		DO		1	0
I067	4	CE	LATE	Equals K056 at 100.5	A		1	110
I068	0				DF	slag (Phase 3 or 4)	1	80
I069	4	CE	LATE		DO		2	150
I070.1	4	CA	EARLY		DF	Split locus, bags I.070.272-274; 30	2	405
I070.2	5				DF	Split locus, bags I.070. 311-314; 31	3	340
I071	4	CE	LATE		S		3	95
I072	4	CE		EAST-WEST WALL	WM		2	90
I073.1	4	CE	EARLY		DO	Split locus, bags I.073. 297-299; 30	2	295
I073.2	5				DO	Split locus, bags I.073.300-302	1	60
I074	4	CE	LATE		WM		1	45
I075	4	CE			WM		0	0
I076	4	CE	EARLY		WM		1	15
I077	4	CE	EARLY		DO		1	70
I078	5				A		1	30
I079	5				DF		2	20
I080	5				A		1	40
I081	4	CA	EARLY	Equals C070.	S		0	0
I082	4	CE	EARLY		WM		1	14
I083	5				DF		1	30
I084	5				A		1	100
I085	5				A		1	50
I086	5				DF		1	75
I087	5				DF		1	100
I088	3	CE	LATE	Stone circle in I047.	I		0	0
J001	0				M		0	0
J002	0				DF		1	45
J003	0				DF		4	95
J004	0				B		3	52
J005	0				B		2	3

Tell El Hayyat Loci

Tell El Hayyat Loci

Locus	Phase	Sector	Subphase	Description	Code	Contents	Number of Bags	Qty sherds excavated
J006	0				B		4	65
J007	0				B		3	70
J008	0				B		4	180
J009	0				DF		1	20
J010	0				S		1	25
J011	1				WS		0	0
J012	0				DM		1	40
J013	1				S		1	20
J014	1				DF		2	22
J015	2	TS	LATE		DF		1	25
J016	1				DF		1	20
J017	0				B		3	130
J018	2	EB		NOTHERN WALL	WS		0	0
J019	1				DF		2	65
J020	1				S		2	32
J021	1				S		1	0
J022	2	EA	LATE		DM		1	20
J023	0				DM		1	40
J024	2	EA	LATE		DM		4	215
J025	0				B		1	25
J026	0			TEMPLE ENCLOSU	WS		0	0
J027	0				B		1	40
J028	0				B		1	40
J029	0				WS		0	0
J030	0				B		1	15
J031	0				S		1	25
J032	2	EA	LATE		DM		2	60
J033	2	EA	LATE		S		1	60
J034	0				B		1	25
J035	2	EA	EARLY	EARLIEST USE SU	S		1	55

Locus	Phase	Sector	Subphase	Description	Code	Contents	Number of Bags	Qty sherds excavated
J036	0				DF		1	30
J037	2	EA	EARLY		S		2	170
J038	0				B		1	30
J039	3	EA			WM		0	0
J040	2	TT		FILL BETWEEN TE	DF		1	20
J041	2	EA	EARLY		DF		2	60
J042	2	EA	EARLY		S		2	260
J043	2	EA	EARLY		TF		0	0
J044	3	EA			WM		0	0
J045	2	EA	EARLY		TF		1	30
J046	2	EA	EARLY	EARLIST PH 2 LOC	S	1 waster	2	340
J047	2	EA	EARLY		S		2	69
J048	2	EA	EARLY	EARLIEST PH 2 SU	S		1	75
J049	3	EA	LATE		S	1 waster	2	290
J050	3	EA	LATE		S		2	400
J051	3				WM		0	0
J052	3	EA	LATE		S		3	885
J053	3	EA	EARLY		DO		1	200
J054	3	EA	EARLY		S		2	350
J055	3	EA	EARLY		S		2	500
J056	3	EA			WM		1	60
J057	4	EA	LATE		S	slag	3	825
J058	3	EA			WM		0	0
J059	4	EA	LATE		S	4 wasters, slag	4	1150
J060	4	EA	LATE		DM		2	475
J061	4	EA	LATE		WM		0	0
J062	4	EA	EARLY		DM		3	600
J063	4	EA	EARLY		DF		1	75
J064	4	EA	EARLY		S		1	150
J065	4	EA	EARLY		S		2	275

Tell El Hayyat Loci

Locus	Phase	Sector	Subphase	Description	Code	Contents	Number of Bags	Qty sherds excavated
J066	4	EA	EARLY		S		1	120
J067	4	EA	EARLY		WM		2	133
J068	5				S		1	50
J069	5				DF		4	497
J070	6				DF		2	16
J071	0				V		2	55
J072	4	EA	LATE		S		1	96
J073	4	EA	EARLY	Equals J062, contains	S		3	900
J074	4	EA	EARLY		A		0	0
J075	4	EA	EARLY	Equals J064.	S		1	200
J076	5				WM		1	50
J077	5				S		2	400
J078	5				S		2	400
J079	5				X		3	426
J080	5				S		1	225
J081	5				A		1	60
J082	5				DO		3	425
J083	5				DO		1	125
J084	5				DO		5	705
J085	5				DO		1	200
J086	5				DO		1	100
K001	0				M		0	0
K002	0				DF		3	75
K003	0				P		1	30
K004	1				WS		1	4
K005	0				DF		2	31
K006	0				B		1	10
K007	0				DF		5	139
K008	0				B		2	35
K009	1				S		1	30

Tell El Hayyat Loci

Locus	Phase	Sector	Subphase	Description	Code	Contents	Number of Bags	Qty sherds excavated
K010	0				B		2	38
K011	0				B		2	11
K012	1				WS		0	0
K013	0				DF		3	50
K014	0				DF		1	30
K015	0				P		2	37
K016	2	EB		CROSS-WALL SEP	WS		3	62
K017	1				S		5	78
K018	0				R		1	10
K019	1				S		1	20
K020.1	2	EB1	LATE		DF	Split locus, bags 46?, 49, 51-52, 91-	2	46
K020.2	0				DF	Split locus, bags 45, 47, 48.	1	80
K021	2	EB		WESTERN WALL	WS		0	0
K022.1	2	EB1	LATE		DF	Split locus, bags 23, 53-58, 63-65,	3	155
K022.2	0				DF	Split locus, bags 59-61, 66-68.	2	195
K023	2	EB1	LATE		DM		0	0
K024	0				B		1	20
K025	0				B		1	15
K026	2	EB1	LATE		S		4	186
K027	2	EB2	LATE	DEBRIS ABOVE PA	DM		1	25
K028	2	EB1	LATE		S		4	197
K029	0				B		1	60
K030	1				WM		1	4
K031	2	EB		DRAIN THROUGH	WS		1	25
K032	0				B		0	0
K033	2	EB			DO		1	75
K034	0				B		1	11
K035	2	EB1	EARLY	EARLIEST USE SU	S		2	155
K036	2	EB2	LATE	DEBRIS ABOVE PA	DM		1	55
K037	2	EB2	LATE	PAVEMENT IN RO	S		1	30

Tell El Hayyat Loci

Locus	Phase	Sector	Subphase	Description	Code	Contents	Number of Bags	Qty sherds excavated
K038	2	EB	EARLY	MAKEUP FOR PH 2	DF		3	49
K039	3				WM		1	7
K040	2	EB	EARLY	MAKEUP FOR PH 2	DF		1	140
K041	3				WM		2	120
K042	2	EB	EARLY		P		1	12
K043	2	EB	EARLY	MAKEUP FOR PH 2	DF		5	234
K044	3	EB	LATE		DF		11	1420
K045	3				WM		1	45
K046	3	EB	EARLY		S		3	77
K047	3	EB	EARLY		S		4	141
K049	3	EB	EARLY		H		1	8
K050	3	EB	EARLY		H		0	0
K051	3	EB	EARLY		H		0	0
K052	0				R		3	113
K053	3	EB	EARLY		S		1	75
K054	4	EB	LATE		TF		0	0
K055	3	EB	EARLY		H		1	4
K056	4	EB	LATE		S		2	120
K057	4	EB	LATE	East-west wall along	WM		0	0
K058	4	EB	LATE		P		1	5
K059	4	EB	LATE		P		1	35
K060	4	EB	EARLY	Mudbrick liner for pit	WM		0	0
K061	4	EB	EARLY		DO		3	235
K062	5				DO		2	200
K063	5				DO		2	120
K064	4	EB			P	2 WASTERS, SLAG	7	1735
K065	5				DO		1	120
K066	5				DO		1	100
K067	5				DO		1	150
K068	0				V		0	0

Tell El Hayyat Loci

Locus	Phase	Sector	Subphase	Description	Code	Contents	Number of Bags	Qty sherds excavated
L001	0				M		1	25
L002	0				DF		3	120
L003	0				DM		3	95
L004	0				B		11	724
L005	0				DM		0	0
L006	1				A		0	0
L007	1				DF		1	20
L008	2	TS	LATE	EARLY=L017 SURF	DF		1	20
L009	2	TS	LATE		DF		3	70
L010	2	T		SOUTHERN WALL	WM		3	32
L011	2	TS	LATE		DO		2	73
L012	2	TS	LATE		A		0	0
L013	2	TS	LATE		DO		2	75
L014	2	TS	LATE		S		0	0
L015	2	TS	LATE		DO		1	160
L016	2	TS	LATE	Except bag 59 which	DO		3	218
L017	2	TS	EARLY	EARLIEST PH 2 SU	S		0	0
L018	2	TS	EARLY	MAKEUP FOR PH 2	DM		4	615
L019	2	TS	EARLY	MAKEUP FOR PH 2	A		0	0
L020	2	T		STONE FOUNDATI	WS		7	335
L021	3	T		East-west enclosure	WS		0	0
L022	2	TS	EARLY	LOWEST PH 2 SUR	DO		3	695
L023	2	TS	EARLY	THIN FILL BELOW	DF		1	140
L024	3	TS	LATE	PHASING FOR L P	S		0	0
L025	3	TS	LATE	Equals L024.	S		2	60
L026	3	TS	LATE		S		2	62
L027	3	TS	MIDDLE		DM		4	158
L028	3	TS	MIDDLE		DF		7	322
L029	3	TS	EARLY	Earliest surface for P	S		1	100
L030	4	TS	LATE		S		2	128

Tell El Hayyat Loci

Locus	Phase	Sector	Subphase	Description	Code	Contents	Number of Bags	Qty sherds excavated
L031	4	TS	LATE				2	400
L032	2	T		Bottom of subfoundat	WF		1	50
L033	3	T		North-south enclosur	WM		0	0
L034	2	T		Bottom of subfoundat	WF		2	9
L035	4	TS	LATE		DM		1	225
L036	4	T		East-west temple wal	WM		0	0
L037	4	TS	LATE		S		1	60
L038	4	TS	LATE		S		1	100
L039	4	T		Temple enclosure wa	WM		0	0
L040	4	TS	LATE		DM		4	700
L041	4	TS	EARLY		S		2	158
L042	4	TS	EARLY		S		2	235
L043	4	TS	EARLY		DM		1	150
L044	5	TS	LATE	Between ph. 4 and 5,	S		5	865
L045	5	TS			S		1	50
L046	5	TS			S		3	700
L047	5	TS			S		2	110
L048	4	TS			WM		0	0
M001	0				DF		1	25
M002	0				DF		3	105
M003	0				B		6	250
M004	0						3	185
M005	0						0	0
M006	0						1	70
M007.1	2	TS	EARLY	INCLUDES MATER	DM	Split locus, bags 22-24, 31, 34-35,	3	58
M007.2	0						3	200
M008	0						0	0
M009	2	T		WALLS M009.1 IS	WM		3	190
M010	0						2	7
M011	2	TS	EARLY		DM		2	89

Tell El Hayyat Loci

Locus	Phase	Sector	Subphase	Description	Code	Contents	Number of Bags	Qty sherds excavated
M012	0				B		0	0
M013	2	TT	EARLY		SP		1	9
M014	0				B		1	14
M015	2	TS	EARLY		DF		3	355
M016	0						1	25
M017	2	TT	EARLY		DF		1	6
M018	0						1	55
M019	0						1	2
M020	3	T			WM		1	15
M021	0						1	15
M022	0						2	45
M023	0						1	7
M024	0						1	60
M025	0						0	0
M026	2	TS	EARLY		DO		1	55
M027	0						0	0
M028	2	TS	EARLY		DF		2	120
M029	0						0	0
M030	2	TS	EARLY		DF		1	50
M031	0						0	0
M032	2	TS	EARLY		DO		1	75
M033	3	TS	LATE	EQUALS M036	S		0	0
M034	3	TS	LATE		DO		1	150
M035	0				B		0	0
M036	3	TS	LATE		DO		3	105
M037	3	TS	LATE		S		1	25
M038	3	TS	MIDDLE		DM		1	18
M039	3	TS	LATE	EQUALS M037	S		1	30
M040	3			LEVELING UNDER	WM		1	40
M041	3	TS	MIDDLE		DM		4	505

Tell El Hayyat Loci

Locus	Phase	Sector	Subphase	Description	Code	Contents	Number of Bags	Qty sherds excavated
M042	3	TS	MIDDLE		DF		2	230
M043	3			SOUTHERN TEMP	WS		0	0
M044	3	TS	EARLY		S		2	290
M045	2	T		SUBFOUNDATION	WF		0	0
M046	0				U		0	0
M047	0				U		0	0
M048	0				U		0	0
M049	0				U		0	0
M050	0				U		0	0
M051	4	TS	LATE		S		3	305
M052	4	TS	LATE		S		3	375
M053	3	TI	EARLY	Earliest Ph. 3 surface	S		1	60
M054	4	TS	LATE		S		1	225
M055	4	T		Southern wall of tem	WM		1	20
M056	4	TS	LATE		S		1	75
M057	4	TS	LATE		S		1	125
M058	4	TS	LATE		DM		2	90
M059	4	TS	LATE		S		2	150
M060	4	TS	LATE		S		2	225
M061	4	TS	LATE		DM		1	100
M062	4	TS	LATE		S		2	750
M063	4	TS	EARLY		S		0	0
M064	4	TS	EARLY		DO		3	280
M065	4	TS	EARLY		S		2	110
M066	4	TS	EARLY		S		2	70
M067	5	TS	LATE	Latest Ph. 5 surface.	S		1	50
M068	5	TS	LATE		S		1	40
M069	5	TS	LATE		S		1	4
M070	0	TS			V		1	125
M071	0				U		0	0

Tell El Hayyat Loci

Locus	Phase	Sector	Subphase	Description	Code	Contents	Number of Bags	Qty sherds excavated
M072	5	TS	LATE		A		0	0
M073	5	TS	LATE		S		1	60
M074	5	TI	LATE		H		0	0
M075	5	TS	LATE		S		1	250
M076	5	TI	EARLY	Mud bench on temple	WM		0	0
M077	5	TS	EARLY		S		1	40
M078	5	TI			S		1	15
M079	5	TI			S		2	65
M080	5	T		Back wall of temple i	WM		0	0
M081	5	TI			S		2	53
M082	5	TI			S		1	50
M083	5	TI			S		2	245
M084	5	TI			S		0	0
N001	0						0	0
N002	0				B		0	0
N003	2	TI	LATE		DM		2	47
N004	2	T		Stone and mudbrick	WS		1	60
N005	2	TI	LATE		SP		1	30
N006	2	TI	LATE		DF		1	90
N007	2	TI	EARLY		SP		2	45
N008	2	T		BACK WALL OF T	WM		1	15
N009	2	TI	EARLY		DF		2	230
N010	2	T		PLASTERED SURF	WM		0	0
N011	2	T		TEMPLE WALL FO	WS		0	0
N012	2	TI	EARLY	EARLIEST PH 2 LO	DF		1	150
N013	3	TB	LATE	EXCAVATED AS A	DM	ONLY BAG N013.043 IS TEMPL	9	645
N014	3	TB	EARLY	MIXED PH 3 AND	DF		2	300
N015	3	T		Mudbrick on stone fo	WS		2	165
N016	3	TI			DO		4	575
N017	3	TI		EARLIEST USE SU	SP		0	0

Tell El Hayyat Loci

Locus	Phase	Sector	Subphase	Description	Code	Contents	Number of Bags	Qty sherds excavated
N018	4	T		Mudbrick back (west	WM		1	175
N019	4	TI	LATE		S		5	800
N020	4	TI	LATE		DO		2	225
N021	4	TI	LATE		DO		3	62
N022	4	TI	EARLY	Mudbrick bench agai	WM		0	0
N023	5	TI			S		3	275
N024	4	T		Mudbrick wall projec	WM		0	0
N025	4	TB	LATE		S		1	275
N026	4	TB	EARLY		DM		4	800
N027	5	TB			S		3	675
N028	5	TB			S		3	450
N029	5	TB			S		3	380
N030	5	PT		Earliest surface, pre-t	S		1	250
N031	5	TI			S		2	105
N032	5	TI		Equals P192, TI	S		4	330
N033	5	TI			S		2	250
N034	5	TI			H		0	0
N035	5			Back wall of temple (	WM		0	0
N036	5	TI			H		0	0
N037	5	TI			H		0	0
N038	5	TI		Mudbrick bench agai	WM		0	0
N041	4	TI	EARLY				0	0
P001	0						0	0
P002	0						0	0
P003	0						0	0
P004	0						0	0
P005	0						0	0
P006	0						0	0
P007	0						0	0
P008	0						0	0

Tell El Hayyat Loci

Locus	Phase	Sector	Subphase	Description	Code	Contents	Number of Bags	Qty sherds excavated
P009	0						0	0
P010	0				B		0	0
P011	0						0	0
P012	2	TI	LATE	LATEST PLASTER	SP		1	9
P013	2	TI	LATE	LATEST PLASTER	SP		1	3
P014	0				B		0	0
P015	2	TI	LATE	LATEST PLASTER	SP		0	0
P016	0				B		0	0
P017	2	TI	LATE	LATEST PLASTER	SP		0	0
P018	2	TI	EARLY	LOWER PLASTER	SP		0	0
P019	0						0	0
P020	0				P		0	0
P021	2	TI	LATE	LATEST PLASTER	SP		0	0
P022	2	TI	LATE	UPPER PLASTER S	SP		0	0
P023	0				B		0	0
P024	0				P		1	25
P025	2	TI	EARLY	LOWER PLASTER	SP		0	0
P026	2	TI	EARLY	EQUALS P070, LO	SP		0	0
P027	0				B		0	0
P028	0				P		2	36
P029	0				P		1	30
P030	0				B		1	175
P031	0				B		0	0
P032	0				P		1	15
P033	2	T		Stone foundation for	WS		1	250
P034	0				P		0	0
P035	0				B		0	0
P036	0				R		1	3
P037	2	TI	LATE		DO		1	8
P038	0						1	5

Tell El Hayyat Loci

Locus	Phase	Sector	Subphase	Description	Code	Contents	Number of Bags	Qty sherds excavated
P039	3				WM		0	0
P040	0				B		1	30
P041	0						0	0
P042	0						0	0
P043	3		LATE		DO		1	1
P044	2	TI	LATE	UPPER PLASTER S	DO		1	16
P045	2	TI	LATE	UPPER PLASTER S	SP		0	0
P046	2	T		Plaster on mudbrick t	WM		0	0
P047	2	T		EASTERN WALL O	WM		0	0
P048	0						0	0
P049	3	TI		Equals P091	S		1	8
P050	0				R		0	0
P051	2	TI	LATE	UPPER PLASTER S	SP		0	0
P052	2	TI	LATE		DF		1	8
P053	2	TI	LATE		DO		0	0
P054	2	TI	LATE		DO		1	15
P055	2	T		EASTERN WALL, P	WM		1	25
P056	0				B		1	15
P057	0				B		0	0
P058	2	T		SOUTHERN WALL	WM		0	0
P059	0				B		0	0
P060	2	TI	LATE	UPPER PLASTER S	SP		1	5
P061	2	T		Plaster on temple wal	WM		0	0
P062	2	T		COMBINE WITH P0	WM		0	0
P063	0				U		0	0
P064	2	TI	LATE		DM		0	0
P065	2	TI	LATE	MAKEUP FOR UPP	DM		1	20
P066	2	TI	LATE	MAKEUP FOR UPP	DF		0	0
P067	2	T		SOUTHERN WALL	WM		0	0
P068	2	TI	LATE	MAKEUP FOR LAT	DF		1	8

Tell El Hayyat Loci

Locus	Phase	Sector	Subphase	Description	Code	Contents	Number of Bags	Qty sherds excavated
P069	2	TI	LATE	MAKEUP FOR LAT	DF		1	25
P070	2	TI	EARLY	EQUALS P026, EAR	SP		1	25
P071	2	TI	LATE		A		0	0
P072	2	TI	LATE	MAKEUP FOR UPP	DM		1	20
P073	2	TI	LATE	MAKEUP FOR UPP	DO		1	30
P074	0						0	0
P075	2	TI	EARLY	MAKEUP FOR LO	DF		1	27
P076	2	TI	EARLY		DF		1	27
P077	2	TI	EARLY		DO		1	20
P078	2	TI	EARLY	MAKEUP FOR LO	DF		1	25
P079	0				B		0	0
P080	2	TI	EARLY	MAKEUP FOR PH 2	DM		1	10
P081	2	TI	EARLY	MAKEUP FOR PH 2	DM		1	25
P082	0				R		0	0
P083	2	T		levelling layer	WM		0	0
P084	2	TI	EARLY	MAKEUP FOR PH 2	DM		1	35
P085	2	TI	EARLY	MAKEUP FOR PH 2	DF		1	20
P086	3	TI		fallen wall	DM		1	100
P087	3	TI			DM		1	29
P088	3	TI		FALLEN WALL	DM		0	0
P089	3	TI			DO		3	327
P090	3	TI			TF		1	2
P091	3	TI			DO		2	350
P092	3	TI			DO		1	200
P093	0				R		0	0
P094	3	TI			DM		3	225
P095	3				WF		0	0
P096	3	TI			DM		0	0
P097	3				WM		0	0
P098	3	TI			S		2	200

Tell El Hayyat Loci

Locus	Phase	Sector	Subphase	Description	Code	Contents	Number of Bags	Qty sherds excavated
P099	3				WM		0	0
P100	3	TI			DO		2	325
P101	2	T		FOUNDATION OR	WF		2	105
P102	3			PLASTER ON WAL	WM		0	0
P103	3				WM		1	455
P104	3				WS		1	1
P105	3				WS		0	0
P106	3			BUTTRESS IN Q?	WS		0	0
P107	3	TI			DO		6	1002
P108	3	TI		EQUALS P109	S		1	200
P109	3	TI			S		0	0
P110	3	TI			A		0	0
P111	3	TI			A		0	0
P112	3	TI			S		2	300
P113	3	TI			S		0	0
P114	3				WM		0	0
P115	3	TI			S		1	200
P116	3	TI			A		0	0
P117	3	TI			A		0	0
P118	3	TI			A		0	0
P119	3	TI			H		1	20
P120	3	TI			S		2	65
P121	3	TI			DO		1	50
P122	3	TI			DO		0	0
P123	3	TI			A		0	0
P124	2	T		PHASE 2 OR 3?	WM		0	0
P125	3	TI			A		0	0
P126	3	TI		LOWEST PH 3 LOC	DM		2	350
P127	0				U		0	0
P128	4	TI	LATE		S		4	556

Tell El Hayyat Loci

Locus	Phase	Sector	Subphase	Description	Code	Contents	Number of Bags	Qty sherds excavated
P129	4	TI	LATE		DO		4	540
P130	3				WF		0	0
P131	4	TI			WM		0	0
P132	4	TI			WM		0	0
P133	0				U		0	0
P134	4	TI	LATE		S		6	522
P135	4	TI	LATE		S		8	1175
P136	4	TI	EARLY	ALTAR	WM		3	26
P137	4	TI	LATE		P		2	40
P138	4	TI	LATE		P		0	0
P139	4	TI	EARLY	ALTAR	WM		0	0
P140	4	TI	LATE		S		1	225
P141	4	TI	MIDDLE		A		1	10
P142	4	TI	EARLY	ALTAR	WM		0	0
P143	4	TI	EARLY		WM		0	0
P144	4	TI			WM		0	0
P145	4	TI	MIDDLE		S		2	325
P146	4	TI	EARLY	ALTAR	WM		0	0
P147	4	TI	MIDDLE		DM		1	300
P148	4	TI	EARLY		DO		1	300
P149	4	TI	EARLY		S		2	160
P150	4	TI	EARLY	CLAY LINED PIT?	H		0	0
P151	4	TI	EARLY		S		1	100
P152	4	TI	EARLY		H		0	0
P153	4	TI	EARLY		A		0	0
P154	4	TI	EARLY	BENCH	WM		0	0
P155	4	TI	EARLY		A		1	8
P156	4	TI	EARLY		A		0	0
P157	4	TI	EARLY		A		0	0
P158	5	TI		COBBLED THRES	WS		0	0

Tell El Hayyat Loci

Locus	Phase	Sector	Subphase	Description	Code	Contents	Number of Bags	Qty sherds excavated
P159	4	T		UNEXCAVATED	DF		0	0
P160	4	TI	LATE		S		1	200
P161	4	TI	MIDDLE		DM		0	0
P162	4	TI	EARLY		DO		2	115
P163	4	TI	EARLY		A		0	0
P164	4	TI	EARLY		A		0	0
P165	4	TI	EARLY	BENCH	WM		0	0
P166	4	TI	EARLY	BENCH	WM		0	0
P167	4	TI	EARLY		S		0	0
P168	4	TI	LATE	N-P BALK, EQUAL	S		3	1125
P169	4	TI	MIDDLE		DM		0	0
P170	4	TI	EARLY		DO		2	145
P171	4	TI	EARLY		A		0	0
P172	4	TI	EARLY	DOORWAY	A		0	0
P173	4	TF	LATE	STEP	WM		0	0
P174	4	TF	LATE	STEP	WM		0	0
P175	4	TI	EARLY	BENCH	WM		0	0
P176	4	TI	EARLY	ALTAR	WM		1	40
P178	5	TI		FOUNDATION TRE	WF		0	0
P179	5	TI			S		7	617
P180	4	TI	EARLY	HEARTH?, IN ALT	WM		0	0
P181	4	TI	EARLY	ALTAR	WM		0	0
P182	5	TI		ALTAR	WM		0	0
P183	5	TI		MUDPLASTER ON	WM		0	0
P184	5	TI		IN ALTAR	P		1	1
P185	5			TEMPLE WALL	WM		0	0
P186	4	TI	EARLY	ALTAR AND JAR C	WM		0	0
P187	5	TI		SURFACE IN DOO	S		0	0
P188	5	TF			A		1	3
P189	5	TF			A		0	0

Tell El Hayyat Loci

Locus	Phase	Sector	Subphase	Description	Code	Contents	Number of Bags	Qty sherds excavated
P190	5				WM		0	0
P191	5				WM		0	0
P192	5	TI		EQUALS N032	S		12	922
P193	5			TEMPLE DOORJA	WM		0	0
P194	5	TI		EARLIEST SURFA	S		1	25
P195	5	TI		CUT FROM P194	H		0	0
P196	5	TF			A		0	0
P197	5	TI			A		0	0
P198	5	TI		CUT FROM P194	H		0	0
P199	5	TI		CUT FROM P194	H		0	0
P200	5	TI			S		1	125
P201	5	TI			H		0	0
P202	5	TI			DF		0	0
P203	0				V		0	0
P204	5	TI			H		0	0
P205	4	TI		ALTAR, EARLY	WM		0	0
Q001	0				M		0	0
Q002	0				B		4	36
Q003	0				B		0	0
Q004	0				B		0	0
Q005	0				B		1	1
Q006	0				B		1	2
Q007	0				B		0	0
Q008	0				B		0	0
Q009	0				B		0	0
Q010	0				B		0	0
Q011	0				B		0	0
Q012	1	TF		PHASE 1 OR 2, SPL	DB		2	34
Q013	2	TF	EARLY	CUTS THROUGH E	X		4	130
Q014	0				P		1	25

Tell El Hayyat Loci

Locus	Phase	Sector	Subphase	Description	Code	Contents	Number of Bags	Qty sherds excavated
Q015	0				B		1	15
Q016	2	TF	EARLY	EARLIEST (LOWES	SP		1	25
Q017	2	TF	LATE		A		0	0
Q018	0				B		0	0
Q019	2	TF	LATE	LATEST OR UPPER	SP		1	5
Q020	2	TF	LATE	LATEST OR UPPER	SP		0	0
Q021	2	TF	LATE	CONTINUATION O	DB		1	14
Q022	0				B		0	0
Q023	2	TF	LATE	DEBRIS BETWEEN	DB		2	25
Q024	2	TF	LATE	NEAR TEMPLE DO	DM		1	30
Q025	2	TF	EARLY		SP		1	3
Q026	2	TF	EARLY	MAKEUP FOR PHA	DB		2	44
Q027	3	TF			A		0	0
Q028	2	TF	EARLY	MAKEUP TO PH 2	DB		1	40
Q029	2	T		EQUALS Q036	WM		0	0
Q030	2	TF	EARLY	MAKEUP FOR PH 2	DB		2	70
Q031	2	TF	EARLY	EARLIES (LOWER)	SP		3	27
Q032	2	TF	EARLY	MAKEUP TO PH 2	DB		0	0
Q033	2	TF	EARLY	MAKEUP FOR PHA	DO		0	0
Q034	3	TF	LATE		DO		2	500
Q035	2	TF	EARLY	MAKEUP FOR PHA	DB		3	90
Q036	2	T		TEMPLE FRONT C	WM		1	11
Q037	2	T		TEMPLE NORTH B	WS		0	0
Q038	2	TF	EARLY	MAKEUP FOR PHA	DB		2	95
Q039	2	TF	EARLY	VOTIVE POTTERY	DB		4	234
Q040	2	TF	EARLY	MAKEUP FOR PH 2	DB		2	150
Q041	3	TF	LATE	MOST IS Q034 & Q	X		2	340
Q042	3	TF	LATE		DO		3	350
Q043	2	T		TEMPLE FOUNDA	WF		2	60
Q044	3	TF	MIDDLE		DF		1	100

Tell El Hayyat Loci

Locus	Phase	Sector	Subphase	Description	Code	Contents	Number of Bags	Qty sherds excavated
Q045	3	TF	MIDDLE		S		2	195
Q046	3	TF	MIDDLE		A		2	150
Q047	3	TF	MIDDLE	EQUALS Q046	DB		0	0
Q048	3	TF	MIDDLE		DO		1	100
Q049	3	TF	EARLY		DF		1	500
Q050	3				WM		1	4
Q051	3				WF		1	9
Q052	3	TF	EARLY	PH 3 SUBPHASING	DO		10	1220
Q053	3	TF		TEMPLE WALL DE	WS		1	12
Q054	3	TF	EARLY	STANDING STONE	SS		1	50
Q055	3	TF	EARLY	STANDING STONE	SS		0	0
Q056	3	TF	EARLY	PEDESTALLED ST	SS		0	0
Q057	4	TF	LATE		DO		8	1025
Q058	4	TF	LATE	POSSIBLY PHASE	DO		1	100
Q059	4	TF	LATE	POSSIBLY PHASE	DO		1	250
Q060	4	T		TEMPLE WALL	WM		0	0
Q061	4	TF	LATE		DM		5	785
Q062	4	TF	LATE	CORNER WALL	WM		2	280
Q063	4	TF	EARLY	STANDING STONE	SS		0	0
Q064	4	TF	EARLY	Contains standing sto	DO		3	465
Q065	4	TF	EARLY	BASIN IN TEMPLE	SS		0	0
Q066	4	TF	LATE	STEP IN TEMPLE D	WM		0	0
Q067	4	TF	EARLY	Surface is under Q06	DO		3	1215
Q068	4	T	LATE	ENCLOSURE WAL	WM		0	0
Q069	4	TF	EARLY	LOWER NORTH TE	WM		0	0
Q070	4	T	EARLY	LOWER TEMPLE E	WM		0	0
Q071	4	TF	LATE	BRICK STEP SOUT	WM		0	0
Q072	4	TF	LATE	CORNER WALL	WM		0	0
Q073	4	TF	LATE	INSIDE CORNER B	DF		0	0
Q074	5	TF	LATE		DO		1	150

Tell El Hayyat Loci

Locus	Phase	Sector	Subphase	Description	Code	Contents	Number of Bags	Qty sherds excavated
Q075	5	TF	LATE		S		0	0
Q076	5	TF	LATE		S		3	500
Q077	5	TF	LATE		DO		2	325
Q078	5	TF		TEMPLE BUTTRES	WM		0	0
Q079	5	TF	EARLY		DO		4	745
Q080	5	TF	EARLY	CORNER WALL	WM		0	0
Q081	5	TF	EARLY	CORNER WALL	WM		0	0
Q082	5	TF	EARLY	NEAR STERILE, PR	DF		1	20
Q083	4	T		TEMPLE WALL, E	WM		0	0
Q084	5		LATE	TEMPLE ENCLOSU	WM		0	0
R001	0				M		0	0
R002	0						0	0
R003	0						0	0
R004	0						2	8
R005	0				B		0	0
R006	0						0	0
R007	0						2	7
R008	0						4	152
R009	0						0	0
R010	2	T		TEMPLE BUTTRES	WM		1	2
R011	2	TF	LATE	UPPER PLASTER S	SP		0	0
R012	2	T		EASTERN TOWER	WM		0	0
R013	2	TF	LATE	ABOVE UPPER PL	DM		1	15
R014	0				B		1	15
R015	2	TF	LATE		DO		1	50
R016	2	T		EASTERN TOWER	WS		1	3
R017	2	TF	EARLY		S		1	60
R018	0				B		1	1
R019	2	TF	LATE	BASALT "COLUM	SS		0	0
R020	3	TF	LATE	LAST SURFACE IN	S		3	76

Tell El Hayyat Loci

Locus	Phase	Sector	Subphase	Description	Code	Contents	Number of Bags	Qty sherds excavated
R021	0				B		0	0
R022	2	TF	LATE	ABOVE PLASTER	DF		1	25
R023	2	T		EASTERN TOWER	WM		2	25
R024	2	T		SOUTH BUTTRESS	WS		1	75
R025	2	T		SOUTH BUTTRESS	WM		1	20
R026	2	T		SOUTH BUTTRESS	WS		0	0
R027	3	TF		MAKEUP FOR PH 2	DF		1	12
R028	2	TF	EARLY	PLASTER SURFAC	SP		0	0
R029	2	T		TEMPLE WALL, E	WM		1	0
R030	2	TF	EARLY	FILL FOR PH 2 MA	DM		2	135
R031	2	TF	EARLY	FALLEN WALL EQ	DM		0	0
R032	3	TF	LATE	COMBINES MATE	X		1	50
R033	0				R		0	0
R034	3	TF	LATE	EQUALS R020	S		1	20
R035	2	T	EARLY	FOUNDATION TRE	WF		1	7
R036	0						0	0
R037	3	TF	LATE		DO		2	71
R038	3	TF	LATE		DO		1	250
R039	3	TF	MIDDLE		DO		2	175
R040	3	TF	MIDDLE		S		1	100
R041	3	TF	LATE		DM		1	40
R042	2	TF	EARLY	MAKEUP FOR PH 2	DM		1	60
R043	3	TF	LATE		DF		1	40
R044	2	T	EARLY	TEMPLE SUBFOU	WF		1	60
R045	2	T	EARLY	FOUNDATION TRE	WF		2	500
R046	3	TF	MIDDLE		DO		3	475
R047	3				WM		0	0
R048	3				WS		1	25
R049	3	TF	MIDDLE		DO		2	450
R050	3	TF	MIDDLE		S		1	100

Tell El Hayyat Loci

Locus	Phase	Sector	Subphase	Description	Code	Contents	Number of Bags	Qty sherds excavated
R051	3	TF	MIDDLE		DO		2	425
R052	3	TF	EARLY		DM		3	675
R053	3	TF	EARLY		DF		5	828
R054	3	TF	EARLY		DO		5	975
R055	3	TF	EARLY	STANDING STONE	SS		2	125
R056	4	TF	LATE		DM		4	650
R057	4	TF	LATE		DO		1	200
R058	4	TF	LATE		S		2	300
R059	4	TF	LATE		DO		2	82
R060	4	TF	LATE		DO		1	125
R061	4	TF	LATE		S		1	125
R062	4	TF	LATE		H		3	450
R063	4	TF	EARLY	R063 & R064 are bui	DO		2	500
R064	4	TF	EARLY	R063 & R064 are bui	S		1	200
R065	4	TF		TEMPLE WALL	WM		0	0
R066	4	TF	LATE	ENCLOSURE WAL	WM		0	0
R067	4	TF	LATE	ENCLOSURE WAL	WM		1	5
R068	5	TF		ENCLOSURE WAL	WM		0	0
R069	4	TF	EARLY	This seems to be the	DO		1	250
R070	5	TF	LATE	LATEST SURFACE	DO		2	125
R071	5	TF	LATE		S		2	500
R072	5	TF	LATE		S		2	180
R073	5	TF	EARLY		S		3	195
R074	5	TF	EARLY	EARLIEST SURFA	S		3	330
R075	4	TF		ENCLOSURE WAL	WM		0	0
R076	5	TF		SOUTH BUTTRESS	WM		0	0
S001	0						0	0
S002	0						0	0
S003	1				TF		0	0
S004	0						0	0

Tell El Hayyat Loci

Locus	Phase	Sector	Subphase	Description	Code	Contents	Number of Bags	Qty sherds excavated
S005	1				DM		1	90
S006	1				S		2	110
S007	1				WM		1	30
S008	1				WM		0	0
S009	1				DM		1	90
S010	0				B		1	50
S011	0				P		1	200
S012	0				B		0	0
S013	0				B		0	0
S014	0				B		0	0
S015	1				A		1	40
S016	1				DM		1	80
S017	0				B		1	100
S018	2	TE		WALL=T017	WM		2	365
S019	1				WM		0	0
S020	1				DO		0	0
S021	2	TF	LATE	LATEST SURFACE	DO		1	20
S022	2	TF	LATE		A		1	60
S023	2	EA	LATE	LATEST PH 2 SURF	DO		2	45
S024	2	EA	LATE		A		2	15
S025	2	EA	LATE		S		1	50
S026	2	TF	LATE		DM		1	25
S027	2	EA	LATE	=S025	S		2	50
S028	2	EA	LATE		DO		2	90
S029	2	EA	LATE		DM		2	100
S030	2	TF	LATE		DF		1	40
S031	2	EA	LATE		S		0	0
S032	2	T		TEMPLE, EASTER	WM		0	0
S033	2	EA	LATE		DM		1	25
S034	2	EA	LATE		S		1	35

Tell El Hayyat Loci

Locus	Phase	Sector	Subphase	Description	Code	Contents	Number of Bags	Qty sherds excavated
S035	2	TT		BALK REMOVAL,	X		1	25
S036	2	TF	EARLY		SP		1	40
S037	2	TF	EARLY		DF		1	150
S038	2	TF	EARLY	EARLIEST SURFA	S		1	100
S039	2	EA	MIDDLE		S		1	125
S040	2	EA	MIDDLE		DF		2	330
S041	3				WM		3	90
S042	2	EB	EARLY	E-W WALL UNDER	WS		1	250
S043	3			BUTTRESS	WM		1	35
S044	2	EA	MIDDLE	ASHY SURFACE, T	S		1	250
S045	3	TF	LATE	=R037	S		1	175
S046	3	TF	LATE	=R038	S		1	60
S047	3	TF	MIDDLE	=R039	DF		1	150
S048	3	TF	MIDDLE	=R040	S		1	200
S049	2	EA	MIDDLE		DO		3	650
S050	2	EA	EARLY	EARLIEST PH 2 US	DO		2	265
S051	3	EA	LATE		DM		2	375
S052	3	EA	LATE		DF		1	80
S053	3	EA	EARLY		DO		4	1050
S054	3	EA	EARLY		S		2	450
S055	3	EA	EARLY		S		2	550
S056	3	EA	EARLY		S		3	800
S057	3			CURB	WM		2	325
S058	3	EA	EARLY		S		7	1850
S059	4	EA	LATE		WM		0	0
S060	0			BALK REMOVAL	X		1	13
S061	3	EA	EARLY	FLOTATION SAMP	S			
S062	4	T		PLASTER TO WAL	WM		3	290
S063	4	T		TEMPLE ENCLOSU	WM		0	0
S064	4	TF	LATE		DF		1	150

Tell El Hayyat Loci

Locus	Phase	Sector	Subphase	Description	Code	Contents	Number of Bags	Qty sherds excavated
S065	4	TF	LATE		DM		2	225
S066	4	TF	LATE		A		1	35
S067	4	EA	LATE		S		10	2000
S068	4	EA	EARLY		S		8	1875
S069	4	EA	EARLY		X		0	0
S070	4	EA	EARLY		DO		1	200
S071	4	EA	EARLY		X		3	950
S072	4	EA	EARLY		S		2	225
S073	5				DO		5	1200
S074	5				DF		2	450
S075	5				DF		1	100
S076	5				DM		6	1225
S077	5			STONE ALIGNME	WS		0	0
S078	5			ENCLOSURE WAL	WM		0	0
S079	5				A		1	125
S080	5				A		3	750
S081	5				A		2	475
S082	6				DO		1	100
T001	0						0	0
T002	0						0	0
T003	0				B		0	0
T004	0				B		0	0
T005	0				B		0	0
T006	0				B		0	0
T007	0				P		0	0
T008	2	EB5	LATE	DEBRIS IN ROOMS	DM		4	215
T009	0				B		0	0
T010	2	EB		N-S CROSSWALL S	WS		0	0
T011	0				B		0	0
T012	0				B		0	0

Tell El Hayyat Loci

Locus	Phase	Sector	Subphase	Description	Code	Contents	Number of Bags	Qty sherds excavated
T013	0				B		0	0
T014	2	EB3	LATE		S		4	62
T015	2	EB2	LATE	FILL AND COBBLE	DO		4	96
T016	2	EB3	LATE		S		2	150
T017	2	EB		=K030	WS		1	3
T018	0			POSSIBLE RODEN	R		2	7
T019	2	EB	EARLY	E-W WALL PARAL	WS		1	20
T020	2	EB	MIDDLE	BEDDING LAYER	DF		3	345
T021	2	EB	EARLY	N-S CROSSWALL F	WS		1	5
T022	2	EB	MIDDLE		DO		6	73
T023	2	EB	EARLY	=S042	WS		0	0
T024	2	EB	MIDDLE		DO		3	275
T025	2	EB	MIDDLE		DO		2	150
T026	2	EB	EARLY	USE SURFACE REL	DF		5	650
T027	3	EC	LATE		A		0	0
T028	3	EC	LATE		DO		1	250
T029	3	EC	LATE		DF		2	325
T030	3	EC	LATE		S		1	75
T031	3	EC	EARLY		DF		4	1050
T032	3	EC	LATE		P		1	6
T033	3	EC	EARLY		H		0	0
T034	3	EC	EARLY		DO		3	700
T035	3	EC	EARLY		H		1	6
T036	3	EC		=K045	WM		1	60
T037	3	EC	EARLY		DF		16	2370
T038	3	EC	EARLY		A		4	580
T039	3	EC	EARLY		DO		4	355
T040	3	EC	EARLY	"BASIN"	I		2	15
T041	4	EC	LATE		DO		7	721
T042	3	EC	LATE	TO T036 WALL	WF		1	8

Tell El Hayyat Loci

Locus	Phase	Sector	Subphase	Description	Code	Contents	Number of Bags	Qty sherds excavated
T043	4	EC	LATE		TF		1	10
T044	3	EC			WM		0	0
T045	4	EC	LATE		DO	RESTORABLE VESSEL	3	303
T046	4	EC	LATE	=S056	WM		0	0
T047	4	EC	MIDDLE		WM		0	0
T048	4	EC	MIDDLE	=T052	DO		2	550
T049	4	EC	MIDDLE		H		1	10
T050	4	EC	MIDDLE		H		1	20
T051	4	EC	MIDDLE		H		1	2
T052	4	EC	MIDDLE		DO		4	975
T053	4	EC	MIDDLE		P		0	0
T054	4	EC	LATE	WALL AND DOOR	WM		0	0
T055	4	EC	MIDDLE		WM		0	0
T056	4	EC	EARLY		DO		3	700
T057	4	EC	EARLY		P		1	6
T058	4	EC	EARLY		DO		2	650
T059	4	EC	EARLY		P		1	3
T060	4	EC	EARLY	CHANNEL	I		0	0
T061	4	EC	EARLY	BIN	I		2	100
T062	5				S		4	750
T063	5				DO		1	250
T064	5				DO		3	850
T065	5				P		2	75
T066	5				H		0	0
T067	5				DO		2	250
T068	5				DO		1	150
T069	5				DO		4	600
T070	5				S		1	125
T071	5				DO		0	0
T072	5				P		1	6

Tell El Hayyat Loci

Locus	Phase	Sector	Subphase	Description	Code	Contents	Number of Bags	Qty sherds excavated
T073	5				A		1	125
T074	5				DO		2	450
T075	5				P		2	225
T076	5				DO		1	150
U001	0				M		0	0
U002	0				B		1	1
U003	2	TFE			DF		0	0
U004	2	TFE		UPPER PLASTER S	SP		4	42
U005	2	TFE			DO		4	78
U006	2	TFE			S		1	25
U007	2	TFE			DF		4	62
U008	2	TFE			DO		5	85
U009	2	TFE		LOWER PLASTER	SP		6	40
U010	2	TFE		LOWER PLASTER	SP		0	0
U011	2	TFE			DO		1	6
U012	2	TFE			X		1	17
U013	2	TFE			X		0	0
U014	2	TFE			DO	BAG U014.31 IS MIXED WITH U	6	76
U015	2	TFE			S		4	22
U016	2	TFE		EASTERN MOST B	WS		1	5
U017	2	TFE			DO		1	22
U018	3	TF		MUDBRICK WALL	DM		8	353
U019	2	TFE			P		0	0
U020	2	TFE			A		0	0
U021	3	TF		BELOW U018 IN N	P		0	0
U022	3	TF		TEMPLE FORECO	DM		0	0

Tell El Hayyat Loci

APPENDIX C:
TELL EL-HAYYAT REGISTERED OBJECTS
(filename: "TH REGISTERED OBJECTS")

Tell El Hayyat Registered Objects

Registration #	Phase	Locus	Bag	Material	Form	Max dim.	Length	Width	Depth	Diameter	Weight	Condition
82.001		A002	006	Stone	Pendant	4.1	4.1	1.2				good
82.002		C003	012	Iron	Point	7.4	6		1.5		7.4	poor
82.004		D015	068	Iron	Knife	103.5	16		2.5		103.5	poor
82.009		E043	179	Clay	Seal Impression	4.5	4.5	2.8				fair
82.020		F029	116	Copper Alloy	Fragment	0.4					0.4	poor
82.021		C092	083	Ceramic	Fragment	8	8	5.1				poor
82.022		A??? ?	???	Ceramic	Cylinder	3.5	3.5			2.5		fair
82.023		B???	???	Ceramic	Oval	5.9				5.9		good
82.024		C010	030	Ceramic	Cylinder	7	7	4.6				poor
82.025		C022	009	Ceramic	Disc	4	4		0.8	4	17.1	good
82.026		C022	009	Ceramic	Disc	3.5	3.5		0.6	3.5	8.3	fair
82.027		C022	009	Ceramic	Disc	3.6	3.6		0.6	3.6	10.5	good
83.001		J010	024	Silver	Earring	1.8	0	0	0	0.6	2.7	fair
83.002		E055	226	Copper Alloy	Ring	1.8				0.4	1.4	fair
83.003		F035	229	Chalk	Spindle Whorl	4.9			1.1	4.9		fair
83.004		H011	023	Stone	Bowl Fragment	4.2	4.2	4	3.6			good
83.005		D056	306	Copper Alloy	Pin	9.9	9.9			1.3	30	poor
83.006		K044	156	Copper Alloy	Pin	8.6	8.6			0.5	4	poor
83.007		I017	057	Copper Alloy	Clasp	3.6	3.6			0.7	2.8	poor
83.008		K022	023	Stone	Scarab	1.5	1.5	1.1	0.6			broken
83.009		J013	041	Ceramic	Thumb-Pot	3.5	3.2			3.5		chipped
83.010		K022	055	Ceramic	Jar	8	8			6		good
83.011		G023	052	Ceramic	Juglet	9.8	9.8			2.3		restored
83.012		J048	160	Bronze	Pin	5.5	5.5			0.2	0.6	poor
83.013		I071	291	Bone	Drilled Bone	9	9			2		?
83.014		I009	016	Ceramic	Jar Handle	7.5	7.5	5				?
83.015		E077	317	Stone	Pendant	4.5	4.5	1.7				good
83.016		A081	106	Stone	Bead	2	2			0.7		good
83.017		C141	184	Bronze	Earring	2	2		0.3	2	1.6	fair

Page 1 of 19

Registration #	Phase	Locus	Bag	Material	Form	Max dim.	Length	Width	Depth	Diameter	Weight	Condition
83.018		I069	275	Bone	Tool	6.5	6.5	1.5				good
83.019		A099	231	Stone	Fragment	4.5	3			4.5		?
83.020		A051	295	Stone	Object	7	7	4.5	2.5			?
83.021		C061	267	Ceramic	Disc	2.5			1.2	2.5		good
83.022		I070	310	Shell	Pendant	3.6	3.6	1.6	0.1			?
83.023		A051	306	Ceramic	Disc	3.3			0.6	3.3	8.8	good
83.024		I069	276	Stone	Spindle Whorl	5.3			0.8	5.3		good
83.025		A077	305	Ceramic	Disc	3.3			1	3.3	14.3	good
83.026		I070	309	Stone	Bead	1.5			0.9	1.5		good
83.027		F054	320	Ceramic	Object	3			3	2.5		?
83.028		K064	258	Stone	Spindle Whorl	4.3			1.1	4.3		good
83.029		K064	250	Ceramic	Bottle Stopper	2.6			0.6	2.6		?
83.030		K064	254	Ceramic	Figurine	3.8	3.8	3.7	2.1			good
83.031		K064	248	Ceramic	Basket	5			5	4.6		?
83.032		I070	314	Bone	Tool	6.8	6.8	1.3				good
83.033		E100	491	Ceramic	Disc	3.4			0.8	3.4	9.4	good
83.034		K062	280	Stone	Spindle Whorl	3.2			0.8	3.2		fair
83.035		C063	279	Ceramic	Lump	4.3	4.3			1.8		?
83.036		K022	056	Copper Alloy	Lump	1.9					1.9	poor
83.037		A051	311	Copper Alloy	Lump	0.3					0.3	poor
83.038		A051	331	Copper Alloy	Fragments	0.4					0.4	poor
83.039		B054	???	Copper Alloy	Lump	11.5					11.5	poor
83.040		K064	247	Copper Alloy	Fragment	1.3					1.3	poor
83.041		E089	436	Copper Alloy	Lump	30.6					30.6	fair
83.042		E089	435	Copper Alloy	Fragment	0.7					0.7	poor
83.043		J057	204	Copper Alloy	Lump	23.4					23.4	poor
83.044		K044	149	Copper Alloy	Lump	12.7					12.7	poor
83.046		A076	060	Ceramic	Oval	6.5	6.5	2				fair
83.047		I050	202	Ceramic	Disc	3.8			0.8	3.8	13.3	good

Tell El Hayyat Registered Objects

Registration #	Phase	Locus	Bag	Material	Form	Max dim.	Length	Width	Depth	Diameter	Weight	Condition
83.048		B053	209	Ceramic	Cylinder	3.5	3			3.5		good
83.049		L018	058	Ceramic	Cylinder	5.5	3.7			5.5		good
83.050		I047	178	Ceramic	Disc	2.5			0.9	2.5	7.2	good
83.051		A043	338	Plaster	Chips	105.1					105.1	poor
83.052		A086	137	Dung	Lump	22.3					22.3	fair
83.053		G063	199	Ceramic	Disc	7.5			0.7	7.5		good
83.054		A086	136	fuel?	Lumps	10.8					10.8	poor
83.055		G057	176	Glass	Piece	0.9	0.9	0.4				good
83.056		J057	208	Ceramic	Disc	4.5			0.9	4.5	20.3	good
83.057		L004	011	Glass	Pieces	4	4	1.5				good
83.058		E086	395	Ceramic	Ball	2.3				2.3		good
83.059		G078	275	Ceramic	Disc	3.5			0.7	3.5	12.4	good
83.060		J046	144	Ceramic	Disc	4.5			0.6	4.5		good
83.061		H025	080	Ceramic	Fragment	1	1			1		poor
83.062		H025	080	Ceramic	Fragment	2	2	1.5				poor
83.063		G086	400	Ceramic	Disc	7	7	4.7				fair
83.064		K044	166	Ceramic	Fragment	3.8	3.8	2.8				fair
83.065		G036	107	Ceramic	Disc	4			0.8	4	13.1	good
83.066		J027	086	Plaster	Chips	12.2					12.2	poor
83.067		K030	086	Stone	Knob	5.5	0		5.5	4.5		good
83.068		I070	311	Ceramic	Disc	2.8			0.6	2.8	5.9	good
83.069		C075	330	Ceramic	Disc	3.8			0.9	3.8	20.3	good
83.070		I009	183	Glass	Pieces	1.5	1.5	0.7				poor
83.071		F035	146	Bone	Tool	11.5	11.5	0.7				good
83.072		I086	353	Ceramic	Kernos	4.8	4.8			3.6		good
85.001		Q039	076	Ceramic	Bowl	10.6			4.2	10.6		good
85.002		Q039	076	Ceramic	Bowl	10.5			4.1	10.5		restored
85.003		Q039	003	Ceramic	Bowl	10.4			3.3	10.4		good
85.004		Q039	006	Ceramic	Bowl	10.5			4.5	10.5		restored

Registration #	Phase	Locus	Bag	Material	Form	Max dim.	Length	Width	Depth	Diameter	Weight	Condition
85.005		Q039	095	Ceramic	Bowl	11			3.5	11		good
85.006		Q039	076	Ceramic	Bowl	6.9			5.2	6.9		restored
85.007		Q039	005	Ceramic	Bowl	7			4.8	7		good
85.008		Q039	096	Ceramic	Bowl	7			5.3	7		restored
85.009		Q039	069	Ceramic	Lamp	8.2		8.2	2.4	4.6		restored
85.010		Q039	076	Ceramic	Lamp	8.5		8.5	2.6	4.6		good
85.011		T022	054	Ceramic	Bowl	10.7			7.5	10.7		restored
85.012		P128	215	Ceramic	Bowl	9.3			7	9.3		restored
85.013		H042	320	Ceramic	Bowl	9.7			9.7	9.6		good
85.014		Q030	002	Ceramic	Jar	7.2			7.2	6.9		good
85.015		P126	015	Ceramic	Jar	8.1			8.1	5.5		good
85.016		U016	032	Ceramic	Pot Stand	10.4			6.8	10.4		good
85.017		U002	001	Ceramic	Juglet	21.8			21.8	11.5		restored
85.018		P043	014	Ceramic	Juglet	14.3			14.3	7.7		good
85.019		T022	048	Ceramic	Juglet	20.4			20.4	8.5		restored
85.020		R008	041	Ceramic	Base Fragment	5.1			5.1	4.8		good
85.021		R004	003	Ceramic	Base Fragment	15.6			4.4	15.6		good
85.022		T016	039	Bone	Astragalus	2.7	2.7	1.3	1.5			good
85.023		T029	093	Bone	Point	1.5	1.5	0.7	0.4			good
85.024		P086	100	Bone	Worked Fragment	2.4	2.4	1.2	0.2			good
85.025		R056	184	Bone	Point	2.8	2.8	0.9	0.4			good
85.026		R049	143	Bone	Point	4.7	4.7	0.8	0.5			good
85.027		T037	142	Bone	Worked Fragment	2.8	2.8	0.4				good
85.028		P147	285	Bone	Point	6.6	6.6	1.3				good
85.029		M052	163	Bone	Point	2.2	2.2	0.9				bood
85.030		T052	226	Bone	Point	2.8	2.8	0.8				good
85.031		T052	231	Bone	Point	5.9	5.9	0.9				good
85.032		Q052	210	Bone	Point	7.1	7.1	0.9				good
85.033		S067	248	Bone	Point	2.4	2.4	0.5				good

Tell El Hayyat Registered Objects

Registration #	Phase	Locus	Bag	Material	Form	Max dim.	Length	Width	Depth	Diameter	Weight	Condition
85.034		S067	248	Bone	Point	1.7	1.7	0.7				good
85.035		S067	248	Bone	Worked Fragment	3.9	3.9					good
85.036		Q057	216	Bone	Worked Fragment	3.2	3.2			1.7		good
85.037		P128	211	Shell	Bead	2.6	2.6			0.8		good
85.038		Q037	148	Glass	Bead							poor
85.039		T064	275	Stone	Bead	1.5			1.4	1.5		good
85.040		P176	342	Stone	Necklace	1.3	1.3			0.9		good
85.041		H058	262	Stone	Bead Fragment	1.8			0.9	1.8		good
85.042		T088	022	Stone	Fragment	2.6	2.6	1.3	0.6			good
85.043		Q039	099	Stone	Drilled Object	3.3				3.3		good
85.044		T034	117	Stone	Worked Object	3.7			3.7	2.8		good
85.045		J075	289	Stone	Fragment	3.8			3.2	3.8		good
85.046		L031	147	Stone	Fragment	2.9	2.9	1.9	0.9			good
85.047		T048	223	Ceramic	tool fragment	7.2			1	7.2		good
85.048		L020	118	Ceramic	Disc	4.8			0.8	4.8		good
85.049		Q042	138	Ceramic	Disc	4.2			1	4.2		good
85.050		S058	189	Ceramic	Disc	5			1.4	5		poor
85.051		J073	277	Ceramic	Tool	4.8	4.8	4.5	0.8			fair
85.052		R054	175	Ceramic	tool fragment	5	5	4.7	1			good
85.053		Q042	132	Ceramic	Cart Wheel	10.5			2.7	10.5		fair
85.054		J067	297	Ceramic	Cart Wheel	14	0		2.6	14		good
85.055		R039	107	Ceramic	Cart Wheel	11			2	11		good
85.056		T039	176	Ceramic	Figurine	6.3	6.3	3.5	2			good
85.057		J081	323	Ceramic	Figurine	6.8	6.8	2.8	3.7			fair
85.058		N025	097	Ceramic	Figurine	5.1	5.1	2.3	2.8			good
85.059		P107	158	Ceramic	Jar	3.9			3.9	2.7		good
85.060		P103	146	Ceramic	Jar	5.8			5.8	5.2		good
85.061		Q049	171	Ceramic	Jar	4.5			4.5	3.6		fair
85.062		L030	146	Ceramic	Jar	3.9			3.5	3.9		good

Tell El Hayyat Registered Objects

Tell El Hayyat Registered Objects

Registration #	Phase	Locus	Bag	Material	Form	Max dim.	Length	Width	Depth	Diameter	Weight	Condition
85.063		R051	155	Ceramic	Jar	4			4	2.5		restored
85.064		N013	045	Ceramic	Jar	3			2.9	3		?
85.065		R052	167	Ceramic	Kernos	20			4.7	20		restored
85.066		L029	140	Ceramic	Kernos	6.5			6.5	4.1		restored
85.067		R045	132	Ceramic	Kernos	5.9			5.9	3.5		good
85.068		L030	146	Ceramic	Kernos	4.9			4.9	4.3		fair
85.069		L030	146	Ceramic	Kernos	5.6			5.6	4.7		restored
85.070		R046	145	Ceramic	Kernos	3.9			3.9	2		?
85.071		Q052	178	Ceramic	Kernos	5.2			5.2	4.9		?
85.072		Q052	183	Ceramic	Jar	5.8			5.8			?
85.073		R062	210	Ceramic	handle fragment	20	6.5	2.9	1.8	20		good
85.074		P134	240	Ceramic	Object	9.9			4.1	9.9		good
85.075		L035	168	Ceramic	Bowl Fragment	12				12		good
85.076		S065	235	Ceramic	Bowl Fragment	7			0	7		good
85.077		S067	245	Ceramic	Bowl Fragment	14				14		good
85.078		T037	146	Ceramic	dish fragment	7.8	7.8	4.7	4.3			good
85.079		J065	294	Ceramic	Crucible Fragme							good
85.080		S056	182	Ceramic	Vessel Fragment	19.5			4.5	19.5		good
85.081		R018	031	Copper Alloy	Coin	2.2				2.2	7	?
85.082		N001	???	Copper Alloy	Figurine	7	7	5.7			121.1	poor
85.083		P128	210	Silver	zoomorphic fig	4.6	4.6	0	2.9		23.1	good
85.084		Q059	225	Copper Alloy	Blade	11.7	11.7	3.6	0.1		31.4	poor
85.085		M052	157	Copper Alloy	Point	5.6	5.6	2.2	0.9		17.6	fair
85.086		M052	165	Copper Alloy	Point	6.8	6.8	2.4			9.5	poor
85.087		P135	261	Copper Alloy	Object	10.1					10.1	fair
85.088		M052	166	Copper Alloy	Tweezers	8.1	8.1	3.1			13.4	fair
85.089		M054	175	Copper Alloy	Object	3.3	3.3	1.7			3.2	fair
85.090		P145	283	Copper Alloy	eyelet	0.8	0.8				0.8	poor
85.091		P179	367	Copper Alloy	Oxhide Ingot	4.1	4.1	2.6			2.6	poor

Registration #	Phase	Locus	Bag	Material	Form	Max dim.	Length	Width	Depth	Diameter	Weight	Condition
85.092		P186	371	Copper Alloy	Oxhide Ingot	2.7	2.7	2			1.2	fair
85.093		R070	242	Copper Alloy	Point	12.2	12.2	2.5	1.1	1.5	34.4	poor
85.094		M052	158	Copper Alloy	Tang	10	10	1.5	0.9	1	15.1	fair
85.095		M052	171	Copper Alloy	Lump	3	3	2.2			17.4	
85.096		P148	292	Copper Alloy	Fragment	1.9	1.9	0	1.5		0.5	fair
85.097		P179	366	Copper Alloy	Fragments	3.7	0.4				1.9	poor
85.098		P177	360	Copper Alloy	Nail	6.1	6.1			0.9	9.1	fair
85.099		P147	287	Copper Alloy	Fragments	2.4	2.4	0.8			2.1	poor
85.100		T058		Copper Alloy	Tang	5	5	0.8		0.3	4.2	fair
85.101		R069	235	Copper Alloy	Fragments	2.1	2.1	0.7			1.2	poor
85.102		P136	338	Copper Alloy	Tip	2.1	2.1	1.9			0.4	poor
85.103		Q059	230	Copper Alloy	Fragments	3	3	0.7		0.7	1.7	fair
85.104		P151	346	Copper Alloy	Fragments	2.7	2.7	0.5			1.3	fair
85.105		Q045	159	Copper Alloy	Fragment	2.1	2.1	1	0.5		6.7	fair
85.106		P177	364	Copper Alloy	Fragments	1.2	1.2	1			4	poor
85.107		R069	233	Copper Alloy	Object Fragment	2.1	2.1			1.2	1.5	poor
85.108		M052	159	Copper Alloy	Lump	3.8	3.8	2.3	1.5		26.5	poor
85.109		P126	205	Copper Alloy	Lump	2.5	2.5	1.3			5.4	fair
85.110		S061	219	Stone	Mortar Fragment	23			5.8	23		fair
85.111		H042	321	Stone	Mortar	22.5			7.2	22.5		good
85.112		Q039	100	Stone	Loom Weight	5			3.5	5		good
85.113		R008	030	Clay	Loom Weight	3.5				3.5		
85.114		R071	243	Clay	Object Fragment	4		3.3	2.2	4.4		
85.115		H066	396	Stone	Oval Object	9.3	9.3	5.8	5			
85.116		L035	168	Stone	cart wheel?	5.7	0	2.1				
85.117		R057	192	Ceramic	Disc	4.7			1.1	4.7	28.6	
85.118		P182	370	Stone	Bead	0.6				0.6		
85.119		J067	297	Stone	Mould Fragment	6.4	6.4	5.6	3			good
85.120		R054	179	Stone	Mould Fragment	8	8	6.1	2.8			fair

Registration #	Phase	Locus	Bag	Material	Form	Max dim.	Length	Width	Depth	Diameter	Weight	Condition
85.121		P177	353	Ceramic	Crucible	11	11	8	3.2			
85.122		P177	353	Ceramic	Crucible	9	9	7	5			
85.123		P179	369	Ceramic	Crucible Fragme	9.5	9.5	7.5		2		
85.124		M082	286	Stone	Bead	2	2			1.4		
85.125		P184	406	Stone	Beads	8	8			6		
85.126		P179	394	Stone	Sphere	4				4		
85.127		N023	140	Ceramic	Bowl	10.5			7.4	10.5		
85.128		N032	139	Ceramic	Bowl	10.2		0	7	10.2		
85.129		N032	145	Ceramic	Bowl	10.4			6.4	10.4		
85.130		N032	146	Ceramic	Bowl	9.8			5.7	9.8		
85.131		N032	144	Ceramic	Incense Burner	12.7			12.7	6.8		
85.132		T064	276	Ceramic	Disc	2.3	0		0.5	2.3	3.6	
85.133		L043	196	Ceramic	Kernos	4			3.6	4		
85.134		N023	159	Stone	Object	4.6			2	4.6		
85.135		P194	427	Stone	Disc	10			7	10		
85.136		M076	277	Copper Alloy	Shaft	7.2	7.2	1.9	2		16.2	
85.137		M076	275	Copper Alloy	Figurine	6.3	6.3	2.2		1.2	15.8	
85.138		M056	276	Copper Alloy	Sheet	2.2	2.2	1.6			1.3	
85.139		P179	390	Copper Alloy	Sheet	2.2	2.2	1.8			0.3	
85.140		Q069	292	Copper Alloy	Point	1	1				1	
85.141		Q079	311	Copper Alloy	Lumps	14.1					14.1	
85.142		M083	294	Copper Alloy	Lumps	15.9					15.9	
85.143		M082	287	Copper Alloy	Wire	0.3					0.3	
85.144		M081	287	Copper Alloy	Lumps	7.6					7.6	
85.145		P179	396	Copper Alloy	Lumps	30.4					30.4	
85.146		Q079	301	Copper Alloy	Pin Fragments	2.6					2.6	
85.147		P192	413	Copper Alloy	Lumps	23.2					23.2	
85.148		M084	300	Copper Alloy	Lump	26.3					26.3	
85.149		M060	193	Wood	Pieces	13.1					13.1	fair

Registration #	Phase	Locus	Bag	Material	Form	Max dim.	Length	Width	Depth	Diameter	Weight	Condition
85.150		T064	???	Copper Alloy	Shaft	8.5					8.5	
85.151		P145	276	Ceramic	Figurine Relief	18.5	18.5	11.5				
85.152		A078	076	Bone	Tube	9.5	9.5			1.4		good
85.153		K044	150	Bone	Tube	5.6	5.6			1.3		good
85.154		C070	313	Bone	Tube	3	3			1.4		good
85.155		H051	210	Bone	Tube	2.8	2.8			1.6		
85.156		K044	150	Bone	Awl	8.3	8.3	1.4		0		good
85.157		L022	077	Bone	Worked Fragment	4	4	1.3		0		
85.158		H051	217	Bone	Awl	6.5	6.5	1.3				
85.159		E106	495	Bone	Worked Fragment	5	5	1				
85.160		C062	275	Bone	Worked Fragment	5.5	5.5	1.2				
85.161		K064	253	Bone	Awl	4.9	4.9	1				
85.162		G078	277	Bone	Worked Fragment	3	3	0.8				
85.163		G081	308	Bone	Worked Fragment	6	6	0.5				
85.164		H048	183	Bone	Worked Fragment	3.4	3.4	0.5				
85.165		I071	292	Bone	Worked Fragment	6	6	1				
85.166		E054	253	Bone	Worked Fragment	2.8	2.8	1.5				
85.167		J048	162	Bone	Worked Fragment	2.4	2.4	1.5				
85.168		C071	314	Bone	Worked Fragment	2.4	2.4	0.6				
85.169		C070	313	Bone	Awl	4	4	0.5				
85.170		A083	110	Bone	Awl	5.4	5.4	1.1				
85.171		G017	265	Bone	Awl	3	3	0.8				
85.172		P194	423	Stone	Disc	3	2.5	3				
85.173		F050	294	Bone	Worked Fragment	5.5	5.5	1.7				
85.174		I060	235	Bone	Worked Fragment	4.5	4.5	1.1				
85.175		K035	114	Bone	Awl	5.9	5.9	1				
85.176		A051	208	Bone	Worked Fragment	3.2	3.2	2				
85.177		B054	216	Bone	Worked Fragment	8.2	8.2	2				
85.178		G081	308	Bone	Awl	5.8	5.8	1.5				

Tell El Hayyat Registered Objects

Registration #	Phase	Locus	Bag	Material	Form	Max dim.	Length	Width	Depth	Diameter	Weight	Condition
85.179		G034	101	Bone	Worked Fragment	3	3	1				
85.180		K064	243	Bone	Awl	5	5	1				
85.181		E086	396	Bone	Awl	5.5	5.5	0.6				
85.182		J069	245	Bone	Worked Fragment	6.5	6.5	1				
85.183		J054	188	Bone	Worked Fragment	4.5	4.5	0.7				
85.184		K064	240	Bone	Worked Fragment	4.8	4.8	0.5				
85.185		C064	288	Bone	Awl	2.9	2.9	0.5				
85.186		K064	240	Bone	Awl	5	5	0.4				
85.187		G077	262	Bone	Worked Fragment	5.6	5.6	1				
85.188		D072	348	Bone	Worked Fragment	4.2	4.2	1.6				
85.189		C078	344	Bone	Awl	4	4	1				
85.190		G077	265	Bone	Drilled Bone	4.3	4.3	1.2				
85.191		N025	091	Ceramic	Cylinder	7.5	7.5			2.9		
85.192		P182	436	Copper Alloy	Lump	1.3					1.3	
85.193		A083	110	Bone	Worked Fragment	7.4	7.4	2.3				
85.194		G011	038	Bone	Worked Fragment	4.1	4.1	1.2				
85.195		D066	339	Bone	Worked Fragment	3.1	3.1	0.8				
85.196		E061	245	Bone	Worked Fragment	11.5	11.5	4.5				
85.197		E086	380	Bone	Worked Fragment	7.7	7.7	2.9				
85.198		E061	245	Bone	Worked Fragment	5.5	5.5	1.8				
85.199		K036	129	Bone	Worked Fragment	6.5	6.5	1.7				
85.200		H005	003	Iron	Object	108					108	
85.209		M081	284	Copper Alloy	Lump	3.1					3.1	
85.210		M083	242	Copper Alloy	Lump	1.4						
85.211		M083	291	Copper Alloy	Lump	5.3					5.3	
85.212		M083	299	Copper Alloy	Lump	3					3	
85.213		M085	302	Copper Alloy	Lump	1.1					1.1	
85.214		P179	388	Copper Alloy	Lump	5.7					5.7	
85.215		P179	391	Copper Alloy	Lump	3.4					3.4	

Tell El Hayyat Registered Objects

Registration #	Phase	Locus	Bag	Material	Form	Max dim.	Length	Width	Depth	Diameter	Weight	Condition
85.216		P184	429	Copper Alloy	Lump	3.2					3.2	
85.217		P192	417	Copper Alloy	Lump	3.7					3.7	
85.218		P200	423	Copper Alloy	Lump	1.4					1.4	
90.001		E082	344	Ceramic	Disc	5.5			0.5	5.5	20.9	
90.002		A081	98	Ceramic	Disc	3.75			1.2	3.75	19.1	
90.003		G064	237	Ceramic	Disc	5.5			0.9	5.5	26.8	
90.004		H048	181	Ceramic	Disc	4.5			0.9	4.5	19.75	
90.005		I071	282	Ceramic	Disc	4			1.1	4	19.1	
90.006		I066	257	Ceramic	Disc	3.75			0.9	3.75	12.6	
90.007		I066	257	Ceramic	Disc	3.25			0.8	3.25	9.9	
90.008		I070	306	Ceramic	Disc	6			1.2	6	39.5	
90.009		J050	173	Ceramic	Disc	3.75			1	3.75	14.4	
90.010		I068	257	Ceramic	Disc	5			0.8	5	20.5	
90.011		J059	211	Ceramic	Disc	2.25			0.6	2.25	3.6	
90.012		J059	211	Ceramic	Disc	5.2			0.8	5.2	26	
90.013		J059	211	Stone	Bowl	5.94	5.2	3.5	1.8	11	43.9	
90.014		K056	221	Ceramic	Disc	4			1	4	22.1	
90.015		K067	257	Ceramic	Disc	5			0.8	5	25.2	
90.016		K061	275	Ceramic	Disc	5			1.1	5	38.8	
90.017		K061	275	Ceramic	Disc	2.9			0.6	2.9	7.2	
90.018		L022	76	Ceramic	Disc	2.9			0.7	2.9	5.4	
90.019		L022	67	Ceramic	Disc	3.5			0.9	3.5	15.75	
90.020		L022	67	Ceramic	Disc	3.4			0.6	3.4	8.1	
90.021		J073	277	Ceramic	Disc	5.5			0.8	5.5	32.7	
90.022		J073	277	Ceramic	Disc	4.3			0.9	4.3	25.2	
90.023		J063	278	Ceramic	Disc	4.9			1	4.9	30.35	
90.024		J063	285	Ceramic	Disc	4.5			1.3	4.5	29.1	
90.025		I050	197	Ceramic	Disc	3.5			0.9	3.5	14.6	
90.026		I069	269	Ceramic	Disc	4.4			1.3	4.4	23.6	

Tell El Hayyat Registered Objects

Registration #	Phase	Locus	Bag	Material	Form	Max dim.	Length	Width	Depth	Diameter	Weight	Condition
90.027		I069	269	Ceramic	Disc	3.4			0.8	3.4	11.6	
90.028		I069	276	Ceramic	Disc	3.9			1	3.9	18.5	
90.029		K059	217	Ceramic	Disc	8.4			1.1	8.4	85.7	
90.030		L030	143	Ceramic	Disc	3.5			0.8	3.5	11.8	
90.031		L030	143	Ceramic	Disc	4.6			1.5	4.6	40.45	
90.032		L030	143	Ceramic	Disc	3.1			0.6	3.1	6.9	
90.033		L031	154	Ceramic	Disc	4.5			1	4.5	19.2	
90.034		L031	154	Ceramic	Disc	3			0.6	3	8.4	
90.035		L031	154	Ceramic	Disc	4.3			0.8	4.3	16.1	
90.036		L031	154	Ceramic	Disc	3.3			0.6	3.3	7.4	
90.037		L031	154	Ceramic	Disc	3	3	2	1		7.2	
90.038		L031	154	Ceramic	Disc	3.5	3.5	3	0.8		9.2	
90.039		K064	242	Ceramic	Disc	4			0.9	4	20.2	
90.040		K064	251	Ceramic	Disc	4			0.7	4	14.5	
90.041		K064	251	Ceramic	Disc	3.7			0.9	3.7	14.2	
90.042		K064	237	Ceramic	Disc	6			0.9	6	42	
90.043		K064	257	Ceramic	Disc	5.7	5.7	5	0.9		37.9	
90.044		K064	242	Ceramic	Disc	4.8	4.8	3.5	0.7		17.6	
90.045		K064	237	Ceramic	Disc	4	4	3	1.1		19	
90.046		K064	251	Ceramic	stopper	6	6	4.2	2.5		52.5	
90.047		K064	251	Ceramic	stopper	6	6	4.8	3.4		72.7	
90.048		K064	258	Ceramic	Disc	3.5	3.5	3	1		15.9	
90.049		K064	237	Ceramic	Disc	4.8			0.69	4.8	27.6	
90.050		K064	257	Ceramic	Disc	3.4			1.3	3.4	13.4	
90.051		K064	257	Ceramic	Disc	3.5	3.5	3	0.6		8	
90.052		K064	258	Ceramic	Disc	3			0.7	3	8.4	
90.053		K064	257	Ceramic	Disc	3	3	2.3	0.8		8.1	
90.054		K064	257	Ceramic	Disc	3	3	2.6	0.5		6.4	
90.055		K064	257	Ceramic	Disc	5.8			1.9	5.8	72.7	

Registration #	Phase	Locus	Bag	Material	Form	Max dim.	Length	Width	Depth	Diameter	Weight	Condition
90.056		K064	251	Ceramic	Disc	3.5	3.5	3	1		13.2	
90.057		H056	245	Ceramic	Disc	4			0.7	4	12.7	
90.058		L035	168	Ceramic	Disc	3.6			0.9	3.6	15.8	
90.059		L035	168	Ceramic	Disc	4			1	4	19.6	
90.060		L035	168	Ceramic	Disc	2.8	2.8	2.3	0.8		8.6	
90.061		L035	168	Ceramic	Disc	5.5			1.2	5.2	40.9	
90.062		L037	161	Ceramic	Disc	4.5			1.2	4.5	30.1	
90.063		L038	185	Ceramic	Disc	4.4			1	4.4	7.5	
90.064		L038	165	Ceramic	Disc	2.9			0.6	2.9	19.1	
90.065		M020	87	Ceramic	Disc	5.5			1.1	5.5	22.6	
90.066		M052	160	Ceramic	Disc	5			0.9	5	23.9	
90.067		Q053	275	Ceramic	Disc	5	5	4.5	1.2		39.3	
90.068		P149	298	Ceramic	Disc	4.3	4.3	3.6	0.8		12.7	
90.069		P168	314	Ceramic	Disc	3.5			0.8	3.5	13	
90.070		S067	245	Ceramic	Disc	2.8			0.9	2.8	7.3	
90.071		S067	245	Ceramic	Disc	3.5			1.1	3.5	16.6	
90.072		S067	250	Ceramic	Disc	6.9			0.9	6.9	68.3	
90.073		S067	250	Ceramic	Disc	3	3	2.7	0.7		5.6	
90.074		S068	260	Ceramic	Disc	4			1.1	4	19.1	
90.075		S068	260	Ceramic	Disc	4.4	4.4	4	1.1		24.5	
90.076		S068	260	Ceramic	Disc	4.04	0		0.75	4	13.8	
90.077		S068	260	Ceramic	Disc	5	5	4.25	1.2		32.7	
90.078		S068	260	Ceramic	Disc	4.6			1.35	4.5	36.7	
90.079		S068	265	Ceramic	Disc	5.7			1.3	5.7	59.55	
90.080		S070	271	Ceramic	Disc	5			1.1	5	36.3	
90.081		S070	271	Ceramic	Disc	4.5			0.8	4.5	20.7	
90.082		S071	271	Ceramic	Figurine Leg	3.38	3.2	2	2.5		11.8	
90.083		T048	218	Ceramic	Disc	4.5	4.5	3.5	1.1		23.4	
90.084		T048	218	Ceramic	Disc	3.7			0.9	3.7	15.9	

Tell El Hayyat Registered Objects

Registration #	Phase	Locus	Bag	Material	Form	Max dim.	Length	Width	Depth	Diameter	Weight	Condition
90.085		T048	218	Ceramic	Disc	3			0.9	3	11.1	
90.086		T052	229	Ceramic	Disc	3			0.7	3	9.1	
90.087		T052	233	Ceramic	Disc	3			0.9	3	12.2	
90.088		T056	234	Ceramic	Disc	5.5			1	5.5	31	
90.089		T056	244	Ceramic	Disc	3.5			1.2	3.5	18.2	
90.090		T056	234	Ceramic	Disc	3.2	3.2	2.8	0.6		6.9	
90.091		T052	244	Ceramic	Disc	3.5			1.2	3.5	19.8	
90.092		H058	313	Ceramic	Disc	4.6			1.2	4.6	30.3	
90.093		H058	207	Ceramic	Disc	4.3			1.1	4.3	26.7	
90.094		H058	329	Ceramic	Disc	4.83	3.5	3.5	0.6	0	8.8	
90.095		T058	249	Ceramic	Disc	3.8	3.8	3	1		12.5	
90.096		T058	255	Ceramic	Disc	2.5			0.8	2.5	7.7	
90.097		T058	255	Ceramic	Disc	5.5			1.1	5.5	44.9	
90.098		T058	255	Ceramic	Disc	4			0.7	4	11.8	
90.099		T058	249	Ceramic	Disc	4.5	4.5	3.7	1		19.6	
90.100		T058	249	Ceramic	Disc	4	4	3.5	0.8	4	11.7	
90.101		H056	246	Ceramic	Disc	4.5	4.5	4	1		22.3	
90.102		Q059	211	Ceramic	Disc	4.5	4.5	3.7	0.8		15.9	
90.103		L040	176	Ceramic	Figurine	4.47	4	3.5	3.5		26.9	
90.104		S067	251	Ceramic	Tray	11	11	3	3.5		71.7	
90.105		I087	356	Ceramic	Incense Burner	10	10	9.5	8.1			
90.106		H056	289	Ceramic	Disc	4			0.6	4	13.9	
90.107		S061	210	Ceramic	Trapezoid	7.4	6.1	4.2	2.3		58.3	
90.108		S061	210	Ceramic	Disc	5.2	5.2	4.7	1	5	31.5	
90.109		S061	210	Ceramic	Disc	4.4	4.4	4	1.1	4.1	21.9	chipped
90.110		S061	209	Ceramic	Disc	4.2	4.2	3.7	0.8	4	17.7	worn
90.111		S071	284	Ceramic	Disc	5.2			0.9	4.8	26.6	
90.112		S071	284	Ceramic	Disc	3.7			1.9	3.5	13.9	
90.113		S071	284	Ceramic	Disc	6				5.1	40.1	

Tell El Hayyat Registered Objects

Registration #	Phase	Locus	Bag	Material	Form	Max dim.	Length	Width	Depth	Diameter	Weight	Condition
90.114		S067	254	Ceramic	Disc	3.25			0.75	3.25	8.2	
90.115		S067	254	Ceramic	Disc	6.13			1.3	5.65	63.35	
90.116		S067	254	Ceramic	spout	7.48	7.1	5.08	1.09		60.4	
90.117		J060	268	Ceramic	Disc	5.32			1.04	5.32	57.8	
90.118		J060	268	Ceramic	Disc	4.18			0.92	4.18	16.4	
90.119		T041	169	Ceramic	Disc	3.67			1.17	3.55	17.1	
90.120		T041	149	Ceramic	Disc	3.86			0.94		9.95	
90.121		T041	198	Ceramic	Disc	3.48			1.07	3.4	10.8	
90.122		J063	223	Ceramic	Disc	4.13			1.2	3.8	22.4	
90.123		S061	219	Ceramic	Figurine Feet	3.91	3.48	3.22	1.78		23.6	
90.124		J059	269	Ceramic	Disc	5.28			0.8		16.5	
90.125		J062	220	Ceramic	Disc	4.32			0.9	4.09	16.6	
90.126		T052	232	Ceramic	Disc	3.5	3.5	3	0.8		12.5	
90.127		T052	229	Ceramic	Disc	5.5	5.5	5	0.8		26	
90.128		T052	224	Ceramic	Disc	4.8	4.8	4.2	0.9		21.4	
90.129		T052	233	Ceramic	Disc	4			0.7	4	14.7	
90.130		T052	224	Ceramic	Disc	6	6	5	1.5		57	
90.131		H056	242	Ceramic	Disc	3.25			0.88	3.25	10.9	
91.006		E086	406	Ceramic	Disc	5.8			1	5.8	32.25	
91.007		E086	412	Ceramic	Disc	5.45			1.25	5.35	37.8	
91.008		E086	390	Ceramic	Disc	5.25			1	5.15	27	
91.009		E086	409	Ceramic	Disc	4.7			0.9	4.6	18.9	
91.010		K064	257	Ceramic	Disc	5.7			0.8	5.7	26	
91.011		E086	392	Ceramic	Disc	6			1.1	5.8	38.1	
91.012		E086	390	Ceramic	Disc	7.75			0.7	7.75	44	
91.013		E086	406	Ceramic	Disc	3.5			0.75	3.45	8.9	
91.014		E086	400	Ceramic	Disc	3.5			0.85	3.5	9.8	
91.015		E086	392	Ceramic	Disc	4			0.9	4	14.7	
91.016		E086	406	Ceramic	Disc	3.8			0.9	3.65	14.4	

Tell El Hayyat Registered Objects

Registration #	Phase	Locus	Bag	Material	Form	Max dim.	Length	Width	Depth	Diameter	Weight	Condition
91.017		E086	400	Ceramic	Disc	4.1			0.6	4.05	10.3	
91.018		E086	387	Ceramic	Disc	4.2			0.7	4.2	12.5	
91.019		E086	387	Ceramic	Disc	2.7			0.7	2.7	5.3	
91.020		E086	387	Ceramic	Disc	3.55			1	3.5	11.8	
91.021		E086	412	Ceramic	Disc	3.55			0.9	3.5	10.5	
91.022		E086	409	Ceramic	Disc	3.25			0.65	3.2	7	
91.023		E086	387	Ceramic	Disc	4.3			0.8	4.3	16.3	
91.024		E086	387	Ceramic	Disc	4.2			1	4.1	16	
91.025		E086	387	Ceramic	Disc	4.3			1.25	4.2	21.6	
91.026		E086	387	Ceramic	Disc	3.6			1	3.6	12.8	
92.001		G074	251	Ceramic	Disc	4.9			0.8	4.5		
92.002		A045	176	Ceramic	Disc	3.9			0.9	3.4		
92.003		G077	263	Ceramic	Disc	4.6			1.2	4.2		
92.004		C066	295	Ceramic	Disc	5.2			0.8	4.9		
92.005		H055	237	Ceramic	Disc	5.4			1.1	5.2		
92.006		H050	196	Ceramic	Disc	4.4			1	4		
92.007		L042	277	Ceramic	Disc	3.9			1.2	3.8		
92.008		G074	254	Ceramic	Disc	3			0.6	2.8		
92.009		G080	303	Ceramic	Disc	4.2			0.8	4		
92.010		G074	251	Ceramic	Disc	3.5			0.6	3.5		
92.011		C066	295	Ceramic	Disc	3.8			0.9	3.5		
92.012		F054	274	Ceramic	Disc	4.5			0.6	4.2		
92.013		H054	232	Ceramic	Disc	4.9			0.6	4.7		
92.014		C066	295	Ceramic	Disc	4.7			0.8	4.7		
92.015		G080	303	Ceramic	Disc	4.1			0.9	4		
92.016		F038	156	Ceramic	Disc	3.6			0.7	3.4		
92.017		H054	232	Ceramic	Disc	6.1			1.3	5.6		
92.018		H054	232	Ceramic	Disc	6.2			1.1	5.5		
92.019		G080	303	Ceramic	Disc	3.2			0.8	3.1		

Registration #	Phase	Locus	Bag	Material	Form	Max dim.	Length	Width	Depth	Diameter	Weight	Condition
92.020		G074	254	Ceramic	Disc	3.4			0.7	3.3		
92.021		G079	281	Ceramic	Disc	3.7			1.1	3.7		
92.022		G073	240	Ceramic	Disc	3.3			0.7	3.1		
92.023		C064	283	Ceramic	Disc	5.2			0.9	2.9		
92.024		C079	283	Ceramic	Disc	3.9			0.7	3.3		
92.025		G074	251	Ceramic	Disc	3.3			0.7	3.1		
92.026		G079	293	Ceramic	Disc	4			0.9	4		
92.027		H054	232	Ceramic	Disc	3.8			0.7	3		
92.028		H060	196	Ceramic	Disc	3.6			0.7	3.3		
92.029		C066	295	Ceramic	Disc	4			0.7	3.5		
92.030		G074	254	Ceramic	Disc	4.1			1.2	3.9		
92.031		G079	286	Ceramic	Disc	3.2			1	3.2		
92.032		C065	289	Ceramic	Disc	4.6			1	4.3		
92.033		G081	306	Ceramic	Disc	5.1			0.9	5.1		
92.034		C067	302	Ceramic	Disc	3.5			0.8	3.3		
92.035		G074	251	Ceramic	Disc	3.6			0.8	3.3		
92.036		G080	303	Ceramic	Disc	3.7			1.1	3.3		
92.037		G081	306	Ceramic	Disc	4.4			1.2	4.2		
92.038		G074	254	Ceramic	Disc	4			0.6	3.9		
92.039		G078	278	Ceramic	Disc	4			0.8	3.9		
92.040		C069	309	Ceramic	Disc	4			0.9	6		
92.041		D055	258	Ceramic	Disc	4.7			0.9	4.4		
92.042		G080	303	Ceramic	Disc	4			0.9	3.3		
92.043		G081	306	Ceramic	Disc	3.6			0.9	3.2		
92.044		C067	302	Ceramic	Disc	2.9			0.8	2.1		
92.045		A048	173	Ceramic	Disc	3.2			0.6	2.9		
93.021		B040	190	Ceramic	Disc	6			1.3	6		
93.022		J078	307	Ceramic	Disc	6.8			1.5	6.8		
93.023		T069	300	Ceramic	Disc	7.4			1	7.4		

Registration #	Phase	Locus	Bag	Material	Form	Max dim.	Length	Width	Depth	Diameter	Weight	Condition
93.024		P192	399	Ceramic	Disc	6			1	6		
93.025		T082	262	Ceramic	Disc	4.6			0.8	4.6		
93.026		H066	372	Ceramic	Disc	4.2			0.6	4.2		
93.027		E107	301	Ceramic	Disc	5.4			0.8	5.4		
93.028		S080	325	Ceramic	Disc	5			1.4	5		
93.029		S081	327	Ceramic	Disc	5.1			1.4	5.1		
93.030		E106	294	Ceramic	Disc	4.3			1.2	4.3		
93.031		T049	211	Ceramic	Disc	3.9			1	3.9		
93.032		T062	266	Ceramic	Disc	4.2			0.8	4.2		
93.033		C073	320	Ceramic	Disc	5			1.6	5		
93.034		H070	449	Ceramic	Disc	3			0.7	3		
93.035		C072	317	Ceramic	Disc	5.8			1.3	5.8		
93.036		B040	190	Ceramic	Disc	7			0.7	7		
93.037		L046	211	Ceramic	Disc	4			1	4		
93.038		H064	366	Ceramic	Disc	3.4			0.8	3.4		
93.039		T069	299	Ceramic	Disc	2.8			0.8	2.8		
93.040		E106	494	Ceramic	Disc	4.3			1.1	4.3		
93.041		S076	308	Ceramic	Disc	4.2			1.5	4.2		
93.042		S080	325	Ceramic	Disc	3.6			1.3	3.6		
93.043		H066	372	Ceramic	Disc	4.2			1	4.2		
93.044		B040	190	Ceramic	Disc	4.4			1.1	4.4		
93.045		H040	449	Ceramic	Disc	3			0.6	3		
93.046		H071	446	Ceramic	Disc	3.8			0.8	3.8		
93.047		S072	319	Ceramic	Figurine	2.3				2.3		
93.048		Q076	392	Ceramic	Scraper	5.8			1.1			
93.049		T065	286	Ceramic	Tube	7.6	7.6		1.8			
93.050		S073	294	Ceramic	Wheel	7			1.5			
93.051		B058	224	Stone	Disc	4.5			1.2	4.5		
93.052		L044	199	Stone	Polished	4.6			1.6			

Tell El Hayyat Registered Objects

Registration #	Phase	Locus	Bag	Material	Form	Max dim.	Length	Width	Depth	Diameter	Weight	Condition
93.053		R074	269	Ceramic	spout	4	4			1.6		
93.054		T062	266	Stone	Cylinder	5	5			1.6		

APPENDIX D:
TELL EL-HAYYAT REGISTERED OBJECT DESCRIPTIONS
(filename: "TH REGISTERED OBJECTS DESCRIPTION")

Registration #	Description	Remarks
82.001	Stone pendant, pink	
82.002	Iron object, thin and tapering, probably a point.	
82.004	Long, thin piece of iron, possibly a knife. VERY corroded and VERY fragile.	
82.009	An impression of a seal, possibly out of clay.	
82.020	Thin, small metal fragment, possibly of a pin.	
82.021	Two pieces of ceramic. The largest piece measures 8.0 X 5.1cm.	
82.022	Ceramic cylinder with central hole.	
82.023	Ceramic oval, smooth, worn edges. Probably scraping tool, 2/3 preserved.	
82.024	Perforated ceramic cylinder.	
82.025	Ceramic disc, roughly chipped edges.	
82.026	Ceramic disc, roughly chipped edges.	
82.027	Ceramic disc, roughly chipped edges.	
83.001	crescent-shaped silver earring	heavily encrusted; needs cleaning
83.002	bronze ring; probably with ends twisted by each other, not joined end to end	
83.003	hard chalk spindle whorl in two pieces, one roughly 1/2 of the whorl, the other roughly 1/4 of the whorl. Outside diameter of the larger piece=4.9cm, inner diam= .8. Thichness= 1.1 at center, .4 at each edge.	Central hole probably drilled from both sides.
83.004	Probably polished porphery. Triangular stone sherd from shallow bowl with flat rim. 4.2cm along the rim X 4.0 toward the center of the bowl X 3.6 toward center of bowl. Sherd represents top 2.3cm of depth of bowl.	
83.005	Heavy copper or bronze pin. Tapers in diameter from one end toward the other. The thinner end has a "head" on it for its final 2.5cm. This head= up to 1.3cm diameter (maybe a point--perhaps the whole thing is a bolt-like projectile point).	heavily encrusted
83.006	Copper or bronze pin, 8.6 cm long, tapering from .5 cm to .3 cm diameter from head to point. Head of pin is looped back to form an eye for the last 1.3 cm of the pin.	
83.007	Copper or bronze clasp. Half of a metal safety pin type clasp forming an "elbow" with a socket at one end which may have been the pivot for the missing stick-pin half of the clasp. Minimum thickness at elbow= .4 cm, thickening to .6 or .7 cm at eith	
83.008	Carved front and back and pierced through long axis. Broken, chipped back. Carved design of human figure, date palm, and two unidentified symbols.	
83.009	Small unfired clay semi-hemispherical bowl with a depression the size of a thumb. Handmade. Inner diameter = 2.5 cm, outer = 3.5 cm, height= 3.2 cm.	slightly chipped exterior
83.010	Small wheel-made vessel, pink-buff color, calcite inclusions. The jar has a disc base, carinated body and flared rim. Part of the rim is broken off to the shoulder. Rim diameter= 6.0 cm, base diameter= 4.0 cm.	

Tell El Hayyat Registered Objects Description and Remarks

Registration #	Description	Remarks
83.011	Small wheel-made vessel, red-buff clay, few inclusions. Pear-shaped body, flat base, narrow neck with single oval handle attached at rim and just below shoulder of jar. Rim diameter= 2.0 cm, base diameter= 2.3 cm, height= 9.8 cm.	broken between neck and shoulder, restored.
83.012	Slightly bow-shaped pin with thickened head.	Very corroded. Broken near head.
83.013	Polished bone (tibia?) with 3 sets of opposing double holes and an extra single hole around one end and one pierced hole at the other end. Diameter= 1.2-2.0cm. Diameter of holes= .4cm.	
83.014	Wheel-made, incised jar handle, coarse cooking pot ware with large calcite inclusions. Incised design consists of a single horizontal stroke and radiating vertical strokes. Length 7.5cm, width 2.0-5.0cm.	Handle and design broken.
83.015	Worked stone pendant, brown-black ground and polished stone rectangle; square in section; pierced through slightly off-center. Length 4.5cm, width 1.5-1.7cm.	Chipped at one end.
83.016	polished red stone cylinder, pierced through center.	Chipped near one end.
83.017	Bronze hoop, oval in section, slightly thicker at bottom of ring. 2.0cm diameter, .15-.3cm thick.	Slightly corroded.
83.018	Polished bone point made from a sheep/goat metacarpal.	
83.019	Soft limestone or chalk fragment with two drilled impressions in the center.	Possible drill-end?
83.020	Soft limestone or chalk pear-shaped object, scored around narrow end and carved and drilled depression in middle. Two drill holes, one complete, one incomplete. Back and sides slightly rounded.	About 1/4 is broken off at larger end. Possible d
83.021	Fired clay disc with hole pierced before baking.	
83.022	Trapezoidal worked shell (mother of pearl?) with double hole drilled through narrower end.	
83.023	Sherd chipped into disc shape, hole drilled from both sides.	
83.024	Ground and pecked grey stone disc with drilled hole.	Broken, only half remains.
83.025	Chipped pottery disc with drilled hole.	
83.026	Round stone bead, polished and drilled. Amber-colored with cloudy white inclusions.	
83.027	Mushroom-shaped object of unbaked clay with round flat head and pinched narrow stem.	Possibly a bottle-stopper?
83.028	Complete stone (probably limestone) spindle whorl. Outer diameter= 4.3cm, central hole= .8cm diameter, 1.1cm thick at center, thinning to .3cm thick at edge.	
83.029	Unbaked, flattened clay circle with central protrusion. Outer diameter= 2.6 cm, central protrusion = .8 cm diameter. Thickness is uneven but generally= .6 cm.	
83.030	Unfired lump of clay apparently molded. Two lateral ears or horns at top of head. Central ridge runs lengthwise between two indentations which appear to be eyes. Squared off muzzle below eyes. Cow's head? Overall length along central axis= 3.8cm,	
83.031	Unfired clay "basket," circular in shape, tapered and closed at bottom, open at top, with 7 loose spherical clay pellets, 1 pellet still stuck at bottom of basket. Outer diameter=4.4-4.6cm. Inner diameter at top of "pocket"=2.4-2.9cm. Overall heigh	

Registration #	Description	Remarks
83.032	Sheep or goat metapodial or radius shaft. Sharpened toward distal end, broken at proximal end. Overall length= 6.8cm. Fresh break into 2 pieces at 3.7cm from proximal end. Maximum width= 1.3cm at proximal end, tapering to point at distal end.	
83.033	Circular shaped sherd with central drilled hole. Outer diameter= 3.2-3.4 cm. Perforation= .6 cm diameter. Thickness= .8 cm.	Broken roughly in half through central perforation
83.034	White stone spindle wholr, probably limestone. Outer diameter= 3.2 cm, diameter of perforation = .4 cm, maximum thickness = .8 cm tapering to 7 cm at edges.	
83.035	Lozenge-shaped lump of shaved white clay ar very soft white chalk. Maximum length= 4.3 cm, diameter/thickness= 1.8 cm, tapering to rounded ends.	
83.036	Corroded metal lump.	
83.037	Small metal lump.	
83.038	Small metal fragments.	
83.039	Large metal lump.	
83.040	Metal fragment.	
83.041	Large metal lump.	
83.042	Metal fragment.	
83.043	Metal lump.	
83.044	Lump of some sort of material, probably metal.	
83.046	Fragment of ceramic oval, edges worn smooth. Only 1/8 intact.	
83.047	Ceramic disc, slightly oval, smoothed edges, slightly bevelled.	
83.048	Perforated ceramic cylinder.	
83.049	Perforated ceramic cylinder.	
83.050	Ceramic disc, roughly chipped then smoothed slightly on edges.	
83.051	Three plaster pieces in very poor condition.	
83.052	Medium-sized lump of dried dung.	
83.053	Fragment of ceramic disc with central hole; hole drilled from both sides. Edges chipped and slightly worn.	
83.054	Five chunks of what may be fuel.	
83.055	One piece of glass.	
83.056	Ceramic disc, smooth edges, bevelled.	
83.057	Ten pieces of broken glass. Largest piece measures 4.0 X 1.5 cm.	
83.058	Spherical ceramic object.	

Registration #	Description	Remarks
83.059	Ceramic disc with central hole only partially drilled through. Chipped edges.	
83.060	Fragment of ceramic disc with central hole, chipped edges.	
83.061	Three ceramic fragments in poor condition. The diameter of the largest is 1.0cm.	
83.062	Ceramic fragment in poor condition.	
83.063	Oblong ceramic disc. It is broken into two pieces, roughly at the halfway point. Probably a scraper.	
83.064	Fragment of ceramic.	
83.065	Ceramic disc with central hole, drilled from both sides. Roughly chipped edges.	
83.066	Four chips of painted plaster in very poor condition. The chips look pinkish-white.	
83.067	Stone object shaped like a knob with one end flat and the other end rounded.	
83.068	Ceramic disc, roughly chipped edges, partially smoothed.	
83.069	Ceramic disc, roughly chipped edges now smoothed. Beginning of drill hole.	
83.070	Two pieces of Roman glass. The largest measures 1.5cm X .7cm.	
83.071	Drilled bone with rows of drilled holes. The maximum length is 11.5cm and the maximum width is .7cm.	
83.072	Small ceramic vessel in the form of an inkwell with a flatish base and rounded sides, probably a kernos attachment.	
85.001	MBIIC votive bowl with string-cut base. Pinky-orange fabric. Complete and intact. Diameter of base= 4.0 cm, diameter of rim= 10.6 cm, and height is 4.2 cm.	
85.002	MBIIC votive bowl with string-cut base. Pinky-orange fabric. Mended from two sherds. Small piece missing from rim. Diameter of base= 4.5 cm, diameter of rim= 10.5 cm, and height= 4.1 cm.	Join made with HMG (cellulose nitrate) adhesive.
85.003	MBIIC votive bowl with string-cut base. Pinky-orange fabric. Approx. 1/3 of rim and upper wall missing. Diameter of base= 5.5 cm, diameter of rim= 10.4 cm, and height= 3.3 cm.	
85.004	MBIIC votive bowl with string-cut base. Pinky-orange fabric. Mended from six sherds. Base and profile complete; approxs. 2/3 of rim and upper wall missing. Diameter of base= 4.4 cm, diameter of rim= 10.5 cm and height= 4.5 cm.	Joins made with HMG (cellulose nitrate) adhesive.
85.005	MBIIC votive bowl with string-cut base. Pinky-orange fabric Slightly less than half the bowl preserved, includes full profile. Diameter of base= 5.5 cm, diameter of rim= 11.0 cm, and height= 3.5 cm.	
85.006	MBIIC carinated votive bowl with string-cut base. Pinky-buff fabric. Complete except for small chips out of rim. Diameter of base= 3.6 cm, diameter of rim= 6.9 cm, and height= 5.2 cm.	Two small sherds from rim rejoined with HMG (cellu
85.007	MBIIC carinated votive bowl with string-cut base. Pinky-buff fabric. Complete and intact. Diameter of base= 3.2 cm, diameter of rim= 7.0 cm, and height= 4.8 cm.	
85.008	MBIIC carinated votive bowl with string-cut base. Pinky-buff fabric. Mended from 7 fragments. Base and profile complete. Approx 2/3 of rim and 1/3 of body wall missing. Diameter of base= 3.2 cm, diameter of rim= 7.0 cm, and height= 5.3 cm.	Joins made with HMG (cellulose nitrate).
85.009	MBIIC votive lamp with string-cut base. Pink-buff fabric. Complete except for small chips from mouth.	Several sherds from mouth rejoined with HMG (cellu

Tell El Hayyat Registered Objects Description and Remarks

Registration #	Description	Remarks
85.010	MBIIC votive lamp with string-cut base. Pink-buff fabric. Complete except for one small chip from rim and fragment from spout.	
85.011	MBIIB-C burnished carinated bowl with ring base. Buff fabric. Vertical burnishing below carination; chevron burnishing above. Mended from many fragments. Largely complete except for small portion of rim and several small fragments from body. Diame	Joins made with HMG (cellulose nitrate).
85.012	MBIIB carinated bowl with slightly concave disk base. Buff fabric. Mended from several fragments. Complete except for small piece from lower body. Diameter of base= 6.1 cm, diameter of rim= 9.3 cm, and height=7.0 cm.	Joins made with HMG (cellulose nitrate).
85.013	MBIIC carinated bowl with three holes drilled in base. Buff fabric. Complete except for small chips from rim. Diameter of base= 5.1 cm, diameter of rim= 9.6 cm, height= 9.7 cm, and diameter of holes= .9-1.0 cm.	
85.014	Fragment of MBII closed jar with string-cut base. Orange-buff fabric. Fragment includes entire base and part of lower body wall. Diameter of base= 3.9 cm, maximum present diameter of body= 6.9 cm, and present height= 7.2 cm.	
85.015	MBIIC votive jar with string-cut base. Orange-buff fabric. Thick walls. Six approx. equidistant flaws on exterior 1/4 up from base. Complete except for small chips from rim. Diameter of base= 4.8 cm, diameter of rim= 5.5 cm, and height is irregula	
85.016	MBIIC pot stand, buff fabric. Complete, but wall cracked through at one point. Diameter of base= 10-10.4 cm, diameter of rim= 9.6-10.2 cm, and height= 6.8 cm.	
85.017	MBIIB-C button-bottom juglet. Neck, rim and parts of upper body missing. Brown-buff fabric. Mended from several fragments. Diameter of base= 2.5 cm, maximum diameter of body= 11.5 cm, and maximum present height= 21.8 cm.	Joins made with HMG (cellulose nitrate).
85.018	MBIIB-C button-bottom juglet with vertical burnishing. Orange-buff fabric. Neck, rim, handle and small chip from shoulder missing. Diameter of base= 1.1 cm, maximum diameter of body= 7.7 cm, and maximum present height= 14.3 cm.	
85.019	MBIIB-C button-bottom juglet. Fine buff ware. Complete to rim; approx. 2/3 of neck, 4/5 of rim missing. Handle and neck rejoined from 3 fragments. Diameter of base= 1.2 cm, maximum diameter of body= 8.5 cm, and height to rim= 20.4 cm.	Joins made with HMG (cellulose nitrate).
85.020	MBIIC tripod base fragment. "Chocolate" ware. Red paint streak in deep depression of base, possible a potter's mark? Only one loop of tripod intact, rest of vessel missing from above base. Diameter of base excluding loops= ~4.8cm, and maximum prese	
85.021	Persian or Hellenistic (?) base fragment from large vessel White slipped orange fabric. Base intact except for small hole, rest of vessel above base missing.	
85.022	Bone astragalus (gaming piece) from sheep/goat. Sides planed to make them flat. Approx 1/4 missing.	
85.023	Worked bone point. Polished point, broken at shaft end. Possible sheep/goat metapodial.	
85.024	Possible worked bone. Flat fragment of sheep/goat rib, apparently polished by or for use as tool. Blackened as if burned. Broken on three sides.	
85.025	Worked bone point. Broken at shaft end. Probably from sheep/goat radius shaft.	

Tell El Hayyat Registered Objects Description and Remarks

Registration #	Description	Remarks
85.026	Worked bone point. Broken off at shaft end.	
85.027	Worked bone. Probably a point but broken off at point and shaft ends. Highly polished. From sheep/goat metapodial or radius.	
85.028	Worked bone point. Broken off at shaft end. From sheep/goat radius or metapodial shaft.	
85.029	Worked bone point. Broken off just above point. Polished, but shows signs of having been gnawed. From sheep or goat limb.	
85.030	Worked bone point. Finely made, polished point, broken off at shaft end. From sheep/goat limb bone.	
85.031	Worked bone point. Polished, sharply tapered to point. Shaft end bevelled. From sheep/goat radius or matapodial shaft.	
85.032	Worked bone point. Worn and weathered at shaft end; lightly polished, probably by use at point. From sheep/goat metapodial shaft.	
85.033	Worked bone point. Highly polished. Broken off at shaft end. From sheep/goat limb bones.	
85.034	Worked bone point, probably a needle. Flattened in section, hole pierced through just below point. Broken off across hole. Highly polished.	
85.035	Fragment of worked bone with pierced holes. Sheep or goat humerus (?) with rows of holes drilled along length. Approx 1/3 of bone's circumference and unknown amount of length missing, but traces indicate three rows of opposing holes. Diameter of h	
85.036	Fragment of polished bone with pierced holes. Sheep or goat humerus shaft with rows of holes drilled along length. Approx. 1/2 of circumference missing and bone is broken off across length. One end bevelled. Traces indicate at least three rows of	
85.037	Tubular bead from grey-white shell, partially chalky on surface.	
85.038	Fragment of blue glass (?) bead. Badly damaged.	
85.039	Carnelian bead, flattened sphere in shape with central hole drilled from both sides. Approx 1/3 of bead is missing. Diameter of hole= .4cm.	
85.040	Group of 17 spherical carnelian beads, and 1 tubular carnelian bead (broken). Highly polished. Diameter of beads varies .7-.9cm, and maximum preserved length of tubular bead= 1.3cm	
85.041	Fragment of highly polished cylindrical, or possible spherical bead with hole drilled through central axis. Varied coloring: orange, cream, pinky-grey. Nearly 1/2 of diameter preserved; broken across center and at both ends. Diameter of hole= .15	
85.042	Small chip of alabaster, polished on one (slightly convex) side, pecked in parallel pattern on the other (slightly concave) side.	
85.043	Roughly circular chalk object (possibly a spindle whorl) with a hole drilled through the central axis. Only roughly shaped, possibly unfinished. Diameter of hole= .8cm.	
85.044	Conically-shaped limestone (?) object, possibly a weight. Flat base, slightly convex sides. Striations or tool marks running down from apex. Chip missing from base.	

Tell El Hayyat Registered Objects Description and Remarks

Registration #	Description
	Remarks
85.045	Fragment of stone (limestone?) object. Roughly triangular fragment consisting of one-half of a circular boss with hole pierced through the central axis, and part of the lower tapering surface from which the boss rises. Possibly an unfinished loom we
85.046	Fragment of flat oval of white stone with deep scratches over surface. Possibly used a sharpening or honing stone. Probably 1/4 of original stone remaining.
85.047	Fragment of ceramic burnishing tool. Approx 1/2 of presumably circular worked sherd with hole drilled through it somewhat off-center. Shows signs of considerable use--smooth bevelled edges. Gently curved, pronounced striations running perpendicular
85.048	Fragment of perforated pottery disc from a base from a small vessel in white fabric, which has been worked to produce regular disc with hole drilled through center. Possibly re-used as spindle whorl. Broken across central hole, slightly over 1/2 rem
85.049	Fragment of perforated pottery disc. Sherd worked into roughly circular shape with central hole drilled from both sides and meeting slightly off-center. White fabric. Possibly a spindle whorl, but central hole very small (.3cm). Broken across ce
85.050	Fragment of perforated pottery sherd. A thick disc with hole through central axis. Broken on two sides of hole, approx. 1/3 of whole remaining. Upper, curved surface crumbled and mostly lost. Diameter of hole= 1.0 cm.
85.051	Fragment of pottery burnishing tool. Curved pottery sherd worked into apparently oval shape and used as burnishing or smoothing tool. Edges and convex surface well worn. Broken on two edges.
85.052	Fragment of pottery tool. A straight-sided, nearly flat, worked sherd, with remaining straight edge worn very smooth. Broken on two sides.
85.053	Fragment of ceramic "cart wheel." Modelled fired clay wheel with axle hub protruding from one side. Briken on two sides, somewhat less than one-quarter original circumference remaining. Some surface loss on side without hub. Outer diameter= 10.5cm,
85.054	Fragment of ceramic cart wheel (?). Approx. 1/5 of a modelled fired clay circle tapering toward rounded edge.
85.055	Fragment of ceramic object, possibly a cart wheel. Roughly triangular fragment, approx. 1/8 of disc-shaped pottery object with rounded edge.
85.056	Fragment of ceramic figurine of woman. Probably portrays Ashtarte-type fertility figure. Left half of female torso with left hand cupped under breast. Broken off lengthwise just to right of navel and at beginning of right breast. Also broken off a
85.057	Ceramic zoomorphic figurine. An unidentified quadraped with long torso. Orange fabric. Tail, head and lower legs missing. Roughly modelled and rather worn.
85.058	Ceramic zoomorphic figurine. Quadraped modelled in brown fabric and fired. Probably a bull, because of traces of dewlap and dorsal hump. Head and ends of legs missing.
85.059	Ritual vessel attachment. Miniature jar with uneven base and traces of having been attached to a larger vessel, possibly of the seven-spouted lamp type. Buff fabric. Complete. Diameter of base= 2.7cm, inner diameter of rim= 1.8cm.

Registration #	Description	Remarks
85.060	Ritual vessel attachment. Small jar with uneven base pierced by an irregular hole and traces of having been attached to larger vessel. Orange buff fabric. Jar broken off at neck level, no rim. Diameter of base= 4.5cm, maximum diameter of body= 5.2c	
85.061	Fragment of ritual vessel attachment (?). Bottom of small jar with uneven base and possible traces of having been attached to a larger vessel. Friable orange-brown fabric. Broken off above base, cracked through on one side.	
85.062	Fragment of ritual vessel attachment. Uneven base of small jar with traces of having been attached to larger vessel. Orange-buff fabric. Broken off just above base.	
85.063	Fragment of ring kernos (?). The bottom of a miniature jar with string-cut base, luted onto outer circumference of ceramic ring. Irregular hole pierced through base of jar, may or may not have been original. Only lower half of jar preserved, broken	Joins made with HMG (cellulose nitrate) adhesive.
85.064	Ritual vessel attachment fragment? One half of bottom of miniature jar with uneven base and traces of having been attached to larger vessel at base; similar type to TH 85.063. Buff fabric.	
85.065	Three non-joining fragments of ritual vessel with "inkwell" attachments. A large vessel of unidentifiable type with a series of attachments around its circumference at the shoulder. The surviving attachments are in the shape of a miniature jar with	"Inkwell" rejoined with HMG (cellulose nitrate) ad
85.066	"Inkwell" attachment for ritual vessel. Miniature jar with base pinched off for attachment to larger vessel (see TH 85.065). Green ware. One half of rim and neck and sections of lower body missing. Mended from several sherds. Very friable. Inne	Joins made with HMG (cellulose nitrate) adhesive.
85.067	"Inkwell" attachment for tirual vessel. Miniature jar with base pinched off for attachment to larger vessel (see TH 85.065) Dark buff fabric. Slightly one-half of neck and rim missing. zinner diameter of rim= 1.4, maximum diameter of body= 3.5cm,	
85.068	"Inkwell" attachment for ritual vessel. Miniature jar with base pinched off for attachment to larger vessel (see TH 85.065). Buff fabric. Rim, neck, and portion of upper body missing. Body cracked. Fragments of luting joining it to larger vessel	
85.069	"Inkwell" attachment for ritual vessel. Miniature jar with base pinched off for attachment to larger vessel (see TH 85.065). Green ware. Rim, part of neck and upper body missing. Mended from several fragments. Traces of luting joining it to larger	Joins made with HMG (cellulose nitrate)>
85.070	Fragment of ritual vessel attachment? Fragment of miniature jar, possibly an "inkwell" type attachment for ritual vessel. Buff fabric. Part of rim and upper body preserved.	
85.071	Fragment of ritual vessel attachment. Part of small jar with uneven base (probably with small hole in the center) and remains of luting joining it to ritual vessel, possibly a ring kernos. Orange-buff fabric. Rim, neck and slightly over one-half of	
85.072	Ritual vessel fragment? Possibly a roughly-shaped small jar with base of attachment luting on interior of break. Buff fabric. Rim, neck, base and over half of body missing.	
85.073	Ceramic handle fragment. Handle from unidentified type of vessel. Consists of shaft, broken off at one end joining rim which flares out away from handle. A square boss decoration occurs at the meeting point of rim and handle. Orange-buff fabric.	

Tell El Hayyat Registered Objects Description and Remarks

Registration #	Description
85.074	A hand-made, irregular squatty conical fired clay object with flat vase. The base is blackened and heavily caked with charred matter (sample taken). Use unknown, but possibly a pot lid, or cover for opening in furnace or kiln. Orange-buff fabric.
85.075	Sherd comprising part of rim and wall of small hand-modelled shallow bowl. Buff fabric, very roughly modelled.
85.076	Part of rim and wall of small hand-modelled bowl. Orange and grey fabric, interior crazed.
85.077	Part of rim and wall of small hand-modelled bowl. Orange-brown fabric.
85.078	Part of a shallow hannd-modelled oval dish with flat base. Base is heavily charred and outer wall blackened; possibly a crucible?? Orange fabric. Fragment included approx. one-quarter of estimated rim circumference and full profile.
85.079	Fragment of extremely thick-walled globular small bowl. Orange fabric with large voids; heavily charred, perhaps by use as crucible. Irregularly shaped, hand-modelled, no discernable base, rim or other feature.
85.080	Base and lower wall fragment of ceramic vessel of unknown type, apparently having a flat base with a large bevel- edged opening in the center and very thick walls. On the interior the wall rises in an even gentle curve from the central opening. Oran
85.081	Byzantine (?) coin showing profile head facing toward right of man wearing wreath and toga-like robe with inscription around edge (....TIVS PF AUG). On verse, a man with spear and shield standing over unidentifiable foe, with inscription around edge (
85.082	Figurine of male quadruped, possibly a ram. feet have pegs at end, as though for affixing animal to a base. Figurine has shallow holes in head, neck, and rump; probably for attaching further decoration. Fissures fun length of underside of body and
85.083	Metal figurine in shape of quadruped, possibly donkey or canid (fox, dog, wolf) with long tail, long ears and square snout. There is a round protuberance over the hind haunches. Condition, color, corrosion and weight of object indicate that it migh
85.084	Leaf-shaped spear (?) blade with central rib. Hollow haft crushed flat with small section missing. several severe cracks along length. Thin cohesive surface over bed of powdery bronze disease (atacamit/paratacamite). VERY FRAGILE!!
85.085	Long narrow point with heavy central rib, probably arrow or small spear head. Tip broken off and shaft end damaged (bent and fractured). Fair condition with some (active) outbreaks of bronze disease (atacamite/ paratacamite).
85.086	Fragmentary long narrow blade with sharp point; one edge of blade lost. No indidcation of central rib, so may be part of dagger blade, but extremely poor condition makes it impossible to tell. In two fragments- broken across below point. Massive out
85.087	Fragment of an unidentified object consisting of a shaft broken off at one end and at the other leading to two other broken off stubs at 45 degrees and 90 degrees (apprcx.) to the first and a tiny protuberance opposite the 90 degree stub. Possibly a

Tell El Hayyat Registered Objects Description and Remarks

Registration #	Description	Remarks
85.088	Tweezers or tongs consisting of two blades, flaring and flattened at the ends and joined at the top. the blades nearly meet at the open end, then are angled away from each other to the shoulder of the tweezers. From the shoulders they close in again t	
85.089	Probably the tang-end of a (dagger?) blade. A short, square-in-section shaft leading to a flat blade, flaring sharply out from tang on one side. Blade broken off just beyond its start.	
85.090	Short length of copper alloy wire bent into U-shape and then each end bent back into loop, as in the eye of a hook and eye fastener. In four pieces; FRAGILE!!	
85.091	Thin sheet of copper alloy metal stamped into shape of oxhide ingot, with two holes punched down the center. Active bronze disease. One of four tips broken off. FRAGILE!!	
85.092	Thin sheet of copper alloy metal in shape of oxhide ingot. Intact. FRAGILE!!	
85.093	Long narrow blade with sharp central rib and hollow haft and several detached fragments from the haft. Warty outbreaks of bronze disease. Maximum preserved length to haft= 12.2 cm, to end of blade= 9.7 cm, width= 2.55 cm, diameter of haft= 1.5 cm, a	
85.094	A long shaft, square in section which curves slightly downward to a rounded, flattened finial. The beginning of a dagger?? blade. Flares out from the other end of the shaft, snapped off just beyond it. Probably a full-hilt tang for a dagger which would	
85.095	Irregular mass, roughly of flattened oval of no discernible type or use. Outbreaks of bronze disease.	
85.096	Small section of wire, heavily eroded.	
85.097	Four fragments, no clear joins, so perhaps not all from one object. There are segments of a thin, hollow shaft, one segment has a sharp point and a hole pierced through the shaft .3 cm above the point. The fourth fragment in a small indeterminate mass	
85.098	Long fairly thick shaft, somewhat flattened at one end, as the head of a nail. Heavy, warty corrosion. Fair condition.	
85.099	Three small fragments. Two appear to be cu alloy sheet rolled into a cylinder partly crushed. The other is irregularly globular. Poor condition. Fragile	
85.100	Tang or rod. The rod is broken off at both ends. From one end, round in section, it graually becomes broader and more rectangular in section until just before the other end, one side flares away, perhaps the beginning of the blade for which the rod wa	
85.101	Three copper alloy fragments. 1) A short segment of wire. 2) Small fragment of very thin sheet. 3) Amorphous lump. Poor condition.	
85.102	Point end of presumably leaf-shaped cu-alloy object. Very thin sheet metal, probably not a weapon tip. Broken across just below tip. Poor condition, very fragile. Bronze disease present.	
85.103	Three copper fragments. 1) thin sheet rolled into cylinder and flattened at one end. 2 & 3) Flat fragments of thin sheet metal. Fair condition. Very Fragile.	
85.104	Two copper fragments. A shaft ending in point (pin?) broken off at shaft end. Large corrosion warts. Round in section. And a amorphous lump.	
85.105	Fragment. Section of rectangular section shaft (perhaps tang?). Broken at both ends. Fair condition.	

Tell El Hayyat Registered Objects Description and Remarks

Registration #	Description	Remarks
85.106	Four copper alloy fragments. 1) Segment of a curved shaft, round-in-section, broken at either end. 2) U-shaped band of flat in section metal, broken at both ends. 3) Short section of rod, appears to be round in section at one end and rectangular at the	
85.107	Thin metal sheet rolled up tightly several times to form multi-layered cylinder. Much broken away. Poor condition.	
85.108	Amorphous copper lump, perhaps related to smelting process. Poor condition. Bronze disease.	
85.109	Amorphous lump. Perhaps related to smelting process.	
85.110	Approximately 1/6 of a basalt mortar with ring base. Interior worn smooth.	
85.111	Complete stone bowl. Basalt. Worn smooth on inside. Concave base.	
85.112	Loom weight ? fragment. Approx. 1/2 of irregularly shaped stone cylinder with hole drilled through axis.	
85.113	Clay loom weight fragment. Slightly more than one quarter unbaked clay sphere with hole through center.	
85.114	Fragment of object, unidentified. Tapering cylinder or cone of pale yellow raw clay or soft stone split in half lenthwise and a design incised on the flat face. Surviving design consists of a parallel rectangular raised areas running the length of the	
85.115	Oval basalt object with shallow depression across middle. Loom weight?	
85.116	Stone cart wheel? Fragment. One-half of white stone disc, elliptical in section. Broken across diameter.	
85.117	Perforated pottery disc. Roughly shaped with hole drilled through the ceter from either side. Edges chipped. Buff fabric.	
85.118	Carnelian bead. Intact spherical bead with hold through central axis.	
85.119	Rectangular block of limestone ? with clef design carved into one face. Relief area is charred black, indicating probably use as mould for molten metal. Absence of any keying probably makes it a cover mould. Block is broken off across top of relief and	
85.120	Rectangular block of limestone ? with relief design carved into two opposing faces. Relief areas are charred black, indicating probabl use as a mould for molten metal. One relief runs the full length of the block which is broken off short at one end. I	
85.121	Several adjoining fragments of a shallow ceramic dish with lumps of copper alloy embedded in the interior of broken edges. Clay is extremely friable. Brown fabric, black core.	
85.122	Four fragments of shallow ceramic dish. Found with 85.121 but no obvious joins between them. Splatters of copper rest on rim. Some vitrification of clay in rim. Clay very friable. Fragments join but not tightly, evidently some deformation after or chan	
85.123	Three joining fragments of a shallow ceramic dish with lumps of copper metal in fissures throughout the fabric. Very friable clay with deep cracks throughout. Brown fabric. Joins are not tight, as though deformation had occured during or after firing.	
85.124	Rock crystal. Tubular bead with tapering ends.	
85.125	Group of 15 carnelian beads, 13 are spherical, one is a large flattened sphere and one a small flat round bead. Largest bead is somewhat chipped. All are highly polished.	

Tell El Hayyat Registered Objects Description and Remarks

Registration #	Description	Remarks
85.126	Stone sphere	
85.127	MB IIA carinated bowl. Shallow concave base. Coarse yellow-buff fabric. Complete except for approx. 2/3 of rim. One sherd from body found inside 85.128.	
85.128	MB IIA carinated bowl. Disc base. Coarse yellow-buff fabric. Complete except for 1/3 of rim and severla chips out of the remainder of rim. Series of shallow incised lines around body below rim. Fabric flaky.	
85.129	MB IIA carinated bowl. Flat disc base. Coarse buff fabric. Rim and part of upper body missing.	
85.130	MB IIA carinated bowl. Coarse buff fabric. In several fragments (now restored). Fabric abraded and flaky. Part of lower body and base missing, no rim preserved.	
85.131	Incense burner base. Flaring column with oval opening just above base connected to central "chimney". Orange fabric. Rim and base broken off.	
85.132	Disc, perforated. Brown fabric. Edge irregularly chipped.	
85.133	Fragment of ritual vessel attachment. Miniature jar for attachment to a larger vessel. Buff fabric. Full profile. Approx. 1/3 of circumference.	
85.134	Smooth, flay round white stone with shallow depression worn in one face.	
85.135	Two joining fragments of polished stone disc. Approx. 1/4 of whole. Also from N033.152.	
85.136	Shaft with flat curving protruberance out to one side (like a key). Another fragment of copper alloy shaft found with it may not be part of it. Poor condition.	
85.137	Probably a humanoid furguring with arms folded across chest. Disc base. Extremely poor condition, one side disintegrating. Very fragile.	
85.138	Fragment of copper sheet broken on three edges. Appears to be folded over on itself on the fourth edge. Fair condition.	
85.139	Fragment of copper sheet broken on all edges.	
85.140		
85.141		
85.142		
85.143		
85.144		
85.145		
85.146		
85.147		
85.148		
85.149		
85.150		

Registration #	Description	Remarks
85.151	Relief figurine on vessel.	
85.152		
85.153		
85.154		
85.155		
85.156		
85.157		
85.158		
85.159		
85.160		
85.161		
85.162		
85.163		
85.164		
85.165		
85.166		
85.167		
85.168		
85.169		
85.170		
85.171		
85.172		
85.173		
85.174		
85.175		
85.176		
85.177		
85.178		
85.179		
85.180		

Registration #	Description	Remarks
85.181		
85.182		
85.183		
85.184		
85.185		
85.186		
85.187		
85.188		
85.189		
85.190		
85.191		
85.192		
85.193		
85.194		
85.195		
85.196	Jaw frag.	
85.197	Jaw frag.	
85.198	Jaw frag.	
85.199	Jaw frag.	
85.200		
85.209		
85.210		
85.211		
85.212		
85.213		
85.214		
85.215		
85.216		
85.217		
85.218		

Registration #	Description	Remarks
90.001	disc. rough edges.	
90.002	disc, combing. rough edges	
90.003	disc, rough edges	
90.004	disk, rough edges	
90.005	disc, rough edges	
90.006		
90.007		
90.008		
90.009		
90.010		
90.011	very smooth edges	
90.012	rough edges	
90.013		
90.014	rough edges	
90.015	rough edges	
90.016	rough edges	
90.017	rough edges	
90.018	rough edges	
90.019	rough edges	
90.020	rough edges	
90.021	rough edges	
90.022	rough edges	
90.023	rough edges	
90.024	rough edges	
90.025	rough edges	
90.026	rough edges	
90.027	rough edges	
90.028	rough edges	
90.029	disc, entire base of a vessel, rough edges	
90.030	rough edges	

Tell El Hayyat Registered Objects Description and Remarks

Registration #	Description	Remarks
90.031	rough edges	
90.032	rough edges	
90.033	rough edges	
90.034	rough edges	
90.035	rough edges	
90.036	rough edges	
90.037	oval disc, rough edges, combing	
90.038	oval disc, rough edges	
90.039	rough edges	
90.040	rough edges	
90.041	strange markings (brush?), rough edges	
90.042	strange markings (brush?), rough edges	
90.043	oval disc, rough edges	
90.044	oval disc, rough edges	
90.045	oval disc, rough edges	
90.046	Oval blob, round on one end, indented on the other end.	
90.047	Oval blob, round on one end, indented on the other end.	
90.048	oval disc, rough edges	
90.049	rough edges	
90.050	rough edges	
90.051	oval disc, rough edges	
90.052	rough edges	
90.053	oval disc, rough edges	
90.054	oval disc, rough edges	
90.055	rough edges	
90.056	oval disc, rough edges	
90.057	rough edges	
90.058	rough edges	
90.059	rough edges	
90.060	oval disc, rough edges	

Tell El Hayyat Registered Objects Description and Remarks

Registration #	Description	Remarks
90.061	rough edges	
90.062	rough edges, combing	
90.063	rough edges	
90.064	rough edges	
90.065	half a disc, smooth circumference with hole? weight?	
90.066	rough edges	
90.067	oval disc, rough edges	
90.068	oval disc, rough edges	
90.069	rough edges, combing	
90.070	rough edges	
90.071	rough edges	
90.072	rough edges	
90.073	oval disc, rough edges	
90.074	rough edges	
90.075	oval disc, rough edges	
90.076	rough edges	
90.077	oval disc, rough edges	
90.078	rough edges	
90.079	rough edges	
90.080	edges somewhat smooth?	
90.081	rough edges	
90.082		
90.083	oval disc, rough edges	
90.084	rough edges	
90.085	rough edges	
90.086	rough edges	
90.087	rough edges	
90.088	rough edges	
90.089	sharp slope, rough edges, chipped around base angle	
90.090	oval disc, rough edges	

Registration #	Description	Remarks
90.091	rough edges, combed design	
90.092	rough edges	
90.093	rough edges	
90.094	one quarter disc, very smooth edges, very flat	
90.095	oval disc, rough edges	
90.096	smooth edges, possibly painted	
90.097	rough edges	
90.098	rough edges	
90.099	oval disc, rough edges, painted stripes	
90.100	rough edges, possibly painted	
90.101	oval disc, rough edges	
90.102	oval disc, rough edges	
90.103	leg of statuette??	
90.104	tray or plaque part; two suspension holes; exterior ridge	
90.105	rough edges	
90.106	Handle to "frying pan"? Four finished sides, one is concave, courseware, broken on two ends.	
90.107	irregular, ovoid disc, a lid or gaming piece? pot marks visible on one side, medium ware, chipped edges, piece is in good condition	
90.108	irregular ovoid chipped disc, corroded interior, medium ware	
90.109	irregular ovoid chipped disc, pot marks visible on one side, medium ware	
90.110	complete disc with rough edges	
90.111	complete disc with rough edges	
90.112	nearly complete ceramic oval with rough edges chipped from jar base	
90.113	complete ceramic disk with rough edges	
90.114	complete ceramic disk with rough edges	
90.115	trough shaped piece broken on three sides, with two non-parallel finished on each edge across the width	
90.116	near complete disc, chipped around handle of vessel. Calcium carbonate applied (while a vessel?)	
90.117	complete disc with rough edges	
90.118	complete disc with rough edges	

Tell El Hayyat Registered Objects Description and Remarks

Registration #	Description	Remarks
90.120	1/4 ceramic disc with smooth worn edge, complete diameter probably between six and seven cm.	
90.121	complete disc with rough edges	
90.122	complete disc with rough edges	
90.123	human figurine feet? broken cylindrical piece with flaring base and slight groove down center length	
90.124	broken ceramic disc with smooth edges, complete diameter would be approx 12 cm.	
90.125	complete ceramic disc with rough edges, incised decoration	
90.126	oval disc, smooth edges	
90.127	oval disc, painted design, rough edges	
90.128	oval disc, rough edges	
90.129	rough edges, painted stripes	
90.130	oval disc, rough edges	
90.131	rough edges	
91.006	Oval shaped with rough edges.	
91.007	This is a round shaped disc with rough edges.	
91.008	This is a round shaped disc with worn, smooth edges.	
91.009	This is an almost round and has rough edges.	
91.010	This is an oblong/ oval shaped disc with rough edges. It has combing on exterior (two horizontal sets of multiple bands).	
91.011	This is an oval shaped disc with rough edges.	
91.012	This is an oval shaped disc with rough edges.	
91.013	This is an oval shped disc with rough edges.	
91.014	This is a fairly well rounded disc whose edges have not been smoothed.	
91.015	This is a fairly round disc with rough edges.	
91.016	This is a fairly round disk whose edges are not worn.	
91.017	This is an oval shped disc with rough edges.	
91.018	This is a round disc with unworn edges.	
91.019	This is a roundish oval with rough edges.	
91.020	This is an oval shaped disc with rough edges.	
91.021	This is a round disc with rough edges.	
91.022	This is an oval shaped disc with rough edges.	

Registration #	Description	Remarks
91.023	This is a round disc with rough edges.	
91.024	This is an oval disc with rough edges.	
91.025	This is a fairly round disc with rough edges.	
91.026	This is a "roundish" disc with rough edges.	
92.001	Oval, smoothed edges.	
92.002	Round, rough edges.	
92.003	Round, rough edges.	
92.004	Oval, angular at one end. Rough edges.	
92.005	Oval, rough edges.	
92.006	Oval, smoothed edges.	
92.007	Round, smoothed edges.	
92.008	Oval, smoothed edges. Red paint on exterior.	
92.009	Oval, smoothed edges.	
92.010	Round, smoothed edges.	
92.011	Oval, smoothed edges.	
92.012	Oval, rough edges.	
92.013	Round, smoothed edges.	
92.014	Round, smoothed edges. Horizontal combing on interior.	
92.015	Round, rough edges.	
92.016	Round, smoothed edges.	
92.017	Oval, smoothed edges.	
92.018	Oval, rough edges.	
92.019	Round, rough edges.	
92.020	Round, smoothed edges.	
92.021	Round, smoothed edges.	
92.022	Oval, smoothed edges.	
92.023	Round, smoothed edges. Imcomplete disc, about half preserved, diam 2.9cm	
92.024	Oval, rough edges.	
92.025	Round, smoothed edges.	
92.026	Round, smoothed edges.	

Tell El Hayyat Registered Objects Description and Remarks

Registration #	Description	Remarks
92.027	Oval, smoothed edges.	
92.028	Round, smoothed edges.	
92.029	Oval, rough edges.	
92.030	Round, rough edges.	
92.031	Round, smoothed edges.	
92.032	Oval, smoothed edges. Exterior has horizontal combing.	
92.033	Round, rough edges.	
92.034	Round, rough edges. Red paint on exterior.	
92.035	Round, smoothed edges.	
92.036	Round, smoothed edges.	
92.037	Round, smoothed edges.	
92.038	Round, smoothed edges.	
92.039	Round, smoothed edges.	
92.040	Smoothed edges. Disc fragment.	
92.041	Round, smoothed edges.	
92.042	Oval, smoothed edges.	
92.043	Oval, smoothed edges.	
92.044	Oval, smoothed edges. Exterior has horizontal combing.	
92.045	Oval, smoothed edges. Exterior has red trickle paint.	
93.021	Slightly irregular, rough edges.	
93.022	Round, rough edges.	
93.023	Round, rough edges.	
93.024	Round, rough edges.	
93.025	Round, rough edges.	
93.026	Round, rough edges.	
93.027	Round, rough edges.	
93.028	Round, rough edges.	
93.029	Round, rough edges.	
93.030	Round, rough edges.	
93.031	Round, rough edges.	

Registration #	Description	Remarks
93.032	Round, rough edges, partial hole drilled in center.	
93.033	Round, rough edges.	
93.034	Round, rough edges.	
93.035	Round, rough edges.	
93.036	Round, rough edges, EB IV.	
93.037	Round, rough edges.	
93.038	Smoothed.	
93.039	Round, rough edges.	
93.040	Round, rough edges.	
93.041	Round, rough edges.	
93.042	Round, rough edges.	
93.043	Round, rough edges.	
93.044	Round, rough edges.	
93.045	Round, rough edges.	
93.046	Round, rough edges.	
93.047	Quadruped animal fig. foot	
93.048	Broken, half round, quite smoothed on edges, perhaps a scraper.	
93.049	Broken, perhaps a tuyere tube.	
93.050	Broken toy wheel	
93.051	Chalk stone disc	
93.052	Broken, perhaps part of a wheel.	
93.053	Eb spout	
93.054	Polished stone cylinder, broken at both ends.	

APPENDIX E:
TELL EL-HAYYAT SEED COUNTS
(filename: "TH FLORA SUMMARY")

Phase or Unit	Volume	Ficus	Olea	Vitis	Pros	Barley	Wheat	Avena	Secale	Wild C	OC	Cult L	Wild L	Weeds	UNID
Niaj	204	254	5	28	79	402	112	134	86	120	3	65	63	869	9
Phase 5	198	240	12	4	33	411	270	41	61	91	0	109	82	351	10
Phase 4	270	129	67	6	33	391	171	34	30	172	4	104	130	520	10
Phase 3	239	670	38	14	14	190	186	122	103	161	8	48	183	245	5
Phase 2	145	155	4	2	92	116	138	36	161	23	0	57	154	1677	8
Hayyat Total	852	1194	121	26	172	1108	765	233	355	447	12	318	549	2793	33
Temple	269	652	3	9	14	128	95	14	20	87	10	47	275	913	4
Outside Temple	583	542	118	17	158	980	670	219	335	360	2	271	274	1880	29
TF	145	593	2	6	12	66	56	9	7	52	4	31	245	683	1
Temple 5	54	41	0	2	9	40	15	3	2	34	0	7	9	130	3
Outside 5	144	199	12	2	24	371	255	38	59	57	0	102	73	221	7
Temple 4	80	22	2	1	1	25	21	0	6	18	3	17	68	285	0
Outside 4	190	107	65	5	32	366	150	34	24	154	1	87	62	235	10
Temple 3	107	554	0	6	3	50	45	9	6	28	7	20	140	146	0
Outside 3	132	116	38	8	11	140	141	113	97	133	1	28	43	99	5
Temple 2	28	35	1	0	1	13	14	2	6	7	0	3	58	352	1
Outside 2	117	120	3	2	91	103	124	34	155	16	0	54	96	1325	7
Surface	726	875	117	21	168	986	698	215	333	393	12	289	504	2734	29
Non-Surface	126	319	4	5	4	122	67	18	22	54	0	29	45	59	4

Tell El Hayyat Flora Summary

Phase or Unit	Volume	Ficus	Olea	Vitis	Pros	Barley	Wheat	Avena	Secale	Wild C	OC	Cult L	Wild L	Weeds	UNID
All Interiors	125	142	53	5	7	293	178	131	231	143	2	37	87	99	4
All Exteriors	390	304	63	10	145	604	399	77	104	118	0	176	156	1656	12
Exterior 5	144	199	12	2	24	371	255	38	59	57	0	102	73	221	7
Interior 4	55	27	49	2	1	185	39	25	13	31	1	17	13	31	3
Exterior 4	97	26	15	2	25	148	64	8	11	31	0	30	23	102	1
Interior 3	34	78	3	3	6	65	87	96	79	109	1	5	25	40	1
Exterior 3	88	38	35	5	5	72	46	17	18	23	0	22	18	53	4
Interior 2	36	37	1	0	0	43	52	10	139	3	0	15	49	28	0
Exterior 2	61	41	1	1	91	13	34	14	16	7	0	22	42	1280	0
Area A	76	97	2	2	6	84	95	11	0	99	0	59	31	129	14
Tabun T,TF	44		72												

Tell El Hayyat Flora Summary

APPENDIX F:
TELL EL-HAYYAT SEED DENSITIES
(filename: "TH FLORA DENSITY")

Tell El Hayyat Flora Density

Phase or Unit	Ficus	Olea	Vitis	Pros	Barley	Wheat	Avena	Secale	Wild C	OC	Cult L	Wild L	Weeds	UN
All Interiors	1136	424	40	56	2344	1424	1048	1848	1144	16	296	696	792	32
All Exteriors	779	162	26	372	1549	1023	197	267	303	0	451	400	4246	31
Exterior 5	1382	83	14	167	2576	1771	264	410	396	0	708	507	1535	49
Interior 4	491	891	36	18	3364	709	455	236	564	18	309	236	564	55
Exterior 4	268	155	21	258	1526	660	82	113	320	0	309	237	1052	10
Interior 3	2294	88	88	176	1912	2559	2824	2324	3206	29	147	735	1176	29
Exterior 3	432	398	57	57	818	523	193	205	261	0	250	205	602	45
Interior 2	1028	28	0	0	1194	1444	278	3861	83	0	417	1361	778	0
Exterior 2	672	16	16	1492	213	557	230	262	115	0	361	689	20984	0
Area A	1276	26	26	79	1105	1205	145	0	1303	0	776	408	1697	184
Tabun T,TF		1636												
Niaj	1245	25	137	387	1971	549	657	422	588	15	319	309	4260	44
Phase 5	1212	61	20	167	2076	1364	207	308	460	0	551	414	1773	51
Phase 4	478	248	22	122	1448	633	126	111	637	15	385	481	1926	37
Phase 3	2803	159	59	59	795	778	510	431	674	33	201	766	1025	21
Phase 2	1069	28	14	634	800	952	248	1110	158	0	393	1062	11566	55

Phase or Unit	Ficus	Olea	Vitis	Pros	Barley	Wheat	Avena	Secale	Wild C	OC	Cult L	Wild L	Weeds	UN
Hayyat Total	1401	142	31	202	1300	898	273	417	524	14	373	644	3278	39
Temple TI,TF,TS	2424	11	33	52	476	353	52	74	323	37	175	1022	3394	15
Outside Temple	930	202	29	271	1681	1149	376	575	617	3	465	470	3225	50
TF	4090	14	41	83	455	386	62	48	359	28	214	1690	4710	7
Temple 5	759	0	37	167	741	278	56	37	630	0	130	167	2407	56
Outside 5	1382	83	14	167	2576	1771	264	410	396	0	708	507	1535	49
Temple 4	275	25	13	13	313	263	0	75	225	38	213	850	3563	0
Outside 4	563	342	26	168	1926	789	179	126	811	5	458	326	1237	53
Temple 3	5178	0	56	28	467	421	84	56	262	65	187	1308	1364	0
Outside 3	879	288	61	83	1061	1068	856	735	1008	8	212	326	750	38
Temple 2	1250	36	0	36	464	500	71	214	250	0	107	2071	12571	36
Outside 2	1026	26	17	778	880	1060	291	1325	137	0	462	821	11325	60
Surface	1205	161	29	231	1358	961	296	459	541	17	398	694	3766	40
Non-Surface	2532	32	40	32	968	532	143	175	429	0	230	357	468	32

Tell El Hayyat Flora Density

APPENDIX G:
TELL EL-HAYYAT FLOTATION SAMPLES AND SEED IDENTIFICATIONS (filename: "TH FLORA ALL PHASES")

Tell El Hayyat Flora - All Phases

Locus	A018	A026	A039	A042	A043	A043	A047	A051	C022
Bag	006	013	015	016	018	019	021	022	009
Phase	2	2	3	4	4	4	4	5	3
Sector									CA
Subphase									LATE
Code	S	A	P	S	K	K	P	DF	T
Qty_saved	2E+02	50	10	0	2E+02	2E+02	1E+02	5E+02	98
Volume	10	10	10	10	8	10	10	8	16
Weight									
C/H# undiff#			1	5		3	1		
C/H# hulled var#		45	2	18		1	1		
C/H# naked var#	1	1				2	2	1	
C/Rachis frag#				15					
C/T# undiff#		22		8		4	4		
C/T# emmer		5		4			1	1	
C/T# einkorn		3	2	4		1	8	1	
C/T# bread		8	6	5		3	5		
C/Spikelet frag#									
OC/Avena		10		1					
OC/Secale									
OC/Panicum									
WC/Phalaris		6	1	87			1		
WC/wild grass				3		1			
OC/undiff#									
CL/Cicer									
CL/Lens		12		1			1		
CL/Pisium						1	14	1	1
CL/V# faba		2	1						
CL/V# ervilia/Lathyrus		3		8		1	14		
CL/Cultivated fragments									
WL/wild legumes	2	3		22		2	2		
F/Ficus		42		50			4	1	
F/Olea		1		1					29
F/Pistacia									
F/Vitis		1		1					
F/Prosopis				2			4		
W/Amaranthus	1		1	4				1	
W/Chenopodium			4	11					
W/Malva		1		59	2	1	2	1	
W/Plantago	1	7		5					
W/Rumex/Polygonum		2		5		2		2	
W/Galium		5	1	9			2		
W/Mollugo									
W/cf#Adonis									
W/cf#Ochthodium									
W/cf#Compositae									
W/cf#Beta									
Unidentified frag#		7		6				1	

Tell El Hayyat Flora - All Phases

Locus	C070	C072	C078	D032	D033	D038	D042	D048	D056
Bag	001	002	003	007	008	010	012	014	265
Phase	4	5	5	3	3	4	4	5	5
Sector	CA			WE	WE	CC	CC		
Subphase	EARLY			EARLY	EARLY	LATE	LATE		
Code	S	DO	DF	A	S	S	TF	A	S
Qty_saved	3E+02	50	2E+02	1E+02	75	20	2	70	2E+02
Volume	4	2	4	20	8	10	10	10	6
Weight									
C/H# undiff#	3	9	6		4			3	8
C/H# hulled var#	1	7	1		4	1	1		23
C/H# naked var#					1				7
C/Rachis frag#									7
C/T# undiff#	1	1			1				22
C/T# emmer		2						1	5
C/T# einkorn			1		1				6
C/T# bread	1	1						2	5
C/Spikelet frag#									10
OC/Avena	1	2		1				1	5
OC/Secale		1	1	2				3	16
OC/Panicum									
WC/Phalaris		1						1	2
WC/wild grass		1			1				3
OC/undiff#									
CL/Cicer									
CL/Lens	1		1	2	1				
CL/Pisium									1
CL/V# faba									
CL/V# ervilia/Lathyrus			2		1		3	5	2
CL/Cultivated fragments									
WL/wild legumes	2	5	1	3	1	2			8
F/Ficus	1	7		1	4				30
F/Olea						1		1	
F/Pistacia									
F/Vitis				1					
F/Prosopis	1								2
W/Amaranthus				1					
W/Chenopodium				3					
W/Malva	1	1	1	1	3		12		8
W/Plantago	1			1	3				2
W/Rumex/Polygonum		2	1		3		2	1	7
W/Galium	4	9			2	2	2		
W/Mollugo									
W/cf#Adonis									
W/cf#Ochthodium									
W/cf#Compositae									
W/cf#Beta									
Unidentified frag#									1

Locus	D060	D065	E089	E092	E102	F030	F040	F040	F040
Bag	293	311	434	457	500	139	162	165	235
Phase	5	5	4	4	5	4	4	4	4
Sector			CR	CR		WR	WR	WR	WR
Subphase			EARLY	LATE		LATE	EARLY	EARLY	EARLY
Code	A	A	S	TF	A	DM	S	S	S
Qty_saved	25	40	75	32	71	2E+02	1E+02	1E+02	1E+02
Volume	5	5	3	2	6	20	8	8	3
Weight				18			1	1	1
C/H# undiff#	1	11	4	5	12	11	2		
C/H# hulled var#		3	1		8	13	3		
C/H# naked var#			1		7				
C/Rachis frag#							1		
C/T# undiff#		4	2		9	1			
C/T# emmer	1	1							
C/T# einkorn		1							1
C/T# bread		4	2		10	2			1
C/Spikelet frag#					3				
OC/Avena			2		7		1		
OC/Secale	2		2	3	7		1		
OC/Panicum									
WC/Phalaris		1	1		8		1		1
WC/wild grass		1			3				
OC/undiff#									
CL/Cicer	5				11				
CL/Lens			9	6	3				
CL/Pisium		2							
CL/V# faba									
CL/V# ervilia/Lathyrus		2	1	1	1				
CL/Cultivated fragments	2	2							
WL/wild legumes	14	8	8	1	8				
F/Ficus	52	17		2	18	4	5		
F/Olea			3	42		2			
F/Pistacia									
F/Vitis				2					
F/Prosopis	1								
W/Amaranthus	1						1		
W/Chenopodium									
W/Malva	8	9			9		2		1
W/Plantago						1			1
W/Rumex/Polygonum	3		3	1	12				
W/Galium		2	3		2				1
W/Mollugo									
W/cf#Adonis			1						
W/cf#Ochthodium									
W/cf#Compositae									
W/cf#Beta									
Unidentified frag#				1			2		

Tell El Hayyat Flora - All Phases

Locus	F044	F045	F046	F048	F049	G025	G045	H029	H031
Bag	256	258	264	307	288	)60&064	152	123	144
Phase	5	5	5	5	5	2	2	2	2
Sector						CA	CA	EA	EA
Subphase						LATE	EARLY	LATE	EARLY
Code	DO	A	DO	DO	DO	A	A	DO	S
Qty_saved	95	0	40	1E+02	69	87	50	4E+02	2E+02
Volume	2	8	10	8	8	12	6	3	4
Weight		17							12
C/H# undiff#		3	17	9	12	1		5	1
C/H# hulled var#		1	11	3	9				1
C/H# naked var#		1		1			3		
C/Rachis frag#									
C/T# undiff#			1		4		7		1
C/T# emmer							4		
C/T# einkorn				1	4	1			1
C/T# bread			1	1		2	1		
C/Spikelet frag#					2				
OC/Avena			1	3	3	8	2		
OC/Secale			1	1	1	4	3		
OC/Panicum									
WC/Phalaris						1	1	1	
WC/wild grass						3			
OC/undiff#									
CL/Cicer									
CL/Lens		1	2	5	2		2	1	
CL/Pisium				3					
CL/V# faba									
CL/V# ervilia/Lathyrus			1		6		15		
CL/Cultivated fragments								1	
WL/wild legumes	1		2	1	2	3	7		
F/Ficus	3	1	2	6	4	4	8	3	
F/Olea			2	1	2				
F/Pistacia									
F/Vitis			2						
F/Prosopis	1	3		1	3			84	
W/Amaranthus									
W/Chenopodium									
W/Malva			2			2E+02	1		
W/Plantago			11				1		
W/Rumex/Polygonum				1	15		5		
W/Galium			7		1		2	2	1
W/Mollugo									
W/cf#Adonis					1				
W/cf#Ochthodium							2		
W/cf#Compositae									
W/cf#Beta									
Unidentified frag#			4		1				

Tell El Hayyat Flora - All Phases

Locus	H037	H052	H054	H061	H061	H067	H073	H073	H074
Bag	104	225	235	297	335	392	482	486	536
Phase	2	3	3	4	4	5	6	6	5
Sector	EA	EA	EA	EA	EA				
Subphase	EARLY	EARLY	EARLY	EARLY	EARLY				
Code	A	P	DO	A	A	A	S	S	DO
Qty_saved	0	8	2E+02	75	75	7	6E+02	6E+02	51
Volume	6	2	2	4	12	6	18	18	8
Weight		8	2	15	6	16	3	2	1
C/H# undiff#		6	5	6	3	15	3		
C/H# hulled var#			1	24		34	4	3	
C/H# naked var#			1	3		5	2		
C/Rachis frag#									
C/T# undiff#	4	5	1	5	2	20	1		
C/T# emmer		1	1	3		13	2		
C/T# einkorn	2	1	1	4		18			
C/T# bread	2	3		5	2	27			
C/Spikelet frag#	2								
OC/Avena	2	10		1		4			
OC/Secale	6	3		9		18	1		
OC/Panicum									
WC/Phalaris		1	1	3	1	8			
WC/wild grass	1			3		3			
OC/undiff#									
CL/Cicer									
CL/Lens	1					6			
CL/Pisium		1		2		2		1	
CL/V# faba				4					
CL/V# ervilia/Lathyrus	1			3		5		1	
CL/Cultivated fragments									
WL/wild legumes		1	4	8				1	
F/Ficus	3	4	2	5		7		4	
F/Olea		1		2		1			
F/Pistacia									
F/Vitis	1								
F/Prosopis	1	1				9			
W/Amaranthus									
W/Chenopodium									
W/Malva	1		2	11				1	
W/Plantago	1	1		3					
W/Rumex/Polygonum				2	1	2		1	
W/Galium		3		3		2			
W/Mollugo									
W/cf#Adonis								4	
W/cf#Ochthodium									
W/cf#Compositae									
W/cf#Beta									
Unidentified frag#									

Tell El Hayyat Flora - All Phases

Locus	I029	I045	I050	I055	I057	I060	J043	J052	J071
Bag	089	152	200	236	217	067	142	179	256
Phase	2	2	3	3	3	3	2	3	0
Sector	CE	CE	CE	CE	CE	CE	EA	EA	
Subphase	LATE	LATE	LATE	MIDDLE	MIDDLE	EARLY	EARLY	LATE	
Code	A	A	DO	P	P	P	TF	S	V
Qty_saved	25	0	5E+02	1E+02	1E+02	37	0	9E+02	55
Volume	6	6	6	6	6	4	6	6	8
Weight	1		3					3	18
C/H# undiff#	9	1	3	4	5	10	1	1	5
C/H# hulled var#	1	2	1	1	6	20		5	5
C/H# naked var#					1				
C/Rachis frag#			3		2	25			
C/T# undiff#	1	1	4	1	21		2	2	4
C/T# emmer	1				1			1	2
C/T# einkorn	3				1	1	1	1	6
C/T# bread	4	2	2		14		3		3
C/Spikelet frag#					3				
OC/Avena		3	1		7	27	2	6	
OC/Secale		5	1		31	4	2	1	
OC/Panicum									
WC/Phalaris		1			9	30		1	2
WC/wild grass			3	1	35	4			3
OC/undiff#					1				
CL/Cicer								1	
CL/Lens	5		2		2				11
CL/Pisium	2	2			1		1		1
CL/V# faba	2								
CL/V# ervilia/Lathyrus		2							3
CL/Cultivated fragments									
WL/wild legumes	42	2		10	3	9	6	1	4
F/Ficus	11	2	7		6	24	9	3	4
F/Olea		1			1	2	1	1	
F/Pistacia									
F/Vitis				1	1				
F/Prosopis					6			1	
W/Amaranthus									
W/Chenopodium					5		1		
W/Malva	1	7	1		9			1	3
W/Plantago			1		2	1	3		
W/Rumex/Polygonum	4		5	1	5	2	1	1	
W/Galium		4	2		2	2	1		4
W/Mollugo									
W/cf#Adonis									
W/cf#Ochthodium									
W/cf#Compositae	1								
W/cf#Beta	1								
Unidentified frag#					1				

Tell El Hayyat Flora - All Phases

Locus	J074	J075	J081	K028	K044	K046	K054	K056	K064
Bag	281	292&293	322	119	155	177	203	212	262
Phase	4	4	5	2	3	3	4	4	4
Sector	EA	EA		EB1	EB	EB	EB	EB	EB
Subphase	EARLY	EARLY		LATE	LATE	EARLY	LATE	LATE	
Code	A	S	A	S	DF	S	TF	S	P
Qty_saved	0	2E+02	60	2E+02	1E+03	77	0	1E+02	2E+03
Volume	18	8	8	2	6	6	4	6	1
Weight	18	11	7	1	12	22	48	56	
C/H# undiff#	9	3	19	2	6	2	1	12	15
C/H# hulled var#	18	8	53	3	6		3	35	56
C/H# naked var#	7		2					18	5
C/Rachis frag#					2			40	
C/T# undiff#	16	6	1			11		1	1
C/T# emmer			1		3	3		21	
C/T# einkorn			4		6	6		2	
C/T# bread		2	2		9	4	2	2	1
C/Spikelet frag#					10			1	1
OC/Avena	5	1	4	2	12	49	1	7	14
OC/Secale			2	2	15	28	1	2	4
OC/Panicum									
WC/Phalaris	11	1	4		16			16	1
WC/wild grass	8	2			8	3		2	9
OC/undiff#								1	
CL/Cicer									
CL/Lens									
CL/Pisium		1							
CL/V# faba									
CL/V# ervilia/Lathyrus	3	3	1						
CL/Cultivated fragments		8					1		
WL/wild legumes	5		10	3	3		2		2
F/Ficus	9		1	3	39	2	2	10	4
F/Olea	4	1							2
F/Pistacia									
F/Vitis					1				
F/Prosopis	21	1							1
W/Amaranthus	1								
W/Chenopodium									
W/Malva	1	1	1		2			7	
W/Plantago		2					1	2	
W/Rumex/Polygonum	3	6		1				4	
W/Galium	11	5	2				1		1
W/Mollugo									
W/cf#Adonis									
W/cf#Ochthodium									
W/cf#Compositae									
W/cf#Beta									
Unidentified frag#		1							

Tell El Hayyat Flora - All Phases

Locus	K066	L006	L012	L019	M041	M052	M053	M056	M066
Bag	272	079	035	056	193	164&167	174	182	228
Phase	5	1	2	2	3	4	3	4	4
Sector			TS	TS	TS	TS	TI	TS	TS
Subphase			LATE	EARLY	MIDDLE	LATE	EARLY	LATE	EARLY
Code	DO	A	A	A	DM	S	S	S	S
Qty_saved	1E+02	0	0	0	5E+02	4E+02	60	75	70
Volume	6	3	8	6	1	8	2	2	2
Weight		1	1	4	1	6	1	7	3
C/H# undiff#	14	4	2	3					
C/H# hulled var#	3	4	2	3					1
C/H# naked var#			1						
C/Rachis frag#									
C/T# undiff#	4		3	3	1		1		1
C/T# emmer		2		1				1	
C/T# einkorn		2		1					
C/T# bread	6	2		2		1	1	1	
C/Spikelet frag#									
OC/Avena	7	1		2					
OC/Secale			2	4				1	
OC/Panicum									
WC/Phalaris			2	1			3		
WC/wild grass	3	2		1					
OC/undiff#							4		
CL/Cicer									
CL/Lens				1		1			
CL/Pisium									
CL/V# faba						1			
CL/V# ervilia/Lathyrus				2		1			
CL/Cultivated fragments									
WL/wild legumes	1	10	2	5		9	1		1
F/Ficus	1	3	5	17			2		2
F/Olea				1					
F/Pistacia									
F/Vitis									
F/Prosopis				1					
W/Amaranthus				2					
W/Chenopodium									
W/Malva	3	1		1E+02		1	2		
W/Plantago									
W/Rumex/Polygonum	1		2	14					
W/Galium									1
W/Mollugo									
W/cf#Adonis									1
W/cf#Ochthodium									
W/cf#Compositae									
W/cf#Beta									
Unidentified frag#			1						

Tell El Hayyat Flora - All Phases

Locus	M067	M078	M081	M084	N006	N009	N021	N030	P065
Bag	252	268	275	302	011	027	128	178	048
Phase	5	5	5	5	2	2	4	5	2
Sector	TS	TI	TI	TI	TI	TI	TI	PT	TI
Subphase	LATE				LATE	EARLY	LATE		LATE
Code	S	S	S	S	DF	DF	DO	S	DM
Qty_saved	50	15	53	0	90	2E+02	62	3E+02	20
Volume	2	1	3	2	2	2	2	3	2
Weight	29	10	16	2	20	1	6		
C/H# undiff#	1		5			2	1		
C/H# hulled var#	3							2	
C/H# naked var#								1	
C/Rachis frag#									
C/T# undiff#			2						
C/T# emmer	1								
C/T# einkorn		1				2			
C/T# bread								1	
C/Spikelet frag#		2							
OC/Avena									
OC/Secale			1						
OC/Panicum									
WC/Phalaris	9	1	3			3		6	
WC/wild grass	1							1	
OC/undiff#									
CL/Cicer									
CL/Lens	2							3	
CL/Pisium									
CL/V# faba									
CL/V# ervilia/Lathyrus									
CL/Cultivated fragments									
WL/wild legumes	2							3	
F/Ficus	10						1	20	
F/Olea									
F/Pistacia									
F/Vitis									
F/Prosopis	1							3	
W/Amaranthus									
W/Chenopodium									
W/Malva	29		2	1	1			63	
W/Plantago			2						
W/Rumex/Polygonum	11		1					7	
W/Galium									
W/Mollugo									
W/cf#Adonis									
W/cf#Ochthodium									
W/cf#Compositae									
W/cf#Beta									
Unidentified frag#									

Tell El Hayyat Flora - All Phases

Locus	P089	P090	P110	P111	P112	P116	P117	P128	P135
Bag	107	111	168	169	176	180	181	209	252
Phase	3	3	3	3	3	3	3	4	4
Sector	TI	TI	TI	TI	TI	TI	TI	TI	TI
Subphase								LATE	LATE
Code	DO	TF	A	A	S	A	A	S	S
Qty_saved	3E+02	2	0	0	3E+02	0	0	6E+02	1E+03
Volume	2	2	2	4	4	2	4	4	3
Weight	2	6	1	14	11	1	2	3	4
C/H# undiff#						1			
C/H# hulled var#		1	2	3	1	1		4	
C/H# naked var#									
C/Rachis frag#									
C/T# undiff#	1				1				
C/T# emmer									
C/T# einkorn									
C/T# bread								1	
C/Spikelet frag#									
OC/Avena			1						
OC/Secale	2							1	
OC/Panicum									
WC/Phalaris	1							2	
WC/wild grass								1	
OC/undiff#							1		
CL/Cicer									
CL/Lcns	1		1						
CL/Pisium			1		1				
CL/V# faba									
CL/V# ervilia/Lathyrus									
CL/Cultivated fragments									
WL/wild legumes				1			1	2	
F/Ficus		1		1		1	3	9	
F/Olea									
F/Pistacia									
F/Vitis				1			1		
F/Prosopis									
W/Amaranthus					1				
W/Chenopodium									
W/Malva				3			1	2	
W/Plantago									
W/Rumex/Polygonum	1	1		1			4		
W/Galium							1		
W/Mollugo									
W/cf#Adonis									
W/cf#Ochthodium									
W/cf#Compositae									
W/cf#Beta									
Unidentified frag#									

Tell El Hayyat Flora - All Phases

Locus	P135	P136	P140	P141	P155	P156	P157	P164	P172
Bag	258	334	267	273	301	303	304	309	325
Phase	4	4	4	4	4	4	4	4	4
Sector	TI	TI	TI	TI	TI	TI	TI	TI	TI
Subphase	LATE	EARLY	LATE	MIDDLE	EARLY	EARLY	EARLY	EARLY	EARLY
Code	S	WM	S	A	A	A	A	A	A
Qty_saved	1E+03	26	2E+02	10	8	0	0	0	0
Volume	3	1	3	20	1	1	1	1	5
Weight	4	5	1	8	4	2	1	1	
C/H# undiff#	1				2				
C/H# hulled var#				1	3				1
C/H# naked var#				1					
C/Rachis frag#									
C/T# undiff#	2			1	1				1
C/T# emmer	1				1	1			1
C/T# einkorn									
C/T# bread			1						
C/Spikelet frag#									
OC/Avena									
OC/Secale						2			
OC/Panicum			1						
WC/Phalaris							1		2
WC/wild grass									
OC/undiff#									
CL/Cicer									
CL/Lens									
CL/Pisium	2								
CL/V# faba									
CL/V# ervilia/Lathyrus			1		1				
CL/Cultivated fragments									
WL/wild legumes	4		1	1					
F/Ficus		2	1		1	1	1	1	
F/Olea									
F/Pistacia									
F/Vitis		1							
F/Prosopis									
W/Amaranthus					1				
W/Chenopodium									
W/Malva			1	2		2	2	1	
W/Plantago									
W/Rumex/Polygonum	1	1				1			
W/Galium	1			1					
W/Mollugo									
W/cf#Adonis	1								
W/cf#Ochthodium									
W/cf#Compositae									
W/cf#Beta									
Unidentified frag#									

Tell El Hayyat Flora - All Phases

Locus	P179	P184	P196	P197	Q017	Q027	Q044	Q048	Q049
Bag	392	414	415	417	012	036	142	178	177
Phase	5	5	5	5	2	3	3	3	3
Sector	TI	TI	TF	TI	TF	TF	TF	TF	TF
Subphase					LATE		MIDDLE	MIDDLE	EARLY
Code	S	P	A	A	A	A	DF	DO	DF
Qty_saved	6E+02	1	0	0	0	0	1E+02	1E+02	5E+02
Volume	5	10	4	1	4	4	8	12	12
Weight	2		4		5	4	16		
C/H# undiff#							2	1	
C/H# hulled var#		12	1				6		
C/H# naked var#		4							
C/Rachis frag#									
C/T# undiff#		1			1	3	2		
C/T# emmer						2			
C/T# einkorn					1				
C/T# bread		2					2		
C/Spikelet frag#									
OC/Avena		2					1		
OC/Secale									
OC/Panicum									
WC/Phalaris			3			1	2		
WC/wild grass		4					1		
OC/undiff#									
CL/Cicer						1			
CL/Lens									
CL/Pisium						1			
CL/V# faba									
CL/V# ervilia/Lathyrus									
CL/Cultivated fragments						1			
WL/wild legumes			2		50	20	10		
F/Ficus			5		10	15	2E+02		
F/Olea									
F/Pistacia									
F/Vitis			1						
F/Prosopis			1						
W/Amaranthus					1		1		
W/Chenopodium					4				
W/Malva			4		6	2	1		
W/Plantago		16			1				
W/Rumex/Polygonum			8		6	1	1		
W/Galium						6	1		
W/Mollugo									
W/cf#Adonis							1		
W/cf#Ochthodium									
W/cf#Compositae									
W/cf#Beta									
Unidentified frag#				2					

Tell El Hayyat Flora - All Phases

Locus	Q057	Q061	Q067	Q074	Q075	Q075	Q079	R040	R050
Bag	218	231	265	288	283	309&310	305&308	122	154
Phase	4	4	4	5	5	5	5	3	3
Sector	TF	TF	TF	TF	TF	TF	TF	TF	TF
Subphase	LATE	LATE	EARLY	LATE	LATE	LATE	EARLY	MIDDLE	MIDDLE
Code	DO	DM	DO	DO	S	S	DO	S	S
Qty_saved	1E+03	8E+02	1E+03	2E+02	0	0	7E+02	1E+02	1E+02
Volume	4	4	9	4	8	8	6	4	12
Weight	2	1	3	5		13		14	
C/H# undiff#				1		2	1	4	2
C/H# hulled var#		2	2	2	1	4	1	2	
C/H# naked var#		1			1	1			
C/Rachis frag#									
C/T# undiff#		1						5	
C/T# emmer				1		1		3	
C/T# einkorn		1		1		1			
C/T# bread					1	3			
C/Spikelet frag#									
OC/Avena						1		1	
OC/Secale		2				1			
OC/Panicum									
WC/Phalaris		2	3		6	6		15	
WC/wild grass					1				
OC/undiff#			2						
CL/Cicer									
CL/Lens			1			1			
CL/Pisium		1	1	1		1		1	
CL/V# faba									
CL/V# ervilia/Lathyrus					2			1	
CL/Cultivated fragments									
WL/wild legumes	45		2	4		1		35	
F/Ficus			3	9	11	6		3E+02	
F/Olea									
F/Pistacia									
F/Vitis						1			
F/Prosopis						7			
W/Amaranthus								3	
W/Chenopodium									
W/Malva	3E+02		1	4	17	4		11	
W/Plantago					17				
W/Rumex/Polygonum			3	2	8	4		18	
W/Galium	1	1						1	
W/Mollugo									
W/cf#Adonis									
W/cf#Ochthodium									
W/cf#Compositae									
W/cf#Beta									
Unidentified frag#						1			

Tell El Hayyat Flora - All Phases

Locus	R051	R051	R052	S021	S024	S047	S061	S065	T014
Bag	158	161	165	042	051	123	208	235	012&013
Phase	3	3	3	2	2	3	3	4	2
Sector	TF	TF	TF	TF	EA	TF	EA	TF	EB3
Subphase	MIDDLE	MIDDLE	EARLY	LATE	LATE	MIDDLE	EARLY	LATE	LATE
Code	DO	DO	DM	DO	A	DF	S	DM	S
Qty_saved	4E+02	4E+02	7E+02	20	15	2E+02		2E+02	62
Volume	8	8	8	4	12	8	4	6	4
Weight	3	3	3	4	9	27	3	11	2
C/H# undiff#		2	1			1	1	3	
C/H# hulled var#	1		1		1	16	3	2	
C/H# naked var#	2								
C/Rachis frag#									
C/T# undiff#	2	1	1			7	1	4	
C/T# emmer	1				1	5			
C/T# einkorn	2				1	3	6		2
C/T# bread						1	4		1
C/Spikelet frag#									
OC/Avena		1				5			
OC/Secale					1	4			2
OC/Panicum									
WC/Phalaris	1	1	1		1	2	3	4	
WC/wild grass							1	3	
OC/undiff#	1	1							
CL/Cicer									
CL/Lens						10		5	
CL/Pisium		1						1	
CL/V# faba									
CL/V# ervilia/Lathyrus		1						1	
CL/Cultivated fragments						3			
WL/wild legumes	34	13	1	1	22	24	2	3	
F/Ficus	5	4	2	3	14	90	1		
F/Olea								2	
F/Pistacia									
F/Vitis	1					3			
F/Prosopis	1				6	2		1	
W/Amaranthus		3		2E+02	2				
W/Chenopodium	3	1			5				
W/Malva	1	2		20	14	3	4		1
W/Plantago	1	1			1			2	
W/Rumex/Polygonum	30	22	1	1	51	5	1	3	
W/Galium	1	1				9	1	4	
W/Mollugo									
W/cf#Adonis									
W/cf#Ochthodium									
W/cf#Compositae									
W/cf#Beta									
Unidentified frag#							1		

Locus	T022	T022	T024	T025	T027	T030	T033	T037	T040
Bag	048	055	133	068	087	100	111	135	162
Phase	2	2	2	2	3	3	3	3	3
Sector	EB	EB	EB	EB	EC	EC	EC	EC	EC
Subphase	MIDDLE	MIDDLE	MIDDLE	MIDDLE	LATE	LATE	EARLY	EARLY	EARLY
Code	DO	DO	DO	DO	A	S	H	DF	I
Qty_saved	73	73	3E+02	2E+02	0	75	0	2E+03	15
Volume	8	4	4	2	2	8	4	4	4
Weight	4	15	1	8	6	17	22	15	2
C/H# undiff#	2	9		2	1		4	2	1
C/H# hulled var#		12				22	4	2	3
C/H# naked var#							1		
C/Rachis frag#									
C/T# undiff#	1	13		2	1	3	2		
C/T# emmer		3		1			2		
C/T# einkorn		13		3		1	5		
C/T# bread		1					2		
C/Spikelet frag#									
OC/Avena	1	3		1					
OC/Secale		1E+02		3	1	9	2		
OC/Panicum									
WC/Phalaris		1		1		2	2	10	
WC/wild grass								1	
OC/undiff#									
CL/Cicer						1			
CL/Lens				1	1		1		2
CL/Pisium				1			3	1	
CL/V# faba						1		1	
CL/V# ervilia/Lathyrus								1	4
CL/Cultivated fragments									
WL/wild legumes				2		5		1	
F/Ficus			1	20		20	2	1	
F/Olea						3			1
F/Pistacia									
F/Vitis						4			
F/Prosopis						2		1	
W/Amaranthus			1						1
W/Chenopodium									
W/Malva		1				1		1	
W/Plantago			1	1		2		3	
W/Rumex/Polygonum				4		4		1	1
W/Galium						4	2	1	1
W/Mollugo									
W/cf#Adonis									
W/cf#Ochthodium									
W/cf#Compositae									
W/cf#Beta									
Unidentified frag#								3	

Locus	T042	T043	T044	T046	T049	T050	T051	T057	T059
Bag		175	248	207	213	215	217	238	253
Phase	3	4	3	4	4	4	4	4	4
Sector	EC	EC	EC	EC	EC	EC	EC	EC	EC
Subphase	LATE	LATE		LATE	MIDDLE	MIDDLE	MIDDLE	EARLY	EARLY
Code	WF	TF	WM	WM	H	H	H	P	P
Qty_saved	8	10	0	0	10	20	2	6	3
Volume	4	4	4	4	4	4	4	8	3
Weight		9		11	2	3	11	9	2
C/H# undiff#		1		19			4	7	
C/H# hulled var#				8			11	3	1
C/H# naked var#				5				2	
C/Rachis frag#									
C/T# undiff#		2		2	2			2	2
C/T# emmer				1			1	1	
C/T# einkorn				2				1	
C/T# bread								1	
C/Spikelet frag#									
OC/Avena									
OC/Secale							2		
OC/Panicum									
WC/Phalaris					1		1		
WC/wild grass									
OC/undiff#									
CL/Cicer									
CL/Lens							2		
CL/Pisium				1				1	
CL/V# faba									
CL/V# ervilia/Lathyrus				1			3	2	
CL/Cultivated fragments									
WL/wild legumes		4					2		
F/Ficus					2		5	4	
F/Olea					1		1	1	4
F/Pistacia									
F/Vitis							2		
F/Prosopis								2	
W/Amaranthus									
W/Chenopodium									
W/Malva		1		1				2	
W/Plantago									1
W/Rumex/Polygonum					2		11	1	
W/Galium				3	1		3	2	
W/Mollugo									
W/cf#Adonis									
W/cf#Ochthodium									
W/cf#Compositae									
W/cf#Beta									
Unidentified frag#									

Tell El Hayyat Flora - All Phases

Locus	T064	T065	T067	T072	T075	T075	U009	U019
Bag	279	304	292	312	327	331	083	)66&069
Phase	5	5	5	5	5	5	2	2
Sector							TFE	TFE
Subphase								
Code	DO	P	DO	P	P	P	SP	P
Qty_saved	9E+02	75	3E+02	6	2E+02	2E+02	40	0
Volume	6	5	5	6	4	5	4	8
Weight	7	5	5	8	8	2	1	22
C/H# undiff#	3	5	1	5		2		
C/H# hulled var#	5		2	3	21			
C/H# naked var#					2			
C/Rachis frag#								
C/T# undiff#	3	3	13	3	7	1		
C/T# emmer		1	3	2	3			
C/T# einkorn	3		9	3	4	1		1
C/T# bread	3		4			2		
C/Spikelet frag#								
OC/Avena				1				
OC/Secale	1		1	2		2		
OC/Panicum								
WC/Phalaris		6			4			
WC/wild grass								
OC/undiff#								
CL/Cicer								
CL/Lens				4	3			
CL/Pisium	4			1	2			
CL/V# faba								
CL/V# ervilia/Lathyrus	2		2	7	4			
CL/Cultivated fragments								
WL/wild legumes	1	4	2		1	1	4	
F/Ficus	6	3	2	12	4	2		
F/Olea		4			1			
F/Pistacia								
F/Vitis								
F/Prosopis	1							
W/Amaranthus								
W/Chenopodium								
W/Malva		1					1E+03	
W/Plantago	1	1						
W/Rumex/Polygonum	3	3			2	1		
W/Galium	1	4	1		2			
W/Mollugo								
W/cf#Adonis								
W/cf#Ochthodium								
W/cf#Compositae								
W/cf#Beta								
Unidentified frag#								

Tell El Hayyat Flora - All Phases